The Questions We Ask God

R. P. PRIDDY

Faith In Texas Press

THE QUESTIONS WE ASK GOD

Copyright © 2026 by R. P. Priddy

Published by Faith In Texas Press

League City, Texas

www.faithintexaspress.com

ISBN: 979-8-9953520-1-3 (Paperback)

ISBN: 979-8-9953520-2-0 (Hardcover)

ISBN: 979-8-9953520-3-7 (eBook)

ISBN: 979-8-9953520-0-6 (Audiobook)

ISBN: 979-8-9953520-4-4 (Enhanced Read-Along Edition)

Library of Congress Control Number: 2026907724

Scripture quotations are taken from the King James Version (KJV) of the Holy Bible. The KJV is in the public domain in the United States of America.

This book is intended for inspirational and educational purposes only. It does not constitute professional counseling, theological instruction, or medical advice. The author and publisher make no warranty, express or implied, with respect to the contents of this work.

For rights and permissions inquiries, contact: publisher@faithintexaspress.com

First Edition, 2026

Printed in the United States of America

Table of Contents

Dedication	V
Acknowledgments	VIII
Preface	X
Opening Prayer	XX
1. Why Do Good People Suffer — And Where Is God In It?	1
2. Why Would God Ever Forgive Evil People?	30
3. If God Already Knew, Why Did He Let It Happen?	65
4. Who Created God — And Where Did He Come From?	91
5. Why Does God Stay Silent When I Need Him Most?	145
6. Why Does God Seem So Different in the Old Testament?	176
7. Has Science Disproved God?	207
8. Why Are There So Many Religions If There Is Only One God?	234
9. Why Is The Church Full of Hypocrites?	263
10. What Is My Purpose — And Did I Fulfill It?	289
11. What Actually Happens When We Die?	321

12. Why Did God Create Me Knowing I Would Struggle?   352

13. Why Does God Allow Children to Suffer?   383

14. How Could a Loving God Send Anyone to Hell?   412

15. Why Does Psychosis Target God?   444

Closing Prayer   470

A Note to The Reader   473

Scripture Reference Index   474

Dedication   479

Dedication

To God — First, Last, and Always.

Without Your presence, nothing is possible. Through Your grace, everything is. You carried me through my weakest moments, corrected me when I strayed, and remained faithful even when I faltered. This book does not exist because of me. It exists because You never abandoned me.

To My Mammaw Z — My Angel.

I saved this space for you because no paragraph tucked inside a list of names could ever be enough. You deserve your own moment. Your own words.

You were not just my grandmother. You were a living demonstration of what it looks like to build an entire life on Christ and refuse to waver regardless of what that life brings. Your commitment was not performed on Sunday mornings and set aside the rest of the week. It was the architecture of everything you were. It shaped the way you spoke, the way you loved, the way you entered a room, the way you held the people God placed in your care.

I was not always easy. There were seasons where I was a handful — where my rebellion and my searching and my stubbornness were enough to exhaust anyone around me. You never saw a lost cause. You saw what God could do. And you prayed accordingly.

I carry those prayers with me still. I believe they are part of why I am standing today.

This book — more than any other thing I have ever attempted — is the one I wish I could place in your hands. Not because of anything impressive about it, but because its entire foundation is the thing you built your life upon. The Word of God. The faithfulness of Christ. The belief that every hard question a human being can carry already has an answer — and that answer is found in Scripture.

You knew that before I did. You tried to show me. And eventually, God made sure I found my way back to what you planted.

I think about your garden often. That enormous, beautiful stretch of earth you kept with such care and devotion. Walking through it with you for hours — you showing me what grew where, how things worked, what God had made — and talking. About life. About faith. About the things that mattered. Those hours were some of the most peaceful of my childhood, and I did not fully understand their value until they were behind me. I understand now. I am grateful for every one of them.

And your voicemails. Whenever I went too long without calling or visiting, the phone would ring — and there you were. That sweet, gentle voice reminding me without a word of accusation that I had been missed. I saved those messages longer than I should admit. They were not just voicemails. They were proof that someone in this world was always thinking about me and always glad I existed.

My mother says you are her angel. I understand that completely — and I would never argue with my mother. But I hope you know that we share you. Because the way you loved us, there was always more than enough to go around. That was just who you were, Mammaw Z. There was always more than enough.

I miss you more than these words can hold. But I do not grieve —
because I know exactly where you are, and I know that I will see you
again.

This book is for you, Mammaw Z. It always was.

"I thank my God upon every remembrance of you." — Philippians
1:3 (KJV)

Acknowledgments

T his book exists because of questions. And questions exist because of people who were willing to ask them honestly.

To every person who agreed to be part of the survey that gave this book its voice — who wrote down the questions they had been carrying in silence and trusted that they would be handled with care — thank you. Your honesty is the reason this book is what it is rather than what it might have been. You are not named in these pages, but you are in every chapter.

To J.V. — who sat with me in one of the hardest seasons of my life, opened Scripture with me, and told me to read the Book of Job. You did not know what you were starting. God did. This book is, in part, the fruit of that conversation.

To my wife — who endured every late night, every obsessive revision, every moment when this book occupied more of my mind than was fair to the people around me. You are the steadiest person I have ever known. Thank you for letting me finish what God started.

To my children — whose lives are woven into these pages in ways they may not fully understand until they are older. You are the reason I want what I write to be true, not just well-written.

To everyone who prayed over this project without knowing its title or its contents — who simply prayed for me because they knew I needed it — I believe those prayers are part of what held this together in the seasons when I was not sure it would.

To the scholars, theologians, pastors, and writers whose work built the intellectual and spiritual foundation of every chapter in this book — you gave me language for things I knew but could not yet say.

And to God — who answered before I finished asking, who was faithful when I was not, and who somehow entrusted a broken man with something this far beyond him.

Any truth in these pages belongs entirely to God. Any error belongs entirely to me.

— R.P. Priddy

Preface

The Night I Stopped Pretending

Before this preface is over, I am going to tell you about a night that changed everything. But to understand that night, you need to understand the road that led me there.

From the time I was a very small child, I was taught about God. I grew up in church, surrounded by family who knew Christ deeply and lived their faith without apology. My grandfather stood behind that pulpit and delivered the Gospel with a conviction that even as a small boy had my full attention. I remember sitting there amazed — a room full of people deeply moved by every word my grandfather spoke. Something stirred deep inside me in those moments that I have never been able to fully explain.

Those early years, those seasons of being immersed in faith and surrounded by people who took God seriously, led me to something real. By the age of nine, I was ready. I gave my life to Christ. I stood before the whole congregation with this amazing feeling — all of these people gathered here, watching me give my life to God. That was one of the proudest moments of my childhood.

But little did I know what was coming.

The older I grew, the more life began to reveal itself for what it truly is — difficult, demanding, and unrelenting in the way it tests everything you were raised to believe. The responsibilities of becoming a man, a husband, a father, a provider — they came with a weight I was not prepared for. And slowly, without fully realizing it, my faith moved from the center of my life to somewhere in the background.

There were seasons — long ones — where I made promises to God I did not keep. Seasons where I called myself a believer on Sunday and lived by my own rules every other day. Seasons where prayer became a last resort rather than the first response. Where I confused controlling my life with taking responsibility for it. Where I carried everything so tightly in my own hands that I left no room for God to lead.

I was not a hypocrite who knew better and did not care. I was a man who genuinely loved God but had not yet learned how to fully surrender to Him. There is a difference. But the results can look exactly the same from the outside — and the people closest to me felt it most.

My wife felt it. My children felt it. The depression. The sleepless nights. The overactive mind that never rested. The intensity that filled every room I walked into — these were the things my family lived beside while I told myself I was doing it all for them. I was present in body and absent in everything that mattered. I am not proud of those years. I still carry the weight of the unnecessary pain I caused the people I love most. God has been gracious enough to redeem those years — but I do not minimize them.

And my body was keeping score of all of it.

For more than ten years I had been dealing with pancreatitis — a condition that quietly worsened over time. The doctors could manage the episodes but they could not stop them. They kept saying it was from external things. But I knew in my spirit that stress was the engine driving this. Years of carrying what I was never designed to carry. Years of internalizing pressure, running on overdrive, refusing to rest. My body had finally begun to reflect what my soul had been enduring.

In recent years it had become an annual reality — in and out of the hospital for pancreatic pain, a rhythm I could not break no matter what I did.

What I did not realize was that God was already orchestrating a moment that would change everything.

I tell you this because the God who carried me through those dark times is the same God who can carry you — and before this book is over, I intend to show you how I know that to be true.

It started as an ordinary day.

My youngest son was only five years old. He was not feeling well — running a fever, a little cold, the kind of thing parents handle without a second thought. My wife took him to the doctor to get some medication. But during that visit, my son started touching his side. The doctor noticed. He asked my son about it. My son said it had been hurting him a little right there. It was the first time any of us had ever heard him mention it.

The doctor decided to do a scan.

What they found on that scan had nothing to do with why they came in that day. What the world would call chance, I know was the hand of God — revealing something that needed to be found: a tumor on my son's kidney. The case was sent to a specialist immediately.

When the specialist called us, the words left little room for hope. The cancer was definitive. The kidney had to come out. A port would be installed in his chest during surgery so that chemotherapy could begin as soon as he recovered. That is how certain the doctors were about what they saw.

Those words — spoken into a phone, landing in the middle of an ordinary day — hit me with a weight I was not prepared for.

I was already in the middle of a pancreatitis episode at the time, one that was not quite bad enough to put me in the hospital. But once

I received that news, it broke me. The pancreatic pain tore through me worse than it ever had. My son's diagnosis was pressing down on everything else at the same time. My family told me I needed to go to the hospital — to get well enough to come back home before my son's surgery so I could be there and be strong for him. I agreed.

I left the house in tears. I spent my time in that hospital in tears. I began to lose hope. I spent hours with God those days — crying, asking why. Why my health. Why my son's health. What did we do to deserve this. I pleaded with God — Lord, let my son be fine. I will take these illnesses. I can handle this pain. I asked God to bless me with enough strength and health to leave that hospital so I could be there for my son's surgery and stand beside him after.

When I was done with that prayer, there was a familiar feeling — a comfort I had felt many times in my life. That same feeling that had come to me in other hard seasons and then slipped away once things stabilized. I had known that feeling my whole life. It was real. But it had never been enough to fully change me.

I left the hospital with a quiet in my spirit. I walked into my son's surgery day as a father who somehow felt things were going to be all right.

We were told the surgery would take roughly two hours. Two hours passed. Then three. Then four. Then five. By this point the questions my wife and I were asking — out loud and in our heads — were unbearable. Every minute that passed, I could feel the hope I had walked in with completely eroding. That familiar comfort was gone. It was not enough for this moment.

By the time my son's surgery was finally over and they allowed us to see him, I was already completely broken. When I walked in and saw him — small, pale, surrounded by tubes and monitors and fresh incisions — I felt something crack open inside me. I was grateful his heart was still beating, but I was devastated that this was happening to my child.

Nothing prepares a parent for a moment like that. There are no adequate words for the helplessness of standing next to your child in a hospital bed right out of surgery, knowing there is nothing you can do to fix them.

Whatever strength I had walked in with was long gone.

I told my wife I needed to leave that room — that if she could sit with our son while he was still under the anesthesia and resting, I needed some time. She said yes. I hugged her. I told her I loved her and that I would see them in a little bit.

I spent a long while searching that hospital for the chapel. I was so upset in that moment that I did not even want to ask anyone where it was. I just walked — floor by floor — until I found it.

It was late. The chapel was dark, cold, and completely empty. Silent. And when I finally found it, I hesitated at the door — the way you hesitate before walking into an office knowing the conversation you are about to have is going to cost you something. I took a deep breath. I walked in. I sat on the very front row.

And I broke.

I wept. I paced. I sat back down. I paced again. I sat back down. I did everything I could to form words and could not. I begged God — please have mercy on me. Please forgive me for whatever I have done. In that moment I was a man who had reached the absolute end of himself and had nothing left to offer God except the truth.

So I gave Him the truth.

I told God about every promise I had made and broken. Every time I made excuses. Every time I tried to control decisions that were never mine to control. Every time I treated prayer like a backup plan instead of the first call. I was honest, raw, unfiltered — and I did not want to negotiate. I was not bargaining with God the way a frightened man bargains. Something was different this time. I was truly ready.

I vowed to God that I would lead my family. That I would stop living for just myself. That this time I would keep God at the center of my life and not drift away from that the moment things stabilized again. That I would become truly present in the lives of the people He had already entrusted to me. That I would steward my health, my mind, and my body as sacred gifts rather than expendable resources.

Then something happened that I have never been able to fully explain in human language.

It felt as though I was enveloped — not threatened, but surrounded. Protected. A comforting presence I can only describe as the fullness of God drawing near. The Father, the Son, and the Holy Spirit surrounding a broken man at the lowest point of his life. For me, it was my soul finally encountering the first truly honest moment of commitment to God that I had felt since the day I was baptized at nine years old. It was a sacred, personal, and completely undeserved moment of grace.

I knew this was not that familiar comfort that had come and gone so many times before.

I remember there was a moment where something told me — grab your phone. Write this down the best you can. This is a defining moment in your life. This is a story you will tell one day. Write it down so you can share it and help others.

So I wiped the tears from my eyes, took a deep breath, and wrote in my notes the best that I could.

After I wrote, I continued talking to God. Confirming that all my faith was in Him. That I would not doubt Him. That whatever happened, I knew it was for a reason. I thanked Him for my wife, for all three of my children. I realized in that moment how many years I had wasted — how many years I had missed being a fully present and involved father. I pleaded with God one more time — please do not take my son. Whatever You do, please do not take him. And I asked Him, one final time before I walked out of that chapel, to give me the strength and health to be there for my son throughout this journey.

Then I walked back.

When I returned to my son's room, my wife was happy to see me. It was almost as if she could sense something different about me. That was the man she did not yet know was becoming.

A couple of days went by. My son was recovering well. But when my wife and I began asking the doctors about starting the chemotherapy, the answers would not come. The doctors kept saying maybe tomorrow — but not today. That same response went on for several days. And my wife and I began to grow genuinely concerned. If the chemotherapy was so urgently needed, why was it not starting? Was the cancer spreading? Was our son's condition being taken seriously? These were real questions, and the silence from the medical team was becoming harder to handle.

I took some time. I comforted my wife. And I quietly said a prayer.

Before I could even finish forming the words, I felt something come over me. An overwhelming certainty — like a light going on — that my son was going to be just fine. That somehow the cancer was going to be gone. There was not a single moment of doubt in it. It was not wishful thinking. It went right back to what I had felt in that chapel — as if God was pointing from that moment to this one, letting me know that what I was sensing was not something I had manufactured in my own head.

I mentioned to my wife — I think God is doing something. I have a feeling the cancer is going to be gone.

She probably heard that the way a mother hears a father wishing for the best. I understood.

A few days later, the doctors delivered the results. The biopsy for the tumor showed zero cancer.

You could see it on the doctor's face — he was physically shaken. He explained that he and no other doctor there had ever seen anything like this. They sent the tumor to another hospital for review. That hospital confirmed the same thing. No cancer in the tumor.

I remember slightly smiling at my wife. Taking a deep breath. I knew what God had told me was true. It was not me talking to myself.

I navigated the tension of that news carefully, though. One of my son's kidneys had been removed unnecessarily. That is damage that cannot be undone. My son's future still carries some uncertainty because of it. My wife carries grief about that and rightfully so. I do not dismiss it. I mourn what was lost too.

But I am also a witness to what was spared.

And until you have pleaded with God alone and broken in a chapel — and then watched Him do something the doctors could not explain — there is a level of confidence and understanding that words cannot fully prepare you for. You now know that God will show up. You know He is always there. And you know that the promise you made to Him that night — this time it is true.

Once my son was well enough to return home and go back to living the life of a normal five-year-old, I decided it was time to follow up on my own health. The doctors had been wanting to do an MRI on my pancreas. What they found was that twenty-five percent of my pancreas was completely dead. They called it necrotizing pancreatitis — the result of over ten years of episodes silently destroying tissue I could not recover. There is no cure, they told me. Once the tissue is gone, it is gone. And the deterioration, they said, would only continue. I should prepare myself for the day I would no longer have a functioning pancreas.

I walked out of that office angry.

I told my wife — I am not going to accept that as a solution or an outcome. With everything in me, I told her I was going to find a way to stop this.

When I got home, God led me to spend hours and days and weeks researching supplements and peptides — things that conventional medicine had not offered and would not offer. I began carefully and slowly incorporating them. Before long, the pain episodes stopped.

Nearly two years later — I have not been hospitalized once. The pain that was a daily reality for over a decade is almost completely gone. I have not felt this way in more than ten years. I am not claiming to be healed — only God knows the full condition of my body. What I know is this: the rapid decline stopped, the excruciating pain is gone, and everything that changed traces directly back to the night I made that promise in that chapel.

I am not a finished man. I still struggle. I still drift. But I am no longer living my life without an anchor. The direction has changed.

This book was not written by a theologian or a man who has lived a perfect life. I am a husband and a father first. I am a man who was once a small boy at nine years old who decided he was going to give his life to Jesus Christ — but who was not fully prepared for the commitment and the cost that came with that. I spent the next couple of decades wrestling with depression, chronic illness, overwork, self-reliance, and the persistent temptation to carry what only God was meant to hold.

I wrote this book because real people — people I know, people who agreed to be part of this — are carrying questions that have become so heavy and so loud that they have stopped asking them out loud. Questions about who God really is. About His silence. About suffering. About why children hurt, why good people struggle, why prayers seem to go unanswered. Questions that feel too big, too dangerous, or too painful to bring into the light.

I understand those questions. I have felt them.

What I discovered — and what I want you to discover — is that none of these questions surprised God. He has had the answers to every single one of them in Scripture. His Word has always held them. We simply need to learn how to look and how to understand what He actually said.

This is not a performance of faith. It is the testimony of a man who found God faithful in the darkest room of his life — who went searching for answers in Scripture and wants to walk you through what he found, question by question, chapter by chapter, with honesty, compassion, and the unchanging truth of God's Word as the only authority.

What this book does is go back behind the English translation to the original Hebrew and Greek — to what God actually said before institutions shaped what most believers receive. What I found did not shake my faith. It deepened it. The God of the original words is not smaller than the God I was taught. He is larger.

This book is not meant to be a theological war. It is not meant to attack any religion or faith. It is meant to help people come to know Jesus Christ and to weather the dark moments in life with faith.

I pray for each reader and I hope my research serves well.

God Bless, R.P. Priddy

Opening Prayer

B efore You Turn to Chapter One, Let Us Pray.

Father God,

Before this reader turns to Chapter One, I come to You on their behalf.

I do not know their name, but You do. I do not know what they are carrying right now — the fears, the doubts, the questions that may have kept them up at night, the wounds they have never spoken aloud, or the skepticism they walked in with. Lord, You know all of it. Every thought forming in their mind in this very moment. Every wall they have built. Every reason they almost did not open this book at all.

But Lord, I ask that You still them now. Quiet every distraction. Silence every voice that is not Yours. Remove every preconceived idea about who wrote these words or why.

Father, I ask that You let them see no man. Let them hear no ego. Let the author completely fade into the background — because this book was never about me, and these pages were never mine to claim. Father, this book belongs to You. I am nothing more than a broken man You chose to write through. A man with flaws, a past, and a faith that has been tested and stretched and has at times barely held on.

Father, if there is anything true and good and healing within these pages, it did not originate with me. It originated with You. And I need the reader to know that before they go any further.

So Father, I pray that as their eyes move across these words, something supernatural takes place. That the noise of the world fades. That the fast-beating heart slows. That the doubts soften just enough to let Your truth in. That this reader will feel not the presence of the writer, but the presence of the living God — who knew they would be sitting exactly where they are sitting, reading these exact words, at exactly this moment in their life.

I pray that this feels like a conversation only You and they are having. That it feels intimate. Safe. Honest. Unrushed.

I ask, Father, that Your Spirit goes ahead of every chapter — before their eyes even reach the words — and prepares their hearts to receive the words You have already spoken. And Lord, I ask that You cover what I have written. Correct anything in these pages that is in error. Amplify anything that is Your truth. And where my human limitations fall short, fill those gaps with Your grace.

I pray for the one who is angry with You. The one who is grieving. The one who has been hurt by religion and is giving it one last chance. I pray for the one who does not yet believe but is still searching. And I pray for the one who believes but has stopped trusting.

I ask You, Lord, that You meet every single one of them exactly where they are right now. Please do not let them leave these pages the same way they arrived.

You are the answer to every question in this book. You always have been, Lord.

I pray that they find You.

In the name of the Father, the Son, and the Holy Spirit.

Amen.

"The LORD thy God in the midst of thee is mighty; he will save, he will rejoice over thee with joy; he will rest in his love, he will joy over thee with singing." — Zephaniah 3:17 (KJV)

Chapter One

Why Do Good People Suffer — And Where Is God In It?

The LORD is nigh unto them that are of a broken heart; and saveth such as be of a contrite spirit. Many are the afflictions of the righteous: but the LORD delivereth him out of them all." — Psalm 34:18–19 (KJV)

The Question

It is the oldest question in human history. It has been whispered in hospital waiting rooms, screamed into empty bedrooms, and pressed against the walls of prison cells. It has risen from the lips of the dying and the grieving, from the hearts of parents who have buried children and from the mouths of the faithful who served God faithfully and still watched everything fall apart.

Where is God when it hurts?

This is not a question born in skepticism, though skeptics have weaponized it for centuries. It is a question born in the deepest chambers of human experience — in the place where love and loss collide, where faith meets the unimaginable, where every theological framework a person has ever constructed is tested against the weight of actual suffering.

Job asked it. David asked it. Jeremiah asked it. The disciples asked it.

And if you are holding this book today, there is a reasonable chance you are asking it too.

The church has not always handled this question well. Too often, well-meaning people have rushed to fill the silence of suffering with theological explanations that, while technically accurate, land in the ears of a grieving person like stones dropped on an open wound.

Suffering is not primarily an intellectual problem to be solved. It is a human experience to be accompanied. And before we say a single theological word about why suffering exists, we owe it to every person carrying this question to sit with them in it for a moment — honestly, quietly, and without rushing toward resolution. But we cannot stay there forever.

Because the question does not go away simply because we refuse to answer it.

And the God of Scripture — the same God who is present in the suffering — has not been silent about it. He has not left us without an answer. The answer is not simple, and it is not painless, and it does not resolve every tension that suffering creates. But it is real. It is true. And for the person willing to pursue it, it changes everything.

That is why this chapter exists. Not to offer cheap comfort. Not to minimize anyone's pain. Not to produce a neat theological formula that wraps suffering in a bow and makes it presentable.

Acknowledging the Pain

Before we go to Scripture — before we open a single commentary or cite a single theologian — we need to say something plainly: Your suffering is real.

And it matters. Whatever brought you to this chapter — the diagnosis, the betrayal, the loss, the depression that will not lift, the prayer that has gone unanswered so long you have stopped counting the days — it is real. It counts. God sees it. And no amount of theological explanation makes it stop hurting.

Suffering comes in forms that defy categorization. Some of it arrives suddenly — in a phone call, a diagnosis, an accident, a moment that divides life permanently into before and after. Some of it is slow and grinding — the kind that wears you down over years until you can barely remember what life felt like before the weight arrived.

Some suffering is physical. Some is relational. Some is financial. Some is the specific grief of watching someone you love suffer and being utterly unable to stop it.

And some suffering — perhaps the hardest kind — comes with the added burden of silence. The kind where God feels absent. Where prayer feels like talking to an empty room. Where every verse that once brought comfort now seems hollow and every sermon feels directed at someone whose life is less broken than yours.

If that is where you are, you are not alone. And you are not outside the reach of God. Suffering does not mean God has abandoned you. It does not mean you have failed spiritually. It does not mean you are being punished for something you did or did not do.

What Scripture Says

Part 1 — The Lie We Were Never Supposed to Believe

The Greek language of the New Testament contains a word — pathema — that refers to suffering, affliction, and the experience of pain. It shares its root with pascho, which means to suffer, to experience, to endure. And the word pathetos — used to describe something that is subject to suffering — is applied in the New Testament to describe the very nature of Jesus Christ before His resurrection.

Destined to suffer. This is not incidental. This is architectural.

Suffering was not an accident that interrupted God's plan for humanity. It was accounted for within it — from before the foundations of the world.

"In the world ye shall have tribulation: but be of good cheer; I have overcome the world." — John 16:33 (KJV)

Notice what He did not say. He did not say tribulation might come, or that tribulation comes only to those who lack faith, or that the spiritually mature can expect to avoid it. He said ye shall have tribulation. Not as a warning delivered with reluctance. As a declaration delivered with confidence — immediately followed by the only adequate response to it: He has overcome the world.

The church has not always preached it this way. There is a version of Christianity that promises the faithful a life of increasing health, wealth, and comfort. That frames suffering as evidence of insufficient faith. That reduces the God of the universe to a vending machine dispensing blessings in proportion to the spiritual currency deposited.

Job's friends believed this. Three men who loved Job — who sat with him in silence for seven days before speaking — ultimately arrived at the same wrong conclusion: that Job's suffering must be the consequence of Job's sin. That the equation of the universe was simple. Obedience produces blessing. Suffering reveals disobedience.

God's response to this theology was not gentle:

"My wrath is kindled against thee, and against thy two friends: for ye have not spoken of me the thing that is right, as my servant Job hath." — Job 42:7 (KJV)

The transactional theology — the idea that faithfulness guarantees comfort and suffering reveals failure — is not just theologically inaccurate. According to God Himself, it is a misrepresentation of His character serious enough to provoke His anger.

Jesus dismantled the same assumption directly. When His disciples asked whose sin was responsible for a man's blindness from birth, Jesus answered with something that reoriented the entire question:

"Neither hath this man sinned, nor his parents: but that the works of God should be made manifest in him." — John 9:3 (KJV)

The man's suffering was not a punishment. It was a preparation. Not for something he had done wrong — but for something God intended to do right.

The One Form of Evil That Cannot Multiply

C.S. Lewis — in his landmark work The Problem of Pain — makes a distinction about the nature of suffering that most people have never encountered, and once heard cannot be forgotten. Lewis observes that the evils of the world can be divided into categories — intellectual evil, which is error, and moral evil, which is sin. And both of these evils share a deeply troubling characteristic: they reproduce themselves.

Error breeds more error. Sin breeds more sin, strengthening sinful habits and slowly eroding the conscience that might otherwise resist them.

Pain, Lewis argues, is fundamentally different. Pain is what he calls the one sterile or disinfected evil — the only form of evil that does not naturally reproduce itself. Once a pain is over, it is over. It has no built-in tendency to generate more pain. And when a person suffers publicly, the natural response in human observers is not corruption. It is compassion. It awakens something good in the people who witness it.

Lewis concludes that when God needs a tool to awaken a sleeping or falling world — He reaches for the one instrument in His hand that destroys itself rather than multiplying. Pain is not God's cruelty. It is, in the most precise theological sense, His mercy. The one form of correction that cannot make things worse.

Philip Yancey — one of the most honest modern writers on the subject of suffering — identifies three questions that suffering tends to generate beneath its surface: Is God unfair? Is God silent? Is God hidden? These questions are not born in theology. They are born in experience. And the Psalms — which contain some of the most raw and unfiltered expressions of human anguish in all of Scripture — validate every one of them.

"My God, my God, why hast thou forsaken me? why art thou so far from helping me, and from the words of my roaring?" — Psalm 22:1 (KJV)

"Awake, why sleepest thou, O Lord? arise, cast us not off for ever. Wherefore hidest thou thy face, and forgettest our affliction and our oppression?" — Psalm 44:23–24 (KJV)

"I am weary of my crying: my throat is dried: mine eyes fail while I wait for my God." — Psalm 69:3 (KJV)

These are not the words of people who have lost their faith. These are the words of people whose faith was real enough to bring their full, unfiltered anguish directly to God.

Part 2 — The Answer Is Not a Philosophy. It Is a Person.

J.I. Packer — one of the most respected theologians of the modern era — made an observation about suffering that deserves to be received slowly. He drew a sharp line between those who merely believe God exists and those who actually know Him. His conclusion was this:

without a genuine, personal knowledge of God's character, the world becomes an incomprehensible place — painful, disorienting, and impossible to navigate with any steadiness.

The problem, Packer argued, is not unbelief. The problem is unfamiliarity. A person can affirm every doctrine in the creeds and still remain a stranger to the God those doctrines describe. And that stranger will suffer the same confusion in hard seasons as the person who never believed at all.

Not for those who do not believe in God. For those who do not know Him.

There is a profound difference between believing God exists and actually knowing who He is. A person can believe in God and still stumble blindly through suffering because they have never gone deep enough into His character to understand how He works, why He allows what He allows, and what He is building in the life of every person He loves.

The answer to suffering is not found in a formula or a theological argument. The answer is found in a Person.

God Has Never Watched Our Pain From a Distance

Before we examine how God entered human suffering through the Incarnation, there is something hidden in the Old Testament that stops most people cold when they encounter it — because it inverts an assumption almost every believer carries without examining it.

When God commanded the Israelites to build the tabernacle in the wilderness — and later when Solomon built the great Temple in Jerusalem — the common understanding is that these were places built for humanity. Places where people could go to find God. Access points to the divine.

But theologians Terryl and Fiona Givens, in their work The God Who Weeps, argue something extraordinary and almost entirely overlooked: the temple was also designed as God's sanctuary. His place of refuge from the agony of being fully present in a broken and sinful world.

Think carefully about what that means. For a being of absolute purity, absolute goodness, and absolute love to descend into a world of darkness, cruelty, injustice, and suffering — that descent is not emotionally neutral. The authors observe that God's love compels Him to draw near to His people in their distress — but that the pain of our world is genuinely agonizing to Him.

God does not observe our pain from a position of comfortable emotional immunity. He feels it.

This is not a God who designed a world of suffering and retreated to a safe distance to watch it unfold. This is a God whose love drives Him into the midst of it at tremendous personal cost — and who then, through the Temple, established a place within that broken world where He could dwell among His people while remaining shielded from the full, unbearable weight of every evil surrounding Him.

And then — in the Incarnation — He set even that shield aside entirely.

God Entered It

"He was despised and rejected of men; a man of sorrows, and acquainted with grief." — Isaiah 53:3 (KJV)

The Son of God — through whom all things were created — became a man of sorrows. Acquainted with grief. Not observing grief from heaven. Not sending a representative. He put on human flesh and walked directly into the full weight of human suffering.

But before the cross — before the nails, before the crown of thorns, before the darkness at noon — there was a garden. And what happened in that garden is one of the most important and most underexamined moments in the entire life of Jesus.

The night before the crucifixion, Jesus withdrew to the Garden of Gethsemane with three of His closest disciples and went a little further from them to pray. And what Luke records happening to His body in that moment is medically extraordinary:

"And being in an agony he prayed more earnestly: and his sweat was as it were great drops of blood falling down to the ground." — Luke 22:44 (KJV)

The Greek word Luke uses here is agonia — the root from which the English word agony descends. It does not mean sadness or anxiety. It describes the full psychological and physiological distress of a person confronting something catastrophic. And the phenomenon Luke describes — sweat becoming as drops of blood — is a documented medical condition called hematidrosis, recorded in ancient medical literature and in modern clinical accounts, in which extreme psychological duress causes the capillaries near the sweat glands to rupture, mixing blood with sweat. It occurs under conditions of absolute, overwhelming terror.

This was not metaphor. This was a body responding to what the soul inside it was facing.

And yet what makes this moment more staggering than the physical detail is what preceded it. Jesus knew exactly what was coming. He was not caught off guard. He had told His disciples three times that He would be handed over, killed, and would rise on the third day. He knew the plan. He knew the purpose. And He chose, in full knowledge, to feel every moment of the anticipation rather than numb Himself to it.

When the soldiers offered Him wine mixed with gall — a pain-dulling substance commonly offered to condemned men before crucifixion — Jesus tasted it and refused. He would not blunt the experience. He bore the full weight of the cross completely awake, completely present, completely conscious of every moment of what was happening to Him.

Why does this matter for a chapter about human suffering? Because the deepest form of suffering most people carry is not the event itself. It is the anticipation of it. The diagnosis you receive on a Tuesday and cannot tell anyone about until Friday. The conversation you know is coming that will end something you love. The medical results you are waiting for in a hallway, alone, not knowing which direction your life is about to turn.

Most human suffering lives not in the worst moment but in the long approach to it.

And Jesus — in Gethsemane — walked that road with His eyes completely open, sweating blood, begging for another way, and then going anyway. He does not meet you in your anticipatory dread as a stranger to it. He has been there. He felt it with a body like yours. And He went through it for you.

He Wept Because He Chose To

John 11:35 is the shortest verse in the English Bible. Three words: Jesus wept.

But the Greek beneath those three words carries a precision that most English readers never encounter. And it changes the entire meaning of the moment.

There are two different Greek words used in that passage for weeping. The crowd surrounding the tomb, and Mary who had fallen at Jesus's feet, were klaio — loud, audible, convulsive weeping. The kind that breaks out of the body involuntarily when grief overwhelms it. It is the same word used to describe Peter's weeping after he denied Jesus three times. Uncontrolled, heaving grief.

Jesus did not klaio. The word used for Jesus in verse 35 is dakruo — a quieter word. The welling of tears. The silent overflow of something deeply felt. Not a performance of mourning for the crowd. Something that moved through Him before He chose whether to display it or not.

Now here is what makes this moment so theologically significant. Just before He wept, the bystanders said something worth reading very carefully:

"Could not this man, which opened the eyes of the blind, have caused that even this man should not have died?" — John 11:37 (KJV)

They recognized His power. They understood that the man standing at Lazarus's tomb could have prevented what was in it. Which means that Jesus wept — dakruo, quietly, involuntarily — while knowing He was four minutes from raising a dead man to life.

He did not weep because He did not know what was about to happen. He wept because grief was real, and the people in front of Him were carrying it, and His love for them moved through His body before His mind could manage it. He chose to feel the weight of their sorrow even standing at the edge of the miracle that would end it.

That is the God who is present in your suffering. Not a God who stands above it looking for the right moment to fix it. A God who stands inside it with you, feeling what you feel, carrying what you carry — even when He already knows how the story ends.

He Bore It as a Physical Load

Isaiah 53 is one of the most precise prophetic descriptions of the Messiah's suffering in all of Scripture — written seven centuries before the crucifixion. Most people know verse 3: He was despised and rejected, a man of sorrows, acquainted with grief. But verse 4 contains a word study that changes the entire understanding of what Jesus did with human suffering — and it is almost never examined in its original Hebrew.

"Surely he hath borne our griefs, and carried our sorrows: yet we did esteem him stricken, smitten of God, and afflicted." — Isaiah 53:4 (KJV)

The Hebrew word translated "borne" is nasa. In Brown-Driver-Briggs, nasa is defined as to lift, to carry, to take up and transport a burden. It is not a metaphor drawn from emotional empathy. It is a word from the world of physical labor. It describes a worker bending down, getting underneath a heavy load, straightening up, and carrying it on his own back so that the one who was carrying it no longer has to.

The Hebrew word translated "carried" is sabal. Sabal is even more vivid. It means to carry as a heavy, pressing, crushing weight — the kind of burden that bows the shoulders of the carrier. It is the word used for carrying loads that were never designed for one person to carry alone.

Isaiah is not saying that Jesus sympathized with human grief. He is saying that Jesus stepped underneath it, lifted it entirely off humanity, and carried it on His own body. Nasa and sabal are not the language of compassion from a distance. They are the language of physical substitution. He took what you were carrying and put it on Himself.

The Hidden Word: What the Oldest Manuscript of Isaiah Reveals

For centuries, readers of the King James Bible have encountered Isaiah 53:11 in this form:

"He shall see of the travail of his soul, and shall be satisfied." — Isaiah 53:11 (KJV)

The servant suffers. The servant sees. The servant is satisfied. It reads as a declaration of endurance rewarded.

But in 1947, when scholars began examining the caves of Qumran near the Dead Sea, a revelation emerged from one of the oldest manuscripts of Scripture ever recovered — the Great Isaiah Scroll, dated to approximately 125 B.C., more than a thousand years older than any Hebrew manuscript the translators of the KJV ever held in their hands. The scroll contained a word the later Masoretic Hebrew tradition had dropped entirely.

That word is ' — □□□or. Light.

The complete text as the Qumran scroll preserves it reads: He shall see light from the travail of his soul, and be satisfied.

And here is what makes this discovery so staggering in its confirmation: the Septuagint — the Greek translation of the Hebrew Scriptures made by Jewish scholars in Alexandria in the centuries before Christ, which the entire Greek-speaking early church used as its Bible — also contains this word. It had been there all along. The Greek reads δεῖξαι αὐτῷ φῶς — to show him light.

Two independent ancient witnesses, the Dead Sea Scrolls and the Septuagint, both preserved a reading the later Masoretic tradition lost. This is why modern translations restored the word light to Isaiah 53:11 based on the scroll evidence — while the faithful KJV reader, following the Masoretic text, has never seen it.

What it means is this. The servant does not merely endure the travail and survive it. He descends into death — real death, the full weight of every human sin carried by nasa and sabal — and he emerges to see light. The resurrection was not an afterthought attached to the cross. It was embedded in the language of Isaiah's prophecy seven centuries before it happened, preserved in the oldest manuscript ever found, confirmed by an independent Greek translation made before the birth of Jesus.

The cross was always going to end in light. And the most ancient copy of Isaiah's own words confirms it.

The Trinity Hidden in the Architecture of the Passage

But there is something deeper still — something the early church fathers who read Isaiah through the Septuagint saw with a clarity that most modern readers have never encountered.

Justin Martyr — writing in the second century, engaging Jewish scholars directly in his Dialogue with Trypho — argued that Isaiah 52:13 through 53:12 cannot be read as a single-person narrative. The passage, he observed, carries three distinct layers of divine agency that the Greek text makes unmistakably clear.

The Father is the One who wills the offering. Isaiah 53:10 declares: it pleased the LORD to bruise him; He hath put him to grief. The sovereign, initiating will comes from above.

The Son is the Servant who bears the burden — who descends, who carries the nasa and the sabal, who sees the light from the travail of His soul and is satisfied.

And the Spirit is present in the passage not in chapter 53 itself but in its direct continuation. Isaiah 61:1 — the very verse Jesus stood up in the synagogue at Nazareth and read aloud as His own mission statement, declaring it fulfilled in that very hour — announces:

"The Spirit of the LORD is upon me; because the LORD hath anointed me to preach good tidings unto the meek." — Isaiah 61:1 (KJV)

Jesus quoted it in Luke 4:18 and then sat down and said: this day is this scripture fulfilled in your ears. The Father anointing. The Spirit empowering. The Son bearing the travail and proclaiming the light on the other side of it.

"The Spirit of the Lord is upon me, because he hath anointed me to preach the gospel to the poor; he hath sent me to heal the brokenhearted, to preach deliverance to the captives, and recovering of sight to the blind, to set at liberty them that are bruised." — Luke 4:18 (KJV)

The atonement of Isaiah 53 was never a solo act. The Father sent. The Spirit sustained. The Son bore every grief and every sorrow all the way down into the darkness.

And in the oldest manuscript of Isaiah ever discovered, the word that tells us where it ends — the word hidden from most readers for centuries — is 'or. Light.

He bore it as a physical load. He carried it all the way to the bottom. And He came back with light.

This is what Hebrews 4:15 confirms when it declares that we do not have a High Priest who cannot be touched with the feeling of our infirmities — but one who was in all points tempted, tried, and tested like as we are. The Greek word sumpatheo — from which the English sympathy descends — does not mean He feels sorry for you from a distance.

All Things — Even the Painful Ones

"And we know that all things work together for good to them that love God, to them who are the called according to his purpose." — Romans 8:28 (KJV)

Notice carefully what this verse does not say. It does not say all things are good. It does not say every experience will feel good or produce immediate visible results. It does not ask you to call your pain a blessing before you have had time to grieve it.

It says all things work together.

The word together is doing enormous theological work in that sentence. Individual threads of a life may look like chaos, loss, and destruction when examined alone. But God is weaving them — all of them — into something that serves His purpose and ultimately the good of those who belong to Him.

Paul describes our present trials as achieving "a far more exceeding and eternal weight of glory" — 2 Corinthians 4:17 (KJV). Whatever you are suffering in this life — however real and however heavy — is light and momentary when placed against the eternal weight of what God is preparing.

"And God shall wipe away all tears from their eyes; and there shall be no more death, neither sorrow, nor crying, neither shall there be any more pain: for the former things are passed away." — Revelation 21:4 (KJV)

Not managed. Not minimized. Wiped away. By God Himself. Personally. Every tear that was ever cried — including yours.

The Answer Is Not a What. It Is a Who.

Packer arrives at a conclusion that brings everything in this chapter into focus. When he asks what human beings were ultimately made for — what the highest aim of life truly is — his answer collapses every intellectual framework down to three words: to know God.

Not to know about God. Not to understand His ways or master His theology. To know Him — personally, directly, the way a person knows someone they have sat with in a dark room and found faithful.

Not to understand suffering. Not to explain it. Not to resolve it intellectually. To know the God who is present in it. To encounter Him in the darkest room. To find — in the moments when a person has finally run out of everything except honesty — that the God of the universe shows up.

The Stories That Prove It

Theology is powerful. But story is where theology becomes undeniable. The Bible is not a collection of abstract principles handed down from a distant God who has never witnessed human pain. It is a living record of real people who suffered deeply, questioned honestly, and found God faithful in ways they never anticipated.

Two of those stories stand above the rest as the clearest and most complete case studies of innocent suffering redeemed by God's sovereign purpose.

Job — The Man Whose Name Was the Question

Before Job ever lost a single thing he owned, God Himself declared him —

"a perfect and an upright man, one that feareth God, and escheweth evil." — Job 1:8 (KJV)

God did not call Job nearly perfect. He called him perfect and upright. And then He allowed everything to be taken from him.

In a single day Job lost his oxen, his donkeys, his sheep, his camels, his servants, and all ten of his children. Then he lost his health — covered from head to foot in painful sores, sitting in ashes, scraping his wounds with broken pottery. His wife told him to curse God and die. His three closest friends told him he must have sinned to deserve this.

And Job — perfect, upright, God-fearing Job — told God exactly how he felt. Without filtering it. Without performing faith for an audience.

"Why is light given to him that is in misery, and life unto the bitter in soul; which long for death, but it cometh not?" — Job 3:20–21 (KJV)

Job did not lose his faith. He brought his faith — raw and bleeding and demanding — directly to God. And God did not reject him for it. What God rejected was the neat theological explanation his friends offered — the comfortable lie that suffering always equals sin.

When God finally spoke to Job out of the whirlwind, His answer was not a theological treatise. God answered Job by revealing Himself. And something extraordinary happened. Job — who had demanded answers — encountered God Himself. And that was enough.

"I have heard of thee by the hearing of the ear: but now mine eye seeth thee." — Job 42:5 (KJV)

Job did not walk away with explanations. He walked away having seen God. And God restored everything Job had lost — double what had been taken. Not because Job earned it. Because God is faithful. And because Job's story was never really about Job. It was written for every person who would ever sit in the ash heap of their own life and wonder if God was still there.

But notice something that the theology of Job's story demands we face honestly. God permitted the suffering. He set its limits. He told Satan exactly how far he could go and drew a line he could not cross. God was not the author of what happened to Job. He was the sovereign who governed it. And that governance was never careless, never cruel, and never without purpose.

Every day in the ash heap was a day inside a story that God was writing toward a conclusion Job could not yet see.

The whirlwind did not answer Job's questions. It answered his need. And his need was not information. It was encounter. The God who speaks from the whirlwind is the same God who is present in your darkness right now — not necessarily to explain it, but to be found in it.

Joseph — The Man Whose Suffering Saved Nations

Joseph's story is examined in full detail in Chapter Three of this book, where it serves as the primary case study for God's foreknowledge working through human history. What matters here — for this chapter's specific question — is not the architecture of God's design across twenty-two years, but the daily experience of a man living inside it.

Joseph did not know he was in the middle of a sovereign story. He knew he was in a pit. He knew he was in Potiphar's prison. He knew he had done nothing to deserve either. And Scripture does not record a single moment where God pulled back the curtain and explained to Joseph what was happening. It simply records that God was with him

—

"But the LORD was with Joseph, and shewed him mercy, and gave him favour." — Genesis 39:21 (KJV)

Not a dramatic rescue. Not an explanation. Just the quiet, faithful, unseen presence of God in the middle of a situation that looked, from the inside, exactly like abandonment.

That is what suffering often looks like from the inside. Not divine absence. God's presence without God's explanation.

And it was enough for Joseph to remain faithful, to serve excellently wherever he was placed, and to arrive — twenty-two years later — at the moment where the full design was finally visible.

"But as for you, ye thought evil against me; but God meant it unto good, to bring to pass, as it is this day, to save much people alive." — Genesis 50:20 (KJV)

You thought evil. God meant it unto good. The distinction does not erase the pain.

The Suffering of the Innocent

There is one dimension of suffering that presses harder than almost any other — and it deserves to be addressed directly rather than folded quietly into a broader theological argument. The suffering of children.

When a child is sick. When an innocent person is abused. When someone who has done nothing wrong endures something they never deserved — every theological framework feels inadequate. Every attempt to explain it feels hollow. And the question shifts from abstract to devastating: how can a loving God allow this?

Scripture does not avoid this tension. Jesus addressed it directly.

"But whoso shall offend one of these little ones which believe in me, it were better for him that a millstone were hanged about his neck, and that he were drowned in the depth of the sea." — Matthew 18:6 (KJV)

The language Jesus chose here is not gentle. It is not diplomatic. It is a declaration of the weight God places on the protection of the vulnerable. Those who harm innocent children face a consequence Jesus describes in the most severe terms available to Him.

But it still does not answer why God allows innocent suffering in the first place.

Here is what Scripture does tell us: that God's heart toward the innocent is not indifference. It is burning, active, protective love. The same God who wept at Lazarus's tomb — who felt the weight of a single family's grief so personally that He cried in front of them — is the same God who is present in every moment of innocent suffering. Not unmoved. Not distant. Present. Grieving. Working.

The question of why God allows children to suffer is addressed fully in Chapter Thirteen of this book, where it receives the direct and sustained treatment it deserves. What this chapter wants to say here is simpler and more foundational: the God who is present in your adult suffering is the same God who is present in the suffering of the most vulnerable. He has not turned away. He has not looked the other way.

God Allows. God Does Not Cause.

This distinction matters more than almost any other in this entire chapter.

God is not the author of evil. He is not the designer of suffering. He did not create sickness, cruelty, abuse, or injustice. These things entered the world through the free choice of created beings — both angelic and human — who exercised the freedom God gave them in directions that violated His character and His design.

But God is sovereign. And His sovereignty means that nothing — not a single event in the entire history of creation — occurs outside of His awareness or beyond His ability to redeem.

He does not cause every painful thing that happens. But He permits what He permits for reasons that His character guarantees are never careless, never cruel, and never without purpose.

The Book of Job makes this architecture explicit. Satan approached God and requested permission to test Job. God set the boundaries. He did not send the suffering — He permitted it within defined limits. And He never abandoned Job inside it for a single moment.

The same pattern holds throughout Scripture. Joseph's brothers chose to sell him. Potiphar's wife chose to lie about him. The cupbearer chose to forget him. At every point the suffering came through the free choices of human beings acting out of their own sin and selfishness. And at every point God was present in it — weaving something through it that the people causing the suffering could not see and would never have chosen.

God never wastes what He permits. Every trial He allows passes through His hands before it reaches you. He does not promise to prevent every painful experience. He promises to be present in every painful experience — and to work within it toward something that serves both His glory and your ultimate good.

"There hath no temptation taken you but such as is common to man: but God is faithful, who will not suffer you to be tempted above that ye are able; but will with the temptation also make a way to escape, that ye may be able to bear it." — 1 Corinthians 10:13 (KJV)

He sets the limit. He provides the way through. And He remains present in every moment between the beginning of the trial and the end of it.

God did not cause your suffering.

The Questions Skeptics Ask

There are people reading this chapter who did not come to it as believers. They came as challengers. As people who have heard the Christian answer to suffering before and found it unconvincing. This section is for them. These are the hardest versions of the question. They deserve a direct and honest response rather than a rehearsed deflection.

"If God Is All Powerful and All Good — He Would Stop Suffering."

This is the problem of evil — perhaps the oldest and most sophisticated philosophical argument against the existence of God. It sounds airtight. It is not.

The argument assumes that an all-good God would necessarily eliminate all suffering immediately and completely. But this assumption contains a hidden premise never examined — that the elimination of suffering is always the highest good. That premise is demonstrably false even within ordinary human experience.

A surgeon causes pain. A loving parent disciplines a child. A coach pushes an athlete past the point of comfort. In each case a person with both the power to prevent suffering and the genuine desire for the other person's good chooses not to prevent it — because they understand the suffering serves a purpose that elimination would destroy.

C.S. Lewis noted that the question is not whether God could create a world without suffering — but whether a world without the possibility of suffering could contain beings capable of genuine moral development, genuine love, and genuine relationship with God. His conclusion was that it could not. A world of perfectly comfortable beings with no capacity for suffering would also be a world of beings with no capacity for courage, compassion, sacrifice, or growth.

The God who removes every obstacle and guarantees every comfort is not a good God. He is an indulgent one. And indulgence is not love.

"If God Knew I Would Suffer — Why Did He Create Me At All?"

This question carries real pain beneath it. Job said something remarkably similar in the depths of his anguish:

"Let the day perish wherein I was born, and the night in which it was said, There is a man child conceived." — Job 3:3 (KJV)

Job cursed the day of his birth. And God did not reject him for the honesty of his despair. He met him in it. And He will meet you in it too.

The question assumes that a life containing suffering is worse than no life at all. But every human being who has ever lived has experienced both suffering and beauty — both pain and joy — both loss and love. The presence of suffering does not negate the value of existence.

Furthermore — God did not create humanity for earth alone. He created humanity for eternity. Paul — who was beaten, imprisoned, shipwrecked, and eventually martyred — described earthly suffering this way:

"For I reckon that the sufferings of this present time are not worthy to be compared with the glory which shall be revealed in us." — Romans 8:18 (KJV)

"Why Do the Wicked Prosper While the Righteous Suffer?"

The Psalmist asked this with raw honesty. He watched the wicked live in comfort and ease while the righteous struggled. And he admitted it almost destroyed his faith. Almost.

"Until I went into the sanctuary of God; then understood I their end." — Psalm 73:17 (KJV)

The turning point was not a philosophical argument. It was a change of perspective. When Asaph saw the full picture — not just the present moment but the eternal destination — everything shifted. God's justice is not absent. It is not yet complete. And when it is complete — nothing will have been overlooked.

"Be not deceived; God is not mocked: for whatsoever a man soweth, that shall he also reap." — Galatians 6:7 (KJV)

"Science Explains Suffering — We Don't Need God To Explain It."

Science explains the mechanism of suffering. It does not explain the meaning of it. Science can tell you that cancer is caused by the uncontrolled division of abnormal cells. It cannot tell you why your mother developed it at sixty-two. It can explain the neurological process of grief. It cannot tell you why love is worth the grief it costs.

Mechanism and meaning are two entirely different categories. And science — by its own definition — operates exclusively in the category of mechanism.

Francis Collins — former director of the Human Genome Project and a committed Christian — put it plainly. Science answers how. Faith answers why. And the human soul in the middle of suffering is not asking how. It is asking why.

"Thy word is a lamp unto my feet, and a light unto my path." — Psalm 119:105 (KJV)

One Final Word to the Skeptic

If you have read this chapter as a skeptic — if you came to it doubtful and you are leaving it still wrestling — that is not a failure. That is honesty. And God has never been afraid of honest wrestling.

Jacob wrestled with God through the night and walked away with both a limp and a blessing. Job demanded answers and walked away having seen God face to face. God is not threatened by your questions. He is not waiting for you to have everything figured out before He will meet you.

"Come unto me, all ye that labour and are heavy laden, and I will give you rest." — Matthew 11:28 (KJV)

That invitation has no prerequisite.

My Reflection

I want to be honest with you before this chapter closes. I am not a finished man.

I did not come to these pages with a credential or a title. What I came with is a story — one I shared with you in the preface — and a God who used that story to break me open in ways I never expected and never would have chosen, but would never trade.

What I want to add here — from the other side of those seasons — is not a retelling of the events. It is what I now understand about them.

My son handled what he went through with a strength that I can only describe as God-given. He was a child. And he carried it with a grace and a peace that shamed me in the most beautiful way. I believe God knew my son before he was born. I believe God pre-ordained a strength in him that would be needed for exactly this moment. And I believe my son's story — whatever it becomes — carries a significance that has not yet been fully revealed. I am his father. And I am watching.

As for my own suffering — the years of pancreatitis, the hospitalizations, the pain that would not let me go — I do not believe God was punishing me. I never believed that. Even in my darkest moments that thought never settled as truth. What I believe now — looking back from the other side of those seasons — is that I was a man who needed to be emptied before I could be filled. I needed the noise stripped away. The self-reliance broken. The control surrendered. And God — in His patience and His mercy — used everything He needed to use to get me there.

None of it was a curse. All of it was a tool.

I want to say something specifically about the Gethsemane section of this chapter, because it is where something became personally clear to me that I want to share with you directly. There were moments during my son's health journey where the suffering was not the worst of it. The worst of it was the waiting. The anticipation. The nights before tests came back. The days between the diagnosis and the surgery. The hours in a hospital corridor not knowing which direction everything was about to turn.

What I felt watching my son was sadness. Deep, helpless, fatherly sadness. The kind that does not live in the body but somewhere underneath it. I would have taken everything he was going through if I could have. I could not. And that — that love with nowhere to go — is a weight no father forgets.

When I finally understood what happened in Gethsemane — not the abstract theology of it but the human reality of it — something settled in me that has not moved since. Jesus did not carry just one kind of suffering on the road to the cross. He carried both. His body was broken — the scourging, the thorns, the nails, the physical agony that no man should have to endure. That was real. It was not symbolic. It was the kind of pain that breaks the body completely.

But before any of that, in the garden, He sweat drops of blood under the weight of something deeper than physical pain. He carried the emotional and spiritual anguish of knowing what was coming — of loving deeply and bearing what love costs when it refuses to let go. Two kinds of suffering. Both fully felt. Neither numbed.

I lived both of those in that season. My body had been through years of pain that brought me to my knees and at times to the floor. That was physical — and it was real. But what I felt watching my son was something that lived in a different place entirely. That was the sadness. The helplessness. The fatherly anguish of a love that would give anything and could not give enough.

Jesus knew both of those places. He chose to enter both of them fully — so that when I am in the pain of my body or in the grief of my heart, I am not in a place He observed from a distance. I am in a place

He walked through first. For me. For my son. For every father who has ever stood helpless in a hallway waiting to hear.

That is not a philosophy. That is a Person. And it is the only answer to suffering that has ever actually reached me where I live.

I have come to believe that after God's grace through Jesus Christ — after the gift of salvation and eternity — the second greatest thing a human being can experience in this life is the moment they finally understand why they are here. Their real purpose. Their actual calling. The thing God designed them for before they were formed. That moment of clarity — when the suffering finally makes sense and the calling becomes undeniable — is one of the most extraordinary experiences available to a human soul on this earth.

That is what my suffering gave me. That is what this book is. Not a punishment. A preparation.

If you are in the middle of your suffering right now — if the question "where is God in this?" is not a theological exercise for you but a desperate, personal, daily cry — I want you to hear this from someone who has sat in that kind of darkness and found God already there.

He is there. He was there before you arrived in this dark place. He entered it before you did — in a garden, in drops of blood, in tears at a tomb, in the darkness of a Friday afternoon that the whole world thought was the end. He knows what it feels like to carry what you are carrying.

"For his anger endureth but a moment; in his favour is life: weeping may endure for a night, but joy cometh in the morning." — Psalm 30:5 (KJV)

A Prayer for the Reader

Father, we come to the end of this chapter the same way we should come to the end of every hard season — not with all the answers, but with our hands open and our hearts turned toward You.

For the person reading this who is in pain right now — whose suffering is not a theological question but a daily reality — I ask that You meet them in this moment. Not with explanations. With Your presence. Let them feel the weight of Your nearness in the very place where they feel most alone.

For the parent who has watched a child suffer and screamed at the sky demanding to know why — remind them that You see every tear. That You count every one. That not a single moment of their child's pain has escaped Your attention or Your love.

For the person who came to this chapter as a skeptic — who picked up this book with doubt in one hand and desperation in the other — I pray that something in these pages cracked something open. That the God they were not sure existed made Himself just real enough to be worth pursuing further.

For the person who has suffered at the hands of another human being — whose pain was not the result of natural circumstance but of deliberate cruelty — remind them that You are not the author of what was done to them. That Your heart toward them has always been protection, restoration, and justice. And that You waste nothing — not even the wounds that were never supposed to happen.

For the person sitting in the waiting right now — in the hours before the results come back, in the days between the diagnosis and the answer, in the long dark anticipation of something they do not yet know how to face — remind them of the garden. That You were there before them. That You chose to feel every moment of that anticipation in a body like theirs. And that the One who went through it for them is the same One who is present in it with them now.

For all of us — remind us that You are not a distant God observing our suffering from a safe and comfortable heaven. You are the God who put on flesh and entered it. Who refused the numbing drink and felt every moment fully. Who cried out from the cross in the darkest hour and still declared victory. Who conquered death so that suffering would never have the final word.

We do not always understand Your ways. We do not always feel Your presence. But we choose — in the middle of the questions, in the middle of the pain, in the middle of the wondering — to trust that You are good. That You are near. And that You are working. Even now.

Amen.

Chapter Two

Why Would God Ever Forgive Evil People?

"**B**ut God commendeth his love toward us, in that, while we were yet sinners, Christ died for us." — Romans 5:8 (KJV)

The Question

It comes from a place most people are afraid to admit. Not from theology. Not from doubt. From something raw and human and honest — the part of us that has watched someone destroy an innocent life, cause irreparable damage, shatter something that can never be fully restored — and then heard that God forgives them anyway.

And something inside us recoils.

Not because we are cruel. Not because we lack faith. But because we are human beings with a God-given conscience that recognizes evil when it sees it and demands that evil be answered for. That instinct is not wrong. In fact it is holy. It is the image of God in you recognizing that what happened was not supposed to happen — and refusing to pretend otherwise.

But here is where the question gets complicated. Because if God only forgives the people we deem worthy of forgiveness — then we have made ourselves the judge. And if we are the judge, then we are also subject to our own standard. And not one of us would survive that courtroom.

This chapter is not going to give you a comfortable answer. It is going to give you a true one. And the truth of what God did to make forgiveness possible — for the worst person you can imagine, for the people who have hurt you most, and for you — is one of the most staggering realities in all of human history.

The Tension Is Real — And God Knows It

Before we go any further, something needs to be said plainly.

If you have ever felt a surge of anger at the idea of God forgiving someone who committed a horrific act — you do not need to apologize for that. You do not need to rush past it or perform a spiritual composure you do not actually feel. God is not offended by your honesty. He is not surprised by your struggle. In fact, the very capacity to feel outrage at evil is itself a reflection of His character living inside you.

The question of how God can forgive evil people is not a sign of weak faith. It is one of the oldest theological tensions in all of Scripture. The prophets wrestled with it. The Psalms are filled with it. Entire books of the Bible exist because human beings — faithful ones — brought this exact confusion before God and demanded an answer.

So bring it. Bring all of it.

Because God has an answer. And it will not just satisfy your mind. If you let it, it will change the way you see everything.

What This Question Is Really Asking

Before we can answer why God forgives evil people, we need to understand what forgiveness actually is — and what it is not.

Most of us carry a version of forgiveness in our minds that sounds something like this: if God forgives someone, then what they did no longer matters. The slate is wiped clean. The damage disappears. Justice is set aside in favor of mercy.

That is not what the Bible teaches. That is not what happened at the cross. And that misunderstanding is the source of most of the confusion people carry when they wrestle with this question.

Because the truth is this — forgiveness did not cost nothing. It cost everything. And the only reason any human being can stand before God forgiven is because every single ounce of justice that their sin demanded was paid. In full. By someone else.

That someone was Jesus Christ.

And until you understand what He actually absorbed on that cross — not just emotionally, but legally, spiritually, and at a cosmic level — the forgiveness of evil people will continue to feel like God looking the other way.

He was not looking the other way. He was looking directly at every act of evil ever committed by every human soul — and absorbing the full weight of the punishment that each one of those acts deserved — into the body of His own Son.

That is not leniency. That is the most severe act of justice in the history of creation.

Why Sin Had to Exist — The Gift That Required a Risk

To understand why God forgives evil people we first have to understand why evil people exist at all. And the answer begins with the greatest gift God ever gave.

Free will.

Look at every other living thing on this earth. Study the animal kingdom, the plant life, the intricate systems of nature that God set in motion. Magnificent. Complex. Ordered. But limited. Every creature operates within the boundaries of its design — instinct, nature, pattern. None of them wrestle with God. None of them choose to love Him. None of them carry the weight and the glory of a soul that can look at its Creator and decide.

The human being is different. Radically, uniquely, breathtakingly different.

The complexity of the human soul — the depth of our emotion, the capacity of our thought, the weight of our conscience, the hunger we carry for meaning and purpose and something greater than ourselves — is not an accident. It is evidence of trust. God designed the human soul with abilities that mirror His own — the capacity to create, to reason, to love, to choose — because He trusted us with something no other created being was given.

The freedom to choose Him.

But here is the theological reality that most people never fully reckon with. You cannot have genuine free will without a genuine alternative. A choice with only one option is not a choice at all. It is a script. It is programming. It is exactly what God refused to give us — because He did not want robots. He wanted sons and daughters. He wanted relationship. He wanted love that was freely given rather than mechanically produced.

And love that is freely given can also be freely withheld.

That is the risk God took. Not because He did not know what would happen — He knew exactly what would happen. But He loved us enough to give us the dignity of choosing our own path, even knowing that many would choose destruction. Even knowing the cost He would have to pay to redeem what free will broke.

Without the possibility of evil, there is no free will. Without free will, there is no genuine love. Without genuine love, there is no relationship with God.

This is why we are here. The entire journey of human life — with all of its suffering, its failure, its beauty, and its redemption — is the soul learning to choose God freely. And the process of purifying and ultimately destroying the sin that had to exist alongside that freedom is what Scripture calls sanctification. It is what Job endured in the wilderness. It is what every honest believer wrestles with between the moment of salvation and the moment of glory.

This body is not our home. It is a shell — temporary, limited, and finite. We are here for a breath in the scope of eternity. The things that feel most enormous to us — the betrayals, the losses, the injustices, the unanswered prayers — feel enormous because we are inside them. Because we experience them with these five senses and these complex emotions and this God-given capacity to feel deeply.

But the Bible serves as a constant reminder that this life, with all of its weight and meaning, is not the destination. It is the process. It is the purifying fire through which the soul is refined before it enters what it was always designed for.

"That the trial of your faith, being much more precious than of gold that perisheth, though it be tried with fire, might be found unto praise and honour and glory at the appearing of Jesus Christ." — 1 Peter 1:7 (KJV)

What God Did About the Problem

So God created free souls. Free souls chose sin. And a perfectly holy God — whose nature cannot coexist with sin any more than light can coexist with darkness — was faced with a reality that demanded a response.

He could have destroyed us. His justice would have permitted it. Every sin ever committed by every human being carries a debt — and that debt, according to Scripture, is death.

"For the wages of sin is death." — Romans 6:23 (KJV)

But destruction was never God's desire. His desire was always restoration. Always redemption. Always relationship.

So He did something that no human mind could have conceived and no other religion on earth has ever offered. He paid the debt Himself. Not by looking the other way. Not by lowering His standard of justice. Not by deciding that sin was not as serious as He originally declared. But by taking every sin — past, present, and future — every act of evil ever committed by every human soul — and placing the full, undiminished, catastrophic weight of the punishment those sins deserved onto the body of His own Son.

Jesus Christ — fully God and fully man — absorbed the complete retributive justice of a holy God on that cross. Every lash. Every nail. Every hour of darkness. Every ounce of separation from the Father that He had never once experienced in all of eternity — He endured it. For us. In our place. As our substitute.

And there is something hidden in the ancient Hebrew text of Scripture that most people have never been shown — something that reveals that this plan was not an afterthought. It was not a response to what went wrong. It was woven into the very fabric of creation before the first human being ever drew breath.

In the opening verse of Genesis — "In the beginning God created the heaven and the earth" — there are two Hebrew letters present in the original text that do not appear in the English translation. The Aleph-Tav. The first and last letters of the Hebrew alphabet, placed directly beside the name of God at the very moment of creation. In standard Hebrew grammar, Aleph-Tav functions as a direct object marker — a grammatical particle pointing to what is being acted upon. Messianic scholars and many early Jewish and Christian readers have noted, with theological significance, that these letters — the first and the last — echo what Jesus declares about Himself in Revelation: I am Alpha and Omega, the beginning and the end. Whether you receive this as a hidden signature of the Son embedded in the first act of creation, or simply as a grammatical feature whose symbolism is deeply meaningful, what it points toward is real: the One who said I am the beginning and the end was present at the beginning of everything.

"I am Alpha and Omega, the beginning and the end, the first and the last." — Revelation 22:13 (KJV)

Christ's signature was present at the moment of creation. Before the fall. Before sin. Before the need for forgiveness ever existed. The Lamb was slain — in the mind and plan of God — before the foundation of the world.

"...the Lamb slain from the foundation of the world." — Revelation 13:8 (KJV)

This was never a rescue plan. It was always the plan.

Satan's Role — The Deceiver Behind the Evil

Before we can fully understand why God forgives evil people we must address something that most conversations about forgiveness completely skip over.

Where does evil actually come from?

Because if we are going to honestly ask why God forgives people who commit horrific acts — we first need to understand what was operating behind those acts. What was influencing that soul. What was working against that person long before the moment of destruction arrived.

Scripture is not vague about this. There is an enemy. He is real. He is active. And his singular purpose — stated plainly throughout the Word of God — is to steal, to kill, and to destroy.

"The thief cometh not, but for to steal, and to kill, and to destroy." — John 10:10 (KJV)

Satan does not force anyone to sin. He cannot override the free will God gave every human soul. But what he can do — and what Scripture shows he does with extraordinary cunning — is deceive. Manipulate. Trick. Exploit weakness, wound, trauma, pride, and pain to lead a soul down a path it never would have chosen with clear eyes and a surrendered heart.

"Be sober, be vigilant; because your adversary the devil, as a roaring lion, walketh about, seeking whom he may devour." — 1 Peter 5:8 (KJV)

This does not remove human responsibility. Every soul that chooses evil is still accountable for that choice before God. Free will means the choice was real. But understanding the enemy's role changes the way we see the people who made those choices. Not excusing what they did. Not minimizing the damage. But recognizing that behind many of the most incomprehensible acts of human evil — there was a force actively working to bring that destruction about.

That is why God's forgiveness is not naive. It is not God pretending evil did not happen or that the person who committed it bears no responsibility. It is God — who sees the full picture, who understands every spiritual dynamic at work, who knows the enemy's hand in every act of destruction — extending grace to a soul He made, that His enemy corrupted, that His Son died to reclaim.

"For we wrestle not against flesh and blood, but against principalities, against powers, against the rulers of the darkness of this world, against spiritual wickedness in high places." — Ephesians 6:12 (KJV)

When you look at the person whose evil you cannot understand — you are not just looking at a human being who made a choice. You are looking at a soul that was targeted by the most sophisticated deceiver in the history of creation. That does not make what they did acceptable. But it does make God's desire to forgive and restore them make complete sense.

Only God Creates the Soul — And Only God Can Redeem It

There is a question that surfaces in our modern world that previous generations never had to wrestle with — and it speaks directly to the heart of why forgiveness belongs to God alone.

We live in an age where human beings are attempting to do things that were never meant to be in human hands. The cloning of animals. The manipulation of DNA. The blurring of lines that God set in place at creation. And with all of that comes a question that sounds like science fiction but is becoming increasingly relevant — if technology advances to the point where a biological human being can be replicated, does that replicated being have a soul?

The answer is no. And the reason matters deeply.

Only God creates souls. That is not a theological opinion. It is a foundational truth of Scripture that runs from Genesis to Revelation without a single contradiction.

"And the LORD God formed man of the dust of the ground, and breathed into his nostrils the breath of life; and man became a living soul." — Genesis 2:7 (KJV)

The soul is not biological. It cannot be grown in a laboratory. It cannot be replicated through genetics. It cannot be manufactured by any technology that human hands could ever devise — because it does not originate in the natural world. It originates in God. He breathed it into existence. He owns it. And He alone has the authority to redeem it.

A clone — if such a thing were ever fully realized — would be a biological shell without the breath of God animating it from within. It would have no soul to sin. No soul to forgive. No soul to redeem.

But you — with all of your complexity, your emotion, your capacity for both profound love and profound failure — you carry the breath of God inside you. You were made by Him. You are known by Him. And regardless of what you have done or what has been done to you — that soul is exactly what Jesus went to the cross to reclaim.

No human technology can create what God breathed into you. And no human sin — regardless of its severity — is beyond the reach of the God who breathed it there.

The Legal Case — How God Can Be Both Just and Merciful

I want to take you somewhere most people never go when they think about forgiveness. Not into emotion. Not into sentiment. Into a courtroom.

Because what happened at the cross was not just a spiritual event. It was a legal transaction. And when you understand the legal architecture God built into the plan of salvation — the forgiveness of even the most evil person stops being a mystery and becomes the most logical conclusion in history.

The Word That Changes Everything — Diatheke

In the original Greek language of the New Testament there is a word used for covenant — diatheke. Most people read that word as simply an agreement between two parties. A promise. A sacred bond.

But diatheke carries a second legal meaning that is just as significant — and almost never discussed in Sunday morning sermons. It also means a last will and testament.

Think about what that means for a moment. When a person writes a last will and testament — the inheritance described in that document cannot be legally transferred to the heirs until one thing happens. The person who wrote it must die.

"For where a testament is, there must also of necessity be the death of the testator. For a testament is of force after men are dead: otherwise it is of no strength at all while the testator liveth." — Hebrews 9:16–17 (KJV)

The New Testament — the new covenant of forgiveness, grace, and eternal life — was a legal document written by God Himself. And the inheritance it promised — the complete forgiveness of sin, reconciliation with the Father, and eternal life — could not be legally transferred to a single human soul until the Testator died.

Jesus was not just the messenger of the new covenant. He was the Author of it. And His death on the cross was not a tragedy that God redeemed. It was the legal requirement that activated the inheritance for every soul who would receive it through faith.

The moment Jesus said "It is finished" — He was not simply announcing that His suffering was over. He was making a legal declaration. The debt was paid. The testament was activated. The inheritance was now available to every human soul — including the most evil person you can imagine — who would receive it through faith and acceptance of Jesus Christ as Lord and Savior.

"In whom we have redemption through his blood, the forgiveness of sins, according to the riches of his grace." — Ephesians 1:7 (KJV)

The King of Righteousness — Melchizedek

There is a figure who appears in Scripture so briefly and so mysteriously that most readers pass right over him. He appears in only a handful of verses in the Old Testament — and yet the writer of Hebrews devotes an entire chapter to explaining his significance.

His name is Melchizedek.

He appears in Genesis 14 — centuries before the Law of Moses, centuries before the Levitical priesthood was established, centuries before Israel existed as a nation. He is described as the King of Salem and the priest of the most high God. And he blessed Abraham — the father of the entire Hebrew nation — without Abraham ever questioning his authority to do so.

"And Melchizedek king of Salem brought forth bread and wine: and he was the priest of the most high God. And he blessed him." — Genesis 14:18–19 (KJV)

His very name is a theological declaration. In the original Hebrew — Melchi means king. Tzedekah means righteousness. His title — King of Salem — means King of Peace.

The King of Righteousness. The King of Peace. Sound familiar?

The writer of Hebrews makes the connection explicit. Jesus Christ is not a priest after the order of Aaron — the earthly Levitical priesthood that served under the Law and offered animal sacrifices that could never permanently remove sin. He is a priest after the order of Melchizedek — a priesthood that existed before the Law, that operates outside of human lineage, and that carries an authority that never expires.

"Thou art a priest for ever after the order of Melchisedec." — Hebrews 5:6 (KJV)

What the Dead Sea Scrolls Reveal About Melchizedek

Most people who know Melchizedek know him only from Genesis 14 and the letter to the Hebrews. But among the Dead Sea Scrolls discovered at Qumran — written before the birth of Jesus — there is a document scholars call 11QMelchizedek. It is one of the most extraordinary texts ever recovered from those ancient caves, and it changes everything about how the original Jewish audience of the New Testament would have heard the name Melchizedek.

This scroll, preserved for two thousand years in the Judean desert, presents Melchizedek not merely as a historical priest-king from Genesis 14 but as a heavenly, transcendent figure — a divine agent appointed to appear at the end of days to execute judgment, proclaim atonement for the righteous, and announce the final Year of Jubilee. The scroll draws directly from Leviticus 25 and the Jubilee laws, presenting Melchizedek as the one who will proclaim liberty to the captives and bring the ultimate release of those bound by sin and death.

And then the scroll quotes Isaiah 61:1 directly. That same verse — the Spirit of the LORD is upon me, to proclaim liberty to the captives — that Jesus stood up in the synagogue at Nazareth and read aloud as His own mission statement, declaring it fulfilled in that very hour.

Think carefully about what this means. When the writer of Hebrews declared that Jesus was a priest forever after the order of Melchizedek — the Jewish readers who knew 11QMelchizedek did not hear a quiet theological argument about priesthood lineage. They heard an explosive claim. They heard someone saying: Jesus is the Melchizedek figure. The heavenly one. The one the scroll said would come at the end of days to execute final judgment, proclaim the great Jubilee, and announce permanent release from the debt of sin.

The Levitical priests had to offer sacrifices repeatedly — every morning, every evening, every year on the Day of Atonement — because their sacrifices were temporary. The blood of animals could cover sin but never permanently remove it.

"For it is not possible that the blood of bulls and of goats should take away sins." — Hebrews 10:4 (KJV)

But Jesus — serving as High Priest after the eternal order of Melchizedek, the order the scroll already described as heavenly and final — offered one sacrifice. Once. For all time. For all sin. For every human soul who would ever live.

"But this man, after he had offered one sacrifice for sins for ever, sat down on the right hand of God." — Hebrews 10:12 (KJV)

He sat down because the work was finished. There is nothing left to add to it. No additional sacrifice required. No annual return to the altar. No waiting for the next Day of Atonement. The heavenly Melchizedek — the one the ancient scroll said would come — had arrived, had offered the final sacrifice, and had taken His seat. The King of Righteousness made a way for every unrighteous soul to stand before a holy God — fully forgiven, fully accepted, fully redeemed.

Including the ones you cannot imagine God forgiving. Including you.

Propitiation — The Word That Explains the Cross

There is one more theological word I need to place in your hands before we move forward. It is the word that explains exactly how God can be simultaneously perfectly just and perfectly merciful — without one quality ever canceling out the other.

The word is propitiation.

"Whom God hath set forth to be a propitiation through faith in his blood, to declare his righteousness for the remission of sins that are past, through the forbearance of God." — Romans 3:25 (KJV)

Propitiation means the complete turning away of wrath through the offering of a perfect sacrifice.

God's wrath toward sin is not a temper tantrum. It is not an emotional overreaction. It is the right and necessary response of a perfectly holy God to the reality of moral evil. If God simply overlooked sin — smiled and waved it away — He would not be good. He would be indifferent. And an indifferent God is not a God worth trusting with your eternity.

Justice demanded that sin be answered for. Every sin. By every soul. With death.

But mercy refused to leave us there.

So God — in a move that no human mind could have designed — satisfied His own justice by absorbing it Himself. Every sin ever committed by every human soul was placed on Jesus at the cross. Every ounce of wrath that perfect justice demanded was poured out — completely, fully, and finally — on the body of His own Son.

The result? God is just — because the penalty was paid in full. And God is the justifier — because He can now legally declare righteous every soul who receives that payment through faith.

"To declare, I say, at this time his righteousness: that he might be just, and the justifier of him which believeth in Jesus." — Romans 3:26 (KJV)

This is why God forgiving evil people is not God compromising His justice. It is God fulfilling it — in the most extraordinary way imaginable. The cross was not mercy instead of justice. It was mercy through justice. Both fully satisfied. Both fully expressed. In one moment. On one hill. Through one Man.

The Hardest Cases — When Forgiveness Feels Wrong

There is a difference between understanding forgiveness theologically and living it out personally.

You can sit in a church pew and nod along to every word of grace preached from a pulpit. You can quote Romans 5:8 from memory. You can believe with every fiber of your being that Jesus paid for the sins of mankind on the cross — and still find yourself standing in front of one specific person, one specific wound, one specific history — and feel the theology drain right out of you.

Because it is one thing to forgive a stranger. It is another thing entirely to forgive someone who sat at your table. Someone who mocked the very faith that holds your family together. Someone whose words landed inside your home — your sacred space — and left damage that does not simply disappear because you choose to believe in a God of grace.

I will not stand here and tell you forgiveness is easy. That would be dishonest and it would not honor what you are actually carrying. What I will tell you is what Scripture tells us — that forgiveness is not a feeling. It is a decision. And it is not optional.

"And when ye stand praying, forgive, if ye have ought against any: that your Father also which is in heaven may forgive you your trespasses." — Mark 11:25 (KJV)

That verse does not offer an exception clause. It does not say forgive unless what they did was bad enough. It says forgive. And Scripture proves through two of the most confronting stories in the entire Bible that God means exactly what He says — even in the hardest cases.

What God Does With Evil People — The Stories That Prove It

There is a king in the Old Testament whose name most people outside of serious Bible study have never encountered. His name was Manasseh. And his story is one of the most confronting passages in all of Scripture for anyone who struggles with the idea of God forgiving evil people.

Manasseh became king of Judah at twelve years old and reigned for fifty-five years — the longest reign of any king in Israel's history. In those fifty-five years he committed acts of evil so severe that Scripture describes them in language that leaves nothing to the imagination.

He rebuilt the pagan altars his father Hezekiah had destroyed. He erected altars to false gods inside the temple of the Lord. He practiced witchcraft and sorcery. He sacrificed his own children in fire as offerings to foreign gods. He filled Jerusalem with innocent blood from one end to the other.

"But Manasseh made Judah and the inhabitants of Jerusalem to err, and to do worse than the heathen, whom the LORD had destroyed before the children of Israel." — 2 Chronicles 33:9 (KJV)

Worse than the heathen. That is the biblical description of this man.

And then God allowed the Assyrian army to capture him. They bound him in chains and dragged him to Babylon. And it was there — in the lowest, most broken place of his life — that Manasseh did something no one who knew his history could have predicted.

He prayed.

"And when he was in affliction, he besought the LORD his God, and humbled himself greatly before the God of his fathers." — 2 Chronicles 33:12 (KJV)

And God heard him. God restored him. God forgave Manasseh — one of the most wicked human beings in the recorded history of Israel.

If something rises up inside you reading that — good. Let it. Sit with that reaction. Because that discomfort is exactly why this chapter exists.

Now consider a man in the New Testament. His name was Saul of Tarsus. Before God transformed him and the world came to know him as Paul — he was a murderer. Not a man with violent thoughts. A man who stood and watched the first Christian martyr, Stephen, be stoned to death and approved of every stone. A man who dragged believers from their homes and threw them into prison. A man who by his own words called himself the chief of sinners.

"This is a faithful saying, and worthy of all acceptation, that Christ Jesus came into the world to save sinners; of whom I am chief." — 1 Timothy 1:15 (KJV)

God did not just forgive Saul. God chose him. Transformed him. And used him — the former murderer of Christians — to write nearly half of the New Testament and plant churches across the ancient world that are still bearing fruit two thousand years later.

God forgiving evil people is not a footnote in Scripture. It is one of Scripture's most consistent and deliberate themes. And it should cause every one of us to stop and ask ourselves — if God forgave them, what exactly do I think disqualifies the person I am struggling to release?

What Forgiveness Does — And What It Does Not Do

This is where the question needs to be answered clearly and without confusion.

God's forgiveness does not erase consequences.

When God completely and fully forgave King David for his adultery with Bathsheba and his orchestration of her husband Uriah's death — David was genuinely and totally forgiven. The prophet Nathan declared it plainly.

"The LORD also hath put away thy sin; thou shalt not die." — 2 Samuel 12:13 (KJV)

But the consequences remained. The physical world operates under laws God set in motion — the principle of sowing and reaping that governs human experience. God does not reach into the natural order and erase every consequence of every forgiven sin. What He does is something far more profound. He walks through the consequences with us. He redeems them. He takes what our choices broke and works it into a purpose that only He could design.

"And we know that all things work together for good to them that love God, to them who are the called according to his purpose." — Romans 8:28 (KJV)

And here is something equally vital to understand. God does not punish His children with wrath. That wrath was fully and finally satisfied on the cross of Jesus Christ. What God brings into our lives is discipline — and the distinction between punishment and discipline is everything.

Punishment looks backward. It is retribution for what was done. God's wrath — which every human being deserved — was poured out completely on Jesus so that it would never have to fall on us.

Discipline looks forward. It is the loving correction of a Father who refuses to let His children destroy themselves. It is not anger. It is not cruelty. It is the hand of a God who loves you too deeply to watch you walk toward destruction and say nothing.

"For whom the Lord loveth he chasteneth, and scourgeth every son whom he receiveth." — Hebrews 12:6 (KJV)

The trials you face are not God's punishment. They are God's process. The pressure that feels unbearable is forming something in you that could not have been formed any other way. The fire that feels like destruction is burning away everything that was never meant to remain.

God is not against you in your suffering. He is in it with you — refining, restoring, and preparing you for something your current circumstances cannot yet reveal.

The Ultimate Example — Jesus Forgave First

If you are still wrestling with whether God's forgiveness of evil people is truly just — I want to take you to one specific moment in history. The moment that answers this question more powerfully than any theological argument ever could.

The cross.

Not as a symbol. Not as a piece of jewelry or a decoration on a church wall. As a real event. A Roman execution. The most brutal form of death the ancient world had designed — reserved specifically for the worst criminals, the most dangerous enemies of the state.

And hanging on that cross was the only innocent man who ever lived.

While the soldiers who had beaten Him, mocked Him, stripped Him, and driven nails through His hands and feet were still standing at the foot of that cross — still in the act of killing Him — Jesus looked down at them and said something that shattered every human understanding of justice and forgiveness that had ever existed.

"Father, forgive them; for they know not what they do." — Luke 23:34 (KJV)

Not after they apologized. Not after they acknowledged what they had done. Not after they changed. While they were still doing it — Jesus issued a blanket forgiveness over the very people who were in the act of murdering Him.

That is not human. That is divine. And it is the standard God calls us toward — not because it is easy, but because it is the only thing powerful enough to break the chain that bitterness forges between the wounded and the one who wounded them.

Forgiveness is not a gift you give to the person who hurt you. It is a gift you receive yourself. It is the moment you stop allowing someone else's sin to have authority over your peace, your prayers, and your future.

The One Sin That Cannot Be Forgiven

There is one passage in Scripture that causes more confusion and fear than almost any other when this topic arises. Jesus Himself spoke it.

"Wherefore I say unto you, All manner of sin and blasphemy shall be forgiven unto men: but the blasphemy against the Holy Ghost shall not be forgiven unto men." — Matthew 12:31 (KJV)

People read that verse and panic. They wonder if they have committed it. They wonder if someone they love has committed it. They wonder if it means God's forgiveness truly does have a limit.

Here is what Scripture actually teaches.

The blasphemy against the Holy Spirit is not a specific word spoken in anger. It is not a moment of doubt. It is not a season of rebellion or a period of walking away from God. The context of that passage shows Jesus speaking to the Pharisees — religious leaders who had watched Him heal the sick, cast out demons, and restore the broken — and declared that His work was the work of Satan.

They were not ignorant. They saw the evidence. They felt the conviction of the Holy Spirit drawing them toward truth — and they made a deliberate, persistent, hardened decision to call that truth a lie.

The unforgivable sin is not a single act. It is a final, permanent condition — the complete and total rejection of the Holy Spirit's drawing toward repentance. It is a heart so hardened over time that it has lost the capacity to recognize its own need for God.

And here is how you know you have not committed it — the very fact that you are asking the question means the Holy Spirit is still working in you. A heart that has truly and finally rejected God does not worry about whether it has rejected God. It simply does not care.

If you care — God is still pursuing you.

"The Lord is not slack concerning his promise, as some men count slackness; but is longsuffering to us-ward, not willing that any should perish, but that all should come to repentance." — 2 Peter 3:9 (KJV)

This Is Why the Cross Changes Everything

I want to bring you back to something that most people have never been shown. Something hidden in the ancient timeline of Scripture that once you see it — you cannot unsee it.

In the Old Testament God commanded the Jewish priests to offer two lambs every single day — one in the morning and one in the evening.

"Now this is that which thou shalt offer upon the altar; two lambs of the first year day by day continually. The one lamb thou shalt offer in the morning; and the other lamb thou shalt offer at even." — Exodus 29:38–39 (KJV)

The morning lamb was bound to the altar at the third hour — nine o'clock in the morning. That is the exact hour the Gospel of Mark records that Jesus was nailed to the cross.

"And it was the third hour, and they crucified him." — Mark 15:25 (KJV)

The evening lamb was slain at the ninth hour — three o'clock in the afternoon. That is the exact moment Matthew records that Jesus cried out from the cross and yielded up His spirit.

"And about the ninth hour Jesus cried with a loud voice...and yielded up the ghost." — Matthew 27:46–50 (KJV)

For over a thousand years before Jesus was born — every single morning and every single evening — the priests of Israel were performing a dress rehearsal for the crucifixion without knowing it. God had written the story of the cross into the daily rhythm of Jewish worship centuries before it happened.

The forgiveness of evil people was never an afterthought. It was never God changing His mind or lowering His standard. It was the plan — written before creation, foreshadowed throughout the Old Testament, and executed on that cross with a precision that only a sovereign God could have orchestrated.

When Forgiveness Feels Humanly Impossible — Four Steps Scripture Supports

I have laid out the theology. I have shown you the legal architecture of the cross. I have walked you through the ancient priesthood and the hidden timeline of sacrifice that pointed to Jesus centuries before He arrived.

But theology alone does not answer the person who is sitting in genuine pain right now. The person who understands everything written above — and still cannot find their way to releasing what was done to them.

So let us get practical. Because Scripture was never meant to stay on a page. It was meant to be lived.

Theologian Lewis Smedes spent his life studying the anatomy of forgiveness — specifically the forgiveness of deep evil. And what he identified aligns precisely with what Scripture teaches about how genuine forgiveness actually moves through a human soul. Not as a single moment. But as a process. A deliberate, Spirit-led journey from wound to release.

There are four movements in that journey.

The First Movement — Surrendering the Right to Get Even

The most natural human response to being wronged is the desire for revenge. Not always in dramatic ways. Sometimes it is simply the quiet satisfaction of imagining justice arriving for the person who hurt you. The hope that one day they will feel what they made you feel.

God does not shame you for that instinct. He understands it. But He calls you out of it — because vengeance was never designed to be carried by human hands.

"Dearly beloved, avenge not yourselves, but rather give place unto wrath: for it is written, Vengeance is mine; I will repay, saith the Lord." — Romans 12:19 (KJV)

Surrendering the right to get even is not saying what happened was acceptable. It is not minimizing the damage. It is placing the scales of justice into the hands of the only One who can actually balance them perfectly — and trusting that He will.

The Second Movement — Giving Their Humanity Back

When someone hurts us deeply enough — we have a tendency to reduce them. To flatten them into the worst thing they ever did. To see them no longer as a complex human soul made in the image of God — but simply as the source of our pain.

That reduction feels justified. But it is spiritually dangerous — because it requires us to see a soul that God made and loves as something less than what God declares them to be.

Giving someone their humanity back does not mean trusting them again. It does not mean pretending the damage did not happen. It means refusing to reduce a human soul — however broken, however destructive — to something beneath the reach of God's redemption.

"For whosoever shall call upon the name of the Lord shall be saved." — Romans 10:13 (KJV)

Whosoever. That word has no exceptions written into it. It does not require a clean record. It does not require a minimum threshold of decency. The same grace that reached you reaches the one who hurt you. And if God has declared that soul a whosoever — then forgiveness must be willing to see them the same way.

The Third Movement — Wishing Them Well

This is the one that costs the most.

Not pretending to wish them well. Not performing a grace you do not yet feel. But genuinely arriving — through prayer, through surrender, through the slow and sometimes painful work of the Holy Spirit inside you — at a place where you can release the person who hurt you into God's hands and mean it.

This does not happen overnight. For some wounds it takes years. For some it is a daily decision made over and over again until the feeling finally catches up with the choice.

But this is exactly what Jesus modeled from the cross. Not after the soldiers repented. Not after they acknowledged what they had done. While they were still doing it — He prayed for them, releasing them entirely to the Father. As He already demonstrated in the most devastating moment of human history, forgiveness does not wait for the other person to deserve it.

The Fourth Movement — Opening to What God Wills

The final movement of forgiveness is the most surrendered. It is releasing not just the person — but the outcome. Letting go of the need to know how God will handle it. Trusting that His justice is real, His mercy is sovereign, and His plan for both you and the person who hurt you is beyond what either of you can currently see.

This is where forgiveness becomes an act of worship. Because it is no longer about you and the person who wronged you. It is about placing the entire situation — the wound, the person, the justice, the future — into the hands of a God who sees the complete picture when you can only see the piece you are standing in.

The Ancient Connection — Prayer as Sacrifice

There is something hidden in the original Hebrew language of the Old Testament that reveals a connection so precise that only God could have designed it.

The Hebrew word 'arak means to arrange or set in order. In the Old Testament this specific word is used repeatedly for the act of arranging wood on an altar in preparation for a blood sacrifice. It is the word used when Abraham laid the wood on the altar before placing Isaac upon it. It is the word used by the priests as they prepared the morning and evening sacrifices.

But here is what makes it extraordinary. The same word — 'arak — is used by the Psalmist to describe the act of arranging a morning prayer before God.

"My voice shalt thou hear in the morning, O LORD; in the morning will I direct my prayer unto thee, and will look up." — Psalm 5:3 (KJV)

The word translated as direct in that verse is 'arak. The same word used for laying a sacrifice on an altar.

God is telling us something profound through that connection. When we bring our prayers before Him — especially the prayers that cost us something, the prayers of forgiveness we offer when every human instinct is pulling us in the opposite direction — we are not simply talking into the air. We are laying something on an altar. We are making an offering. We are participating in the same sacred act that pointed to Christ for thousands of years before the cross ever existed.

Your prayer of forgiveness is a sacrifice. And God receives it as one.

When You Cannot Even Find the Words

There will be moments — perhaps you are in one right now — where the wound is so deep and the weight so heavy that you cannot even form a prayer. Where you sit before God with nothing but silence and pain and the faint desperate hope that He can hear what your broken heart cannot yet speak.

God has already made provision for exactly that moment. C.S. Lewis reflected that the most authentic prayer a broken soul can offer is sometimes nothing more than showing up empty. The words do not have to come. The understanding does not have to be there. The Holy Spirit steps into the exact place where human language collapses and does what we cannot do for ourselves. He breathes through the empty vessel, giving voice to thoughts the soul itself never knew it carried.

When you are too broken to pray — the Holy Spirit prays through you. When you are too wounded to forgive — He intercedes on your behalf with a language beyond what human words can carry.

"Likewise the Spirit also helpeth our infirmities: for we know not what we should pray for as we ought: but the Spirit itself maketh intercession for us with groanings which cannot be uttered." — Romans 8:26 (KJV)

You do not have to arrive at the altar with everything figured out. You do not have to feel the forgiveness before you offer it. You simply have to show up — empty, broken, willing — and let God do what only He can do.

He will meet you there. He always has.

The Root of All Sin — Why We Needed That Transaction

C.S. Lewis identified something in his study of human nature and sin that cuts beneath every surface explanation and reaches the root of the problem.

At the core of every sin — from the smallest act of selfishness to the most horrific act of evil — is one fundamental desire. The creature wanting to be independent from the Creator. The soul wanting to operate as if it is the source of its own existence rather than the recipient of it.

Lewis described it as the difference between a noun and an adjective. God alone is a noun — self-existent, independent, the only true source of being. Every created thing — including every human soul — is an adjective. Dependent. Derivative. Existing only because God sustains it moment by moment.

Sin is the adjective declaring itself a noun. The creature saying to the Creator — this corner of the universe is mine. This decision belongs to me. This life is my own business and not Yours.

But here is the theological reality that makes that declaration not just rebellious but impossible. You cannot actually be independent from the God who is sustaining your very existence in this moment. The attempt to be independent from Him does not make you free — it makes you lost. Because you are trying to exist without the only One who makes your existence possible.

This is why the cross was necessary. Not just legally. Not just judicially. But at the deepest level of what the human soul actually is and what it was designed for. Sin had severed the connection between the created soul and the Creator who sustains it. And that severed connection required a divine act to restore it.

The cross was God reaching across the gap that human rebellion created — not because He was obligated to — but because the soul He made was never designed to exist in that separation. And His love refused to leave it there.

"For God so loved the world, that he gave his only begotten Son, that whosoever believeth in him should not perish, but have everlasting life." — John 3:16 (KJV)

Even Your Repentance Is a Gift

There is one final truth I need to place in your hands before we close this chapter. And it is perhaps the most humbling of everything we have covered.

You might be reading this and thinking — I understand everything written here. I believe the cross was real. I believe Jesus paid the price. But I do not feel the repentance I know I need. I want to surrender but I cannot find my way to it. I want to release what I am carrying but the willingness is not there yet.

The Puritan writer John Flavel identified something in Scripture that answers that exact struggle with extraordinary precision.

We are commanded by God to repent. To surrender our will. To subject ourselves to Him. But Flavel pointed to a profound paradox — we cannot actually produce genuine repentance on our own. The very power by which we repent is not generated inside us. It is given to us by the God who is asking for it.

Even our repentance is a gift of grace.

The Holy Spirit does not simply wait for you to gather enough willpower to turn toward God and then reward you for your effort. He is the one who initiates the turning. He draws you. He convicts you. He softens what has become hard. He opens what has become closed. And then — when you respond to that drawing by taking even the smallest step toward God — He meets you with the full force of heaven's grace.

This means that the very desire you feel right now — the hunger to be right with God, the weight of knowing something needs to change, the part of you that picked up this book and kept reading — that is not you working up enough religion. That is the Holy Spirit already working in you.

Do not resist it.

"No man can come to me, except the Father which hath sent me draw him." — John 6:44 (KJV)

You did not find God. He found you. He has been finding you — through every difficult season, every moment of breaking, every question you have ever carried about why life looks the way it does.

He has been answering before you finished asking. And He is answering still.

What This Means For You Right Now

I want to bring everything we have covered in this chapter down to the most personal level possible. Because theology that does not land in the real world — in your real life, in your real pain, in your real struggle — is just information. And this book was never meant to be just information.

If you are struggling to accept that God forgives someone who hurt you —

The justice you are crying out for was not ignored by God. It was satisfied. Completely. Finally. At the cross. Every act of evil ever committed carries a price — and that price was paid in the body of Jesus Christ. God did not look the other way. He absorbed it Himself. Trust that. And trust that the God who sees all things — every hidden act, every secret sin, every wound inflicted in darkness — will handle what you cannot.

"For nothing is secret, that shall not be made manifest; neither any thing hid, that shall not be known and come abroad." — Luke 8:17 (KJV)

If you are carrying something you believe is too dark for God to forgive —

Remember Manasseh. Remember Paul. Remember that the very fact you are reading these words means the Holy Spirit is still pursuing you. A soul that has truly and finally rejected God does not search for Him. The searching itself is evidence that God has not given up on you.

The cross was not built for people who had it mostly figured out. It was built for the broken. The guilty. The ones who had run out of options and out of excuses and out of any reasonable argument for why they deserved another chance.

It was built for you.

"Come now, and let us reason together, saith the LORD: though your sins be as scarlet, they shall be as white as snow; though they be red like crimson, they shall be as wool." — Isaiah 1:18 (KJV)

If you are trying to forgive someone and cannot find your way there
—

Start where you are. Not where you think you should be. Bring God the honest truth of what you are carrying — the anger, the grief, the injustice, the part of you that does not want to forgive — and lay it on the altar exactly as it is. You do not have to arrive with a cleaned-up version of your heart. You simply have to arrive.

The Holy Spirit will do the rest. He has been doing it since the moment you first believed.

And remember this — forgiving someone does not mean what they did was acceptable. It does not mean you trust them again. It does not mean the consequences of their actions disappear. It means you are releasing the weight of their sin from your hands and placing it into the hands of God — where it always belonged. And in doing that — you are not doing them a favor. You are doing yourself one.

"And be ye kind one to another, tenderhearted, forgiving one another, even as God for Christ's sake hath forgiven you." — Ephesians 4:32 (KJV)

The Answer to the Question

So why would God ever forgive evil people?

Because He is not surprised by evil. He has seen every act of it since the beginning of time and He has never once been caught off guard. Because He understands the enemy's role in deceiving and corrupting the souls He made. Because free will — the greatest gift He ever gave — carried with it the unavoidable possibility of catastrophic misuse. And because the plan to redeem what free will broke was never an afterthought.

It was written before the foundation of the world. Foreshadowed in every morning and evening sacrifice. Hidden in the ancient Hebrew letters at the very first verse of Genesis. Revealed in a heavenly

Melchizedek whose coming was already known to the ancient scrolls. Declared by a mysterious king of righteousness who appeared before Israel even had a law. Purchased legally and finally by the death of the Testator who authored the new covenant with His own blood.

God forgives evil people because the price of that forgiveness has already been paid. Because justice has already been satisfied. Because the cross was not God compromising His holiness — it was God fulfilling it in the most extraordinary act of love the universe has ever witnessed.

And because the soul you are convinced is beyond redemption — is the exact kind of soul Jesus went to the cross to reclaim.

Every single one of us arrived at the foot of that cross with nothing to offer but our need. That is all God ever required. That is all He requires still.

"For by grace are ye saved through faith; and that not of yourselves: it is the gift of God: Not of works, lest any man should boast." — Ephesians 2:8–9 (KJV)

My Reflection

I want to be honest with you about something before this chapter closes. And I want to say it plainly, because the honesty of it is the only thing that makes it worth saying.

I am not a man who came to this chapter from the outside looking in. I came to it from the inside.

For a long stretch of my adult life, I was the person this chapter is about. Not in the most dramatic sense — I was not Manasseh sacrificing children or Saul dragging believers from their homes. But I was a man who had been given a covenant with God, who had stood before a congregation at nine years old and declared his life surrendered, and who then spent the next two decades doing what he wanted with that life while carrying the language of faith like a credential he had not earned.

I made promises to God I did not keep. I prayed when I needed something and went quiet when I had it. I called myself a believer on Sunday and lived by my own rules every other day. I treated the people closest to me — the people who deserved the best of me — to the version of myself that was left over after I had already given everything to my own ambitions, my own anxiety, my own need to control every outcome. That is not a dramatic confession. It is simply the truth of what low-grade spiritual rebellion looks like when it has a respectable surface.

And here is what I know now that I did not fully understand then. That kind of life — the life of a man who belongs to God on paper but not in practice — is not a neutral condition. It is its own kind of evil. Not the evil the world looks at with horror. The quiet kind. The kind that does the most damage to the people you love because it wears the face of someone they thought they could trust.

I needed the forgiveness this chapter describes. Not theoretically. Personally. The kind that covers the promises broken in private. The kind that reaches the man who was too proud to admit he was lost because he had never technically left. The kind that does not wait for you to have cleaned yourself up before it moves toward you.

What broke me open — and you have read parts of that story in the preface — was not a single moment of dramatic moral failure. It was the slow, accumulated weight of being a man who had spent years trying to carry what only God was designed to hold. The body keeps score of that kind of thing. And mine did.

But what I want to say here — specifically in the context of this chapter — is this. The night everything finally broke open inside me, the thing I was most afraid of was not that God would refuse to hear me. It was that I had waited too long. That the years of half-kept promises and self-managed faith had used up whatever patience God had for me. That I was, in the most private and specific sense, the evil person the chapter title asks about.

And what I found — what I want you to hear from someone who has sat in that specific dark — is that the answer to this chapter's question is not abstract. It is not a theological framework you study from a comfortable distance. It is a God who showed up at the lowest moment of a broken man's life, for a man who had given Him every reason to be finished, and was not finished.

The cross did not become real to me in a classroom or a church pew. It became real in the moment I finally stopped pretending I did not need it.

If you are reading this and you are carrying the weight of who you have been — the specific, private inventory of what you know about yourself that most people in your life do not — I want you to hear this from someone who has held that same inventory.

The chapter you just read was written for you. Not for someone worse than you. Not for someone whose failures are more dramatic or more visible. For you. The cross was not built for people who had it mostly together. It was built for the person standing exactly where you are standing right now.

God is not surprised by your history. He was not caught off guard by any of it. And the same love that absorbed everything I brought to that moment is the same love that is present in whatever room you are sitting in right now.

He forgives evil people because He is in the business of making new ones.

I know. Because I am one of them.

A Prayer for the Reader

Father —

I come before You on behalf of every person holding these pages right now. Every soul wrestling with this question from a place of real pain and real confusion.

For the one who cannot understand how You could forgive what was done to them — give them the grace to trust that Your justice is not absent. That the cross was not weakness but the full weight of Your righteousness poured out so that mercy could reach every soul You made. Let them release what they are carrying into Your hands and find the freedom that only forgiveness can bring.

For the one who believes their own sin is too great — too dark, too repeated, too shameful — remind them of Manasseh in chains crying out from the lowest place of his life. Remind them of Paul — the murderer You turned into the greatest voice for the Gospel the world has ever known. Let them see themselves not through the lens of what they have done but through the lens of what Your Son already paid for.

For the one who wants to forgive but cannot find their way there — meet them in that broken place. Breathe through their dumb lips when their springs run dry. Intercede through them when they have run out of words. And lead them step by step through the surrender that sets them free.

Let every soul that has carried this question — Why would God ever forgive evil people — leave these pages knowing the answer with absolute certainty.

Because You already did. At the cross. Before any of us ever asked.

In the name of the Father, the Son, and the Holy Spirit.

Amen.

"But God commendeth his love toward us, in that, while we were yet sinners, Christ died for us." — Romans 5:8 (KJV)

Chapter Three

If God Already Knew, Why Did He Let It Happen?

"I am God, and there is none like me, Declaring the end from the beginning, and from ancient times the things that are not yet done." — Isaiah 46:9–10 (KJV)

The Question

It arrives quietly at first. A passing thought in the middle of a hard season. A question whispered in the dark after a diagnosis, a betrayal, a loss that rewrote everything.

If God knew this was coming — if He truly knew before the world began that this moment would happen, that this child would suffer, that this family would shatter, that this prayer would go unanswered for years — then why did He build the world this way? Why did He set it all in motion? Why did He let it happen?

This is not a question born in casual curiosity. It is forged in the crucible of real suffering. And it carries within it two separate accusations that deserve to be separated and answered honestly.

The first accusation is about God's knowledge: that He saw it coming and did nothing. The second is about God's character: that a God who designed a world containing this much pain cannot truly be good.

Both deserve a direct and honest answer. Not a rehearsed deflection. Not a theological dodge wrapped in comforting language. A real answer — grounded in Scripture, in ancient text, in the deepest layers of what God has actually revealed about Himself and about the path He designed for every human soul.

That is what this chapter is.

Acknowledging the Honest Struggle

Before we go anywhere near an answer, something needs to be said clearly.

The anger beneath this question is not a sign of weak faith. It is a sign of a soul that takes both God and suffering seriously. The prophets felt it. The psalmists cried it. Job screamed it into the sky and God did not rebuke him for the volume of his anguish. He rebuked the friends who offered neat explanations instead of honest presence.

If you are carrying this question from a place of real pain — if it is not a philosophical exercise but a daily wound — then sit with this for a moment before we continue.

God is not surprised by your question. He is not offended by it. He did not design a universe in which honest wrestling with hard reality is a sign of spiritual failure. In fact, as we are about to discover, the wrestling itself is part of the path.

The question "If God already knew, why did He let it happen?" is not a question that threatens the existence of God. It is a question that, when answered fully and honestly, reveals the most extraordinary dimensions of His character, His love, and His sovereign design.

Let us begin at the deepest possible level.

What Scripture Says

Part 1 — God Does Not Exist Inside Time. He Governs It.

The first thing we must understand — and this single truth reframes the entire question — is that God does not experience time the way human beings do.

We experience life as a sequence: past, present, future. Events arrive, unfold, and recede. We remember what has happened, we navigate what is happening, and we dread or anticipate what is coming. Time, for us, is a river we are always floating down — unable to see around the next bend.

God does not float. He stands above the river and sees all of it simultaneously. Thomas Aquinas, in the Summa Theologica, calls this the nunc stans — the "eternal present." God does not look forward into your future. He does not look back at your past. He is fully, actively present in your past, your present, and your future at the same exact eternal moment. All of human history — from the first breath of creation to the final trumpet — exists before Him in a single, simultaneous, eternal Now.

This is precisely what Isaiah recorded when God spoke through him:

"I am God, and there is none like me, Declaring the end from the beginning, and from ancient times the things that are not yet done." — Isaiah 46:9–10 (KJV)

The Hebrew word for "ancient times" here is qedem — meaning the absolute front, the earliest conceivable point of existence. God is not saying He can predict the future as a skilled forecaster predicts weather. He is saying He declared the end before the beginning existed. He sees it all. He governs it all. He is outside of the timeline He created.

There is a sixth-century philosopher and statesman named Boethius who arrived at exactly this truth through a different path than Aquinas — not through abstract theology, but through prison. Condemned to death by the emperor Theodoric, Boethius wrote what became one of the most important philosophical works in the history of Western thought from a cell while awaiting execution. His imaginary companion, Lady Philosophy, explained God's foreknowledge with an image that has never been surpassed in its accessibility.

Imagine, she said, a man standing on a hilltop watching a road below. He can see the entire procession at once — those who have already passed, those directly below him, and those still approaching from a distance — all of them visible simultaneously. Those in the procession, meanwhile, can only see what is directly in front of them. They experience the road as a sequence. The man on the hilltop experiences it as a complete picture.

God's foreknowledge, Boethius argued, works exactly this way. He does not know the future because He watches it arrive in sequence from a privileged vantage point. He knows it because He inhabits an eternal present from which every moment of created time is simultaneously visible. When we say "God knew this would happen," we are using the language of sequence for a Being who experiences no sequence at all. He did not look ahead and see your suffering and write it into the script. From where He stands, every moment of your life — birth to death and all the days between — is simply present.

This completely dismantles the premise embedded in our question. When we ask "Why did God let it happen?" we are imagining God watching events unfold in sequence — seeing a tragedy approaching, having the power to intervene, and choosing not to. But that is not who God is. He is not a passive observer watching your timeline from a safe distance. He is the sovereign Author who sees the entire story — beginning, middle, and end — simultaneously, and who governs every thread of it according to a design that was finalized before a single atom of creation was spoken into existence.

Part 2 — The Path Was Designed Before the Traveler Was Born

Long before you entered this world, before your parents were born, before the nation of your birth existed, before the ground beneath your feet was formed — God knew you. Not knew of you. Knew you.

The Hebrew word used in Jeremiah 1:5 — "Before I formed thee in the belly I knew thee" — is yada. In the original language, yada does not mean simple cognitive awareness. It carries the deepest possible layers of intimate, relational, covenantal knowing. The same word is used to describe the closeness between a husband and wife. God is not saying He had data about you before you were born. He is saying He was in intimate, loving relationship with your soul before your body existed.

"Before I formed thee in the belly I knew thee; and before thou camest forth out of the womb I sanctified thee." — Jeremiah 1:5 (KJV)

Psalm 139 presses this even deeper. The Hebrew word golem — translated as "my substance, yet being unperfect" — describes the pre-formed, unfinished state of the body in the womb. And yet even at that stage — before the body was fully knit together — God had already written every day of that life in His book.

"Thine eyes did see my substance, yet being unperfect; and in thy book all my members were written, which in continuance were fashioned, when as yet there was none of them." — Psalm 139:16 (KJV)

The Apostle Paul, writing to the church at Ephesus, took this truth even further back than conception. He reached behind the very founding of the physical universe to locate the origin of God's design for every human soul:

"According as he hath chosen us in him before the foundation of the world, that we should be holy and without blame before him in love." — Ephesians 1:4 (KJV)

The Greek phrase translated "before the foundation of the world" is pro kataboles kosmou. The word katabole literally means something thrown down — the moment the foundational bedrock of the universe was laid. Pro means before. Before the universe's foundation was thrown down, your soul's purpose, path, and calling was already fully formed in the mind and heart of God.

Your life is not a reaction to the universe. The universe was created as a stage for your predestined life.

And in Romans 8:29, Paul reveals the precise two-step architecture of God's design using two distinct Greek words that most English translations flatten into one meaning:

"For whom he did foreknow, he also did predestinate to be conformed to the image of his Son." — Romans 8:29 (KJV)

Proginosko — foreknew — means God had intimate, relational, loving awareness of the soul before time. Proorizo — predestinated — comes from the word orizo, meaning to set a boundary, to mark out a horizon. God first knew you with intimate love, and then based on that eternal relationship, He marked out the boundaries and ultimate destination of your path.

This is the most important distinction the original languages make on this entire subject, and it is one the English translation has flattened almost completely. Yada — the Hebrew word for God's knowing — does not mean God possesses a complete locked database of every choice every soul will ever make, all of it predetermined before the first breath was drawn. It means He knows intimately, relationally, personally. The same distinction holds in the Greek. The word progi-nosko — foreknew — chosen by Paul in Romans 8:29 is the word for relational, covenantal, chosen knowing. The Greek New Testament had a different word available for prior possession of complete set-tled information. The writers chose the relational word instead. That choice is not an accident.

This matters because Scripture itself shows God genuinely re-sponding to what His creatures do rather than executing a script He wrote before they existed. Genesis 6:6 records that the LORD regret-ted making man — the Hebrew word nacham, genuine grief, genuine sorrow over an outcome. You cannot genuinely grieve an outcome you predetermined and locked in before it happened. Genesis 22:12 records God saying to Abraham: now I know that you fear God — the Hebrew attah yadati, now at this moment I know. Not: I always had this filed as a settled fact. Now I know, because of what this moment has revealed. Jeremiah 19:5 records God saying of the worst evil committed in the Valley of Hinnom: it did not enter my mind — lo alah al libbi, it did not come up upon my heart. The God of the original words genuinely responds. He genuinely grieves. He is genuinely affected by the choices of the souls He made. His knowing is real and total — but it is the knowing of a Father who is intimately invested in every soul, not the knowing of a programmer who wrote every soul's choices into the code before creation began.

The destination is specific. It is not vague. It is not accidental. The path He marked out is designed to conform you, through everything it contains — the valleys as much as the peaks — to the image of His Son.

Part 3 — The Soul He Breathed Into You Is Not Accidental

Ancient Hebrew anthropology recognized three distinct levels of the human soul. The Nefesh — the basic life force that animates the physical body. The Ruach — the spirit, the seat of emotion and intellect. And above both of these, the Neshamah.

The Neshamah is found in Genesis 2:7. The word breath here is neshamah. It is the transcendent spark of the Godhead itself, breathed directly and personally into each human being by the Creator. It is not a biological byproduct. It is not a mass-produced spiritual unit. It originates from God's own breath.

"And the LORD God formed man of the dust of the ground, and breathed into his nostrils the breath of life; and man became a living soul." — Genesis 2:7 (KJV)

This means you are not an accident assembled by chance within a universe that did not know your name. You are a specific, intimate, individually designed impartation of God's own essence. The breath He placed in you descended with a specific mission to fulfill. The path He marked out for you is not a generic template. It is yours. It was written for you before the universe was founded.

The Community Rule scroll discovered among the Dead Sea Scrolls at Qumran — written before the New Testament — states this with extraordinary precision: "From the God of Knowledge comes all that is and shall be. Before ever they existed He established their whole design, and when, as ordained for them, they come into being, it is in accord with His glorious design that they accomplish their task without change."

From the God of Knowledge. Every single thing that is and shall be. Established before they existed. This is not a New Testament innovation. This is ancient Jewish theology, confirmed across Testaments and centuries, declaring the same unchanging truth: the path was designed before the traveler was born.

The Thanksgiving Hymns — A Soul Crying Out From the Ancient Scrolls

But the Community Rule scroll is not the only voice from those Qumran caves that speaks to this truth. Among the Dead Sea Scrolls there is a second collection that most people have never encountered — one that does not read like a doctrinal rule but like a prayer torn from the deepest place of a human soul.

The Hodayot — known to scholars as 1QH, the Thanksgiving Hymns — are among the most intimate devotional texts ever recovered from the ancient world. Written by a leader of the Qumran community, likely the Teacher of Righteousness himself, they are personal psalms composed two centuries before the birth of Christ. They were not written for publication. They were written in the dark, by a man in hiding, for an audience of one.

One passage in the Hodayot stops every serious reader cold. The author writes of himself — and by extension every human soul — as a vessel fashioned by God before breath entered the body. He describes being shaped from dust and clay, formed in the womb by sovereign hands, given a specific calling before he could speak or understand. He uses the Hebrew word yatsar — the potter's word, the word of deliberate shaping — and declares that the same God who arranged the stars arranged him.

And then he says something that lands with the full weight of everything this chapter is built around. He writes that God established his standing before the congregation of the righteous not because of anything he produced — but because of the design God carried for him before his existence began. The path, the purpose, the calling — all of it was God's work before it was his.

This is a man two thousand years in his grave, writing from a desert cave, in a language most people alive today cannot read — and he is saying the same thing Paul would say in Romans 8:29, the same thing Jeremiah heard in chapter 1:5, the same thing this chapter has been building toward. The soul that God breathed into existence carries a design He authored before the first breath. Not as a limitation. As a love letter written before the recipient existed to read it.

The Hodayot confirm what Scripture has always declared: the path was not designed after you arrived. You were designed for the path before the path began.

How Evil Entered the Path

If God designed the path perfectly — if every soul is known, every day written, every boundary marked with sovereign love — then where did the corruption come from? Why does the path contain so much darkness? Why does it run through regions of suffering, betrayal, and injustice that no loving father would choose for his children?

Scripture answers this directly. The darkness did not originate with God. It was introduced into the human story through a catastrophic act of cosmic rebellion that most people have never been fully taught.

Genesis 6:1–4 records it with deliberate brevity:

"When men began to multiply on the face of the earth, and daughters were born unto them, that the sons of God saw the daughters of men that they were fair; and they took them wives of all which they chose." — Genesis 6:1–2 (KJV)

The sons of God in this passage are not human beings. They are divine beings — angels — who abandoned their assigned domain, violated the boundaries God set, and corrupted the human bloodline. The offspring of this union — the Nephilim, described as giants — brought systemic violence and wickedness into the world that Scripture describes as the direct cause of the great flood.

But the corruption went deeper than physical violence. The ancient Book of 1 Enoch, quoted directly by the Apostle Jude in the New Testament — the only place in Scripture where a non-canonical text is cited as prophetic — provides the detailed record of what these fallen Watchers actually introduced into the human story.

Before we go further into this material, I want to say something directly to the reader who may already be raising a question.

The Book of 1 Enoch is not part of the Protestant biblical canon. Scholars debate its authorship, and serious theologians — including men and women with advanced degrees who love Scripture deeply — have raised legitimate concerns about its historical timeline and the accuracy of its claims. I am aware of those debates. I do not present what follows as having the same authority as Scripture. What I present it as is ancient Jewish historical and theological context — material that was widely known and respected in the world of the first-century church, that Jude considered credible enough to cite directly in his New Testament letter, and that illuminates what Genesis records without replacing or overriding it. You do not have to accept every detail of Enoch to receive what this section is offering. The foundation is Genesis and Jude. Everything else is context.

Two hundred angels descended upon the summit of Mount Hermon, led by Semyaza, and swore a mutual oath to take human wives. But the violation was not merely physical. Each leader of this rebellion transmitted specific categories of forbidden, destructive knowledge to humanity that had been stolen from heaven. Azazel taught the art of warfare along with vanity, seduction, and the corruption of beauty. Semyaza taught sorcery. Baraqel taught astrology. Kokabel taught false cosmology. Others taught the manipulation of natural elements, the reading of omens, and the practice of enchantments.

The result was precisely what the enemy intended: humanity began worshipping the knowledge the Watchers gave them rather than the God who had designed them. Ancient polytheism — the sudden explosion of false gods, star worship, idol sacrifice, and occult practice across every ancient civilization — traces directly to this event.

The darkness on your path did not originate in God's design. It was introduced by the rebellion of beings who chose to corrupt what God created. But here is the truth that changes everything: those forces do not operate outside of God's sovereignty. Not one of them can touch you, test you, or oppose you without passing through the hands of a God who has already determined the limits of what they are permitted to do.

Just as Satan could not touch Job without explicit divine permission — and was given specific boundaries he could not cross — the forces that oppose your path are not loose cannons operating in a universe God has lost control of. They are constrained, governed, and ultimately used by a sovereign God who, as Thomas Aquinas declared, would in no wise permit evil to exist in His works, unless He were so almighty and so good as to produce good even from evil.

Free Will — The Gift That Required a Risk

God could have created a universe with no possibility of rebellion, no capacity for evil, no free choices that could go wrong. He could have made every created being — angelic and human — incapable of choosing against Him.

He did not. And the reason matters more than most people ever stop to consider.

A being with no capacity to choose against God has no capacity to genuinely choose God. A choice with only one option is not a choice. It is a script. It is programming. It is exactly what God refused to give us — because He did not want mechanisms. He wanted sons and daughters. He wanted love that was freely given rather than mechanically produced.

"I have set before you life and death, blessing and cursing: therefore choose life, that both thou and thy seed may live." — Deuteronomy 30:19 (KJV)

God described His desire not for "toy soldiers" but for real sons. The difference between a tin soldier and a living child is the capacity to make genuine choices — including the capacity to choose wrongly. God granted the Watchers genuine freedom. He granted humanity genuine freedom. And genuine freedom means the path through this life contains real moral conflict, real spiritual warfare, and real consequences for real choices.

The Community Rule of the Dead Sea Scrolls understood this. It taught that God placed two spirits within every human soul — the Spirit of Truth and the Spirit of Falsehood — and that until the final judgment, these two spirits wage a relentless war inside the human heart. The path God designed is not a smooth, conflict-free highway. It is a designed crucible — a place of genuine moral testing where the soul must choose, again and again, between light and darkness.

This is why Paul's confession in Romans 7 is not a confession of spiritual failure. It is a description of the designed human condition:

"For the good that I would I do not: but the evil which I would not, that I do." — Romans 7:19 (KJV)

God did not build the path to be easy. He built it to be transformative. And A.W. Tozer captured the heart behind this design with a single stunning phrase — what he called the enthusiasm of God. Tozer observed that we are the only part of creation made in the exact image of God. And our greatest spiritual struggle is this: we do not believe that God is overwhelmingly, passionately, infinitely delighted with us. He created this world — knowing its cost — because He is enthusiastically, completely, eternally in love with the prospect of living in communion with you.

The Story That Proves It

Joseph — Twenty-Two Years of Hidden Design

This chapter is about a specific and precise claim: that God's foreknowledge did not merely observe what would happen — it governed it. That the painful events He permitted were not failures of His design but expressions of it. That the suffering of the righteous, channeled through the free and sinful choices of broken human beings, can be the very instrument by which God accomplishes purposes that could not have been reached any other way.

No story in all of Scripture proves this claim more completely than the story of Joseph.

In the previous chapter we met Job — the man who sat in the ashes and asked God why, and found that God's presence was a more complete answer than any explanation. Joseph's story asks a different question. Not where is God in my suffering, but how exactly is God working through it. The twenty-two years from the pit to the palace are not merely a story of endurance. They are the most detailed case study Scripture gives us of foreknowledge translating into sovereignty translating into purpose — executed through the freely chosen sins of broken people who had no idea they were building anything at all.

Joseph was seventeen years old when his own brothers — acting out of genuine jealousy and hatred, exercising their full and real free will — stripped him of his coat, threw him into a pit, and sold him to slave traders for twenty pieces of silver. He was taken to Egypt. He served faithfully and was falsely accused. He refused sin and was imprisoned. At every point where righteous behavior should have produced visible reward, it produced deeper suffering instead.

And yet Scripture records, simply and without dramatic flourish, that God was with him:

"But the LORD was with Joseph, and shewed him mercy, and gave him favour in the sight of the keeper of the prison." — Genesis 39:21 (KJV)

John Flavel, the Puritan theologian, wrote about this story in The Mystery of Providence with an observation that cuts to the heart of how God governs a designed path through evil instruments: Sometimes God makes use of instruments for good to his people, who designed nothing but evil and mischief to them. Thus Joseph's brethren were instrumental to his advancement in that very thing wherein they designed his ruin.

Joseph's brothers did not plan to position him in Egypt. They planned to destroy him. Potiphar's wife did not intend to advance God's purposes. She intended to satisfy her own agenda. The cupbearer who forgot him did not serve God's timeline. He simply forgot. And yet every single one of these free, self-interested, sinful human choices was woven by sovereign hands into the precise positioning required for Joseph to stand before Pharaoh, interpret his dream, oversee the storage of grain during seven years of abundance, and distribute it during seven years of devastating famine that would have destroyed the known world.

Twenty-two years. That is how long the path ran from the pit to the palace. From betrayal to purpose. And when the full picture was finally revealed, Joseph himself named what God had been doing all along:

"But as for you, ye thought evil against me; but God meant it unto good, to bring to pass, as it is this day, to save much people alive." — Genesis 50:20 (KJV)

You thought evil. God meant it unto good. The path was not accidental. The suffering was not wasted. The twenty-two years of darkness were not God abandoning His design. They were the design

— precise, specific, and sovereign — working through the free choices of broken human beings toward a purpose that only God could have architected and only hindsight could finally reveal.

Flavel also wrote about what he called the "rub in the green" — a term from lawn bowling describing the tiny, unexpected bump that redirects the trajectory of the ball. He observed that the majority of our most significant turning points in life were not the result of our own planning or skill, but of some unforeseen providence — a delay, a coincidence, a door that closed, a stranger who appeared at exactly the right moment. God's foreknowledge does not just govern the rise and fall of empires. It governs the tiny, seemingly random redirections that change the course of individual lives.

This is not comfortable theology. It is costly theology. It means the thing that broke you was not outside God's knowledge. It means the betrayal, the loss, the unanswered prayer, the years in the dark — He saw all of it. He permitted all of it. And He was present in all of it, weaving something through the choices of the people who wounded you that they never intended and that you cannot yet fully see.

That is not a reason to minimize your pain. Joseph did not minimize his. He named what his brothers had done for what it was — evil. But he also named what God had been doing all along — good. Both truths stood together. The evil was real. The sovereignty was real. And the sovereignty was larger.

Your tomorrows are God's yesterdays. He has already been in the hardest section of your path, laying the purpose before you arrive.

Navigating the Path — With God Versus Without

Understanding that the path is designed does not remove the pain of walking it. And the research for this chapter points to one of the most practically important truths in all of Scripture: the same event produces completely different outcomes depending on whether the soul navigating it is oriented toward God or toward the world.

Augustine, in The City of God, framed this distinction with remarkable clarity. He observed that the same suffering — the same trial, the same loss, the same persecution — produces completely different fruit depending on the orientation of the soul experiencing it. A soul anchored in God emerges from suffering refined, deepened, and more fully conformed to Christ. A soul anchored in worldly thinking emerges from the same suffering bitter, broken, and further from truth than when it entered.

The Greek word dokime, translated as "experience" in Romans 5:4, captures the exact spiritual product God is building through the hard places of the path. Dokime does not mean survival. It means proven character — the specific quality of a soul that has been tested, held, and emerged with demonstrated faith. It is the only kind of character that can be produced through trial. It cannot be manufactured through comfort.

"And not only so, but we glory in tribulations also: knowing that tribulation worketh patience; and patience, experience; and experience, hope." — Romans 5:3–4 (KJV)

James used the same framework at the opening of his letter:

"My brethren, count it all joy when ye fall into divers temptations; knowing this, that the trying of your faith worketh patience. But let patience have her perfect work, that ye may be perfect and entire, wanting nothing." — James 1:2–4 (KJV)

The Greek word teleios — translated as "perfect" — means complete, mature, fully formed. Ancient theology described this as the very purpose for which the soul descends into the material world: to be refined through real moral conflict, real obedience, and real suffering until it is fully formed — complete in a way that only the journey through this life could produce.

The Enoch prophecies mapped the entire arc of human history before it unfolded — from the flood to Abraham, from Moses to the Temple, from the scattering of the elect to the final judgment. The events of the New Testament and Revelation were already chronologically structured in Jewish apocalyptic literature centuries before they occurred. The path of history, like the path of the individual soul, is not random. It is written.

The Worldly Voices That Make the Path Dark

There is one more dimension of this that must be addressed honestly, because it is the source of most of the darkness that feels unbearable on the path God designed.

The path itself is not the problem. The voices interpreting the path are the problem.

"And be not conformed to this world: but be ye transformed by the renewing of your mind, that ye may prove what is that good, and acceptable, and perfect, will of God." — Romans 12:2 (KJV)

The Greek word suschematizo — conformed — means pressed into a mold from the outside. The world presses against the believer's mind with a constant, relentless interpretation of events: this is loss, this is failure, this is punishment, this is the end, this is proof that God is absent or cruel or fictional. And metamorphoo — transformed — means changed from the inside out, at the deepest level of the soul's structure.

When a hard event arrives on the path God designed, there are two voices immediately competing for the interpretation. The world says: this is meaningless suffering in a chaotic universe and there is no sovereign hand in it. God says: I knew this was coming before the foundation of the world. I have already been in this moment. I am building something in you that could not be built any other way. Your tomorrows are My yesterdays.

Richard Sigmund, reflecting on the nature of divine foreknowledge, described it this way: God does not observe our future from the same limited vantage point we occupy. He has already been there. He has already walked the ground ahead of us and laid His purposes in place before we arrive.

"Be careful for nothing; but in every thing by prayer and supplication with thanksgiving let your requests be made known unto God. And the peace of God, which passeth all understanding, shall keep your hearts and minds through Christ Jesus." — Philippians 4:6–7 (KJV)

The peace that passes understanding is not the absence of hard circumstances. It is the presence of a God who stands outside of time, sees the complete picture you cannot yet see, and has already determined that the path He designed for you ends in something far greater than anything the present moment can threaten.

The Questions Skeptics Ask

"If God designed the path, then I have no real choices. I am just following a script."

This is the oldest philosophical tension in theology, and it deserves a direct answer.

The fact that God foreknew your choices does not mean your choices are not real. It means He is outside of the timeline in which you make them. The man on Boethius's hilltop watching the procession does not control the choices of the people walking below him. His comprehensive view does not eliminate their freedom. It simply means someone sees the full picture that they cannot see from inside it.

Deuteronomy 30:19 makes the reality of genuine human choice unmistakable: "I have set before you life and death, blessing and cursing: therefore choose life." God does not command you to choose if the choice is not real. Joshua 24:15 — "Choose you this day whom ye will serve" — presents a genuine fork in the road with genuine consequences for genuine choosing. The path is designed. The destination is marked. But the quality of the journey, the depth of the relationship, and the eternal weight of what is built through the navigation of it — these are shaped by real choices made by real souls.

"If God already knows who will end up in heaven and who will end up in the lake of fire — why does any of it matter?"

This question deserves a direct and honest answer because it is not a fringe question. It is one that serious, faithful people carry in silence.

Yes. God knows. His foreknowledge is total and it is not partial. Revelation 13:8 and 17:8 both reference names written in the Lamb's Book of Life before the foundation of the world. Ephesians 1:4 places His choosing before creation existed. Romans 8:29 says He foreknew. Not some. Not approximately. He foreknew.

And yet. 2 Peter 3:9 declares that God is not willing that any should perish, but that all should come to repentance. Ezekiel 33:11 records God saying He has no pleasure in the death of the wicked. These are not contradictions. They are two truths held together by a God whose ways are higher than our ways.

Here is the only framework that holds both truths without breaking either one. God's foreknowledge does not cause what He foresees. The man on Boethius's hilltop seeing the whole procession at once does not control the steps of the people walking below. God sees, from His eternal vantage point, every soul that will freely and finally receive His Son — and every soul that will freely and finally reject Him. He created both knowing the outcome. He extended the cross to both without exception. Whosoever believeth — John 3:16 does not qualify that word. It is the most open invitation in all of Scripture.

What this means practically is this: you are not living inside a predetermined script with a destination already stamped on your soul without your participation. You are living inside a genuine story with a genuine choice at its center. God sees how that choice resolves. You are living toward that resolution. The urgency is real. The invitation is real. The choice is yours. And God, who takes no pleasure in any soul's destruction, is longsuffering — patient, merciful, pursuing — because He wants every soul to turn.

"If God knew and designed the path, then my suffering served His purposes — which makes me a tool, not a person He loves."

This is the hardest version of the question, and it deserves to be answered honestly rather than deflected.

The objection assumes that being part of a design automatically reduces a person to a means to an end. But that is not how personal love works, and it is not how God works. A father who shapes his child through difficulty — who allows them to struggle, fail, and grow — does not love the child less because the struggle serves a purpose. He loves the child, and from that love he refuses to protect them from everything that would break them open into something better. The design and the love are not competing. The design is the expression of the love.

The theologian Thomas Torrance, whose work on the personal nature of God's covenant love stands as one of the most careful treatments of this question in the twentieth century, argued that God's relationship to His creatures is never merely instrumental. God does not use you. He loves you — and the difference is everything. An instrument is valued for what it produces. A person who is loved is valued for who they are. Your suffering did not happen because God needed something from it. It happened because God loves you enough to build into your story the exact conditions required to produce in you what comfort alone could never produce.

Paul Jewett, writing on the personal nature of God's covenant relationship with humanity, made the point with precision: the God who foreknew you did not foreknow a function. He foreknew a person. The intimacy of yada — that covenantal knowing we examined in Jeremiah 1:5 — is the knowing of a Father who loved you before the first moment of your existence and whose design for your path has never been separate from that love. You are not on the path because God needed you there. You are on the path because God loved you before the path existed.

"If God let evil enter the path through the fallen angels, He is responsible for the result."

Aquinas answered this with philosophical precision that has never been improved upon. Evil, he argued, is not a substance. It is not a thing God created. It is a privation — a corruption or absence of good. God only creates good. The Watchers who rebelled and the humans who have followed their corruption exercised genuine free will to choose the corruption of good. God did not author that choice. He permitted it within defined boundaries, and then — in the most staggering act of sovereign genius in all of history — He designed a system so profoundly sovereign that even evil is forced to serve the purposes of grace.

Augustine described this with an image that is almost too beautiful to absorb: for as the beauty of a picture is increased by well-managed shadows, so, to the eye that has skill to discern it, the universe is beautified even by sinners. The darkest threads are not accidents that damaged God's design. They are the precise tension required to manifest the highest attributes of His character — mercy, grace, redemption — which could never have been displayed in a universe where nothing ever went wrong.

"If the path was pre-designed, prayer is pointless."

Philip Yancey addressed this with a framework that changes the entire posture of prayer. He observed that God operates through what he called a partnership — having given humanity genuine free will and genuine agency, God invites human beings to participate as partners in the unfolding of His sovereign design. Prayer is not an attempt to change God's mind about His plan. It is the act of a soul reaching into the sovereign future God has already secured and pulling its reality into the present.

Paul declared in 2 Corinthians 1:20: "For all the promises of God in him are yea, and in him Amen." Every promise is already yes. Prayer is not persuasion. It is claiming what has already been guaranteed by a God who exists in the eternal present of a future that is already secured.

"Call unto me, and I will answer thee, and shew thee great and mighty things, which thou knowest not." — Jeremiah 33:3 (KJV)

My Reflection

There is a question this chapter forced me to sit with longer than any other in this book. Not the philosophical question. Not the one about foreknowledge and free will. The personal one. The one that sounds like this: if God designed the path, and if the path runs through everything mine has run through — does that mean He planned it? Does that mean He looked at what was coming and chose not to redirect it?

For a long time I could not sit with that. There is a version of "God designed this" that feels like betrayal if you hold it the wrong way. If God is the Architect and the suffering was in the blueprint, then what does that make of the relationship? It can feel, in the darkest hours, like finding out someone you trusted had more information than they were sharing. Like the love was real — but there was a plan underneath it you were never shown.

I worked through that slowly. Not through theology first — through something more personal. I thought about the way my own father raised me. The hard things he allowed. The disappointments he could have shielded me from and did not. The moments where I was convinced he was not on my side and later understood that he was so completely on my side that he refused to rob me of the growth the difficulty was producing. There was a plan. He knew more than I did. And the plan was never separate from the love. The plan was the love working in the only way love that is serious about your future can work.

That is the moment this chapter's question stopped being a wound for me and became an anchor. Not because the pain disappeared. Because I finally stopped reading the design as evidence against the love and started reading it as the evidence of it.

God did not let it happen because He was absent. He built it into the path because He is present. He governs everything that touches you before it reaches you. He sets the limits on what can pass through His hands into yours. And He has already been in your tomorrow, laying the victory before you ever arrive.

The Fibonacci sequence — that extraordinary mathematical pattern woven into the architecture of shells and galaxies and flower petals and the spiral of the human ear — is the fingerprint of a God who coded precision, beauty, and order into the deepest structure of creation. He did not throw a universe into existence and step back to see what happened. He embedded His signature into the mathematics of reality before the first atom existed. And if He was that precise about the structure of a flower, He was that precise about the structure of your life.

He knows. He designed. He governs. And He is building something in you — through everything the path contains — that your current circumstances cannot yet reveal.

Though the words below were first spoken to the nation of Israel in Babylonian captivity, the God whose character they reveal is the same God who governs your path:

"For I know the thoughts that I think toward you, saith the LORD, thoughts of peace, and not of evil, to give you an expected end." — Jeremiah 29:11 (KJV)

A Prayer for the Reader

Father —

I come to You on behalf of every soul holding these pages right now — every person carrying this question from a place of real pain and real confusion.

For the one who is looking at their life right now and cannot see how any sovereign design could include what they are walking through — open their eyes. Not to remove the darkness, but to reveal Your presence in the middle of it. Let them feel what Joseph felt when the full picture was finally revealed: that the years in the pit and the prison were not God abandoning the design. They were the design.

For the one who is carrying anger at You for a path they would never have chosen — meet them in that anger with the patience of a Father who is not threatened by honest wrestling. Remind them that the question itself is a form of faith — because it is addressed to You, not away from You.

For the one who fears that being part of a design makes them less than a person You love — speak the truth of yada into their spirit. That before You designed anything, You knew them. Not as a function. As a person. The design was never separate from the love. The design was the love, working in the only way love that is serious about a person's future can work.

For the one who has been told their suffering is meaningless, accidental, random — let the truth of this chapter land like an anchor in their soul. You knew. You designed. You govern. Nothing that has touched them passed through the world without passing through Your hands first. Not one moment of it was wasted. Not one tear has escaped Your count.

For the one who is navigating the path alone — driven by their own strength, carrying what You designed to be shared with You — I pray for the moment of surrender. The moment they throw up the sponge. Not in defeat, but in the greatest act of wisdom a human soul can perform: the recognition that You must do what they cannot.

And for all of us — remind us that our tomorrows are Your yesterdays. That You have already been in the hardest section ahead of us. That You have already laid the victory in the path before we arrive.

We do not need to see the full map. We need to know the Mapmaker. And we do.

In the name of the Father, the Son, and the Holy Spirit.

Amen.

"Before I formed thee in the belly I knew thee; and before thou camest forth out of the womb I sanctified thee." — Jeremiah 1:5 (KJV)

Chapter Four

Who Created God — And Where Did He Come From?

"Before the mountains were brought forth, or ever thou hadst formed the earth and the world, even from everlasting to everlasting, thou art God." — Psalm 90:2 (KJV)

"In the beginning was the Word, and the Word was with God, and the Word was God." — John 1:1 (KJV)

The Question

It is the question that has been aimed at believers like a weapon for centuries. It arrives in college classrooms and late-night arguments, in comment sections and quiet moments of personal doubt. It is delivered sometimes with intellectual arrogance, sometimes with genuine confusion, and sometimes with the raw desperation of a person who desperately wants there to be a God but cannot figure out how to get past the logic.

Who created God? If everything has a cause, what caused Him? If He has always existed, what does that even mean? And if the answer is that He simply always was — how is that any more satisfying than saying the universe simply always was?

These are honest questions. And this chapter will not dismiss them.

But here is what you need to know before we go any further. The question "Who created God?" is not actually a challenge to the existence of God. It is evidence of one. Because the moment you ask what caused the universe — the moment you feel the intellectual pressure of that question and demand an answer — you are already standing at the threshold of the most important discovery a human mind can make.

Something is responsible for all of this.

The question is not whether that Something exists. The question is whether you are willing to follow the evidence far enough to understand what it must be.

This chapter will take you there. Not through religious pressure. Not through emotional manipulation. Through philosophy, through science, through the ancient languages of Scripture, and through the kind of honest, clear-eyed reasoning that has driven the greatest thinkers in human history to the same undeniable conclusion.

There is a God. He has always existed. He requires no cause. And the human mind — in its current form — was never designed to fully comprehend that. Not yet.

But one day it will.

Acknowledging the Challenge

Before we build the case, something needs to be said plainly to every person carrying this question — whether you are a believer who has wrestled with it privately, or a skeptic who has used it to keep God at arm's length.

The fact that your mind cannot fully grasp how God could exist without a beginning does not mean He doesn't. It means you are human.

Think carefully about what you are actually doing when you ask who created God. You are applying the rules of the physical universe — the rules of cause and effect, of before and after, of things requiring other things in order to exist — to a Being who is, by definition, the author of those rules. You are taking the measuring instruments of a created world and attempting to measure the One who created the instruments.

C.S. Lewis addressed this with characteristic precision. He pointed out that words like "before," "created," and "caused" only carry meaning within the boundaries of linear time. To ask what came before the Creator of time is like asking what is north of the North Pole. The question sounds reasonable. It is not. It contains a hidden assumption — that God exists inside the same kind of reality you do — and that assumption is the very thing that needs to be examined.

Your inability to imagine a Being without a beginning is not evidence that such a Being doesn't exist. It is evidence that your imagination is finite.

And here is the comfort in that. The same God who gave you a mind capable of asking this question also promised that there is a day coming when the limitation is removed. When what you now see through a glass darkly you will see face to face. When every question that your earthly mind could not contain will find its perfect answer in the presence of the One who designed you to ask it.

Until that day — what you have is enough. More than enough.

What Scripture Says

Part 1 — The Name That Contains the Answer

When Moses stood before the burning bush on the mountain of God, he asked a question that no human being had ever dared to ask directly.

He asked God His name.

Not out of arrogance. Out of necessity. Moses was being sent back to Egypt — back to the most powerful empire on earth, back to the people who had enslaved his family, back to a Pharaoh who answered to no one — and he needed to know whose authority he was carrying. The people would ask. What would he tell them?

God's answer was not what Moses expected. It was not a title. It was not a genealogy. It was not a description of power or a recitation of deeds. It was something that stopped Moses — and has stopped every honest thinker who has truly considered it ever since.

"And God said unto Moses, I AM THAT I AM: and he said, Thus shalt thou say unto the children of Israel, I AM hath sent me unto you." — Exodus 3:14 (KJV)

Three words in English. Two in Hebrew. And contained within those two Hebrew words is the most complete theological statement ever spoken.

In the original Hebrew, God declares Himself as Ehyeh Asher Ehyeh. The name derives directly from the Hebrew root verb hayah — meaning simply to be, to exist, to become. According to the ancient Hebrew lexicons, this root reveals something extraordinary about God's nature. He does not possess existence the way a tree possesses roots or a river possesses water. He does not have existence as a quality or an attribute. He does not hold existence as something separate from Himself that could theoretically be removed.

He is existence.

Not a being who exists. The act of existing itself. The ground of all being. The reason anything is rather than nothing.

And then God does something remarkable. He shifts the grammar.

When God speaks of Himself, He says Ehyeh — I AM. First person. Present. Absolute. But when He gives Moses the name by which all of Israel will call Him throughout history — the name that will appear nearly seven thousand times in the pages of the Old Testament — He uses the third person form of the same verb.

YHWH. He IS. He WAS. He WILL BE.

Not because God changed. Because God is speaking to creatures who exist inside time, and a name must be pronounceable by the ones who carry it. God says I AM. Humanity says He IS. The grammatical shift is not a contradiction — it is a window. It shows us, with breathtaking precision, the difference between how the Eternal speaks of Himself and how finite creatures must speak of the Infinite.

The ancient Jewish scribes understood the weight of this name so completely that they refused to speak it aloud. The Tetragrammaton — the four Hebrew letters Yod, Heh, Vav, Heh — was considered too sacred to pass through human lips. To avoid breaking the commandment against taking the Lord's name in vain, they substituted the word Adonai (Lord) whenever YHWH appeared in public reading. They would bathe before writing the name. Some would not allow any other letters to touch it on the page. Not superstition. Reverence. The reverence of people who understood that this name did not merely identify God — it described His nature.

When the ancient Jewish scholars translated the Hebrew Scriptures into Greek — producing what is known as the Septuagint — they rendered Exodus 3:14 as Ego eimi ho on. I am the One who is. The Being. Thomas Aquinas seized upon this Greek translation and built one of the most powerful arguments in the history of theology upon it. He declared that this name — He Who Is — is the most perfect and most proper name for God that human language can produce. Because God's existence knows no past tense and no future tense. He does not remember existing yesterday. He does not anticipate existing tomorrow. He simply, purely, eternally IS.

This is not poetry. This is architecture.

And it completely dismantles the question "Who created God?" Because the question assumes that God is a contingent being — something that exists conditionally, the way you and I exist, the way the mountains exist, the way the stars exist. Contingent things require causes. Contingent things have beginnings. Contingent things depend on other things for their existence.

But God is not contingent. He is the Necessary Being. The One whose very essence is existence. To ask who created the source of all existence is to ask who created creation before creation existed. The question folds back on itself and collapses — not because God cannot be examined, but because the human categories being applied to Him were never designed to reach this far.

The God Who Is Everywhere at Once — and Yet Contains Everything

Ancient Jewish theology grappled with the immensity of this reality through a concept that most Western Christians have never encountered.

They called it HaMakom. The Place.

It is one of the oldest and most profound titles ever given to God in Hebrew thought. And its meaning is not what you might expect. God is not called The Place because He dwells somewhere. He is called The Place because He is the location in which all existence occurs.

Space does not contain God. God contains space. Time does not surround God. God surrounds time. The universe does not house God. God houses the universe.

When we ask where God came from, we are assuming He arrived somewhere from somewhere else — that there was a location prior to Him, a before into which He stepped. But HaMakom declares that there is no location prior to God because location itself is a feature of the world He created. There is no before God because before is a category of time, and time is something He authored.

The question "Where did God come from?" is not a challenge to God. It is a revelation of the questioner's framework. It shows that the person asking is still inside the created order, measuring the Creator by the rules of creation.

God is not inside the universe looking for room. The universe is inside God, existing only because He permits it to, sustained only because He wills it to be.

"The LORD possessed me in the beginning of his way, before his works of old. I was set up from everlasting, from the beginning, or ever the earth was." — Proverbs 8:22–23 (KJV)

Before the earth. Before the mountains. Before the oceans were poured into their basins and the stars were scattered across the darkness — He was. Not waiting. Not preparing. Simply, completely, eternally present in Himself.

Me'olam ad olam. From everlasting to everlasting.

The ancient Hebrew word olam points to a dimension of existence so vast that it disappears beyond the horizon of human comprehension — a vanishing point in both directions with no origin and no destination. Not a very long time. A different kind of time altogether. A duration that was never measured because it was never begun. The Septuagint renders this concept using the Greek word aionios —

eternal — pointing to a condition that has neither entrance nor exit. A mode of existence so complete that the concepts of start and finish simply do not apply.

This is who sent Moses back to Egypt. Not a very old God. Not a God who has existed longer than anything else. A God for whom the categories of old and new, before and after, beginning and end, were things He invented — tools He gave to the universe He created so that creatures like us could navigate the story He was writing.

The Earliest Christian Voice — What the Odes of Solomon Declare

Before the church built its creeds. Before the councils formalized their theology. Before most of the letters we call the New Testament had been copied and circulated to every community of believers — there were people who had heard the Gospel within living memory of the apostles themselves, and they were singing.

The Odes of Solomon are the earliest collection of Christian devotional hymns ever discovered. Written in Syriac — the language most closely related to the Aramaic that Jesus spoke — they date to approximately 100 A.D. They were found in 1909 among a collection of ancient manuscripts, and they contain forty-two hymns of extraordinary theological depth that predate almost everything the Western church has ever considered early Christian writing.

Ode 12 stops every serious reader cold. The Odist writes of a Word that existed before the world was spoken into being — a Word not bound by the categories of before and after, not contained by the space it fills, not measured by the time it inhabits. This eternal Word, the Odist declares, is the dwelling place of all things rather than a thing that dwells somewhere. It is the fullness that fills without being filled. The ground of reality that requires no ground beneath it.

This is a believer writing within living memory of those who walked with Jesus, reaching for the same theological reality that Moses encountered at the burning bush and that Aquinas would later articulate in the Summa — that God does not occupy existence the way creatures do. He is the existence that everything else occupies.

The earliest Christians did not need centuries of philosophical development to arrive at this truth. They sang it. Because they had met the One it described.

The Name That Cannot Be Named

There is one more layer to this that the ancient Jewish mystics preserved with breathtaking depth.

In the Kabbalistic theology of the Zohar, the ultimate reality of God is given a name that means precisely that it cannot be named.

Ein Sof. Without end.

The Zohar teaches that before any act of creation, before any revealed attribute or sacred name, before even the concept of divine relationship existed — God dwelt in a state of pure, infinite, undefinable being that surpasses every category, every description, and every name the human mind could produce. The names of God — YHWH, Elohim, El Shaddai, Adonai — are not the ultimate reality of God. They are His garments. The interfaces through which a finite world can encounter an infinite Being without being destroyed.

Ein Sof is God as He is in Himself. Boundless. Nameless. Beyond.

This is not contradiction. This is completion.

The biblical God is simultaneously the most personal Being in the universe — who calls us by name, who counts the hairs on our heads, who wept at a graveside and prayed in a garden and breathed His final breath on a cross for love — and the most transcendent, incomprehensible, infinite Reality that exists. Personal enough to meet you in the lowest moment of your life. Vast enough that no angel can look upon His face.

The question "Who created God?" is answered not by an argument but by an encounter with the magnitude of what is actually being asked. We are not asking about a very large, very old object that requires an explanation. We are asking about the ground of all reality. The source of all being. The I AM who was before before existed.

And that — as Aquinas recognized, as Moses discovered, as every honest philosopher and every broken-hearted believer who has ever stepped past the limits of their own understanding has found — is not a problem to be solved.

It is a Person to be known.

Part 2 — What the Greatest Minds in History Concluded

There is a version of this conversation that never opens a Bible. It never quotes a prophet or invokes the name of Jesus. It never appeals to faith or tradition or personal experience. It operates entirely within the rules of logic, philosophy, and modern science — and it arrives at the exact same destination.

Something uncaused, eternal, and immeasurably powerful is responsible for the existence of everything.

The brightest philosophical and scientific minds in human history did not stumble accidentally into this conclusion. They were driven there by the evidence. And the path they walked is worth following — because when a person understands why reason itself demands a First Cause, the question "Who created God?" stops feeling like a challenge to faith and starts feeling like a doorway into it.

Aristotle and the Unmoved Mover

Twenty-three centuries ago, the Greek philosopher Aristotle sat down with nothing but observation and logic and asked one of the most important questions ever posed: Why is anything moving?

Not moving in the sense of traveling from place to place. Moving in the broader sense — changing. Becoming. A seed becoming a tree. A child becoming an adult. Water becoming vapor. Everything around us is in a constant state of transition from what it is to what it is becoming.

Aristotle made a deceptively simple observation. Nothing moves itself. For something to transition from potential to actual — from what it could be to what it is — something else must act upon it. The wood does not spontaneously become fire. The fire acts upon the wood. The stick does not move the stone on its own. The hand moves the stick.

Follow this chain backward and you immediately encounter a problem. If every mover requires another mover behind it, and that mover requires another, and that one another — where does it end? Aristotle recognized that an infinite regress of movers is logically impossible. Not difficult. Not unlikely. Impossible. Because if there is no first mover, there can be no motion at all. Just as a row of dominoes cannot fall unless the first one is pushed, no subsequent cause in history can produce an effect unless something at the beginning of the chain acted without being acted upon.

There must be, Aristotle concluded, a First Mover. Unmoved. Uncaused. Pure actuality with no potentiality — a Being who does not move because something moved Him, but who simply, eternally, IS.

He got remarkably close to the God of Scripture. He correctly deduced that this First Cause must be singular, immaterial, and perfect. But Aristotle fell short of the full revelation in two critical ways. He believed the universe itself was eternal — that the First Cause had never created anything from nothing, but merely organized what had always existed. And his First Cause was not personal. Not relational. Not loving. It was an abstract philosophical principle, a God entirely absorbed in self-contemplation, with no awareness of or interest in the creatures of the world it had set in motion.

Philosophy had found the address. It had not yet met the Person who lived there.

Thomas Aquinas and the Five Ways

Eight centuries ago, the theologian Thomas Aquinas took Aristotle's framework and built upon it something far more complete. In his masterwork Summa Theologica, Aquinas presented five arguments for the existence of God that remain among the most powerful and precisely constructed in the history of human thought.

The First Way mirrors Aristotle's argument from motion. Things change. Change requires a cause. The chain of causes cannot be infinite. Therefore there is a First Cause of all motion, put in motion by nothing and no one — and this, Aquinas writes, everyone understands to be God.

The Second Way deepens this through efficient causation. We observe an ordered chain of causes in the world. Nothing is the efficient cause of itself, because it would have to exist before it existed to cause its own existence — which is a logical absurdity. Remove the first cause and you remove every subsequent effect. Therefore there must be a First Efficient Cause that is itself uncaused.

But it is Aquinas's Third Way that delivers the most devastating blow to the idea of a universe without God.

He distinguishes between two kinds of beings. Contingent beings — things that are possible to exist or not to exist, things that come into being and pass away. And a Necessary Being — a Being whose existence requires no external cause, whose non-existence is logically impossible.

If every single thing that exists were contingent, Aquinas argues, there would have been a moment in the past when absolutely nothing existed. And here is the logical trap from which there is no escape. If nothing existed, nothing could bring anything into existence. Because from nothing — absolute, total, genuine nothing — nothing comes. The Latin is precise: ex nihilo nihil fit. Out of nothing, nothing is made.

The fact that anything exists at all proves that something has always existed. Something whose existence is not borrowed from anything outside itself. Something that does not merely have existence the way a stone has weight or a river has motion — but something that is existence in itself.

Aquinas called this being Esse Ipsum Subsistens. Subsisting Being Itself. The act of existing, standing alone, requiring nothing, owing nothing, dependent on nothing.

This is not a philosophical nicety. This is the bedrock of reality. And it matches with precision the God who answered Moses from a burning bush and declared His name to be I AM.

The Universe Had a Beginning — And That Changes Everything

For centuries, atheist philosophers relied heavily on the idea that the universe itself was eternal. If matter has always existed, they argued, then there is no need to invoke a Creator. The universe simply is, and always has been, and always will be.

Modern science destroyed that argument completely.

In the early twentieth century, astronomer Edwin Hubble discovered that the universe is expanding in every direction. If you run that expansion backward through time like a film played in reverse, every galaxy, every star, every atom of matter converges on a single point of infinite density at a specific moment in the finite past. The universe did not always exist. It began.

The Big Bang was not a rearrangement of existing matter. It was the sudden, explosive origin of matter, energy, space, and time simultaneously. Before it, there was no before. Not empty space waiting to be filled. Not darkness waiting to be illuminated. Not time waiting to be started. Nothing. And then — everything.

The astronomer Robert Jastrow, himself no religious believer, described the theological implications with remarkable candor. The scientist who follows the trail of evidence backward through time eventually climbs the mountain of discovery, pulls himself over the final ridge — and finds a group of theologians who have been sitting there waiting for him for centuries.

The Second Law of Thermodynamics confirms this from a different direction. Every closed system moves from order toward disorder. Usable energy decreases. Stars burn out. Structures decay. The universe is running down like a wound clock. If the universe were infinitely old, it would have wound down to cold, dead, absolute disorder an eternity ago. The fact that stars still burn, that energy still moves, that life still exists — proves that the clock was wound at a specific moment. There was a beginning.

Stephen Hawking acknowledged what the Big Bang model implies: that the initial state of the universe was so extraordinarily, precisely arranged that it points toward the act of a God who intended to create beings like us. Augustine had reached the same conclusion seventeen centuries earlier — that God must exist outside of time, because time itself began with creation.

The Borde-Guth-Vilenkin theorem of 2003 closed the final mathematical escape hatch. Cosmologists Arvid Borde, Alan Guth, and Alexander Vilenkin proved mathematically that any universe which has been expanding throughout its history cannot be infinite in the past. It must have an absolute beginning. Vilenkin himself, no religious believer, stated the conclusion plainly: cosmologists can no longer hide behind the possibility of a past-eternal universe. The beginning is not a theological assumption. It is a mathematical proof.

And a universe with a beginning demands a Cause that exists outside of it.

The God the Universe Requires

Here is where philosophy and science converge on something remarkable.

If the universe — all of space, all of time, all of matter — had an absolute beginning, then whatever caused it must exist outside of space, time, and matter. It must be spaceless. Timeless. Immaterial. Enormously, incomprehensibly powerful.

And it must be personal.

This is the point that most people miss. An impersonal, mechanical cause — a blind force, an unconscious energy — would produce its effect automatically and eternally. If the cause were simply a brute, impersonal power, its effect would never have had a beginning. It would have always been producing universes, because nothing would have stopped it and nothing would have started it. The fact that the universe began at a specific moment, out of nothing, by a definite act — requires a cause that possesses will. A cause that chose to act. A cause that is not a force but a Person.

And then look at what that universe produced.

The fine-tuning of the physical constants of nature is one of the most staggering facts in modern science. The cosmological constant — the energy density of empty space — is calibrated to a precision that physicists describe as one part in ten raised to the power of one hundred and twenty. The gravitational constant. The ratio of proton to electron mass. The strength of the strong nuclear force. Every one of these constants must be set to an almost incomprehensibly precise value for atoms to exist, for stars to form, for chemistry to be possible, for life to emerge.

Physicist Richard Feynman, in his work on quantum electrodynamics, described the fine structure constant — the number governing the interaction of light and matter — as one of the greatest mysteries in physics. No theory he knew could account for where this number came from or why it held the precise value required for matter to exist. Its precision, he observed, pointed to something beyond the reach of ordinary physical explanation.

The mathematical odds of these constants arriving at their precise values by chance are not slim. They are not astronomically slim. They are so far beyond any conceivable probability that chance ceases to be a coherent explanation. What they point to is not a lucky accident. They point to forethought. Intelligence. A Mind that knew exactly what it was building and designed the building blocks accordingly.

Aristotle found the address through logic. Modern cosmology confirmed the building exists. Fine-tuning science revealed that someone extraordinarily intelligent designed it. And the God of Scripture — the self-existent, personal, infinite I AM who declares the end from the beginning — is the only explanation that satisfies every single requirement the evidence demands.

Not a very old thing. Not a very powerful force. The uncaused, eternal, personal, infinitely intelligent source of all reality. The One who IS.

Part 3 — The Argument That Closes Every Door

There is one more philosophical argument that belongs in this chapter before we turn toward the personal and the pastoral. It was first articulated in precise form by the medieval Islamic philosopher Al-Ghazali in the eleventh century and has been formalized and defended in the modern era by philosopher and theologian William Lane Craig with a rigor that has withstood every serious academic challenge mounted against it.

It is called the Kalam Cosmological Argument. And it is perhaps the most elegant and decisive logical case for the existence of an un-caused Creator ever constructed in the history of human thought.

The argument has three steps. Each one is simple. Each one is defensible. And together they produce a conclusion that no honest thinker can dismiss without abandoning the basic principles of rational thought.

Everything that begins to exist has a cause. This is not a controversial premise. It is the foundational assumption of every scientific investigation ever conducted. Every experiment, every observation, every causal explanation in the history of science rests on this principle. Things do not simply pop into existence from nothing without cause. To deny this premise is to make science itself impossible.

The universe began to exist. This was once the contested premise. For centuries atheist philosophers relied on the assumption of an eternal universe to avoid the implication of a Creator. That assumption has been demolished. The Borde-Guth-Vilenkin theorem of 2003 proved mathematically that any expanding universe must have an absolute beginning. The Second Law of Thermodynamics confirms it from thermodynamics. The cosmic microwave background radiation maps it from observational astronomy. The universe had a beginning. This is no longer a matter of reasonable scientific dispute.

Therefore the universe has a cause. The logic is airtight. And it immediately produces the question that every serious philosopher and cosmologist must then face: What kind of cause does a universe require?

The cause of the universe cannot be physical. Because all physical reality came into existence with the universe. The cause must therefore be non-physical — immaterial.

The cause of the universe cannot be temporal. Because time itself came into existence with the universe. The cause must therefore be timeless — eternal.

The cause of the universe cannot be spatial. Because space itself came into existence with the universe. The cause must therefore be non-spatial — not located anywhere.

The cause of the universe must be enormously, incomprehensibly powerful. Because it produced everything that exists from nothing.

And — most critically — the cause of the universe must be personal. This is the point that stops every purely mechanical explanation in its tracks. An impersonal, mindless force operating outside of time would produce its effect automatically and eternally. If a timeless, non-physical force were the cause of the universe, it would have always been producing universes — because nothing would have stopped it and nothing would have started it. The fact that the universe began at a specific moment, with a definite act, from a state of absolute nothingness — requires a cause that possesses will. The capacity to choose. The freedom to act or not to act.

A mindless force does not choose. Only a Person chooses.

The Kalam Cosmological Argument does not prove every attribute of the God of Scripture. But it proves the non-negotiable foundation. The cause of the universe is eternal, immaterial, non-spatial, incomprehensibly powerful, and personal.

Compare that to the God who spoke to Moses from the burning bush. The God who declares in Revelation 1:8 that He is the One who is, and who was, and who is to come. The God whose Son declares in John 8:58 that before Abraham was, I AM.

"I am Alpha and Omega, the beginning and the ending, saith the Lord, which is, and which was, and which is to come, the Almighty."
— Revelation 1:8 (KJV)

"Jesus said unto them, Verily, verily, I say unto you, Before Abraham was, I am." — John 8:58 (KJV)

The universe requires a cause that matches God's description with a precision no alternative can come close to. The Kalam argument does not lead to a philosophical abstraction. It leads to a Person. And the testimony of Scripture has been telling us His name for thousands of years.

The Case Is Made

Philosophy followed the chain of causes backward and found a First Cause that was uncaused. Science followed the expansion of the universe backward and found an absolute beginning that demands a Creator outside of space and time. Fine-tuning mathematics pointed to a Mind of incomprehensible intelligence that designed the building blocks of reality.

Every road, followed honestly, leads to the same place.

Something uncaused, eternal, immaterial, personal, and incomprehensibly powerful brought everything that exists into being from nothing. That description matches the God of Scripture — the I AM of Exodus, the Alpha and Omega of Revelation, the One before whom the seraphim cover their faces — with a precision that no other explanation can approach.

"Thus saith the LORD the King of Israel, and his redeemer the LORD of hosts; I am the first, and I am the last; and beside me there is no God." — Isaiah 44:6 (KJV)

The question "Who created God?" has been answered by the accumulated weight of every serious mind that has pursued it honestly to its conclusion. The God of Scripture requires no cause. He is the cause. He does not fit into the category of things that need explaining. He is the explanation.

But the case does not end with philosophy and science. God did not leave the question of His eternal nature as a philosophical abstraction. He declared it. He demonstrated it. He stepped into human history and spoke it in the first person — at the cost of His life. Because the God who IS was not content to be known only through argument. He came in person.

Part 4 — The Son Who Was Before the Beginning

In the first part of this chapter, we followed philosophy and science to the edge of what reason can reach. Aristotle found the First Cause. Aquinas proved the Necessary Being. The Borde-Guth-Vilenkin theorem closed every scientific escape route. The Kalam argument sealed the logical case.

Something uncaused, eternal, immaterial, personal, and incomprehensibly powerful brought everything into being from nothing. The argument from reason is complete.

But the God of Scripture was not content to be known only through argument.

He declared His eternal nature. He demonstrated it. He stepped into human history in the person of Jesus Christ and spoke it in the first person — in the middle of the temple courts of Jerusalem, surrounded by witnesses, at the cost of His life. And in doing so, He transformed the question "Who created God?" from a philosophical puzzle into a personal encounter.

Before we go further, there is something worth pausing on. That name — Jesus — is itself a translation of a translation. He was never called Jesus in His lifetime. His actual name, the name His mother gave Him, the name the disciples called out across the Sea of Galilee, the name written above the cross in Hebrew, was Yeshua. It is a Hebrew name meaning the LORD saves — or simply, salvation. Every time someone called His name they were speaking salvation itself. The name Jesus came through Greek, then Latin, then English. Yeshua is what God named His Son.

The Name That Nearly Got Him Killed

It is one of the most electrically charged moments in the entire Gospel of John. Jesus is in Jerusalem, in the temple courts, engaged in a heated exchange with the Pharisees about His identity and His authority. The conversation escalates. The Pharisees are looking for a way to discredit Him. And then Jesus says something that stops the entire exchange cold.

He speaks about Abraham — the founding father of the entire Hebrew nation. A man who lived two thousand years before this moment. A man whose bones have been in the ground for twenty centuries. And Jesus makes a claim that shatters every category they have for Him.

"Your father Abraham rejoiced to see my day: and he saw it, and was glad." — John 8:56 (KJV)

The Pharisees are incredulous. They respond with the obvious objection: Thou art not yet fifty years old, and hast thou seen Abraham?

And Jesus answers them.

"Jesus said unto them, Verily, verily, I say unto you, Before Abraham was, I am." — John 8:58 (KJV)

Read that sentence again carefully. Because Jesus did not say what the grammar of that sentence should say.

If Jesus were simply claiming to be very old — older than Abraham — the natural grammatical construction in Greek would be ego eimi in the past perfect tense. Before Abraham was, I was. That would be remarkable enough. It would be a claim to supernatural age.

But that is not what He said. He said Before Abraham was, I AM.

Past tense for Abraham. Present tense for Himself. In a single sentence, Jesus collapses the entire timeline of history — twenty centuries of human generations — and places Himself outside of it. Not at the beginning of it. Not before it in the sense of earlier along the same timeline. Outside of it entirely. Existing in a perpetual, uninterrupted, eternal present tense that the passage of human time does not affect.

The Greek words recorded in that moment are Ego eimi. I AM. The exact same words used by the Septuagint translators — the Jewish scholars who translated the Hebrew Scriptures into Greek — when they rendered God's answer to Moses in Exodus 3:14.

The Pharisees knew their Scriptures. They knew exactly what those words meant and exactly who had used them last. They did not treat this as a metaphor or a misstatement. They did not ask for clarification. They reached for stones.

"Then took they up stones to cast at him." — John 8:59 (KJV)

Not because He had claimed to be very old. Because He had claimed to be the I AM of Exodus 3:14. Because He had taken the most sacred name in all of Hebrew theology — the name too holy to be spoken aloud — and applied it directly to Himself.

Jesus was not making a poetic statement about His importance. He was making an ontological claim about His nature. He was declaring that He stands in the same eternal present tense as the Father. That He does not merely exist inside time. That He is the same self-existent, uncaused, eternal Being whose name is existence itself.

And He said it in the middle of the temple. In front of witnesses. With full knowledge of what it would cost Him.

He Was Before Everything — And He Holds Everything Together Now

The Gospel of John opens with one of the most theologically dense passages in all of Scripture.

"In the beginning was the Word, and the Word was with God, and the Word was God. The same was in the beginning with God. All things were made by him; and without him was not any thing made that was made." — John 1:1–3 (KJV)

In the beginning was. Not in the beginning became. Not in the beginning appeared. Was. Already present. Already existing in complete relationship with the Father before the first syllable of creation was spoken.

The Apostle Paul builds upon this foundation in his letter to the Colossians with language so cosmologically staggering that it has never been fully absorbed by the casual reader.

"For by him were all things created, that are in heaven, and that are in earth, visible and invisible, whether they be thrones, or dominions, or principalities, or powers: all things were created by him, and for him: And he is before all things, and by him all things consist." — Colossians 1:16–17 (KJV)

Every word in that passage carries enormous weight. But it is the final phrase that stops every physicist and every theologian who encounters it with fresh eyes.

By him all things consist.

The Greek word translated consist is sunistemi. It is a compound word built from sun — together — and histemi — to stand, to hold, to maintain in position. It does not simply mean that Christ created everything in the past and then stepped back. It means that Christ is actively, continuously, presently holding everything in existence right now.

Every atom of matter in the universe is being held together in this moment by the sustaining power of Jesus Christ.

Every electron maintaining its orbit around its nucleus. Every strong nuclear force preventing the protons packed into every atomic nucleus from flying apart under the electromagnetic repulsion that should, by any natural reckoning, tear them to pieces. Every gravitational constant maintaining its precise value across billions of light years of space. Every physical law operating with the consistency that makes science possible and life sustainable.

All of it. Held. Right now. By Him.

Modern physics identifies four fundamental forces that hold the universe together — gravity, electromagnetism, the strong nuclear force, and the weak nuclear force. Every attempt to find a unified theory that explains how all four of these forces relate to a single underlying principle has thus far eluded the finest mathematical minds in human history. The deepest question in theoretical physics is essentially — what holds everything together?

Paul answered it two thousand years ago. Sunistemi. He is holding it together. Not held it together. Not will hold it together. Holds it together. Present tense. Active. Continuous.

And if He is holding it all together right now — then He was never a contingent being who required a cause outside of Himself. He is the cause that everything else requires. The question "Who created God?" collapses entirely when you encounter the God who is not maintained by anything outside of Himself but who is Himself maintaining everything that exists.

The Universe Was Created From Nothing — And That Requires a Creator Outside of Everything

"Through faith we understand that the worlds were framed by the word of God, so that things which are seen were not made of things which do appear." — Hebrews 11:3 (KJV)

The Greek word translated framed is katartizo — a word that means to complete, to prepare, to equip perfectly for its intended purpose. Not assembled from pre-existing components. Not reshaped from existing raw material. Framed. Called into existence from nothing.

Created with such precision that every component serves its intended purpose exactly.

So that things which are seen were not made of things which do appear.

This is the doctrine of creation ex nihilo — creation from nothing. Every ancient culture that ever thought seriously about origins assumed that the Creator worked with pre-existing material. The idea that everything — matter, energy, space, time — was called into existence from absolute nothingness was a uniquely Hebrew theological claim.

And modern cosmology has confirmed it.

The Big Bang is not the reorganization of pre-existing matter. It is the moment at which matter, energy, space, and time simultaneously came into existence from a state in which none of them existed. Before the Big Bang there was no before. There was no space in which a before could have occurred. There was no matter to fill a before. There was no time to measure how long before lasted.

Things which are seen were not made of things which do appear. The writer of Hebrews was describing the Big Bang two thousand years before Edwin Hubble pointed a telescope at the night sky and discovered that the universe was expanding.

The God Who Encompasses All of Time at Once

"I am Alpha and Omega, the beginning and the ending, saith the Lord, which is, and which was, and which is to come, the Almighty."
— Revelation 1:8 (KJV)

Alpha and Omega. The first and last letters of the Greek alphabet. Everything that can be expressed in language begins with Alpha and ends with Omega. God is declaring that He encompasses everything that can be communicated. He is not the first chapter of a story. He is the Author of every chapter.

But look more carefully at the Greek of that passage. The declaration which is, and which was, and which is to come is not simply a flowery way of saying God exists across time. It is a deliberate grammatical construction that places God in simultaneous relationship with every point of time at once.

Ho on — the One who is. Present participle. Eternally present. Kai ho en — and the One who was. Past tense. Completely encompassing all of history. Kai ho erchomenos — and the One who is coming. Future. Already present to the One who stands outside of time.

Past, present, and future are not stages God moves through sequentially the way you and I experience Monday and then Tuesday and then Wednesday. They are dimensions of created reality that He simultaneously encompasses. He is eternally, simultaneously present to every moment of time that has ever existed or ever will exist.

This is what the ancient theologians described as God's eternal simultaneity — His complete, undivided presence to all of time at once. Not frozen. Not static. Perfectly, completely alive and active — but entirely outside the sequential movement of created time.

This is why prophecy is possible. God is not predicting the future. He is describing what He can already see.

And this is why the question "Who created God?" finally and completely dissolves in the light of Revelation 1:8. You cannot ask who created the One who encompasses all of time simultaneously. You cannot ask where He came from because the concept of coming from somewhere requires a before — and there is no before to the One who already encompasses all of time at once.

He does not have an origin. He IS the origin.

From everlasting to everlasting. He is God.

Part 5 — What the Ancient World Knew and Could Not Name

There is a question that serious students of world religion and ancient history eventually ask — and it is one that most Sunday morning sermons never address.

Why do so many ancient cultures, spread across every continent and every century of recorded human history, independently arrive at the concept of an ultimate, supreme, transcendent Being that surpasses all other powers and all other gods?

The Egyptians had Amun — the Hidden One, the unseen force behind all visible reality, so vast that even the other gods did not fully know Him. The ancient Mesopotamians had Anu — the cosmic sky deity whose authority transcended the entire pantheon. The early Chinese philosophical tradition had Tian — Heaven, the supreme moral force underlying all of existence. The ancient Indians had Brahman — the single, infinite, self-existent reality from which all apparent multiplicity arises.

Not borrowed from each other. Not copied from a common source. Independently arrived at.

Paul understood what this meant.

"Because that which may be known of God is manifest in them; for God hath shewed it unto them. For the invisible things of him from the creation of the world are clearly seen, being understood by the things that are made, even his eternal power and Godhead; so that they are without excuse." — Romans 1:19–20 (KJV)

God embedded the knowledge of Himself into the structure of creation so thoroughly that every culture in human history — regardless of whether they had access to Scripture — has produced some version of the same conclusion. There is something behind everything. Something infinite. Something that cannot be named because it is larger than every name. Something that everything else depends on but that depends on nothing.

They were reaching toward the right answer with the wrong hands.

The Throne Room No Angel Can Enter

The Book of 1 Enoch is one of the most ancient Jewish texts outside of the canonical Scriptures. It was found among the Dead Sea Scrolls, confirming its presence and influence in Second Temple Jewish thought. It is quoted directly in the New Testament letter of Jude. And it contains something that stops every serious reader cold.

A description of the throne room of God that no angel has been permitted to enter.

Enoch describes being taken through the heavens in vision, passing through successive realms of increasing majesty and terrifying holiness — until he arrives at a structure that defies every category of description he possesses. The walls are like crystal. The floor is like fire. The ceiling blazes with lightning. And surrounding the innermost chamber is a silence and a heat and a weight of holiness so absolute that the text records something extraordinary.

The angels — beings of pure spirit, beings of incomprehensible power compared to any human creature, beings who exist in permanent proximity to the divine — do not enter this innermost place. They stand outside it. They worship from a distance. They cannot approach the full unveiled presence of the One who dwells there. Even they, in all their created glory, are overwhelmed into silence and reverence at the boundary of the Uncreated.

Enoch enters. Not by his own merit or his own strength. Because he is taken. Carried. Brought in by a grace that bypasses every natural law of access. And what he encounters inside is beyond the capacity of the text to fully describe. He falls on his face. He cannot stand. He cannot speak.

Why does this matter for the question of God's origin? Because the Book of 1 Enoch, written centuries before the New Testament, already understood something that the question "Who created God?" completely misses. The God of Scripture is not simply the most powerful being in a universe of beings. He is not the top of a pyramid that could theoretically be extended further. He is categorically, ontologically different from everything that exists.

The angels who stand outside that throne room are not kept out because of a rule. They are kept out because the unveiled presence of the Uncreated would be to their created nature what the full force of the sun at zero distance would be to human flesh. It is not restriction. It is the natural consequence of the infinite encountering the finite without mediation.

A being like that does not have an origin story. A being like that does not fit into the category of things that require causes. The question is not who made the One inside. The question is whether you are willing to come as Enoch came. Empty-handed. Face down. Carried by grace.

Ein Sof — The Infinite Beyond All Names

In the Kabbalistic tradition of Jewish mysticism, preserved most completely in the Zohar — the foundational text of Jewish mystical thought compiled in the thirteenth century but drawing on traditions far more ancient — there is a description of God that approaches the question of divine origin from a direction that most Western thinkers have never encountered.

Before any act of creation. Before any revealed attribute. Before even the concept of relationship existed. Before the first of the divine names — YHWH, Elohim, El Shaddai — could be applied. There was Ein Sof.

Without end.

The Zohar teaches that Ein Sof is God as He is absolutely in Himself. Not God in relationship with creation. Not God as revealed through His actions. God as He simply and infinitely IS — prior to any distinction, prior to any attribute, prior to any mode of being that a created mind could recognize or name.

The names of God, in this framework, are not the ultimate reality of God. They are what the Zohar calls kelim — vessels. Interfaces. The points at which the infinite light of Ein Sof is stepped down, filtered, shaped into a form that finite creatures can receive without being destroyed by its full intensity.

The Zohar describes the process of revelation using an image of breathtaking precision. A buzina de-kardinuta — a lamp of darkness, or a lamp of obscure light. Not darkness in the sense of absence. Darkness in the sense of a light so concentrated, so intense, so absolute in its purity that it appears dark to any eye that cannot bear its full brightness. Like staring directly into the noonday sun — the very excess of light produces the experience of blindness.

God is not hidden because He is absent. He is veiled because His full presence, fully unveiled, would exceed the capacity of any created being to receive.

This is not contradicting Scripture. This is the same reality Paul describes in 1 Timothy:

"Who only hath immortality, dwelling in the light which no man can approach unto; whom no man hath seen, nor can see: to whom be honour and power everlasting." — 1 Timothy 6:16 (KJV)

Unapproachable light. Not darkness. Not absence. An excess of presence so complete that it exceeds the capacity of any created nature to bear it directly.

The Zohar's Ein Sof answers the question "Who created God?" in a way that is both intellectually precise and theologically profound. You cannot ask who created the Infinite because the Infinite, by definition, has no outside. No boundary. No edge from which a creating force could have operated. Creation is something God did within the overflow of His own infinite being. The universe is not something that exists alongside God in a larger space that contains both of them. The universe is something that exists within God's creative act — something He brought into being from the overflow of His own existence.

Ein Sof is not a concept borrowed from another tradition and imported into Jewish theology. It is the native Jewish attempt to describe in human language the same reality that Exodus 3:14 describes in two Hebrew words. The I AM who simply, infinitely, eternally IS — without cause, without boundary, without outside.

Plotinus and The One — How Close Philosophy Can Get

In the third century of the common era, a philosopher named Plotinus produced what many historians of thought regard as the greatest philosophical system ever constructed outside of Scripture. His work — collected after his death into a series of treatises called The Enneads — represents the absolute summit of what human reason, unaided by divine revelation, can reach when it pursues the question of ultimate reality with total seriousness and total commitment.

Plotinus posited as the foundation of all reality a principle he called The One.

The One is not a being among beings. It is not even Being itself — because Being, as Plotinus understood it, is already a kind of limitation. The One transcends even Being. It is beyond existence as we can conceive it. It is so completely beyond all categories that the only honest philosophical language for it is negative — describing what it is not, because every positive description immediately limits it to something less than what it actually is.

Sound familiar?

The Jewish concept of Ein Sof. The Christian tradition of negative theology — the via negativa of the great mystics who concluded that every positive statement about God is simultaneously an inadequate statement about God. Across traditions, across centuries, across cultures — the deepest thinkers arrive at the same boundary.

There is something at the foundation of all reality that surpasses every category the human mind can generate. And the only honest response when you arrive at that boundary is not to manufacture more categories. It is to stop. To recognize that you have reached the limit of what reason can carry you. And to ask whether the One who exists beyond that limit has chosen to speak.

But here is where Plotinus falls short of the biblical God — and where the distance between the greatest human philosophy and the living God of Scripture becomes unmistakable.

Plotinus's One does not know you. It does not love you. It does not weep at a graveside or sweat drops of blood in a garden or breathe its final breath on a cross for love of the creatures it made. The One of Plotinus is so far beyond relationship that it cannot even be said to care.

The God of Scripture emanates nothing. He creates. He wills. He speaks. He acts. He enters. He weeps. He bleeds. He rises.

Plotinus found the address. He stood at the door and described it with extraordinary precision. But the door was never opened to him — because he did not know whose name to call.

The name is Jesus Christ. And He is not the impersonal emanation of an abstract absolute. He is the eternal Son of the eternal Father — fully God, fully personal, fully relational — who stepped out of the unapproachable light and into human flesh so that the creatures who could never reach the Infinite could be reached by it.

"No man hath seen God at any time; the only begotten Son, which is in the bosom of the Father, he hath declared him." — John 1:18 (KJV)

Declared. Revealed. Made visible and accessible and personal. Not because the Infinite became less than infinite. But because Love, in its infinite nature, refused to remain unapproachable.

The Corpus Hermeticum — When Ancient Paganism Points to John 1

There is one more ancient text that deserves a place in this chapter. Not because it is inspired Scripture. But because it demonstrates something remarkable about how God has written the fingerprints of His truth into traditions that had no knowledge of the Hebrew Bible.

The Corpus Hermeticum is a collection of ancient philosophical and spiritual texts attributed to a legendary figure called Hermes Trismegistus. The texts are Egyptian-Greek in origin, produced somewhere in the first few centuries of the common era, blending Greek philosophy with Egyptian religious tradition. They were widely read across the ancient Mediterranean world.

The most famous of these texts is called the Poimandres. The Poimandres opens with a vision of a boundless light. Within that light, a darkness appears — a coiling, churning primordial chaos that will become the material world. And then, from the divine mind, a Logos — a Word, a rational principle, a creative intelligence — descends from the realm of pure light into the darkness to bring order, form, and life into being.

Light. Darkness. The Word that brings creation into being from the primordial void.

Compare this to the opening of the Gospel of John.

"In the beginning was the Word, and the Word was with God, and the Word was God... In him was life; and the life was the light of men. And the light shineth in darkness; and the darkness comprehended it not." — John 1:1, 4–5 (KJV)

The parallels are not accidental. John wrote his Gospel for a world that was reading texts like the Corpus Hermeticum. He used the framework his audience already carried — the Logos, the Light, the creative Word — and then declared something that shattered every version of that framework they had ever encountered.

The Word became flesh.

"And the Word was made flesh, and dwelt among us, and we beheld his glory, the glory as of the only begotten of the Father, full of grace and truth." — John 1:14 (KJV)

The divine Logos of Greek and Hermetic philosophy had always been an abstract principle. A cosmic force. An impersonal rational order. It organized the universe but it did not love the universe. It was not personal enough to weep. It was not relational enough to bleed. It was not humble enough to be born in a stable and die on a criminal's cross for love of the creatures it had organized into existence.

John's declaration that the Logos became flesh was not a borrowing from pagan philosophy. It was a confrontation with it. He took the highest concept the ancient philosophical world had produced — the divine creative Word that stands at the foundation of all reality — and declared that this Word had a name, a face, a body, a voice that said Come unto me, and hands that were nailed to wood for the sake of people who did not deserve it.

The ancient world had been circling the truth for centuries. In Egypt and in Greece and in the courts of pagan philosophers who never opened a Hebrew scroll — something kept driving the deepest thinkers back to the same conclusion. There is a divine intelligence behind everything. There is a Logos. There is a light that the darkness cannot overcome.

John looked at all of it and said — I know His name. I ate breakfast with Him. I watched Him die. I saw Him walk out of His own tomb.

His name is Jesus. And He is not an abstraction. He is the answer.

Part 6 — Why Is There Something Rather Than Nothing?

There is a question that the German philosopher Gottfried Wilhelm Leibniz asked in the seventeenth century that has never been answered by any system of thought except one.

It is perhaps the most fundamental question that human reason can produce. More fundamental than the question of God's origin. More fundamental than any question about the nature of the universe. It is the question that sits beneath every other question like bedrock beneath soil.

Why is there something rather than nothing?

Not — why does the universe look the way it does? Not — why do the physical constants have the values they have? Not — why does life exist? Those are all downstream questions. They all assume that something already exists and ask about its properties.

Leibniz's question goes deeper. It asks why anything exists at all. Why is there a universe to study? Why are there physical constants to measure? Why is there matter and energy and space and time? Why is there something rather than the absolute, total, complete absence of everything?

Every other philosophical and scientific framework eventually arrives at this question and stops. The universe can be explained in terms of prior physical states. Prior physical states can be explained in terms of earlier ones. Follow the chain back far enough and you reach the Big Bang — the beginning of everything physical. And then the question becomes not what caused the Big Bang but why there was anything capable of causing anything at all.

Physics has no answer to this question. Mathematics has no answer to this question. Philosophy, at its honest best, can only state the question with precision. It cannot answer it from within its own resources.

Leibniz identified the only coherent answer.

There must be a Sufficient Reason for the existence of anything at all. And that Sufficient Reason cannot itself be contingent — cannot be something that might or might not have existed — because then it too would require a Sufficient Reason. The chain of Sufficient Reasons must terminate somewhere. And the only place it can rationally terminate is in a Being whose existence is necessary. A Being who does not merely happen to exist but who could not possibly not exist. A Being whose very essence is existence — so that asking why this Being exists is as incoherent as asking why triangles have three sides. It is simply what they are.

There is something rather than nothing because there is a Being for whom non-existence is not an option. A Being who is not one item among the contents of reality but the ground of reality itself. The reason there is a universe to study is that the self-existent, necessary, eternal God chose to create one.

"Thou art worthy, O Lord, to receive glory and honour and power: for thou hast created all things, and for thy pleasure they are and were created." — Revelation 4:11 (KJV)

For His pleasure they are and were created. Not because He needed them. Not because He was incomplete without them. But because the God who is love, in the fullness of His infinite being, chose to create creatures who could receive that love and return it freely. The universe exists because God wanted it to. And that wanting — that sovereign, free, loving choice to create rather than to remain alone in His infinite self-sufficiency — is the Sufficient Reason that Leibniz was looking for.

Philosophy found the shape of the answer. Scripture gives it a name.

I AM THAT I AM.

"By the word of the LORD were the heavens made; and all the host of them by the breath of his mouth." — Psalm 33:6 (KJV)

The Stories That Prove It

Moses — The Man Who Asked and Was Answered

Moses was eighty years old, tending sheep on the back side of the desert, when he encountered a bush that burned without being consumed. He was not in a season of spiritual ambition. He was in a season of obscurity — forty years removed from the Egypt he had fled, long past any reasonable expectation of doing anything significant with his life.

God spoke from the fire.

And Moses — the man who had grown up in the greatest palace on earth, who had been educated in all the wisdom of Egypt, who knew the names and the stories of every god in the Egyptian pantheon — asked the question this entire chapter has been built around.

What is your name?

He was not asking out of ignorance. He was asking because he understood the ancient world's framework for divine beings. In that world, names were not labels. Names were natures. To know a god's name was to understand what kind of god it was, what domain it operated in, what limits it had. The gods of Egypt had names that described their particular domain — Ra, the sun god. Osiris, the god of the dead. Each name was a container that defined the size and shape of the deity it belonged to.

And God answered with a name that broke every container in the world.

I AM THAT I AM.

Not a domain. Not a jurisdiction. Not a particular area of specialization. Existence itself. Being itself. The Cause behind every cause and the Ground beneath every ground.

Moses went back to Egypt. Not as a man who had finally received a theological credential. As a man who had encountered the One for whom all of Egypt's gods were shadows — pale, borrowed reflections of a Reality so far beyond them that comparison was almost meaningless.

And what followed that encounter rewrote the history of the world.

The ten plagues of Egypt were not random demonstrations of power. They were a systematic, deliberate, public dismantling of the Egyptian pantheon — each plague targeting a specific Egyptian deity, demonstrating that the God of Israel held absolute authority over every domain that Egypt's gods were believed to govern. Ra, the sun god, could not prevent the darkness. Heket, the frog goddess, could not control the frogs. Khnum, the guardian of the Nile, could not protect the river.

The God who spoke from the burning bush was not competing with the gods of Egypt. He was demonstrating, in the most public and undeniable terms available, that there was no competition. That the uncaused, eternal, self-existent I AM stood in a different category entirely from every divine being that human religion had ever invented.

"That ye may know that there is none like me in all the earth." — Exodus 9:14 (KJV)

Isaiah — The Prophet Who Saw the Throne

In the year that King Uzziah died, the prophet Isaiah had an encounter that shattered every human framework he possessed.

"In the year that king Uzziah died I saw also the Lord sitting upon a throne, high and lifted up, and his train filled the temple." — Isaiah 6:1 (KJV)

King Uzziah had reigned for fifty-two years. He was the fixed point of the political world Isaiah had always known. The continuity.

The stability. And when Uzziah died, everything that felt permanent proved temporary. Everything that felt stable proved contingent.

And in that moment of cosmic disorientation — when the thing Isaiah had anchored himself to in the natural world was suddenly gone — he saw what was actually anchored. What was actually permanent. What had been there before Uzziah's first breath and would be there long after his last was forgotten.

The Lord. Sitting on a throne. High and lifted up.

The seraphim above the throne — angelic beings of fire and holiness — covered their faces with their wings. Not from fear. From reverence. The unveiled presence of the One on the throne exceeded even their capacity to look upon directly. And they called to one another with words that have echoed through every century of worship since that moment.

"Holy, holy, holy, is the LORD of hosts: the whole earth is full of his glory." — Isaiah 6:3 (KJV)

Three times holy. In Hebrew literary tradition, repetition indicates emphasis. To say something twice is to stress it. To say it three times is to declare it absolute, complete, and beyond all qualification. Kadosh, kadosh, kadosh. Set apart. Other. Beyond. Entirely unlike anything else that exists.

Isaiah's response to this vision was not theological reflection. It was collapse.

"Then said I, Woe is me! for I am undone; because I am a man of unclean lips, and I dwell in the midst of a people of unclean lips: for mine eyes have seen the King, the LORD of hosts." — Isaiah 6:5 (KJV)

Undone. The Hebrew word is damah — to be silenced, to be destroyed, to cease. Isaiah did not say he was humbled. He said he was undone. The proximity of the Absolute to the contingent did not produce a mild sense of inadequacy. It produced the overwhelming recognition that everything Isaiah was made of was finite, flawed, and utterly unworthy to stand in the presence of the One who simply, eternally, infinitely IS.

This is the God the question "Who created God?" is asking about. And Isaiah's reaction — the collapse, the silence, the undoing — is the only honest response of a creature who has actually encountered what the question is really pointing toward. Not an argument to be won. A Presence to be undone by.

"To whom then will ye liken me, or shall I be equal? saith the Holy One. Lift up your eyes on high, and behold who hath created these things, that bringeth out their host by number: he calleth them all by names by the greatness of his might, for that he is strong in power; not one faileth." — Isaiah 40:25–26 (KJV)

Job — The Man Who Demanded an Answer and Received Something Better

Job had lost everything. His children. His wealth. His health. And through thirty-seven chapters of extraordinary theological debate with his friends, Job had done something that no polished religious performance would ever permit. He had demanded that God show up and explain Himself.

He wanted answers. He wanted reasons. He wanted to stand before God and make his case and hear God's response.

And God showed up. Not with answers. With questions.

"Where wast thou when I laid the foundations of the earth? declare, if thou hast understanding. Who hath laid the measures thereof, if thou knowest? or who hath stretched the line upon it?" — Job 38:4–5 (KJV)

For four chapters God speaks from the whirlwind, and every sentence is a question. Where were you when I set the boundaries of the sea? Have you entered the springs of the sea? Have you perceived the breadth of the earth? Can you bind the Pleiades or loose Orion's belt? Do you know the ordinances of heaven?

Question after question after question. Not to humiliate Job. Not to silence him cruelly. But to expand his frame. To take the man who had been measuring God against the standard of human fairness and place him in front of the actual scale of what God is.

Job had been asking God to justify Himself within Job's framework. And God was gently, inexorably, lovingly dismantling that framework altogether.

And then something remarkable happened. Job stopped demanding answers.

"I know that thou canst do every thing, and that no thought can be withholden from thee." — Job 42:2 (KJV)

He had heard about God. He had theology about God. He had arguments about God. He had been defending God in front of his friends and questioning God in private for thirty-seven chapters.

And then he encountered God. And everything changed.

Not because his questions were answered. Because the One the questions were about became real to him in a way that no answer could have produced. The question "Where did God come from?" was not answered in the whirlwind. It was made irrelevant by the encounter. Because no one who has truly seen the God who lays the foundations of the earth and calls the morning into being walks away asking about His origin story. They walk away, like Job, simply having encountered Him. And having encountered Him, they are changed.

Part 7 — Meeting People Where They Are: The Theology Behind the Method

The Apostle Paul built his entire missionary method upon a principle that this chapter demonstrates in practice.

"For though I be free from all men, yet have I made myself servant unto all, that I might gain the more. And unto the Jews I became as a Jew, that I might gain the Jews; to them that are under the law, as under the law, that I might gain them that are under the law... I am made all things to all men, that I might by all means save some." — 1 Corinthians 9:19–20, 22 (KJV)

The Greek phrase Paul uses — tois pasin gegona panta — means literally I have become all things to all people. Not I have pretended to agree with everyone. Not I have compromised the Gospel to make it more palatable. But I have become — genuinely entered, genuinely engaged, genuinely learned and listened and understood — whatever the person in front of me needed me to be in order to create the conditions where truth could reach them.

Paul did not abandon the truth when he entered a Greek philosophical framework. He brought the truth with him into that framework and demonstrated from within it that the truth he carried was the fulfillment of the best their framework had been reaching toward. He did not tear down Mars Hill. He walked through it, read every inscription, and found the one that gave him a doorway.

"For as I passed by, and beheld your devotions, I found an altar with this inscription, TO THE UNKNOWN GOD. Whom therefore ye ignorantly worship, him declare I unto you." — Acts 17:23 (KJV)

The Unknown God. The Athenians had erected an altar to cover every divine power they had not yet managed to name. Paul looked at that altar and recognized something extraordinary. They were reaching. Imperfectly. Blindly. In a direction that their existing frameworks could not complete. But they were reaching. And rather than condemning the reach, Paul honored it — and then completed it.

This is not theological compromise. This is theological precision. It requires a deeper knowledge of truth than a defensive posture ever produces. You can only guide someone from where they are standing to where they need to go if you are willing to first stand where they are standing and look at the world through their eyes.

Scripture provides not just the method but the theology behind why that method sometimes requires two entirely different approaches depending on the soul in front of you.

"And of some have compassion, making a difference: And others save with fear, pulling them out of the fire; hating even the garment spotted by the flesh." — Jude 1:22–23 (KJV)

Some souls require compassion. Patient, slow, relational, listening compassion. These are the ones who are not hostile to God but have been wounded by religious people, who have wandered into strange places not out of rebellion but out of genuine hunger for truth that the church failed to satisfy. With these you enter slowly. You sit down. You ask questions before you answer them. You learn their language before you speak your own. You earn the right to be heard.

Other souls require urgency. Fire. The kind of intervention that does not wait for the slow work of relationship because the flames are already too close. Some people are not wandering. They are falling. And with them, the compassionate response is not patient listening. It is the outstretched hand that pulls regardless of whether they think they want to be pulled.

Jude's wisdom is that a faithful witness must be able to discern which soul is standing in front of them. The same approach that rescues one person destroys the opportunity with another. Paul became all things to all men not out of inconsistency but out of love precise enough to know that different conditions require different responses.

Part 8 — The Creaturely Voice: What the Ancient Scrolls Knew

There is a document that was buried in the caves above the Dead Sea for two thousand years before it was discovered in 1947. A document written by a Jewish community that had withdrawn from the corruption of Jerusalem and committed themselves to radical devotion to God in the wilderness of Judea. A document that was not written for publication or argument. It was written for prayer.

The Thanksgiving Hymns — known to scholars as the Hodayot or 1QH — are among the most moving devotional texts ever produced outside of canonical Scripture. And within them is a description of the human being standing before the eternal God that captures, in ancient language, the lived experience of every person who has ever truly encountered the One this chapter has been describing.

The author of the Hodayot describes himself and every human creature this way: an edifice of dust kneaded with water. A framework of clay. A vessel formed from the earth, subject to decay, dependent on the breath of God for every moment of its existence.

Not false humility. Not performed religious self-deprecation. The simple, clear-eyed recognition of what a human being actually is when measured against the eternal, self-existent, uncaused Creator of everything.

An edifice of dust kneaded with water.

The phrase carries weight precisely because it is not poetic exaggeration. It is biological fact rendered in ancient language. The human body is composed of elements drawn from the earth. Carbon. Nitrogen. Oxygen. Hydrogen. Elements that existed in stars before they existed in you. Elements that will return to the ground when your last breath is drawn. You are, in the most literal sense, a temporary arrangement of borrowed materials.

And yet into this edifice of dust God breathed the breath of life. Into this temporary arrangement of borrowed elements He placed an eternal soul. Into this frame that returns to the ground He placed the capacity to ask the most profound questions in the universe — including the question of who He is and where He came from.

The ancient writer of the Hodayot understood something that modern intellectual arrogance often forgets. The proper posture of a creature before its Creator is not challenge. It is awe. Not the awe of someone who has been silenced by power. The awe of someone who has been overwhelmed by love so vast that it chose to breathe itself into dust and call that dust beloved.

This is what the question "Who created God?" sounds like from the perspective of a soul that has actually encountered what it is asking about. Not an intellectual puzzle to be solved. Not a weapon to be wielded. A whisper of wonder from an edifice of dust standing in the presence of the I AM — asking not to win an argument, but simply to understand more of the One in whose hands every borrowed element of its being rests.

C.S. Lewis pressed this truth from the other direction with remarkable precision. He observed that every human soul — however ordinary, however unremarkable they appear in the crowded flow of daily life — is an immortal being of staggering eternal weight. There are no ordinary people. Every soul you have ever encountered is either moving toward an incomprehensible glory or away from it.

Think carefully about what that means for the question we have been answering. The Being who created those immortal, radiant, glory-destined souls — what must He be? If the creatures made in His image carry that kind of eternal weight and that kind of incomprehensible potential — what is the nature of the One whose image they bear?

The question "Who created God?" dissolves not because it cannot be asked but because every honest attempt to fully answer it reveals a reality so vast, so far beyond the reach of created language and created imagination, that the only honest response is the one that has been given by every prophet, every mystic, and every broken soul who has ever truly stood in His presence.

Not an answer. Worship.

"Great is the LORD, and greatly to be praised; and his greatness is unsearchable." — Psalm 145:3 (KJV)

The Grand Synthesis

Every stream in this chapter flows to the same river.

Every line of honest inquiry arrived at the same address. The philosopher following reason. The scientist following evidence. The mathematician following probability. The ancient mystic pressing beyond the edge of language. The prophet standing before what no human being can adequately describe. They did not all start from the same place. They arrived at the same Person. A Being uncaused, eternal, personal, and incomprehensibly powerful — whose name is I AM, whose face is Jesus Christ, and whose reach extends from before the first word of creation to the last breath of every soul He ever made.

And in the middle of all of it — in the burning bush and the whirlwind and the throne room vision and the temple courts of Jerusalem where a man named Jesus spoke two words in Greek that sent a crowd reaching for stones — the answer was never a theorem.

It was always a Person.

The question "Who created God?" is not answered by accumulating enough arguments that the doubter is finally cornered into submission. It is answered the way every great question about the Infinite is answered — by encountering the One the question is really about.

Moses asked the question and was answered with a name. Isaiah saw the throne and was undone. Job demanded an accounting and received a vision.

This is the witness of Scripture from beginning to end. The God who has no origin, who requires no cause, who existed before before was possible — is not a philosophical abstraction to be argued into existence. He is a Person who is actively, perpetually, personally drawing every soul He made back toward Himself. Through the structure of the cosmos. Through the precision of the physical constants. Through the ancient longing embedded in every culture that ever reached toward the divine. Through the testimony of prophets and apostles and broken men who found Him faithful in the darkest moments of their lives.

He is not hiding. He is calling.

"Thus saith the LORD the King of Israel, and his redeemer the LORD of hosts; I am the first, and I am the last; and beside me there is no God." — Isaiah 44:6 (KJV)

"Before me there was no God formed, neither shall there be after me." — Isaiah 43:10 (KJV)

No God before Him. No God after Him. No origin. No succession. No replacement. The First and the Last. The Alpha and the Omega. The I AM who was speaking from the fire before Moses arrived and will be speaking long after the last star burns cold.

The universe did not create Him. He created the universe. Time did not produce Him. He produced time. Existence does not contain Him. He contains existence.

And He knows your name.

"Fear thou not; for I am with thee: be not dismayed; for I am thy God: I will strengthen thee; yea, I will help thee; yea, I will uphold thee with the right hand of my righteousness." — Isaiah 41:10 (KJV)

My Reflection

I did not come to this chapter as a philosopher. I came as a father.

There were moments in the years I have described in this book — the medical waiting rooms, the sleepless nights, the seasons where every certainty I had built my life upon was being tested in ways I had not anticipated — where the question of this chapter was not abstract for me. It was personal. Not "who created God" in the academic sense. Something more raw than that. Something that sounds, if I am honest, less like a philosophical inquiry and more like a man in the dark asking whether there is anyone actually there.

Is the I AM big enough for this? Is the God who contains the universe also the God who sees this specific room, this specific moment, this specific fear that I have not been able to say aloud to anyone?

What I found — not through argument, though the arguments came later and mattered — was that the God who is too vast to be caused is simultaneously the God who is too personal to miss. The same Being who existed before time authored is the same Being who was fully present in the moments of my life that time will never let me forget.

That is not a theological deduction. That is an encounter. And it is the only kind of knowing that survives the hardest seasons.

I want to say something to the person who picked up this chapter as a skeptic — the person for whom the arguments were the point, who followed the Kalam and the Five Ways and the Borde-Guth-Vilenkin theorem carefully and honestly. I want to say: the arguments are real. They are not invented to comfort religious people. They are the conclusions that the evidence demands, and serious thinkers who had every reason to want a different answer have arrived at them against their own preferences.

But here is what I also know. The arguments can take you to the threshold. They cannot carry you across it. The step from "something uncaused must exist" to "I know the One who is" is not a logical step.

It is a personal one. It is the moment you stop examining God as a philosophical problem and allow Him to examine you.

The God this chapter describes — the I AM who contains all of space and time, who existed before before was possible, who is both HaMakom and Father, both Ein Sof and the One who counts every hair on your head — this God did not build a universe and retreat behind its physics. He put on a body. He walked into the world He made. He let the creatures He created nail Him to the wood He created. For love of the ones who still did not know who He was.

That is not what an abstract First Cause does. That is what a Father does.

And if there is one thing I know after everything I have walked through — it is that the God who requires no explanation is also the God who offers the only explanation that reaches all the way down into the place where the real questions live.

He is not a conclusion at the end of an argument. He is a Person waiting at the end of an honest search. And He has already seen you coming.

Something shifted in me the day I stopped trying to win this argument and started letting it undo me.

For most of my life, the question "Who created God?" was not something I carried as a skeptic. I carried it as a believer who had not yet been given the language to answer it. I knew what I believed. I knew whom I had encountered. I knew that the presence I had met at the lowest point of my life was not a psychological event or a product of exhaustion or desperation. I knew it was real. I knew He was real.

But when someone across a table looked at me and asked the question — where did God come from? — there were years of my life where I could not give a satisfying answer. And the inability to answer it did not shake my faith. But it did something that I now recognize as important. It humbled me. It reminded me that knowing God and being able to fully explain God are two entirely different things. And that the gap between those two things is not a problem with God. It is a feature of what it means to be a creature encountering a Creator.

I eventually came to understand that the inability to fully explain God is not a weakness of faith. It is actually evidence of genuine faith. Because if I could fully explain God — if I could wrap Him completely in human language and human categories and human logic — He would not be God. He would be something small enough to fit in a human mind. And the God I encountered was not small.

What changed for me was not finding a better argument. What changed was studying the ancient languages and the ancient thinkers and the ancient texts until I understood that every serious mind that has ever pursued this question to its honest conclusion — whether Jewish, Greek, Christian, or secular — has arrived at the same boundary. A boundary where the categories run out. Where the language fails. Where every measuring instrument ever invented reaches its limit and stops.

And on the other side of that boundary — not as a philosophical abstraction, but as the most personal and present reality I have ever encountered — is the I AM who spoke to Moses from the fire.

I spent years reading texts that most Christians would never touch. Not because I doubted. Because God gave me an unusual hunger to understand the world that the lost were living in. The ancient cosmologies. The pagan frameworks. The mystical traditions. The philosophical systems. I read them not to adopt them but to understand the genuine reaching they contained — the universal human hunger for the One that every tradition was circling without fully finding. And what I discovered, across every tradition, every century, every culture that ever produced serious thought about ultimate reality, was this.

They were all reaching toward the same One.

They were reaching imperfectly. With corrupted instruments. With frameworks that had been distorted over centuries. But the reaching was real. The hunger was genuine. And the God of Scripture is the only explanation that satisfies every requirement that every tradition's reaching was actually pointing toward.

Ein Sof. The One. The Unmoved Mover. The Unknown God. The Lord of Spirits. The Head of Days. Different names. Different languages. Different centuries. The same boundary. The same unanswerable question pointing in the same direction.

He was there before any of them started looking. He was there before the first human hand reached toward the sky. He was there before the first star burned and before the first morning broke over a world that had not yet learned to ask questions.

And He is here now.

In a world full of people who are still reaching — still asking who He is, where He came from, whether there is anything real on the other side of the questions they cannot quiet — He is still the same answer He has always been.

I am not a man with credentials behind my name. I am a man who wrestled with ancient questions and found — every single time — that the God of Scripture was already there. Already present in the reaching. Already ahead of the arrival. Already knowing the name of the person who would one day come through the door.

That is who He is. That is the God this chapter is about. Not a Being who requires an explanation. A Being who IS the explanation.

"O LORD, thou hast searched me, and known me. Thou knowest my downsitting and mine uprising, thou understandest my thought afar off. Thou compassest my path and my lying down, and art acquainted with all my ways." — Psalm 147:5 (KJV)

He knew you before you were formed. He knows you now. He knows every question you are carrying. Every doubt you have been too afraid to say out loud. Every moment of reaching toward something real in a world that keeps offering you things that are not.

He is not hiding from your questions. He is in them. He has been drawing you toward Himself through every single one.

Come.

A Prayer for the Reader

Father —

For every person who has carried this question — the ones who asked it as a weapon and the ones who asked it as a wound. For the believer who has been asked this question and could not answer it — give them peace. The peace of knowing that you do not have to explain the Infinite to trust the Infinite. That knowing God and being able to fully articulate God are two entirely different things. That every prophet who ever stood in His presence came away not with a complete theological system but with a changed life. You were not asked to explain Him. You were asked to follow Him. And following Him is more than enough.

For the skeptic — the one who has sharpened this question into a blade and used it to keep You at a distance. I do not ask You to force an answer past their defenses. I ask You to do what You have always done. Reach past the argument and touch the soul underneath it. The soul that built those defenses because something hurt it. The soul that is asking this question not because it does not want You to exist but because it is terrified of what it would mean if You do. You are not afraid of their resistance. You were not afraid of Paul's. You simply waited. And You sent someone who was willing to sit down instead of fight. Raise up more of those people, Lord. People willing to enter the world of the searching instead of demanding the searching come to them.

For the one who is somewhere in between — who believes and doubts in the same breath, who has encountered something real but cannot fully name it, who picked up this book not entirely sure why but found themselves still reading — I ask that something in this chapter landed differently than everything else they have encountered on this question. Not an argument that defeated them. A reality that drew them.

For the one who has wandered into strange places, who has read the ancient texts and followed the ancient paths and found something real in the reaching even when the direction was wrong — remind them that You were present in the reaching too. That You are the One every tradition was circling without fully finding. That the hunger that drove them into those ancient shadows was the same hunger You placed in them before they were born — the hunger that was always meant to lead them home to You. Bring them home, Lord.

You are the uncaused Cause. The unmoved Mover. The self-existent, eternal, necessary Being whose non-existence is not even logically possible. The I AM who spoke to Moses and shattered every category the ancient world had for divine beings. The One before whom seraphim cover their faces. The Ein Sof behind every name, the Light behind every light, the Word that was before the beginning and will be when every beginning is finished.

You are the answer to every question this chapter has raised. And You are personal enough, close enough, and present enough to meet every reader of these words exactly where they are sitting right now.

You have been there all along. You are there now. And You always will be.

In the name of the Father, the Son, and the Holy Spirit.

Amen.

"Before the mountains were brought forth, or ever thou hadst formed the earth and the world, even from everlasting to everlasting, thou art God." — Psalm 90:2 (KJV)

Chapter Five

Why Does God Stay Silent When I Need Him Most?

"Be still, and know that I am God." — Psalm 46:10 (KJV)

The Question

You have prayed. You have waited. You have prayed again.

You have gotten out of bed at three in the morning and walked to a quiet room and poured out everything you had — every fear, every honest confession, every desperate plea — into what felt like empty air. You have opened your Bible searching for a word that felt personal, and the pages felt like a stranger's mail. You have sat in a church pew surrounded by people singing about a God who speaks, who moves, who shows up — and felt completely, terrifyingly alone.

And the silence stretched on.

Maybe it lasted days. Maybe it lasted years. Maybe it is lasting right now, at this very moment, as you hold this book in your hands and wonder whether the God you were told is always near has simply stopped listening.

This question — Why does God stay silent when I need Him most? — is not a question born in laziness or indifference. It is born in the deepest place of human yearning. It is the cry of a person who actually believes, who actually came to the altar, who actually showed up — and received what felt like nothing in return.

It is one of the most common experiences in the history of the Christian faith. And it is one of the least honestly discussed.

The church has not always done well with this question. Too often we have responded to honest expressions of spiritual silence with cheerful platitudes: just keep praying, just trust the process, God's timing is perfect. And while these things are true, they land like stones dropped on an open wound when the person hearing them has been waiting in the dark for months and the ceiling still feels like concrete.

So this chapter will not begin with the answer. It will begin with the truth: God's silence is real. The experience of it is painful. The confusion it generates is legitimate. And the God of Scripture — who has never once been threatened by honest questions — has more to say about it than most people have ever been shown.

Acknowledging the Pain

Before we go anywhere else, something needs to be said plainly.

If you have ever sat in the middle of a crisis — a diagnosis, a broken marriage, a child in danger, a financial collapse, a depression that would not lift — and cried out to God with everything you had and heard nothing back, you are not alone. You are not spiritually defective. You are not being punished. And you are not the first person of genuine faith to feel what you are feeling.

The greatest figures in the history of Scripture felt it.

Job felt it. David felt it. Jeremiah felt it. Habakkuk stood in the ruins of what God had promised and screamed at the sky:

"O LORD, how long shall I cry, and thou wilt not hear?" — Habakkuk 1:2 (KJV)

The prophet did not whisper this politely. He used the Hebrew word za'aq — the same desperate, violent cry Israel used under the bondage of Egypt. He was not asking a theological question. He was demanding an answer from a God who appeared to have gone completely deaf.

And God did not rebuke him for it.

That matters. It matters enormously.

God did not strike Habakkuk down for the honesty of his anguish. He did not respond with a divine lecture about the prophet's lack of faith. He engaged with him. He answered him — in His own time, in His own way, with an answer that Habakkuk admitted he would not have believed if told in advance.

The God of Scripture is not offended by your silence breaking into a cry. He is not threatened by your confusion. He has never once walked away from a soul that was desperate enough to keep showing up even when showing up felt pointless.

What He is asking you to do — what this chapter exists to help you do — is to understand what is actually happening in those seasons when the heavens feel like bronze and the silence feels like abandonment.

Because what is actually happening is nothing like abandonment.

What Scripture Says

Part 1 — The Silence Is Not What It Sounds Like

When the English language describes God as silent, it flattens something profound into something ordinary. Silence, in English, is simply the absence of sound. A room with no one in it is silent. A phone that has been turned off is silent.

But the Hebrew language of the Old Testament had no patience for that shallow a definition.

The word David uses in Psalm 28:1 when he cries out "Be not silent to me" is the Hebrew word charash. And charash does not mean the silence of an empty room.

In Brown-Driver-Briggs — one of the most authoritative Hebrew lexicons in existence — charash is defined with a root meaning that has nothing passive about it. At its core, the word means to scratch, to engrave, to plow. It is the exact word used for a craftsman working metal or wood. A farmer driving a blade through hard ground. A master engraver cutting precise lines into stone.

This is the word for what God is doing when He appears to say nothing.

He is not absent. He is not asleep. He is not indifferent. He is working beneath the surface with the focused, intense silence of a craftsman — cutting something precise, building something exact, plowing furrows in soil that was never going to yield its harvest without the blade going through it first.

When God is charash — when He goes silent — He is doing it the way a surgeon goes silent. Not because the patient does not matter. Because what is being built requires that kind of attention.

The Old Testament also uses two other words for the experience of God's hiddenness that are essential to understanding what silence actually is. The word sathar means to hide by covering, to conceal. And the word alam means to veil from sight. These are not words that describe absence. They describe deliberate concealment. A veil over a face that is still present. A door that has been quietly closed, not because the person on the other side has left, but because what is being built on your side of the door requires the darkness to set properly.

The theological distinction between these three concepts is everything.

When God is silent — He is the craftsman at work beneath the surface, saying nothing because He is doing. When God is hidden — He has placed a veil between His presence and your perception, demanding that your faith operate on something deeper than your senses. When God is absent — this, according to Scripture, is a theological impossibility. It does not exist as a category for the person who belongs to Him.

There is something else hidden in the Hebrew that must be named here. The ancient concept of hester panim — the hiding of God's face — appears across the Old Testament in passages that most believers have never been shown side by side. Deuteronomy 31:17–18. Isaiah 45:15. Psalm 44:24. In each of these passages God warns of or laments a season when His face will be hidden from His people.

But look carefully at what hester panim is and is not. The hiding of a face is not the departure of a person. In the ancient Hebrew world, paneh — the face — represented the unmediated presence, the favor, the relational intimacy of God. The highest blessing in all of Scripture was for God to make His face shine upon you. And the deliberate withdrawal of that shining — the hiding of the face — was never the same as walking away.

It was God standing directly in front of you, placing a veil between your experience of Him and the reality of Him.

Because of a truth that ancient Jewish theology preserved with extraordinary precision: if God made His presence overwhelmingly, undeniably obvious at every moment, human obedience would be driven by sensory compulsion rather than covenantal love. The hiding of the face is not cruelty. It is the exact surgical withdrawal designed to test whether what you have is faith — or whether what you have is merely an addiction to the feeling of God.

Centuries before these Old Testament passages were compiled into the canon as we know it, a community of Jewish scribes at Qumran was preserving texts that did not make it into the final Hebrew Bible. Among those texts — discovered among the Dead Sea Scrolls in the Psalms Scroll (11QPsa) — is a psalm designated Psalm 155, a communal prayer of striking directness:

"Lord, I cried to You; turn not Your face from Your servant. Do not cast me away in the day of distress. Incline Your ear to my plea in the darkness of my suffering." — Psalm 155 (11QPsa Psalms Scroll, Qumran, c. 100–50 BC)

This psalm was not preserved by accident. A community living in the wilderness, separated from the Temple, pressed this prayer into leather because they had known what it was to cry in a season of divine silence. The hester panim — the hidden face of God — was not a theological abstraction to them. It was the lived experience of covenant people who kept praying anyway. Their prayer survives because God intended it to. It belongs here, in this conversation, exactly as much as it belonged in that desert.

And then there is the word that governs how we are meant to survive all of it.

The Hebrew word qavah — translated wait in Isaiah 40:31, "they that wait upon the LORD shall renew their strength" — carries nothing of the passive resignation that the English word implies. The root of qavah means to bind together by twisting. It carries the image of a cord pulled taut, a bowstring under maximum tension. Biblical waiting is not sitting in a room doing nothing. It is the agonizing, excruciatingly active posture of twisting your breaking soul around the unbreakable character of God and holding on.

And what happens to the person who holds on?

The verse does not promise that they will be refreshed, or comforted, or given an explanation. It promises something more violent and more magnificent than any of those things. The word translated renew is chalaph — which literally means to exchange. Not a refill. A replacement. The believer who binds themselves to God in the tension of waiting does not merely get their human strength topped off. They trade it. They exchange their exhausted, depleted, finite human frailty for the inexhaustible omnipotence of the Divine.

But that exchange has a price. The price is human bankruptcy. You cannot chalaph with full hands. God's silence is the exact tool designed to empty them.

Part 2 — The Biblical Language of Unanswered Prayer

There are one hundred and fifty Psalms in the biblical canon. Scholars who have studied them with technical precision have identified that approximately a third of them are laments — expressions of raw, desperate, sometimes accusatory anguish directed at a God who appears to have gone silent.

This is not accidental. God did not put these Psalms in Scripture by mistake. He canonized them. He preserved them across thousands of years of manuscript transmission. He ensured they sat alongside the hymns of praise and the declarations of triumph — because He wanted every person who would ever suffer to find their own voice inside them.

This tradition of honest, canonical lament did not end with the Psalms. In 4 Ezra — also known as 2 Esdras, a text preserved in the Latin Vulgate Apocrypha and rooted in the same theological tradition as the Qumran manuscripts — the prophet Ezra stands before God with a question that every believer who has ever felt abandoned has formed somewhere in the silence:

"Wherefore hast thou dishonoured and scattered thy chosen? Why dost thou not give answer to their cry? Why hast thou forgotten us utterly?" — 4 Ezra 5:28–30 (Apocrypha, c. 100 AD)

What is remarkable is not the question. The question is familiar. What is remarkable is that God answered it. Not with silence continued indefinitely. With an encounter that remade Ezra's entire framework for understanding suffering. The God who appears to have forgotten always answers those who will not stop asking — in His own time, in the register His purposes require.

The structure of a biblical lament follows a remarkable five-part architecture. It begins with an address to God — the sufferer does not scream into the void; they direct their pain specifically to the Covenant God. It moves into a complaint — a detailed, honest, often hyperbolic enumeration of everything that is wrong. Then comes a confession of trust — the theological anchor that holds the entire prayer together, a deliberate turning of the mind toward what God has done before even while He appears to do nothing now. Then a petition — a direct, urgent, sometimes demanding request for God to act. And finally a vow of praise — an anticipatory commitment to worship God in the assembly once He moves, made before the deliverance has arrived.

Psalm 13 moves through this entire architecture in six verses. David opens with "How long wilt thou forget me, O LORD? for ever?" — a cry so raw and so human it requires no translation. He argues his case. He anchors himself in the character of God. And he arrives, by the final verse, at something he did not feel when he started: "I will sing unto the LORD, because he hath dealt bountifully with me." Not because circumstances had changed. Because the process of honest lament before God had moved something.

Psalm 22 takes the experience further.

"My God, my God, why hast thou forsaken me? why art thou so far from helping me, and from the words of my roaring?" — Psalm 22:1 (KJV)

The Hebrew word for forsaken here is azab — to leave, to abandon, to leave destitute. And when the Septuagint translated this word into Greek and when the New Testament recorded Jesus quoting it from the cross, the word used was enkataleipo — which means to separate connection with someone entirely, to desert, to abandon.

This is what it felt like to David. And when Jesus spoke these words from the cross He was doing something that every Jewish ear present would have immediately understood. In the ancient Jewish teaching tradition, quoting the opening line of a Psalm was the accepted way of referencing the entire text. Jesus was not crying out in confusion or weakness. He was declaring — from the cross, in the final moments of the greatest act in all of history — that Psalm 22 was being fulfilled in that moment. He was pointing every witness at Calvary to a Psalm written a thousand years before that described the crucifixion in precise detail and ended not in abandonment but in worldwide worship.

The theological turning point is verse three: "But thou art holy, O thou that inhabitest the praises of Israel." David wrenched his focus off his own torment and forced it onto the throne. And the Psalm that begins in the darkest abandonment ends with nations turning to the Lord.

Even from the cross, in the darkest moment in the history of creation, Jesus was declaring the ending of the story. Not in weakness. In authority. The Psalm He cited ends not in abandonment but in worldwide worship — nations turning to the Lord, a people yet to be born hearing that He has done this. He knew exactly where the Psalm finished. So did every Jewish witness standing at the foot of that cross.

And then there is Psalm 88 — the one that does not end in victory.

Every other lament Psalm in the biblical canon contains a turn. At some point, the darkness gives way to something. The sufferer remembers God's faithfulness. The vow of praise emerges. Some thread of hope catches the light.

Psalm 88 has none of this. It opens in darkness — "O LORD God of my salvation, I have cried day and night before thee" — and it ends in darkness. The final word of the entire Psalm is the Hebrew choshek — darkness. The lover and the friend have been removed. The acquaintance is darkness. And nothing else comes.

Theologians who have wrestled honestly with this have arrived at a conclusion that should permanently reshape how any believer approaches a season of unresolved suffering: God put Psalm 88 in Scripture on purpose. He preserved this Psalm through every copying, every translation, every council that decided which texts belonged in the canon — because He wanted every person who has ever lived through a season of darkness that did not resolve on any human timeline to find themselves in it and know that they are not outside the will of God.

You can endure lifelong suffering. You can experience chronic depression. You can pray for decades without a visible answer. And still be perfectly within the purposes of a God who validates your pain by putting it in His book.

There is one more word in the Psalms that speaks directly to the nature of divine silence — and it is a word most people have walked past their entire lives without stopping.

The word is Selah.

It appears seventy-one times across the Psalms — a musical instruction embedded in the text, interrupting the flow of prayer and praise with a single command. According to the Hebrew lexicons, Selah derives from a root meaning to suspend — and by implication, to weigh or to value. It is a deliberate pause in the music. A moment of enforced silence built directly into the song.

And what it reveals is this: silence is not the interruption of worship. Silence is one of its highest expressions.

When God appears to say nothing, He is instituting a divine Selah. He is not abandoning the song. He is inserting a pause that demands something the music itself cannot demand — that the listener stop their own noise, suspend their own performance, and weigh the value of what has just been spoken against the weight of what they are currently carrying.

God's silence is never just silence. It is always communication. The question is whether we are still enough to receive what the pause is saying.

Part 3 — Three People Who Survived the Silence

Theology is most powerful when it becomes story. And the God of Scripture did not leave us without case studies. He preserved, across thousands of years of human history, the detailed accounts of real people who walked into the silence of God and came out the other side — not unscathed, but undefeated. Three of those accounts stand above the rest as the clearest, most complete portraits of what divine silence actually looks like from the inside.

Job — The Man God Bragged About and Then Went Quiet On

Before Job lost a single thing, before the first wave of catastrophe arrived, the opening words of the book establish him in terms that require no qualification:

"There was a man in the land of Uz, whose name was Job; and that man was perfect and upright, and one that feared God, and eschewed evil." — Job 1:1 (KJV)

God did not call Job nearly perfect. The opening declaration is absolute: perfect and upright. And then God permitted everything to be taken from him in a single day, and went silent for thirty-seven chapters.

Thirty-seven chapters.

While Job sat in ashes scraping his wounds with broken pottery, while his wife told him to curse God and die, while three men who called themselves his friends constructed increasingly elaborate theological arguments for why Job's suffering must be the product of Job's hidden sin — God said nothing.

What was He doing?

The philosopher Peter Kreeft, in his rigorous examination of this question, identified something that cuts beneath every surface answer: God was not absent from Job's suffering. He was hollowing out a space. He was excavating. The silence and the suffering were working together to dig out a cavern in Job's soul large enough to hold what God intended to pour into it — not an explanation, but an encounter. Not a theological treatise, but the raw, unmediated presence of the Living God.

When God finally broke His silence and spoke to Job from the whirlwind in chapters 38 through 41, He did something that every person who has ever demanded answers from heaven should sit with very carefully. He did not answer a single one of Job's questions. Not one. Instead, He asked His own.

"Where wast thou when I laid the foundations of the earth?" — Job 38:4 (KJV)

Question after question after question — pulling Job's perspective further and further from the narrow tunnel of his own suffering and into the vast, incomprehensible architecture of a universe that operates on a scale the human mind cannot hold. God was not being cruel. He was being gracious. He was showing Job that if a textbook answer to the problem of evil had been given, Job would have asked another question. And another. And the conversation would have spiraled inward forever, tightening around the wound rather than releasing it.

The ultimate answer to human suffering is not an explanation. It is an encounter.

And Job understood. Not because his questions were answered. Because he saw God. And what the encounter produced was not triumph. It was something more honest and more complete than triumph:

"Wherefore I abhor myself, and repent in dust and ashes." — Job 42:6 (KJV)

Job did not leave the whirlwind with answers. He left it demolished. The silence had done what no explanation could have done — it had made him so desperate, so emptied of every human comfort and every theological certainty he had constructed, that when God finally showed up, the only possible response was total, undone surrender. Not victory. Worship. And in that surrender, Job received something far greater than the resolution he had demanded: the direct, unmediated presence of the God he had accused.

Elijah — The Man Who Won the Battle and Collapsed in the Silence After

Elijah had just called fire from heaven on Mount Carmel. He had stood alone against four hundred and fifty prophets of Baal and watched God vindicate him in the most dramatic fashion available in human history. He had won the greatest public victory any prophet of God had ever witnessed in the Northern Kingdom.

And then he ran.

Jezebel sent him a single message — one woman's death threat — and the prophet who had stared down an entire apostate nation collapsed under a juniper tree in the wilderness and asked God to take his life.

"It is enough; now, O LORD, take away my life; for I am not better than my fathers." — 1 Kings 19:4 (KJV)

And God went silent.

But the silence of God in this moment is a theological masterpiece precisely because of what God did inside it. He did not thunder from heaven. He did not rebuke Elijah for his collapse. He sent an angel who touched Elijah gently — and let him sleep. Then the angel came back and gave him food and water. And let him sleep again. The text records simply:

"The journey is too great for thee." — 1 Kings 19:7 (KJV)

God recognized something that the church has not always been willing to say out loud: physical exhaustion and spiritual despair are not separate problems. They are connected. And sometimes what looks like a crisis of faith is a crisis of a human body that has been pushed past its breaking point. Before God spoke a single theological word to Elijah, He fed him and let him rest.

What follows is the most famous articulation of divine presence in silence in all of Scripture. God directed Elijah to stand on the mountain. And He sent a great wind — powerful enough to break rocks. Then an earthquake. Then a fire. Three spectacular, adrenaline-soaked displays of raw divine power, one after another.

"But the LORD was not in the wind." — 1 Kings 19:11 (KJV)

"And after the earthquake a fire; but the LORD was not in the fire." — 1 Kings 19:12 (KJV)

And after the fire — a still small voice.

The Hebrew behind that phrase carries breathtaking precision. The word for still is demamah — related to damam, meaning to be struck dumb, to be rendered speechless, to be brought to an absolute halt. And small is daq — thin, fine, barely perceptible. What Elijah heard was not a whisper that could be missed. It was the voice of God arriving in a register so pure, so intimate, so stripped of all spectacle that the only way to receive it was to become completely still first.

God was teaching His servant something that would define the rest of his prophetic ministry: the most sustaining encounters with God do not arrive in the spectacular. They arrive in the quiet. The wind and the earthquake and the fire were the prelude — the noise that burned off the last of Elijah's reliance on the dramatic. The still small voice was the reality.

When Elijah heard it, he pulled his mantle over his face and stood at the entrance of the cave. He did not run. He did not demand more. He covered his face in the presence of the Holy and listened.

The silence before that voice was not abandonment. It was preparation.

Habakkuk — The Man Who Learned to Rejoice in the Ruins

"O LORD, how long shall I cry, and thou wilt not hear! even cry out unto thee of violence, and thou wilt not save!" — Habakkuk 1:2 (KJV)

The Hebrew word for cry here is za'aq — a violent, desperate cry for help in a situation of injustice and suffering. It is the same word used when Israel cried out under the crushing bondage of Egypt. Habakkuk was not filing a polite complaint. He was screaming at a God who appeared to be watching violence and injustice triumph over the righteous — and doing nothing about it.

God's answer, when it finally came, was not what Habakkuk expected. God told him that He was raising up the Chaldeans — a nation even more violent and wicked than what Habakkuk was complaining about — to execute His sovereign purposes. The answer to Habakkuk's prayer was an answer that made things look, on the surface, considerably worse.

What does a prophet do with that? He climbs a watchtower and waits.

"I will stand upon my watch, and set me upon the tower, and will watch to see what he will say unto me." — Habakkuk 2:1 (KJV)

He does not storm away in anger. He does not decide that God has proven Himself untrustworthy. He positions himself to listen — even when the last thing God said made no earthly sense.

And then the book ends with one of the most extraordinary declarations of faith in all of human literature.

"Although the fig tree shall not blossom, neither shall fruit be in the vines; the labour of the olive shall fail, and the fields shall yield no meat; the flock shall be cut off from the fold, and there shall be no herd in the stalls: Yet I will rejoice in the LORD, I will joy in the God of my salvation." — Habakkuk 3:17–18 (KJV)

Nothing resolved. The figs are still not blooming. The vines are still barren. The herds are still gone. Nothing in the external world has changed. And Habakkuk has arrived at a place where none of that determines what he does next.

This is the destination that divine silence is designed to produce. Not a faith that holds on because circumstances improved. A faith that holds on because the character of God has been settled — finally, permanently, below the level of circumstance — in the bedrock of the soul. Habakkuk did not detach from reality. He simply stopped allowing reality to be the final authority on whether God was good.

Part 4 — Why God Is Never Truly Absent

There is a truth that every person who has ever felt abandoned by God needs to hear — stated plainly, without softening, because the weight of it is the very thing that makes the silence survivable.

God cannot leave you. Not will not. Cannot.

The New Testament does not simply promise that God will try to stay near. It makes a claim that is ontological — rooted in the very structure of what is true — about the permanent, unbreakable presence of God within every believer.

Jesus, in the hours before His crucifixion, gathered His disciples and made them a promise so absolute that it requires the most intense language available in the Greek to contain it. He told them He was going away. He told them they would not be able to follow Him immediately. And then He said this:

"I will not leave you comfortless: I will come to you." — John 14:18 (KJV)

The English word comfortless is a catastrophic understatement of the original Greek. The word Jesus used was orphanos. Orphaned. Fatherless. Destitute and without a guide or protector in a hostile world. Jesus was speaking directly into the specific, devastating terror His disciples were about to face — the terror of being left alone as spiritual orphans in a world that was about to kill them for His name.

And He promised He would not do that to them.

He fulfilled that promise by sending the Holy Spirit — whom He called Parakletos in John 14:16. The Greek word Parakletos means one called alongside to help — an advocate, a counselor, a helper who comes specifically to the side of the one who is overwhelmed. And Jesus specified that this was allos — another of the exact same kind. Not a substitute. Not a lesser substitute. The same divine presence, the same companionship, the same protection — now dwelling not beside them but within them.

"Know ye not that ye are the temple of God, and that the Spirit of God dwelleth in you?" — 1 Corinthians 3:16 (KJV)

The word Paul uses for temple here is not hieron — the general temple complex. It is naos — the specific, inner sanctuary. The Holy of

Holies. The room where the manifest presence of God dwelled, where only the High Priest could enter, and only once a year. Paul is saying that the individual believer's body has become that room. Not the outer courts. The innermost chamber. The place where God uniquely, personally, permanently dwells.

When God appears to be silent — when the ceiling feels like concrete and the prayers seem to bounce back — the Holy Spirit is not absent from that room. He has not packed and left. He is there, doing something that Romans 8:26–27 describes with a Greek word so precisely constructed it demands to be broken apart.

The verse tells us that the Spirit intercedes for us with groanings that cannot be uttered. The Greek word for intercedes is hyperentugchano — a compound word whose architecture says everything. Entugchano means to approach or appeal to someone on behalf of another. The prefix hyper means over, beyond, super. The Holy Spirit does not merely pray for you. He super-intercedes. He steps into the precise gap where your human language has collapsed entirely — where you have nothing left to say, where the words will not come, where you are sitting in silence because the pain has taken the voice — and He takes over the legal and spiritual advocacy required before the throne of God.

The groanings that cannot be uttered — stenagmos in Greek — are the deep, involuntary sounds wrung from a soul in profound anguish. The sounds that are too broken and too raw to be called words. And the Scripture says that in those exact sounds, in those fractured, wordless moments of total collapse, the Holy Spirit is praying with a precision and a power that human language could never achieve.

You think you have gone silent. Heaven is listening to the most perfect prayer you have ever offered.

And then there is the promise in Hebrews 13:5 — a verse that, in the English translation, reads as a simple, steady reassurance:

"I will never leave thee, nor forsake thee." — Hebrews 13:5 (KJV)

The English is beautiful. The Greek is a fortress.

When the author of Hebrews recorded this promise, he did not use a single negative to deny the possibility of abandonment. He stacked five. Five distinct negatives in a single sentence — building a grammatical wall of absolute impossibility around the lie that God ever leaves. The word used for forsake is enkataleipo — the same word Jesus quoted from Psalm 22 on the cross. The full weight of cosmic abandonment that Jesus endured at Calvary is the exact thing God declares, with five stacked negatives, that He will never — not, no, never, nor, by no means — allow to fall on you.

Because Jesus absorbed it so you would not have to.

C.S. Lewis — writing in the raw season after the death of his wife — pressed against what felt like a door that would not open, trying to find God in the way a desperate man finds someone he needs. He described going to God in desperate need and finding not comfort but what felt like locked doors and drawn curtains. A presence gone from the windows.

And then he discovered something that changed everything he thought he knew about silence.

The door was never bolted to keep him out. The silence was not an empty house. God had not retreated behind a locked door because He did not want Lewis's grief. He had gone quiet — in the exact way a loving surgeon goes quiet during the most critical phase of an operation — because what was being built required that kind of focused, undistracted, uninterrupted work.

Lewis realized, in the crucible of that grief, that he had been coming to God primarily for the feeling of God's presence — the emotional warmth, the sense of companionship, the neurological comfort of knowing someone was there. And God, in His mercy, had quietly removed that feeling. Not to harm Lewis. To cure him of a subtle idolatry he had not even noticed: the tendency to love the feeling of God more than God Himself.

The silence was God locking Lewis safely inside the process that would produce something the comfortable, feeling-filled version of his faith never could have produced alone.

Part 5 — What God Is Building When He Says Nothing

The question is not only whether God is present in the silence. The question is what He is doing there.

Because the silence is never random. It is never careless. It is never the absence of a plan. The God who numbers the hairs on your head and notes the fall of every sparrow does not accidentally lose track of you in a season of suffering. Every period of divine silence in the life of a believer has an architecture — a purpose being built beneath the surface that the noise of God's visible activity would have drowned out if He had not gone quiet first.

John Flavel — the Puritan theologian who spent a lifetime studying the hidden workings of God's providence — identified something that most people never think to ask in the middle of a silent season. He observed that God is always doing two things simultaneously in a season of apparent inactivity. He is preparing the mercy for the believer. And He is preparing the believer for the mercy.

Both halves of that statement matter equally.

The first half — God preparing the mercy — explains why the answer does not arrive when we demand it. Flavel used an image that is simple enough to dismiss and precise enough to stop you cold: a foolish child would pull the apple from the tree while it is still green. But when the apple is ripe, it drops of its own accord, and it is more pleasant and more wholesome than anything the impatient hand could have seized early. God's delays are not denials. They are the time required for the answer to become what it needs to be before it reaches you.

The second half — God preparing the believer for the mercy — is the more uncomfortable truth. Because it means the silence is not just about what God is building. It is about what God is removing. Flavel taught that God uses the agonizing silence to break the stubbornness of the human will — to pry open the clenched fist of self-reliance until the believer finally arrives at a posture of surrender rather than demand.

The silence forces the believer into a corner where the only remaining option is surrender. And surrender — true, unperformed, whole-hearted surrender — is the exact posture God has been waiting for all along.

The Apostle James describes this process with a Greek word drawn directly from the ancient metallurgical tradition. The word is dokimion — the intense, sustained fire applied to raw metal to burn away the dross and reveal the pure substance beneath. This is what God is doing in the silence. He is applying the heat. He is not burning you. He is burning away everything in you that was never meant to remain — the self-reliance, the false comforts, the layers of performance and pretense that accumulated in the seasons when life was manageable.

And what the fire produces — what survives it — is something the Greek calls dokime. Proven character. The spiritual status of a soul that has been through the furnace and come out the other side not destroyed but refined. A faith that is no longer theoretical. A trust that is no longer contingent on comfort.

Paul traces the entire chain of this transformation in Romans 5:3–5 with four Greek words that build on each other like the links of a forged chain. Thlipsis — the crushing, pressing, squeezing weight of tribulation, like olives being pressed to release the oil. From that crushing comes hupomone — not the passive resignation that the English word patience suggests, but the militant, muscular endurance of a soldier holding the line under sustained assault. From that endurance comes dokime — proven character, the certification of a soul that held under pressure. And from proven character comes elpis — not the wishful thinking that the English word hope implies, but the Greek meaning: solid, unshakeable, confident expectation. An anchor that does not move.

You cannot leapfrog the steps. You cannot arrive at elpis without passing through thlipsis. You cannot obtain proven character without exercising endurance. And you cannot practice endurance unless you are first placed under the crushing weight of silence and suffering. God is not torturing you. He is forging you.

And then there is the story of Lazarus — which is not primarily a story about a resurrection. It is a story about what God is doing in the days before He moves.

"Lord, behold, he whom thou lovest is sick." — John 11:3 (KJV)

They did not demand a specific outcome. They spread the need before Him and trusted Him to act as He saw best. And the response of heaven was silence.

John 11:6 records it with a simplicity that makes it more devastating, not less: when He had heard therefore that he was sick, He abode two days still in the same place where He was. Jesus heard. And stayed. Deliberately. The man He loved crossed the threshold from sick to dead while Jesus remained where He was.

Why?

Jesus answered that question before He ever left:

"This sickness is not unto death, but for the glory of God, that the Son of God might be glorified thereby." — John 11:4 (KJV)

If He had rushed to Bethany and healed a sick man, it would have been a great miracle — one of many. But by waiting in silence until four days of death and decay had made human intervention not just unlikely but mathematically and biologically impossible, Jesus set the stage for something that a healing could never have been.

A resurrection.

"I am the resurrection, and the life." — John 11:25 (KJV)

This declaration was not made in the abstract. It was made at a tomb. In front of grieving sisters. After days of terrible silence. And it required every one of those days of silence to become the declaration it was.

The silence before the miracle was not the absence of the miracle. It was the preparation for a weight of glory that the miracle, if it had come early, could never have carried.

Part 6 — You Are Not an Orphan

There is a lie that divine silence is designed to produce — not by God, but by the enemy who watches the silence and moves into it with the oldest whisper in his arsenal: He has left you. You are on your own. Whatever you thought you had with God was an illusion, and this silence is the proof.

The Scripture does not argue with that lie delicately. It destroys it.

The posture God commands in the middle of silence is described in Psalm 46:10 with a Hebrew word that has been profoundly softened in translation. The verse reads in English: "Be still, and know that I am God." The Hebrew word behind be still is raphah. And raphah does not mean sit quietly and breathe deeply.

Raphah is a military command. It means to drop your weapons. To release your grip. To let your hands fall limp to your sides. God is standing on a battlefield where a frantic soldier is flailing — trying to fix, trying to force, trying to manufacture an outcome through sheer human will — and He is shouting: Stop. Drop it. Let go.

Because the prerequisite to truly knowing God — "know that I am God" — is the total surrender of the human grip on the situation. The silence is the test of whether you will keep striving in the flesh, or whether you will raphah — release it entirely — and allow Him to be what He has always been.

Jeremiah, writing from the smoking ruins of a destroyed Jerusalem, captured the posture that survives the silence in a passage that contains two Hebrew words that deserve to be held side by side. In Lamentations 3:26 he writes of one who hopes — the Hebrew word yachal, which means not cheerful optimism but agonizing, painful endurance, staying at a post of suffering without abandoning it. And he writes of one who quietly waits — the Hebrew dumam, which carries the connotation of being struck so speechless by the weight of God's hand that the mouth simply closes and the soul goes still.

The posture of survival in divine silence is yachal combined with dumam. Agonizing, painful hope that refuses to abandon its post. Combined with a holy silence that stops demanding explanations and lets the weight do its work.

And when the weight has done enough — when the casual seeker has finally become the desperate hunter — God breaks His silence.

"Ye shall seek me, and find me, when ye shall search for me with all your heart." — Jeremiah 29:13 (KJV)

God does not promise to be found by the person who casually adds Him to their list of concerns. He promises to be found by the person whose darash — their formal, thoughtful seeking — has been so broken open by the silence that it has transformed into baqash. The desperate hunt. The cry of a person who has finally arrived at the place where there is no plan B, no backup, no human alternative left on the table.

That moment — the moment of baqash — is not the moment God begins to care. He has been caring the entire time. It is the moment the silence has accomplished what it was sent to accomplish. The clenched fist has finally opened. The self-reliant soul has finally reached the end of itself. And what happens next is not God rushing in from a distance. It is God revealing that He was never at a distance.

He was there the entire time. The Holy Spirit was super-interceding inside the room you thought was empty. The naos — the Holy of Holies of your own body — was occupied the entire time by the One who promised with five stacked negatives that He would not, no, never, by no means, leave or forsake you.

You were never an orphan. You were in surgery.

What This Means For the Skeptic

There are people reading this chapter who have been waiting for a long time. Not days. Years. Decades. And the idea that God's silence is purposeful and productive does not land as comfort — it lands as a theological argument that seems designed to make peace with a situation that deserves to be confronted.

This section is for you. Not with argument. With honesty.

Philip Yancey spent years examining the most common versions of this exact objection. He pointed to something that permanently dismantled his own version of it — the account of the Israelites in the wilderness. Here were people who had everything a sufferer claims to want from God. An audible voice. A visible pillar of fire by night. A cloud by day. Daily miraculous provision. A God who was, by no reasonable definition, silent.

And they rebelled. Ten distinct times. Across the entire Sinai journey. With every sensory proof of God's presence available to them — they doubted, complained, built idols, and demanded to go back to Egypt.

Yancey's conclusion was not comfortable, but it was precise: signs addict us to signs, not to God. If God broke His silence with a visible miracle every time you suffered, your faith would not be in the character of God. Your faith would be in the experience of miracles. And the first time a miracle did not arrive — the first time the sign was delayed or absent — everything would collapse.

God's silence is not a failure of His love. It is the refusal of His love to produce in you a faith that cannot survive darkness.

The faith God is building in the silence is the only kind that lasts. It is the faith that says what Habakkuk said from the ruins: even though nothing has resolved, even though the answer has not come, even though the silence continues — yet I will rejoice in the LORD. Not because the circumstances changed. Because the soul has been anchored below the level of circumstance. And nothing that happens on the surface of life can move what has been secured that deep.

My Reflection

The silence I am about to describe was not something that happened to me. It was something I built, one year at a time, without realizing what I was constructing.

There was a season of my life — a long one — where my relationship with God was transactional in ways I did not have the self-awareness to recognize. I believed. I prayed. I called myself a man of faith. And underneath all of it, at a level I was not examining, I had constructed a version of faith that was really a version of expectation. I expected God to perform in proportion to my belief. I expected the life I was building to reflect the God I was serving. I expected that being a husband, a father, a man who showed up — even imperfectly — would result in a life that held together.

And for a long time, God was gracious enough to let me live inside that illusion.

Then it came apart.

My body began to fail me — years of pancreatitis, hospitalizations that became a rhythm I could not break. And then, before I had any margin left in my own body or spirit, the news came about my son. I have told both of those stories in detail elsewhere in this book. What I want to tell you here — from the other side of it — is what I now understand about the silence I experienced in that season.

I had been living what I now recognize as a darash faith. A formal inquiry. I was seeking God in the way a man checks a box. Sunday. Prayer at the right moments. The language of faith without the desperation of it.

The illness stripped one layer of that away. The hospitalizations stripped another. And then my son's surgery took what was left. What I found in that chapel — on the front row of an empty room at the lowest moment of my life — was not God arriving. I understand that now. He had been there the entire time. What arrived in that room was the first moment I had been empty enough to receive Him.

What I walked into that chapel was not a man of deep, tested, battle-worn faith. It was a man who had finally, completely run out of himself. The self-reliance was gone. The performance was gone. The carefully managed version of strength I had always maintained for the people around me was gone. For the first time in my adult life I was purely and completely a baqash — a desperate, whole-hearted, have-nothing-left hunt for the God I had been formally seeking for years without ever fully finding.

And what happened in that room — the presence, the weight of it, the words that landed in my spirit — was not God rushing in from a distance. God had not been absent during the years of darash faith. He had not been absent during the hospitalizations or the long months of confusion or the season when my family felt the weight of my unresolved self-reliance more than they ever should have.

He had been the craftsman working in charash silence. He had been the surgeon operating in the dark. He had been the architect building, beneath every painful layer that was stripped away, a man I had not yet met — a man I am still becoming — but a man I am finally, genuinely proud to be on the days when I look in the mirror.

The silence was not punishment. It was not abandonment. It was preparation that I would never have chosen and would never trade.

I want to say something I have never heard said out loud, though I suspect others who have walked through dark seasons have quietly thought it.

I am glad I suffered.

Not in a performative, theologically tidy way. Not because suffering is good in itself. But because the man on the other side of that suffering is a better husband, a better father, a better steward of everything God has given me than the man who walked into it.

I want to speak to someone specific before this section closes. Someone who is in the middle of the silence right now — not the end of it, not the reflection of it, but the raw and suffocating middle of it.

He is there.

He was there before you arrived in this dark place. He was there during every day of the silence that preceded this moment. He is there right now, in the room you are sitting in, in the body you are inhabiting, super-interceding for you in a language so precise and so powerful that your broken, wordless groaning is being translated into the perfect will of God before the throne of heaven.

You are not an orphan. You are not forgotten. You are not being punished.

You are in surgery. And the Surgeon has never once lost a patient He was operating on.

The Master Craftsman has not set down His tools. He is still working.

There is one more thing to be said before you turn to the next chapter — something that bridges the ground we have just covered and the ground ahead.

The chapters behind us have been personal. They have lived close to the bone. Suffering. Silence. Forgiveness. Foreknowledge. These are questions that arrive in hospital rooms and dark chapels and the middle of the night, and the answers required that kind of closeness to reach the places they were aimed at.

The chapters ahead ask questions that arrive from a different direction — from the mind more than the heart, from honest reading of the Bible more than from personal crisis. Why does the Old Testament look so different from the New? Has science disproved God? Why are there so many religions? These are harder questions in a different way. They require evidence, precision, and a willingness to follow an argument all the way to its honest conclusion.

But do not mistake the change in register for a change in the person asking. The pastoral voice does not leave when the intellectual question enters. The warmth that sat with you in the silence is the same warmth that will walk with you through every chapter that follows. The God we have been searching for in the dark is the same God we will be examining in the light. And the answers we are going to find together are, if anything, even more staggering than the ones we have already held.

Come on. There is more.

A Prayer for the Reader

Father,

I come before You on behalf of every person holding these pages right now — and especially those who are reading this chapter from the inside of the silence rather than the memory of it.

For the person who has been praying for months and heard nothing — who has gotten out of bed in the dark and poured out everything they had into what felt like empty air — meet them in this moment the way You met me in that chapel. Not with a spectacular sign. With Your presence. Let them feel the weight of the nearness of a God who has never, not once, taken His eyes off them.

For the person whose faith has been reduced to arguing with You — who is angry and confused and cannot reconcile the God they were taught to trust with the silence they are living inside — remind them of Job. Remind them that You did not rebuke his honesty. You engaged it. Bring them to the whirlwind. Show them not an explanation but Yourself.

For the person who has confused Your silence with Your absence — who has begun to believe the whisper that says they have been abandoned and left to manage alone — let the truth of five stacked Greek negatives land in their spirit tonight. You will not, no, never, by no means leave them. The promise was made with a grammatical violence that leaves no room for the lie. Seal that truth in them.

For the person who has been in the silence so long they have stopped believing the other side of it exists — remind them of Lazarus. Four days in the tomb was not the end of the story. It was the setup for the resurrection. The delay was the requirement for the weight of glory that followed. Let them hold on for four more days.

For the person who cannot find words — whose prayer has collapsed into silence because the pain has taken the voice — remind them that the Holy Spirit is super-interceding in the exact place where their language has failed. Their groaning is a prayer. Their emptiness is a sanctuary. The Spirit is at work in the room they think is empty.

And for all of us — in every season of silence that comes — forge in us the faith of Habakkuk. The faith that says: even though the fig tree does not blossom, even though the fields yield nothing, even though everything I was trusting in the natural world has gone quiet — yet I will rejoice in the LORD. I will joy in the God of my salvation.

Not because circumstances changed. Because You are God. And You have never once stopped working.

In the name of the Father, the Son, and the Holy Spirit.

Amen.

"Be still, and know that I am God." — Psalm 46:10 (KJV)

Chapter Six

Why Does God Seem So Different in the Old Testament?

"For I am the LORD, I change not; therefore ye sons of Jacob are not consumed." — Malachi 3:6 (KJV)

In the chapters behind us we have been in close, personal territory — sitting with the kind of questions that arrive in the dark and refuse to leave. Why do good people suffer. Why does God go silent. Whether the foreknowledge of God makes the pain of our lives meaningful or inevitable. Those questions pressed against the heart first.

This chapter asks a different kind of question. It begins in the mind, not the chest. It is the question of a person who has sat down with the whole Bible — both Testaments in hand — and encountered something that genuinely stops them. Two pictures of God that do not appear, at first reading, to belong to the same frame.

What follows is one of the most important chapters in this book. Because if you cannot hold the God of Sinai and the God of Calvary in the same hands — if they feel like two different Gods rather than one — then the foundation trembles beneath everything else. We are going to hold them together. And what you find when you do will not make the difficult passages disappear. It will make them more luminous than you expected.

The Question

It is one of the most honest questions a person can bring to the Bible.

You open the Old Testament and you find a God who commands the total destruction of entire cities. A God who sends plagues on Egypt. A God who opens the earth and swallows families whole. A God who orders the stoning of people for violations that modern Christianity would barely pause over. A God who commands Abraham to kill his own son on an altar of wood.

And then you turn to the New Testament. And you find a God who tells a story about a father who runs down a road to embrace a son who wasted everything he was ever given. A God who stops a woman from being stoned and tells her simply to go and sin no more. A God who weeps at a graveside. A God who washes the feet of the men He created the universe.

The question is not born in skepticism. It is born in honest reading. And it deserves an honest answer.

Because if these are two different Gods — one of wrath and one of grace, one of law and one of love — then the entire foundation of the Christian faith trembles. You cannot trust a God who changed His mind about what He requires or who He is. You cannot build your life on a character that shifts between the pages of the same book.

But if they are the same God — if the God of the burning bush and the God of the empty tomb are the exact same "I AM" — then something else is happening in the Old Testament that most people have never been shown. Something that does not make the difficult passages disappear, but that transforms them entirely. Something that reveals that what looks like contradiction is actually preparation. What looks like cruelty is actually protection. What looks like the absence of love is actually love in its most fierce, most uncompromising, most costly form.

That is what this chapter is about.

The Oldest Accusation

The idea that the God of the Old Testament is fundamentally different from the God of the New Testament is not a new thought. It is nearly two thousand years old.

In the second century A.D., a man named Marcion of Sinope proposed exactly this. He taught that the God of the Old Testament was a lower, inferior deity — a strict, harsh Creator-God of law and judgment — while the God of the New Testament, revealed by Jesus, was a higher God of love and grace. He went so far as to physically remove the entire Old Testament from his version of the Bible, along with any New Testament passages that too closely referenced it.

The early church condemned this view as heresy. Not cautiously. Not reluctantly. With the full force of its theological conviction. Every major theologian of the early church — Irenaeus, Tertullian, Justin Martyr — wrote extensive refutations of Marcionism because they understood what was at stake. If the God of the Old Testament is not the same God as the New Testament, then Jesus was lying when He said the Scriptures testified of Him. Moses was wrong. The prophets were wrong. The entire sacrificial system that the cross was designed to fulfill becomes meaningless.

Marcionism was declared heresy because it is heresy. But in the twenty-first century, it has crept back in through the side door. Not always with a theological label. But whenever a person says "I prefer the God of the New Testament" — whenever someone describes Jesus as having corrected or replaced the God of the Old Testament — they are, knowingly or not, walking the same road that Marcion walked eighteen hundred years ago.

The answer to this question begins with something most people have never been taught. The God of the Old Testament and the God of the New Testament are not two different characters in two different stories. They are the same eternal being — and the entire Bible, from Genesis to Revelation, is one single, unified, perfectly orchestrated story of that being's relentless pursuit of the human soul.

What Never Changed

Before we examine why God's actions in the Old Testament look the way they look, we need to establish something foundational. Something that no honest reading of Scripture can avoid.

God does not change.

Not slightly. Not occasionally. Not in His essential character. Not at all.

The prophet Malachi records it in the plainest Hebrew language available. The original text reads: lo shaniti — I have not changed. This is not a poetic claim. It is a theological absolute. The Hebrew root shanah means to alter, to repeat in a different form, or to be different. God's declaration through Malachi is that His character, His nature, His fundamental being has never altered, never shifted, and never taken a different form. He is the same today as He was the day He breathed the breath of life into Adam's nostrils.

"For I am the LORD, I change not." — Malachi 3:6 (KJV)

The theologian Thomas Aquinas, in his Summa Theologica, describes this divine quality with a Latin phrase: Actus Purus — pure actuality. Aquinas argues that God is not a being in the process of becoming something. He is not developing, growing, learning, or changing His mind. He is the only being whose essence is entirely complete and entirely actual, with nothing unrealized, nothing in potential, nothing in development. He is not moving toward anything. He arrived at perfection in Himself before time began.

A.W. Tozer — one of the most penetrating theological minds of the twentieth century — observed that God's immutability is not the cold immovability of a stone. It is the perfect, self-consistent stability of a being who is already everything He can possibly be. With God there is no yesterday or tomorrow, no before or after. He simply is. The God who spoke from the burning bush is the same God who spoke from the empty tomb. The same character. The same love. The same holiness. The same justice. The same mercy. Without the slightest variation.

Charles Spurgeon put it this way: if God could change, He could only change in two directions — for better or for worse. He cannot change for the better, because He is already perfect. He cannot change for the worse, because He is perfectly good. Therefore He cannot change at all.

If God cannot change — and the Scripture declares He cannot — then the grace and mercy we see so vividly in the New Testament were not invented at the manger in Bethlehem. They were the eternal disposition of God long before the first human being drew breath. The question is not whether God changed between the Testaments. The question is why He appears different. And the answer is not about God at all.

The answer is about us.

The World Was Young

To understand why God responded the way He responded in the Old Testament, you have to understand the world He was responding to.

That world was young. Not just in age. In spiritual development. In moral comprehension. In the capacity of the human race to understand who God was and what He required.

Think about what God was working with. When He called Abraham out of Ur, He was calling a man out of a culture steeped in polytheism — a world where every city had its own god, every harvest required its own ritual, every disaster was the temper tantrum of some jealous deity demanding blood. When God delivered the Israelites from Egypt, He was not leading a theologically sophisticated people into the wilderness. He was leading a traumatized, culturally conditioned group of former slaves who, within days of their miraculous deliverance, melted their jewelry into the shape of a golden calf and held a pagan festival before it.

The apostle Paul provides the perfect theological lens for reading this reality. Writing to the Galatians, he describes the Old Testament law using a single Greek word that changes everything:

"Wherefore the law was our schoolmaster to bring us unto Christ, that we might be justified by faith. But after that faith is come, we are no longer under a schoolmaster." — Galatians 3:24–25 (KJV)

The word translated "schoolmaster" in that verse is paidagogos. In the ancient Greco-Roman world, a paidagogos was not a teacher in the academic sense. He was a strict household servant whose specific duty was to supervise the moral conduct and physical safety of his master's minor child. The paidagogos was responsible for restricting the child's freedom, applying the rod of discipline when necessary, and guarding the child from destructive influences until he reached the age of maturity. His methods were firm. His boundaries were inflexible. And his entire purpose was temporary — not to be the child's permanent relationship with authority, but to guard that child until he was old enough to understand and embrace a deeper kind of relationship.

That is what God was doing in the Old Testament. He was not displaying a different character than the one we see in Jesus. He was applying the strict, disciplinary framework necessary to keep a spiritually infantile humanity alive long enough for the Messiah to arrive.

The ancient world was not a place where the gentle invitation of the Sermon on the Mount would have been sufficient to keep a people anchored to the one true God. The surrounding cultures practiced child sacrifice. They institutionalized temple prostitution. They worshipped gods who demanded blood and offered nothing in return except the illusion of control over a terrifying world. And Israel — surrounded by all of it — had a deeply human tendency to look over the fence at what their neighbors were doing and want it for themselves.

God's strict demands in the Old Testament were not the expression of a tyrant who enjoyed restriction. They were the expression of a Father who understood exactly how dangerous the world was and exactly how young and fragile His people were inside it. The paidagogos does not hate the child he disciplines. He is the reason the child survives to meet the Father.

The Captain and the Crew

There is an image that captures this dynamic with a clarity that theology alone sometimes cannot reach.

Imagine a ship carrying the most precious cargo in the history of the universe — the entire lineage through which the Savior of the world would one day be born. The ship is sailing through a hurricane of pagan culture, idolatry, and moral destruction. The crew — God's chosen people — are gifted, loved, and deeply precious to the Captain. But they are also young, undisciplined, and dangerously prone to jumping overboard every time the seas calm down and another ship sails past flying a more colorful flag.

In that environment, the Captain does not run the ship the way He would run it on a calm sea. He issues strict orders. He maintains rigid discipline. He deals harshly with mutiny because mutiny in a hurricane does not just endanger the mutineer — it endangers the entire vessel and the cargo that the survival of the entire human race depends upon. His commands are demanding. His corrections are severe. And to a crew member who has never seen the end of the journey, who cannot see past the next wave, the Captain can seem harsh.

But the Captain is not harsh. The Captain is desperate. He loves every member of that crew with a love they cannot yet fully comprehend. And He knows something they do not — that if He relaxes the discipline for even a season, the ship goes down. The lineage is broken. The Savior never arrives. And every soul who would have been reached by that arrival is lost.

The God of the Old Testament was that Captain. Not a different God than the Father who ran down the road toward the prodigal son. The same God — in a different season, with a different set of requirements imposed by the desperate fragility of the situation. His love never changed. His methods had to.

God's Heart Was Always Bleeding

The greatest proof that God's character never changed between the Testaments is not found in the New Testament. It is found in the most dramatic moment of the Old Testament — a moment so often misread that most believers have never understood what God was actually saying.

In Exodus 32, while Moses is still on the mountain receiving the Law, the Israelites melt their gold, build a golden calf, and worship it with a pagan festival. The very people God just delivered through ten impossible plagues and a parted sea have, within forty days, abandoned Him entirely.

If the God of the Old Testament were simply a God of wrath with no capacity for grace, this would be the moment He would have ended Israel. The legal justification was complete. The evidence was overwhelming. The sentence was obvious.

Instead, God did something that should permanently silence every accusation of Old Testament cruelty. He descended on Mount Sinai to the very people who had just betrayed Him, stood before Moses, and declared His own character with words that the Hebrew language had to strain to hold:

"And the LORD passed by before him, and proclaimed, The LORD, The LORD God, merciful and gracious, longsuffering, and abundant in goodness and truth, keeping mercy for thousands, forgiving iniquity and transgression and sin." — Exodus 34:6–7 (KJV)

Every word of this declaration deserves to be read slowly. In the original Hebrew, this is not a list of theological attributes presented in the abstract. Each word is a living, weighty declaration of who God was — not who He would one day become in the New Testament, but who He had always been and still was in that very moment, even as His people burned incense to a metal cow in the valley below.

The word translated "merciful" is rachuwm — a word derived from the same root as rechem, the Hebrew word for a mother's womb. Rachuwm describes a deep, maternal, visceral compassion — the kind a mother feels for the child she carried in her own body. God is describing His love for Israel using the most intimate biological image in the human experience.

The word translated "gracious" is channun — describing a love that bends down toward the one who does not deserve it. A love that moves toward the undeserving, not away from them.

The phrase translated "longsuffering" is erek appayim — which in Hebrew literally means long of nose, or slow to flare the nostrils. In ancient Hebrew, the flaring of the nostrils was the physical image of anger about to erupt. God is saying: I am a God whose anger takes a very, very long time to build. I am slow to reach that point. I hold back for longer than you can comprehend.

And the word translated "abundant in goodness" is rab chesed — an overflow of chesed. That word chesed appears 249 times in the Old Testament alone. The same God that critics claim is all wrath in the Old Testament used His most defining self-description word — relentless, covenant-keeping, unbreakable love — more than two hundred times before Jesus was born.

What is remarkable is that this understanding of God's mercy was not confined to the Hebrew prophets alone. The Jewish wisdom tradition — preserved in the Septuagint and venerated among the communities whose writings were found among the Dead Sea Scrolls — understood the same God in precisely the same terms. The Wisdom of Solomon, written in Greek by a Jewish author steeped in the same theological stream as the Old Testament, declares of this same God:

"But thou hast mercy upon all; for thou canst do all things, and winkest at the sins of men, because they should amend themselves. For thou lovest all the things that are, and abhorrest nothing which thou hast made... But thou sparest all: for they are thine, O LORD, thou lover of souls." — Wisdom of Solomon 11:23–26 (Apocrypha, Septuagint)

Lover of souls. This was not a New Testament innovation. It was the settled conviction of ancient Jewish wisdom about the God they had worshipped for generations. The communities that preserved and transmitted the Old Testament Scriptures understood their God as one whose mercy encompassed even those who wandered from Him — waiting with open hands for any soul willing to turn. The God that critics describe as the God of pure wrath was being called the lover of souls by His own people before Jesus was born.

This is not the vocabulary of a God who was secretly angry and waiting for the New Testament to discover grace. This is the vocabulary of a God who had been gracious, compassionate, longsuffering, and overflowing with love from the very beginning — and who declared that character most loudly in the very moment His people deserved it least.

The God who wept over Jerusalem. The God who ran down the road toward the prodigal son. The God who washed the disciples' feet the night before the cross. That God was present on Mount Sinai. He has always been present. The New Testament did not create Him. It revealed what the Old Testament had been pointing to all along.

The Gardener Pulling Weeds

The most difficult passages in the Old Testament are not the ones where God is gracious. Those are easy. The most difficult passages are the ones where God orders the destruction of entire people groups — the Canaanites, the Amalekites, the cities of Sodom and Gomorrah.

These passages require a direct answer. Not a deflection. Not an apology. A direct answer that begins with two things: God's consistent pattern of warning, and the degree of evil that had taken root before the judgment arrived.

God never acted without warning. The prophet Jeremiah records that God had been sending messengers to Israel "rising early and sending them" for years upon years before judgment fell.

"Since the day that your fathers came forth out of the land of Egypt unto this day I have even sent unto you all my servants the prophets, daily rising up early and sending them." — Jeremiah 7:25 (KJV)

The destruction of Jerusalem came after centuries of prophetic warning that was rejected, mocked, and ignored.

This pattern of warning before judgment was so central to the ancient Jewish understanding of God's character that it was preserved in the Dead Sea Scrolls. The Damascus Document — a community rule text discovered among the Qumran manuscripts and copied across multiple generations of Jewish scribes — records the theological conviction that God had consistently raised up teachers and messengers to make His ways known to His people before allowing any judgment to fall. The community at Qumran understood what modern critics have overlooked: God warns before He acts. Always. Without exception. His judgment is never the first word. It is always the last — spoken only after every avenue of mercy has been opened, every messenger sent, and every invitation refused.

And in the case of the Canaanites — the most difficult judgment of all — there is a remarkable Hebrew word that explains the timing of God's action. In Genesis 15, God told Abraham that his descendants would not yet possess the Promised Land because "the iniquity of the Amorites is not yet full." The Hebrew word used there is shalem — meaning complete, whole, or brought to its full measure. God was not waiting impatiently for an excuse to destroy the Canaanites. He was waiting an additional four hundred years for the full measure of their evil to manifest, giving every possible generation within that culture the opportunity to turn.

But there is one more dimension of the Canaanite commands that the English translation almost entirely conceals — and it is perhaps the most important of all. The Hebrew word that governs the total-destruction commands is not merely a military term. It is a theological category.

That word is herem. It appears throughout the Old Testament — translated variously as "utterly destroy," "devoted to destruction," or "accursed." But in Brown-Driver-Briggs, the comprehensive Hebrew lexicon, herem is defined with a precision that changes everything: something set apart as absolutely belonging to God, removed from ordinary human use, consecrated exclusively to Him. The same root word is used for sacred dedications to the sanctuary. The same concept governs a vow of complete consecration to God.

When God issued herem commands regarding Canaan, He was not issuing the theological equivalent of ethnic cleansing. He was declaring a sacred excision — announcing that a specific system, not simply a collection of individual people, but an entire organized structure of child sacrifice, temple prostitution, occult warfare, and deliberate defiance of the living God that had been building for four centuries, had reached the point where it could not be reformed from within and could not coexist alongside Israel without destroying her.

Consider what herem also meant for individuals within that system. The account of Rahab — a Canaanite woman in Jericho who hid the Israelite spies and whose entire household was explicitly spared from the herem judgment — demonstrates that the command was never about race, ethnicity, or national origin. Rahab and her family lived, were folded into Israel, and she appears in the genealogy of Jesus Christ in Matthew chapter one. The herem was a moral verdict rendered against a specific system of institutionalized evil. Any individual who turned from that system was received. The door was always open.

The same principle governs 1 Samuel 15 — the command against the Amalekites that has troubled careful readers for centuries. God commanded Saul to utterly destroy the Amalekites. When Saul spared the Amalekite king Agag and the best of the livestock, the prophet Samuel declared this a catastrophic act of disobedience.

This passage is impossible to understand without knowing who the Amalekites were in the long arc of redemptive history. The Amalekites were not a passive, unrelated nation that happened to live near Israel. They were the first nation to attack Israel — in the wilderness in Exodus 17 — and they did so by targeting specifically the weakest members of the march: the exhausted, the elderly, the stragglers at the rear. God declared at that moment: "I will utterly put out the remembrance of Amalek from under heaven." This was not tribal hatred. It was a judicial declaration against a system that had specifically, repeatedly, and without provocation hunted God's most vulnerable people — and continued doing so for four hundred years after that declaration.

Matthew Henry, the eighteenth-century biblical commentator whose pastoral precision has guided believers for generations, observed that God's commands against nations like Amalek must always be read in the light of their complete history — not as isolated snapshots but as verdicts rendered after the full weight of centuries. God does not issue herem hastily. He issues it after the ledger has been kept, every warning has been sent, and every avenue of mercy has been offered and refused.

The hardest honest answer to these passages is this: God took precisely what He declared He would take, after precisely the patience He demonstrated He had, with precisely the exceptions for repentance He consistently offered. The difficulty is not that His actions were arbitrary or cruel. The difficulty is that they are total — and our modern instinct toward selective mercy feels violated by the completeness of a holy judgment we cannot fully see from where we stand in history.

What was that evil? It was not mere moral failure of the kind that every human culture exhibits. It was the institutionalized, systematic sacrifice of children burned alive in fire. It was temple prostitution woven into the structure of religious practice. It was evil that had been given four hundred years to metastasize and had used every moment of that grace to go deeper into darkness.

C.S. Lewis offered an image for this that is simple and devastating. He described God in the Old Testament as a gardener who loves his garden. A gardener who refuses to pull weeds is not compassionate — he is negligent. Weeds do not stay in their corner. They spread their roots under the soil, choke the good plants, steal the nutrients from everything healthy, and ultimately destroy the garden entirely if left unchecked. A gardener who pulls weeds is not expressing hatred for the garden. He is expressing love for it. The pulling is an act of preservation.

And even in those judgments, God's mercy operated in ways that are easy to miss. The book of Jonah records that God sent His reluctant prophet to Nineveh — the capital of the Assyrian Empire, a culture so violent that they were infamous for skinning their enemies alive and stacking skulls as monuments. When Nineveh fasted and repented, God relented. The Hebrew word used in Jonah 3:10 is nacham — describing a shift in God's providential posture when humanity's posture shifted. Jonah was furious. He threw God's own words from Exodus 34 back at Him in frustration: "I knew that thou art a gracious God, and merciful, slow to anger." Even God's own prophet found the depth of His mercy toward the worst of sinners to be almost incomprehensible.

God's judgment was never random. It was never the first resort. It was always the last resort of a God who had exhausted every avenue of patience, warning, and grace — and who still, even in the act of judgment, left the door open to any soul willing to walk through it.

The Holding Cell

There is one more dimension to this question that most people never consider — and it may be the most important of all.

Every time we read an Old Testament judgment and feel the weight of the innocent lives that were lost in it, we are making an assumption so deeply embedded in the modern worldview that we rarely notice we are making it. We are assuming that physical death is the ultimate tragedy. That the end of an earthly life is the worst possible outcome.

The Bible does not share that assumption.

In his letter to the Corinthians, the apostle Paul describes the worst physical suffering he endured — beatings, imprisonments, shipwrecks, stonings, hunger, and near-death experiences — and calls it a "light and momentary trouble." The Greek word he uses for what that suffering is producing is the word aiōnios — eternal, unending, belonging to the very nature of God's permanent existence. What feels like catastrophe to human eyes is, in the calculus of eternity, a microscopic investment in an infinite return.

"For I reckon that the sufferings of this present time are not worthy to be compared with the glory which shall be revealed in us." — Romans 8:18 (KJV)

Saint Teresa of Ávila — writing in the sixteenth century from the center of a life consumed by both suffering and profound contemplation — captured this with an image so simple it requires a moment to land: in the light of heaven, even a life full of the most atrocious suffering on earth will be seen as no more serious than one night in an inconvenient hotel. The inconvenience was real. The discomfort was genuine. But it was one night. And what follows it has no end.

This reframes everything in the Old Testament that looks harsh when viewed through a purely earthly lens.

This life is not the destination. It is the holding cell. And God, in His mercy, has made the holding cell survivable. He has given us relationships and beauty and laughter and the taste of good food and the warmth of sunlight through a window. He has given us the capacity to love and be loved, to create, to dream, to pray, to hear His voice through His Word. He has given us access to Him even from this temporary place.

A life without God in the holding cell is a different experience entirely. It is a padded, dark, soundproof cell — nothing but silence and your own thoughts in the dark, no window, no light, no connection to anything beyond the four walls closing in around you. With God, even the holding cell has a bed and a window with sunlight, and a phone you can pick up at any moment to hear the voice of the One who is waiting for you on the other side.

But the holding cell is still a holding cell. It is not home. And the God who designed it was not designing a permanent dwelling — He was designing a temporary preparation for something that human language does not yet have adequate words to describe.

Jesus Himself validated this framework in one of the most vivid accounts He ever gave. In Luke 16, He describes the moment after death for two men — a rich man who had enjoyed every earthly comfort while ignoring God, and a beggar named Lazarus who had suffered disease and starvation at the rich man's gate while clinging to faith. When both men die, the reversal is total and instantaneous. Lazarus is carried by angels to Abraham's bosom — a Hebrew image of warmth, intimacy, and honored rest at the feast of the righteous. The rich man lifts his eyes in Hades, the intermediate realm of departed spirits, in torment.

Both are in a holding state — the final judgment has not yet come. But the direction of each soul's eternity is already fixed. And the God who allowed Lazarus to suffer every earthly indignity while the rich man feasted in comfort was not absent from that situation. He was building in Lazarus something that no earthly comfort could have built. He was preparing a soul for a welcome that will make every moment of earthly suffering look, in retrospect, like the price of the greatest ticket ever given.

Some of the souls who died in the Old Testament judgments — particularly the young, the innocent, the ones who had not yet had time to choose the evil of their culture — may have been the most fortunate of all. Their purpose was fulfilled. Their souls were received. What looks to human eyes like a tragedy interrupted from the outside may, from the perspective of eternity, look like an early and merciful arrival at the place every human soul was made for.

God does not waste what He permits. Not a single moment of suffering in the Old Testament — not a single judgment, not a single death, not a single tear — was outside His awareness, beyond His purpose, or beneath the reach of His love.

The Shadow and the Substance

There is one final architectural reality that permanently resolves the apparent contradiction between the two Testaments. And it is found in the book of Hebrews.

"For the law having a shadow of good things to come, and not the very image of the things, can never with those sacrifices which they offered year by year continually make the comers thereunto perfect."
— Hebrews 10:1 (KJV)

The Greek word translated "shadow" in that verse is skia — a silhouette, an outline, the two-dimensional dark shape cast by a three-dimensional reality approaching from behind. And the word used for the true "image" of what was coming is eikon — the exact manifestation, the precise substance, the full reality that the shadow could only hint at.

A shadow is not a lie. A shadow is not an error. A shadow is not a primitive, inferior version of the real thing. A shadow is what you see when the real thing is behind you, when the light is shining forward, and when the substance has not yet arrived in your view. The shadow does not contradict the body that casts it. It proves the body exists. And the closer the body gets, the clearer the shadow becomes.

The entire Old Testament is a shadow. Every bleeding lamb on every altar. Every high priest entering the Holy of Holies once a year with blood on his hands. Every morning and evening sacrifice laid on the altar at the third hour and the ninth hour. Every Passover lamb slaughtered without a broken bone. Every word of Isaiah 53, written seven centuries before Calvary, describing a servant who would be crushed for iniquity and pierced for transgression and led as a lamb to slaughter. All of it — every piece of it — was the shadow of the cross.

And when the cross came — when the Substance arrived — something extraordinary happened. Matthew records it in a single sentence that most people read past without understanding the magnitude of what it describes.

At the moment Jesus yielded up His spirit on the cross, the thick, impenetrable curtain that separated the Holy Place from the Most Holy Place in the Temple was torn in two — from the top to the bottom.

That curtain — the paroket in Hebrew, the katapetasma in Greek — had stood for over a thousand years as a physical reminder that sin separates humanity from a holy God. Only the High Priest could pass through it. Only once a year. Only with the blood of a substitute. And God tore it from the top to the bottom — not from the bottom up, which would suggest a human hand — but from the top down. The initiative came from heaven. The barrier was destroyed by God Himself the moment the final sacrifice was complete.

This was not God changing His mind about the Old Testament system. This was God declaring that the Old Testament system had perfectly accomplished what it was always designed to accomplish. The shadow had finished its job. The Substance had arrived. And there was no longer any need for what had only ever been preparation.

The God who demanded the blood of bulls and goats for a thousand years was the same God who then offered His own blood to make those offerings permanently unnecessary. The God of the Old Testament was not cruelty eventually replaced by grace. He was grace preparing humanity, through the vocabulary of sacrifice and substitution, to comprehend the magnitude of what He was about to do on a hill outside Jerusalem.

Jesus and the Same God

Jesus Christ did not leave this question unanswered. He addressed it directly, repeatedly, and with a clarity that should permanently close the case.

"For had ye believed Moses, ye would have believed me: for he wrote of me." — John 5:46 (KJV)

He was not gently suggesting a connection between Himself and the Old Testament. He was declaring absolute ownership. The God who gave Moses the Torah was the same God standing in front of them. If they had truly understood what Moses wrote, they would have recognized Him.

And in John 8, when the religious leaders challenged His identity and His authority, Jesus made the most staggering declaration in the entire Gospel. He did not offer a new name or a new identity. He reached back to the oldest, most sacred name in the Hebrew Scriptures — the name God declared from the burning bush on the mountain of God:

"I AM THAT I AM." — Exodus 3:14 (KJV)

When Jesus said "Before Abraham was, I am," He did not use the past tense. He did not claim mere pre-existence. He used the Greek phrase ego eimi — the absolute, timeless formula that every Jewish ear in that room would have immediately recognized as the divine name of Exodus 3:14. He was not saying: I existed before Abraham. He was saying: I am the God who spoke to Moses. I am the burning-bush God. I am the I AM. The religious leaders understood immediately and picked up stones to execute Him for blasphemy — because they knew exactly what He was claiming. Jesus of Nazareth was publicly, deliberately, and unambiguously identifying Himself as the same God who had been speaking through every page of the Old Testament from the very beginning.

"Think not that I am come to destroy the law, or the prophets: I am not come to destroy, but to fulfil." — Matthew 5:17 (KJV)

The Greek word translated "fulfil" is pleroo — to fill to the brim, to complete, to bring to its fullness. Jesus did not come to abolish what God had established in the Old Testament. He came to fill it with the three-dimensional reality that the two-dimensional shadow had always been pointing toward.

When He said "Ye have heard that it was said by them of old time... But I say unto you," He was not correcting the Old Testament God. He was the Old Testament God. He was correcting the shallow, external, legalistic interpretations that the Pharisees had layered over the

Law and rescuing the Law's original, internal intent — an intent He had written into it from the beginning. The Law had always been about the heart. The Pharisees had reduced it to the hands.

There is only one God in this story. He has always been the same. What changed between the Testaments was not His character. What changed was the clarity with which He could reveal it — because for the first time, the shadow was no longer necessary. The Substance had arrived.

The New Vocabulary of Love

There is something that has stayed with me through years of studying this question: when Jesus walked, something happened to the concept of love itself. Something for which the ancient world had no adequate words and which the ancient world, encountering it, did not at first know what to do with. The linguistic evidence confirms it with a precision that should stop every reader cold.

The ancient Greek language had multiple words for love. There was storge — the natural affection between family members. There was eros — romantic, passionate desire (significantly, the New Testament never uses this word, because its cultural associations were too corrupted to carry what God needed to say). And there was philia — the warm, mutual friendship between people who find each other pleasant and beneficial.

None of these were adequate. None of them could hold the weight of a God who would leave the throne of heaven, put on human flesh, walk through betrayal and abandonment and torture without defending Himself, and then ask the Father to forgive the people who were killing Him while they were still doing it.

So the early church reached for a Greek word that had been lying mostly dormant, barely used in secular literature — a colorless, nearly blank word — and they filled it with the bleeding reality of the cross.

That word was agape.

R.C. Trench, in his landmark work Synonyms of the New Testament, states a fact about this word that is almost impossible to overstate: there is no trace of agape in any heathen Greek writer whatever. It was born within the bosom of revealed religion. It was not borrowed from the culture. It was not adapted from an existing concept of love. It was a word that effectively did not exist until the reality of Jesus Christ required it.

Agape is not love drawn out by the excellence of the one being loved. Agape does not require the object to be attractive, worthy, or deserving. Agape flows entirely from the nature of the One doing the loving. It is love directed toward the unlovely. Love extended toward the hostile. Love that acts in behalf of the enemy, the stranger, the one who has nothing to offer in return.

"Herein is love, not that we loved God, but that he loved us, and sent his Son to be the propitiation for our sins." — 1 John 4:10 (KJV)

This is agape — love that flows entirely from the character of the Giver, never from the worthiness of the recipient. And this love — this agape that had no name before Jesus walked — was not invented at the Incarnation. It was revealed at the Incarnation. The God who expressed rachuwm (maternal womb-compassion) for Israel in the wilderness, who declared chesed over His people 249 times, who waited four hundred years for a sinful people group before moving in judgment, who ran to embrace a repentant Nineveh — that God had always been an agape God. He was simply waiting for a vocabulary adequate to describe it fully. And when the Word became flesh and dwelt among us, the vocabulary arrived.

Jesus told a story that carries agape in every sentence.

A father has two sons. The younger demands his inheritance early — which in the culture of that day was essentially telling his father he wished he were already dead. He takes the money, travels to a far country, and wastes every penny in reckless living until he is reduced to feeding pigs and envying what they eat.

And then he comes to himself, and he turns toward home.

"But when he was yet a great way off, his father saw him, and had compassion, and ran, and fell on his neck, and kissed him." — Luke 15:20 (KJV)

The Greek word translated "had compassion" in that verse is splagchnizomai. It is derived from the word for the intestines, the bowels, the inward parts of the body — the place where in ancient Greek understanding the most violent, gut-wrenching emotions resided. Jesus is attributing to God the Father a love so deep it is felt in the physical center of the body. A love that moves before reason does. A love that cannot see its child at a great way off without already beginning to run.

And the father runs. In first-century Middle Eastern culture, a respected patriarch never ran. To hike up his robes and sprint down a road was an act of profound social humiliation. Augustine, meditating on this parable, observed that the Father was heedless of his own dignity. The God who created the universe set aside His dignity to sprint through the dust toward a child who had squandered everything He gave him.

That Father was always there. In the Old Testament, in the wilderness, in the captivity, in the centuries of prophetic warning, in the patience of a God who waited four hundred years. The running did not begin with the New Testament. The running has never stopped.

Mercy Hiding in Plain Sight

If a person reads the Old Testament looking only for its severity, they will find it. If they read it looking for its mercy, they will find something that will make their theology fundamentally larger.

Consider Hagar. She was an Egyptian slave — not a Hebrew, not a member of the covenant people, without standing before any court in the ancient world, without a name that any god of the ancient Near East would have paused to remember. She was used by Abraham and Sarah to provide an heir when faith in God's promise faltered. When Sarah's jealousy ignited, Hagar was cast out — driven into the wilderness of Beersheba with her son Ishmael and provisions that would not last more than a day. In a world where gods cared only for their chosen kings and their chosen people, no one would have expected what happened next.

God heard her cry.

Not the cry of Abraham, the covenant patriarch. Not the cry of Sarah, the mother of promise. The cry of the Egyptian slave woman that God's own people had thrown into the desert to die.

He opened her eyes to a well of water she had not seen. He spoke to her personally. He promised to make a great nation from the son that His own people had discarded. And then He told her something that no other person in all of Scripture ever did or was able to do in return.

She named Him.

"And she called the name of the LORD that spake unto her, Thou God seest me." — Genesis 16:13 (KJV)

El Roi. The God who sees. In the entire canon of Scripture — across every patriarch, every prophet, every king, every priest — Hagar is the only human being who ever gave God a name. Not because she was the most important figure in redemptive history. Because in a moment when she was the most invisible, the most discarded, the most utterly alone person in the ancient world — God found her. And she was so undone by the encounter that she had to name what she had just experienced. The God who sees. This is the Old Testament. This is the God His critics have not read carefully enough.

Consider David. He committed adultery with Bathsheba and then arranged the murder of her husband Uriah to cover it. Under the Mosaic Law, both crimes carried the same mandatory penalty: death. There was no prescribed animal sacrifice for deliberate, premeditated murder. There was no loophole. There was no exception clause.

Yet when the prophet Nathan confronted David and David responded with the simple, unguarded words "I have sinned against the LORD" — Nathan's immediate response was: "The LORD also hath put away thy sin; thou shalt not die."

God suspended the strict letter of the Law because He saw the genuine, shattered contrition in David's heart. The Law was the paidagogos — the strict disciplinarian. But the God behind the Law had always been the Father. And when the Father saw the heart of His child, the Father responded the way fathers respond to genuine repentance. With forgiveness that the Law never promised and that the child had no right to expect.

And then there is Nebuchadnezzar — not an Israelite, not a member of God's covenant people, but the king of Babylon. A man who had conquered Jerusalem, destroyed the Temple, and carried God's own people into exile in chains. A man whose pride was so absolute that God struck him with a form of divine madness — he was driven from among men, ate grass like an ox, and lived in the wilderness for seven years. If the God of the Old Testament were the calculating tyrant His critics describe, the exile of Nebuchadnezzar's mind would have been permanent.

Instead, God waited. He waited the full measure of what was required. And when Nebuchadnezzar's years in the wilderness had accomplished their work — when the man who had called himself the greatest king on earth finally lifted his eyes toward heaven — this is what came back:

"And at the end of the days I Nebuchadnezzar lifted up mine eyes unto heaven, and mine understanding returned unto me, and I blessed the most High, and I praised and honoured him that liveth for ever, whose dominion is an everlasting dominion, and his kingdom is from generation to generation." — Daniel 4:34 (KJV)

The conqueror of Jerusalem — the man whose armies had burned the house of God to the ground — lifted his eyes to heaven and was restored. This is the Old Testament God His critics have not read carefully enough. No soul was too far. No pride was too deep. No distance was too great. The moment Nebuchadnezzar looked up, God met him where he was.

The Old Testament is full of these moments. Full of them. The God who critics describe as the God of pure wrath is the same God who left a ram in the thicket so Abraham's son would not die. Who gave Joseph a dream to sustain him through thirteen years of slavery and imprisonment. Who fed Elijah under a juniper tree when he was suicidal with exhaustion. Who sent an angel to touch Daniel and call him "greatly beloved." Who let the sun stand still for Joshua, who shut the mouths of lions for Daniel, who parted a sea for Moses.

This is not the record of a harsh God. This is the record of a God who has been relentlessly, creatively, extravagantly merciful from the very beginning — and who was waiting, through every generation of human history, for the moment when He could finally reveal the full depth of that mercy in the person of Jesus Christ.

One Rescue Mission

When you put all of this together — divine immutability, progressive revelation, the paidagogos, the consistent pattern of warning, the chesed that never stopped, the agape that the cross finally named, the shadow and the substance, the ego eimi of Jesus declaring Himself the burning-bush God made flesh — the picture that emerges is not two

Gods, or a God who changed His mind, or a primitive deity eventually replaced by a more enlightened version.

The picture that emerges is one God. One love. One rescue mission.

"God, who at sundry times and in divers manners spake in time past unto the fathers by the prophets, hath in these last days spoken unto us by his Son." — Hebrews 1:1–2 (KJV)

The Greek behind "sundry times and in divers manners" is poly-merōs kai polytropōs — many partial fragments delivered in many different forms. That is what the Old Testament is. Not a different God speaking. The same God speaking — in the fragments and forms that the spiritual infancy of humanity could absorb at the time. And then, in the fullness of time, He spoke in the most complete, most direct, most undiluted way possible. He spoke in a Son.

The God who shouted over Sinai and the God who whispered "peace, be still" to a storm on a Galilean sea are the same God. The God who rained fire on Sodom and the God who said "neither do I condemn thee" to a woman dragged before Him in the act of adultery are the same God. The God who ordered the sacrifice of bulls and goats and the God who became the sacrifice are the same God.

He was not harsh and then kind. He was never harsh. He was a Father doing whatever was necessary — in every generation, at every cost to Himself — to keep the door open long enough for every soul He loved to find their way home.

"The LORD hath appeared of old unto me, saying, Yea, I have loved thee with an everlasting love: therefore with lovingkindness have I drawn thee." — Jeremiah 31:3 (KJV)

An everlasting love. Not a New Testament love. Not a love that began in Bethlehem. An everlasting love — spoken through the prophet Jeremiah, in the Old Testament, to a people in exile, surrounded by the consequences of their own rebellion. The same love. The same God.

The same unbreakable, centuries-deep, shadow-casting, cross-bound, resurrection-anchored love.

It was always there. It will never end.

My Reflection

I did not grow up reading the Old Testament with suspicion. I grew up reading it with longing.

I have sometimes wished I could have lived in the Old Testament times. Not in any romanticized way — I understand that the ancient world was brutal and the margin for survival was thin and the theological clarity we have today did not exist in the same form. But there is something in me that has always been drawn to the rawness of those encounters. The burning bush. The still small voice to Elijah. The whirlwind that spoke to Job. The moments where God showed up without ceremony and without filter and changed the entire trajectory of a human life in a single conversation.

I think the people of the Old Testament knew something about that. The men and women whose stories we read from a distance — they were not reading stories. They were living them. They were in the wilderness, without a completed Bible, without two thousand years of church history to lean on, without the full revelation of a God who had not yet taken human form. And they held on anyway. They held on to what they had. And what they had — even in fragments, even in shadows, even through the disciplinary framework of a paidagogos — was enough. Because what they had was Him.

I do not believe God was harder in the Old Testament. I believe the world was harder in the Old Testament. And God met it where it was, with what it needed, at the cost that would be required. Just as He meets every soul in exactly the season and the form that the soul's particular darkness requires.

He does not change. That is not a theological abstraction. That is one of the most stabilizing truths I have ever held. The God I called out to in that hospital was the same God who called out to Abraham, who spoke to Moses, who wept over Jerusalem, who walked out of a garden tomb on a Sunday morning. He did not suddenly become more available in the New Testament. He has always been available. He has always been present. He has always been exactly what every broken, confused, questioning human soul needed Him to be.

And He has always been running down the road before we were close enough to see the house.

If you have been spiritually wounded by the Old Testament — if the harsh passages have built a wall between you and the God you want to believe in — I want to ask you to try something. Not a theological exercise. Not a study project. Just a quiet, honest request.

Ask Him to show you who He actually is. Not who the critics say He is. Not who the harshest passages seem to suggest He is when read in isolation from everything else. Ask Him directly. He has never been afraid of the question. He has been waiting for it.

And He already has the answer.

A Prayer for the Reader

Father —

We come to the end of this chapter carrying something heavier than a theological question. We carry wounds. We carry years of reading passages that confused us and frightened us and made us wonder whether the God we wanted to trust was the same God we found on those pages.

For the person who has walked away from the Old Testament and refused to go back — meet them in that refusal. Do not shame it. Understand it. And in Your patience and Your mercy, draw them gently back into the story they have been trying to avoid. Let them see what is actually there. Not a harsh God waiting to condemn. A Father who spent thousands of years doing whatever was necessary to keep the door open long enough for His children to find their way home.

For the person who is angry at the Old Testament passages they cannot reconcile — remind them that their anger at injustice is not an obstacle to faith. It is a reflection of Your own image inside them. The same righteous anger that they feel at the suffering of the innocent is a shadow of the love that drove You to the cross to end it permanently.

For the person who has been told that Jesus corrected or replaced the God of the Old Testament — let the weight of His own words settle into their spirit. I AM THAT I AM. He was not offering an alternative. He was revealing the fullness of what had always been there.

For the person who has experienced something devastating and who is asking whether the God they are addressing today is the same God who allowed the harsh things they have read in Scripture — yes. He is the same God. And He is also the God who ran down the road, who tore the veil from top to bottom, who left the grave empty. He has been all of those things at the same time. He always will be.

For all of us — let this truth become a foundation, not a conclusion. Let it be the beginning of a deeper reading, a longer conversation, a more honest pursuit of the One who has never been hiding and has never been other than He has always declared Himself to be.

Loving. Gracious. Longsuffering. Abundant in goodness and truth. The same yesterday, today, and forever.

In the name of the Father, the Son, and the Holy Spirit.

Amen.

"For I am the LORD, I change not." — Malachi 3:6 (KJV)

Chapter Seven

Has Science Disproved God?

"The heavens declare the glory of God; and the firmament sheweth his handywork." — Psalm 19:1 (KJV)

The Question

It arrives in different forms, but it always carries the same weight.

Sometimes it comes from a college freshman who has just taken their first biology course and been told that Darwin's theory of evolution has made the Genesis account of creation scientifically obsolete. Sometimes it comes from a man in his fifties who has spent a lifetime quietly believing, only to read a headline declaring that physicists have now mapped the origin of the universe without needing a God to explain it. Sometimes it comes from a teenager who has been mocked in class for believing the Bible, with no theological training to defend what they feel but cannot articulate.

Has science disproved God?

It is one of the defining questions of the modern era. And it deserves an answer that takes both the science and the faith seriously — not one that dismisses the scientific evidence, and not one that surrenders the faith to avoid an argument.

Here is the answer this chapter will build, piece by piece, until the evidence is undeniable: No. Science has not disproved God. In fact, the more deeply science has probed the microscopic engines of the living cell, the macro-architecture of the cosmos, and the ancient dirt of the biblical lands, the more the illusion of a Godless universe has collapsed. The scientists who set out to bury God have been returning, one after another, with shovels in their hands and astonishment on their faces — not because they found an empty grave, but because they found fingerprints everywhere they dug.

That is not a theological claim. That is a pattern. And it is a pattern that the evidence demands we examine honestly.

The War That Was Invented

Before we examine the evidence, we need to dismantle a myth. Because the most powerful weapon in the arsenal of those who claim science has disproved God is not a scientific discovery at all. It is a historical narrative. And that narrative is false.

The idea that science and the Christian faith have always been locked in a perpetual, zero-sum war — that enlightened scientists have spent centuries battling oppressive, anti-intellectual theologians — did not emerge from actual history. It was deliberately manufactured in the second half of the nineteenth century by two men: John William Draper, who published a book in 1874 titled History of the Conflict Between Religion and Science, and Andrew Dickson White, whose 1896 book A History of the Warfare of Science with Theology in Christendom weaponized the Galileo affair and the Darwinian controversies to argue that science and faith were fundamentally incompatible.

Modern historians of science have completely dismantled this conflict thesis. It is not a disputed finding on the fringes of academic debate — it is the settled consensus of the field. The relationship between science and the Christian faith across history has been predominantly one of mutual support, not combat. The supposed war was a rhetorical smokescreen designed to smuggle an atheistic philosophy into the culture under the guise of objective science.

The most powerful proof of this is not an argument. It is a list of names.

Galileo Galilei, the father of observational astronomy, was a devout believer who declared that God endowed us with sense, reason, and intellect and clearly intended us to use them. Johannes Kepler, who discovered the laws of planetary motion, described his scientific work as simply thinking God's thoughts after Him. Sir Isaac Newton, who formulated the laws of gravity and motion, wrote more on biblical theology than he ever did on physics and declared that the magnificent system of the sun, planets, and comets could only proceed from the counsel of an intelligent and powerful Being. James Clerk Maxwell, the genius who unified electricity and magnetism, built his entire scientific framework on a deep, settled Christian faith. Gregor Mendel, the undisputed father of modern genetics, was an Augustinian monk who conducted his revolutionary experiments in the garden of his monastery.

These are not peripheral figures in the history of science. They are its founders. And not one of them experienced their scientific discoveries as a threat to their faith. Every single one of them experienced their discoveries as an act of worship — as the breathtaking privilege of tracing the blueprints of the Divine Architect.

Alister McGrath holds Oxford doctorates in both molecular biophysics and Christian theology. He did not begin his academic life as a believer. He began it as a committed Marxist atheist, convinced that the natural sciences had rendered God unnecessary and that rational people had moved beyond religion. His journey from that position to orthodox Christian faith was not the result of an emotional crisis or a sudden supernatural experience. It was the result of following scientific inquiry to its honest conclusion.

As McGrath immersed himself in the intricacies of molecular biophysics at Oxford, he found that atheism offered a severely impoverished framework for explaining what he was observing. The elegance of the natural order, the mathematical intelligibility of the universe, the fact that human minds shaped by blind evolutionary processes could somehow perceive and describe the deep structure of reality — none of it fit comfortably inside a worldview that reduced everything to accident. McGrath concluded that the Christian doctrine of creation provided the only adequate explanatory framework: the universe is rationally ordered and humanly comprehensible because both the ordering mind and the comprehending mind were designed by the same rational Creator. Science was not the enemy of theology. Far from being enemies, they are reading the same book of reality from two necessary and complementary strata — the natural sciences addressing the creation, theology addressing the Creator known through that creation.

The war was invented. The evidence was always on the same side.

In the Beginning God Created

The opening sentence of the Bible is not an introduction. It is a declaration of war against every false cosmology the ancient world had produced — and, as it turns out, against every false cosmology the modern world has produced as well.

"In the beginning God created the heaven and the earth." — Genesis 1:1 (KJV)

To understand what that sentence actually claims, you have to go beneath the English and examine the Hebrew words that carry the weight of it.

The word translated created is bara. In the entire Old Testament, this verb is never used with a human subject. Not once. A carpenter can make a table. A potter can form a vessel. A builder can assemble a structure. But only God can bara. The word denotes the bringing into existence of something entirely new, entirely unprecedented, and entirely without pre-existing material. Theologians call this creatio ex nihilo — creation out of nothing. God did not rearrange existing matter. He did not organize an eternal universe that had always been there. He spoke existence itself into being from the absolute void of non-existence.

To feel the full weight of bara, compare it to two other Hebrew words for making. The word asah means to make or manufacture out of already existing material. The word yatsar means to form or mold, as a potter presses wet clay into a specific shape. Both asah and yatsar describe what creatures do with what already exists. Bara describes what only God can do: originate.

This single linguistic distinction permanently destroys the atheist's most comfortable assumption. The assumption is that matter has always existed in some form, that the universe is self-explanatory, and that God is at best a hypothesis for explaining what science has not yet figured out. Genesis 1:1, in its original Hebrew, refuses that assumption completely. The universe is not eternal. Matter is not self-originating. Time itself had a beginning. And the One who initiated that beginning was not constrained by the laws of physics because He authored the laws of physics. He was not working with existing material because the existing material was what His voice produced.

This understanding of God as the originating, rational source of all creation was not unique to the Hebrew prophets. Among the wisdom writings preserved in the Septuagint — the Greek translation of the Hebrew Scriptures revered by the early church — the book of Sirach, also known as Ecclesiasticus, contains one of the most remarkable hymns to God as Creator in all of ancient literature. Written by a Jewish sage in the second century before Christ and preserved intact through the centuries, it declares:

"I will now call to mind the works of the Lord, and will declare the things that I have seen: in the words of the Lord are his works... He beholds the whole world, and perceives the ends of the earth. Who can say enough in his praise? He is greater than all his works." — Sirach 42:15, 43:28 (Apocrypha, Septuagint, c. 180 BC)

The Septuagint communities understood what the Hebrew bara declared: creation is not an accident to be investigated in isolation from its Creator. It is a word — spoken by a Person who is greater than everything He made, and who embedded within His creation the precise testimony required for honest investigators to find their way back to Him. The heavens were always declaring. The question in every generation has only ever been whether anyone was listening.

Augustine of Hippo grasped this with remarkable precision in the fifth century. He recognized that time itself requires movement and transition, and that therefore God did not create the universe after spaces of time had elapsed. There was no "before" the creation because before is a temporal concept, and time was part of what was created. The world was made, Augustine concluded, not in time but simultaneously with time. The verse declares this in its Hebrew structure: Bereshit, the creation of time. Hashamayim, the creation of space. Ha'aretz, the creation of matter. All three, simultaneously, from nothing, by a voice.

Modern cosmology, through Einstein's General Relativity and the implications of Big Bang physics, confirmed this exact architecture fifteen centuries after Augustine described it. Space, time, and matter are not independent entities. They are inextricably linked in a single continuum called spacetime. You cannot have matter without space. You cannot have space without time. They had to come into existence simultaneously. The biblical text declared this reality before science had the mathematics to describe it — not because the biblical writers were scientists, but because the One who spoke it into existence also inspired the account of it.

The Mountain and the Theologians

For most of modern history, the most powerful argument against the existence of God was the assumption that the universe had always existed. An eternal universe needs no Creator. If matter and energy have simply always been here, the question of what caused them becomes unnecessary. This was not merely a convenient assumption; it was the scientific establishment's preferred position, held with something approaching religious devotion.

That position was permanently destroyed in the twentieth century — not by theologians, but by physicists.

The discovery of the expanding universe by Edwin Hubble, and the subsequent development of Big Bang cosmology, forced science to confront a reality it had spent decades trying to avoid: the universe had a beginning. Not a rearrangement of existing matter. Not a new phase of an eternal cycle. A beginning — a moment before which there was literally nothing, and after which there was everything. The entire physical universe — all matter, all energy, all space, and time itself — came into existence in a single, sudden, incomprehensible explosion of light and energy.

The theological implication is inescapable. Whatever begins to exist has a cause. The universe began to exist. Therefore the universe has a cause. And because that cause must exist outside of time, space, and matter — since it is the cause of time, space, and matter — it must be timeless, spaceless, immaterial, uncaused, and unimaginably powerful. Furthermore, because a purely mechanical, impersonal cause would automatically produce its effect from eternity, the only way to explain a universe with a chosen beginning is a Personal Agent endowed with free will who deliberately initiated the act of creation. The philosopher William Lane Craig calls this the Kalam Cosmological Argument. Its three premises are devastatingly simple. Every step of the logic is sound. Every step of the physics confirms the second premise. And the conclusion points directly at the God of Genesis 1:1.

No one captured the weight of this moment more honestly than Dr. Robert Jastrow — the founder of NASA's Goddard Institute for Space Studies and a self-described agnostic who had no theological agenda and every professional incentive to avoid this conclusion. In his book God and the Astronomers, Jastrow described the profound crisis that Big Bang cosmology produced in the scientific community. Scientists, he observed, carry a deep faith of their own — the conviction that every event in nature can be explained rationally as the product of a prior natural event. The Big Bang shattered that faith completely, because it proved the universe began under conditions where the known laws of physics break down entirely, driven by forces science cannot investigate or describe. Jastrow concluded that the rational scientist, having spent a lifetime scaling the mountains of inquiry, pulls himself over the final rock at the summit of the universe's origin — and finds the theologians already seated there, having arrived centuries before. An agnostic NASA astronomer acknowledged that modern astrophysics had climbed to the summit of cosmic origins and found Genesis 1:1 waiting at the top.

The Fine-Tuned Universe

The discovery that the universe had a beginning was only the first piece of evidence. The second was, if anything, more devastating to the case for a Godless cosmos.

As physicists began to map the fundamental constants of the universe — the strength of gravity, the strong nuclear force, the cosmological constant, the ratio of the proton to electron mass — they made a discovery that has never been adequately explained by any atheistic framework. Every single one of these constants is calibrated with a precision so extreme that it defies any reasonable probability of accident.

If the gravitational constant were slightly stronger, stars would burn too quickly for life to develop. If it were slightly weaker, they would never ignite at all. If the strong nuclear force were fractionally different, atoms themselves would be impossible. If the cosmological constant were adjusted by even one part in ten to the power of one hundred and twenty, the universe would either collapse back on itself or expand too rapidly for galaxies, stars, or planets to ever form.

Stephen Hawking — not a man inclined toward theological concession — acknowledged the weight of this evidence directly. He wrote that these fundamental constants appear to have been adjusted with extraordinary precision to permit the development of life, and that it would be exceedingly difficult to account for why the universe began in exactly this configuration by any means other than the deliberate act of a God who intended to produce beings capable of knowing Him. The acknowledgment came from one of the most brilliant and most publicly skeptical scientific minds of the twentieth century. The fine-tuning demanded a response. He gave it.

Oxford physicist Roger Penrose calculated the odds of the universe's initial low-entropy state occurring by chance. His answer was one in ten to the power of ten to the power of one hundred and twenty-three. That number is so incomprehensibly small that it is mathematically indistinguishable from zero. It does not represent improbability. It represents impossibility.

And then there is Sir Fred Hoyle. He coined the term Big Bang — originally as a term of mockery, designed to ridicule the idea of a universe with a sudden beginning. He spent his career as a committed atheist. And then he discovered something about carbon. Carbon is the building block of all biological life. For carbon to exist in the quantities necessary for life, the nuclear resonance of the carbon atom must be calibrated to an almost impossibly precise level. When Hoyle calculated this resonance, he found it sitting at exactly the right value. The mathematical precision was so staggering that Hoyle publicly abandoned his atheism. He declared that the evidence pointed unmistakably to a superintelligence having arranged the physics of the universe with deliberate precision. The man who named the Big Bang as a joke ended his career acknowledging the Maker.

To escape the crushing weight of this evidence, some scientists have proposed the multiverse theory — the idea that an infinite number of random universes bubble into existence, and we simply happen to live in the one that won the cosmic lottery. But the multiverse is not a scientific theory. It is a philosophical escape hatch. These alternate universes are, by definition, impossible to detect, impossible to measure, and impossible to test. The multiverse is not science. It is metaphysical blind faith, requiring belief in infinite unobservable realities for the sole purpose of avoiding the conclusion that this one was designed.

The universe we live in — the one we can measure, the one that exists — bears every mark of intentional, precise, purposeful creation. As the Psalmist declared three thousand years before the invention of the radio telescope: the heavens are declaring something. The Hebrew word translated declare is saphar — not a word for casual announcement, but a mathematical, technical term meaning to enumerate, inscribe, or count exactly. It is the root from which the Hebrew word for book is derived. And the word translated glory is kabod, whose literal root meaning is heavy, weight, mass, gravity. David was not writing a poem. He was making a cosmological statement: the physical universe is mathematically enumerating the infinite mass and gravity of its Creator. Three millennia before Hawking and Penrose, a shepherd-king described precisely what they would spend their careers measuring.

The Language of God

If the cosmos points to a Creator, the cell shouts His name.

When Charles Darwin published On the Origin of Species in 1859, the living cell was assumed to be a simple blob of protoplasm — a microscopic droplet of organic material that could plausibly have assembled itself from the chemical soup of the early earth. Darwin himself acknowledged that his theory would absolutely break down if it could be demonstrated that any complex organ existed which could not have been formed by numerous, successive, slight modifications. He offered that as a hypothetical challenge. The twenty-first century answered it.

Dr. Francis Collins began his career as an atheist. He was one of the most accomplished geneticists of his generation, and when he was chosen to lead the Human Genome Project — the international effort to map the complete chemical sequence of human DNA — he brought no religious agenda to the work. What he brought was a commitment to following the evidence wherever it led. What he found changed everything.

The human genome contains 3.1 billion letters of chemical code. It is not a random sequence. It is not a pattern. It is a message — a highly specific, intricately structured, functional instruction manual that tells the living cell how to build every protein, regulate every biological process, and maintain the staggering complexity of a human body through every moment of its existence. Collins concluded that this code is the language of God — not metaphorically, but literally: an information-bearing system of this complexity requires an intelligent source, and the intelligence required to write 3.1 billion letters of functional biological code exceeds anything the natural world can produce unguided.

The scientist Hubert Yockey stated the critical distinction with precision: the relationship between DNA and a written text is not one of surface resemblance or loose analogy. DNA does not merely resemble a message in the way a river pattern resembles a painting. DNA functions as a message in the full, technical, information-theoretical sense of the term. A river creates patterns through natural forces, and those patterns carry no information. A code — a system in which specific sequences of symbols carry specific functional meaning — is categorically different. And DNA is a code.

Information theory has established one foundational law from which there are no known exceptions: specified complexity — functional, semantic information — never arises from random, unguided processes. Not sometimes. Not rarely. Never. Every piece of specified information ever observed by science has a single type of source: an intelligent mind. DNA is a code. Codes require a Coder.

What is remarkable is that this instinct — to read the created order as the deliberate inscription of an intelligent mind — was not a modern theological invention. Among the Dead Sea Scrolls discovered at Qumran is a text known to scholars as 4QInstruction (4Q418), a wisdom document in which the community instructs its members to study the mystery of existence embedded in the created order. The text calls the community to examine what has been engraved in the foundations of creation — the hidden intelligence inscribed into the structure of the natural world — as both an intellectual obligation and an act of worship. The Qumran community believed, centuries before the invention of the microscope, that the physical world had been written. That what appeared to be mere matter was, on careful examination, a text with an Author. Modern molecular biology did not discover this idea. It confirmed it.

Biochemist Michael Behe took this argument into the machinery of the cell itself. He introduced the concept of irreducible complexity: a system composed of multiple interacting parts in which the removal of any single part causes the entire system to stop functioning completely. The bacterial flagellum — a microscopic rotary motor attached to a bacterium, complete with rotor, stator, drive shaft, and propeller, all constructed from precisely arranged proteins — is exactly such a system. Remove any single protein component and the motor does not work at reduced efficiency. It does not work at all.

Darwin's mechanism of natural selection only preserves traits that provide an immediate survival advantage. An incomplete flagellum provides zero survival advantage. Natural selection would discard every partial step immediately. The only way to build an irreducibly complex system is to assemble all of its parts simultaneously toward a functional goal — and the only force in the universe capable of coordinating non-functioning parts toward a future functional goal is an intelligent mind that can envision the finished product before the first piece is in place. The engines inside our cells are the fingerprints of a Divine Engineer who designed the end before He laid the foundation.

There is one more detail worth pausing on. When researchers measured the physical dimensions of the DNA double helix, they found it measures 34 angstroms long by 21 angstroms wide. The ratio of those two numbers is 1.619 — astonishingly close to the Golden Ratio, the mathematical proportion that appears throughout nature in the spiral of a nautilus shell, the branching of a tree, and the proportions of the human face. The Master Designer did not merely write the code of life. He signed it.

And within that code, something remarkable operates that is worth understanding clearly. The genome contains built-in mechanisms for adaptive variation — the capacity for living creatures to adjust to changing environments while remaining entirely within the boundaries of their created kind. In Genesis 1, God commands the earth to bring forth living creatures after their kind. The Hebrew word is min — a biological boundary God established that creatures can adapt within but cannot cross. A dog can produce enormous variety within its kind. Bacteria can develop resistance to antibiotics. Human populations carry genetic diversity suited to different climates. But a fish does not become a reptile. A reptile does not become a bird. The boundaries of the min hold, in the fossil record and in the observable present, without exception.

This adaptive capacity is not evidence of blind, random mutation. It is evidence of brilliant pre-engineering. A static organism with no genetic flexibility would go extinct at the first environmental shift. God built into the genome a vast reservoir of latent genetic information that can be activated or deactivated in response to environmental pressure. Adaptation is not an accident. It is a feature. It is the genius of a Designer who built survivability into the very architecture of life before the first environment ever changed.

The Brain That Cannot Trust Itself

Before we move to the archaeological evidence, there is one more argument that deserves its full weight. It comes not from a laboratory or an excavation site but from pure philosophical reasoning. And it may be the most devastating blow to atheistic naturalism ever delivered.

C.S. Lewis identified it with the precision of a surgeon finding the single point of failure in a complex system. Atheistic naturalism claims that the physical universe is all there is, and that human beings — including our brains and our thoughts — are nothing but the accidental by-products of blind, irrational, purposeless physical forces. On this view, the human mind is simply what happens when unguided chemistry reaches a certain level of complexity.

Lewis pointed out the fatal contradiction hiding inside that claim.

If the human mind is purely the product of irrational, unguided processes — if there is no Designer who shaped the brain to perceive truth, no rational Logos who structured the universe to be comprehensible, no intended correspondence between the mind that thinks and the reality it thinks about — then what possible basis do we have for trusting the conclusions of that mind? An accidental brain was not designed to find truth. It was shaped by survival pressures to produce behaviors that kept the organism alive long enough to reproduce. There is no guarantee — and no logical reason to expect — that a brain built by blind evolution would produce accurate beliefs about the deep structure of reality rather than merely useful ones.

Lewis observed that trusting the output of an accidental brain is no more rational than trusting the time displayed on a clock assembled by a tornado. The instrument was not designed for the purpose you are relying on it for.

Here is the irony that is almost too sharp to look at directly. The atheist uses scientific reasoning to argue against God. But scientific reasoning requires that we trust the human mind's capacity to perceive reality accurately. And the only philosophical framework that gives us a reason to trust the human mind is the one the atheist is rejecting: the belief that a rational Creator designed both the rational universe and the rational mind that investigates it. Naturalism defeats itself. The atheist borrows the epistemological furniture of the Christian worldview to argue against the Christian worldview, entirely unaware that without the worldview, the furniture collapses beneath the argument.

The universe is rationally ordered. The human mind is capable of perceiving that rational order. The correspondence between the two is not an accident. It is the signature of a single, rational, intelligent Author who designed the investigating mind and the investigated reality at the same time, for the same purpose: that the creature would know the Creator through the creation.

"For the invisible things of him from the creation of the world are clearly seen, being understood by the things that are made, even his eternal power and Godhead; so that they are without excuse." — Romans 1:20 (KJV)

God engineered the visible world to point the honest investigating mind toward the invisible reality behind it. Modern science, at its most rigorous and most honest, has been doing exactly that. The problem has never been a shortage of evidence. The problem has been a shortage of willingness to follow it to its destination.

The Earth Speaks

The cosmos points to a Creator. The cell shouts His name. And the ground beneath our feet has been quietly confirming His Word for over a century.

In the nineteenth century, the dominant position among academic historians was that the New Testament was largely mythological — a collection of legends and theological inventions assembled well after the events it claimed to describe. This view was held with considerable confidence by scholars trained in the German historical school, whose skepticism toward the biblical text had become, in certain academic circles, the intellectually respectable default position.

Sir William Ramsay was one of those scholars. Born in 1851, educated at Aberdeen, Oxford, and Göttingen, he was one of the most eminent archaeologists of his era and a committed skeptic of the biblical record. He was firmly convinced that the Book of Acts was a fabrication of the mid-second century — not a first-century historical document but a later theological invention. He entered his archaeological work in Asia Minor with a mind, as he put it himself, unfavourable to the biblical account.

His own spade destroyed that position.

As Ramsay excavated the ancient cities and trade routes of Asia Minor, he found himself repeatedly confronted with the same uncomfortable reality: Luke's geographical, political, and societal references were astoundingly accurate. Luke correctly identified the civic assembly meeting in a theater in Ephesus. He correctly named Erastus as the city treasurer in Corinth — a detail confirmed in 1929 when archaeologists uncovered a pavement inscription reading: Erastus, curator of public buildings, laid this pavement at his own expense. Luke named thirty-two countries, fifty-four cities, and nine islands across his two-volume account, and he got every single one of them right. After thirty years of meticulous excavation, Ramsay published his conclusion: Luke is a historian of the first rank — this author should be placed along with the very greatest of historians. The man who set out to disprove the New Testament became one of its most formidable defenders. Not because he changed his standards. Because the evidence met them.

The pattern Ramsay represents has repeated itself across every discipline of biblical archaeology. For decades, critical scholars insisted that King David was a legendary figure with no basis in verifiable history. In 1993, archaeologist Avraham Biran excavating at Tel Dan in northern Israel uncovered a ninth-century basalt victory stele explicitly referencing the House of David. The legend was a king. The myth was a man.

In 1961, at Caesarea Maritima, archaeologists uncovered a limestone block inscribed in Latin: Pontius Pilate, Prefect of Judea. The Roman official who condemned Jesus to death, confirmed in stone. In 1990, construction workers in Jerusalem accidentally uncovered a first-century tomb containing an ornate limestone ossuary inscribed in Aramaic: Yehosef bar Qafa — Joseph, son of Caiaphas. The burial box of the High Priest who presided over the trial of Jesus was sitting in the ground beneath Jerusalem, waiting.

And while stone and bone were confirming the people of the biblical record, the ancient manuscripts were confirming the text itself. In 1947, a Bedouin shepherd stumbled upon a series of caves near the Dead Sea at a site called Qumran. What he found inside those caves would become one of the most significant archaeological discoveries in human history: the Dead Sea Scrolls. Among them was the Great Isaiah Scroll — a complete manuscript of the book of Isaiah dated to approximately 125 B.C., making it over a thousand years older than any previously known manuscript of the Hebrew Scriptures. When scholars compared the Great Isaiah Scroll against the Masoretic

Text — the Hebrew manuscript tradition used to translate modern Bibles, which dated to approximately A.D. 1000 — they found word-for-word identity in over ninety-five percent of the text. The remaining five percent consisted almost entirely of minor spelling variations and obvious scribal slips that carried no doctrinal or historical weight whatsoever. Scholars examined Isaiah 53 specifically — the great Messianic chapter describing a suffering servant who was wounded for our transgressions and bruised for our iniquities, written seven centuries before the birth of Christ. Of the one hundred and sixty-six words in that chapter, not a single word affected any point of doctrine or history across a thousand years of hand-copying. The Bible that believers hold today is the same Bible that was in circulation before the birth of Jesus. The scribes who copied it were not rewriting it. They were preserving it with a fidelity that no other ancient document in human history can match.

And then there is Tall el-Hammam. In the Jordan Valley, northeast of the Dead Sea, archaeologists excavating a massive Middle Bronze Age city found evidence of what happened there around 1650 B.C. A 2021 peer-reviewed study published in Scientific Reports documented the findings: defensive walls sheared off their foundations, pottery melted into glass at temperatures exceeding 3,600 degrees Fahrenheit, trinitite — the same glassy material produced at the Trinity atomic bomb test site — shocked quartz that only forms under extreme instantaneous pressure, human remains blown apart and severely burned, and salt contamination from the partially vaporized Dead Sea that rendered the entire valley barren for six hundred years. No earthquake produces these temperatures. No human army of the ancient world generated 3,600 degrees of instantaneous heat. Lead archaeologist Dr. Steven Collins argues the geographical indicators, chronological timeframe, and method of destruction precisely match the Genesis account of Sodom and Gomorrah. Scholarly debate about the specific identification continues, as honest scholarship requires. But the physical mechanics of what happened at that site match the biblical description with a precision that cannot be dismissed.

Dr. Nelson Glueck, one of the most eminent biblical archaeologists of the twentieth century, stated the pattern categorically: no archaeological discovery has ever controverted a biblical reference. Not one. In two centuries of modern archaeological investigation, with every incentive to find the exception, not a single discovery has succeeded in disproving a properly understood biblical statement. The ground keeps confirming the Word. The pattern holds without exception.

The Word That Holds Everything Together

John's Gospel opens with one of the most intellectually audacious sentences ever written. In the beginning was the Word — and the Greek term John uses for Word is Logos.

That word choice was not accidental. It was a deliberate, brilliant act of theological capture.

In the ancient Greek philosophical tradition, originating with Heraclitus and developed by the Stoics and Platonists, the Logos was the organizing, rational principle of the cosmos. The Greek philosophers looked at the universe — the predictable movement of the stars, the mathematical regularity of the seasons, the consistent laws governing physical reality — and concluded that an impersonal divine Reason permeated and ordered everything, preventing the cosmos from descending into chaos. For the Greeks, the Logos was a force, an equation, a transcendent rationality. It was the closest the secular philosophical mind had ever come to describing the God of the Bible without knowing it.

John took that concept — the highest intellectual achievement of Greek rational inquiry — and delivered it to its proper destination. He told the Greek philosophers: you are right. There is a rational, mathematical, ordering principle holding the universe together. The laws of physics are consistent because something sustains them. The universe is intelligible because something made it so. But that something is not a blind equation or an impersonal force. He is a Person. And He just pitched His tent among us.

The opening of John's Gospel declares that in the beginning was the Word, and the Word was with God, and the Word was God — and that all things were made by Him, and without Him not anything was made that was made. This is not poetic introduction. It is a cosmological claim: the rational ordering principle the Greek philosophers had been reaching for without the revelation to find was not a force. He was a Person. And He is the same I AM who spoke from the burning bush, the same Creator whose bara brought spacetime into existence from absolute nothing.

"Who being the brightness of his glory, and the express image of his person, and upholding all things by the word of his power." — Hebrews 1:3 (KJV)

Upholding all things by the word of his power. This is the answer to every question the fine-tuning evidence raises about why the physical constants hold. Why does gravity remain consistent? Why does the strong nuclear force not fluctuate? Why do the laws of physics not simply dissolve into chaos between one moment and the next? Not because they are self-sustaining. Because He is sustaining them. The universe is not running on its own momentum. It is being held together, moment by moment, by the same Word that spoke it into existence.

This is the answer to the deepest question embedded in the science and faith debate: why is the universe rational at all? Why do the laws of physics hold? Why is mathematics the language of the cosmos? Why does the investigating human mind correspond to the investigated reality? None of these questions have answers inside a Godless framework. They are simply assumed, taken for granted, treated as brute facts that require no explanation.

But the Logos answers every one of them. The universe is rational because it was spoken into existence by a rational Person. The laws of physics are consistent because they reflect the character of the One who authored them. Mathematics describes reality because the One who designed reality thinks in the language of precise, ordered truth. And the human mind corresponds to the universe it investigates because both were designed by the same Author, who intended the creature to know the Creator through the creation.

"He stretcheth out the north over the empty place, and hangeth the earth upon nothing." — Job 26:7 (KJV)

Written centuries before the invention of the telescope or the calculation of gravitational physics, this verse describes the earth suspended in empty space — hanging upon nothing. The solid, visible world rests on invisible foundations, exactly as the ancient text declared before science had the instruments to confirm it. The chair you sit on is almost entirely empty space. The body you inhabit is comprised of atoms, built on protons and neutrons, built on quarks, which ultimately dissolve into vibrating fields of quantum energy — invisible, immaterial, and real. The visible world rests on invisible foundations. The Word that holds it all together was always there, upholding what appears to hold itself.

The Logos is not a concept that the church borrowed from Greek philosophy. The Logos is what Greek philosophy was reaching for without the revelation to find. Science has been reaching for it too. Every physicist who describes the rational order of the universe, every biologist who marvels at the information density of the genome, every archaeologist who lifts a stone from the ancient Near East and finds the biblical record confirmed beneath it — they are all, in their own way, tracing the fingerprints of the Logos who made it all and holds it all together still.

My Reflection

The moment I stopped trying to protect my faith from the evidence was the moment the evidence stopped feeling like a threat.

I have spent years reading. Not just Scripture. Not just the voices that confirmed what I already believed. I have read the arguments of the skeptics, the claims of the atheists, the most sophisticated challenges that secular philosophy and modern science have produced against the existence of God. I did not do this because my faith was weak. I did it because my faith was real enough to survive the questions, and because I believed — and still believe — that truth does not need to be protected from scrutiny. Truth is what remains when scrutiny is finished.

What I want to invite you to is not an argument. It is a process.

Take off every label for a moment. Set aside what your professors told you, what your pastor told you, what your parents told you, what the headlines told you. Set aside the tribal loyalty to whatever camp you have been assigned to. Set aside the emotional investment in being right. Set aside the social cost of changing your mind.

Go somewhere quiet. And say this, or something close to it, in whatever words feel honest: Whatever or whoever created me — I am asking You to clear my previous assumptions and help me see the truth. I am not here to defend a position. I am here to find one.

Then read. Read the evidence from both directions. Read the cosmology and the biology and the archaeology. Read the arguments of the skeptics and the responses of the believers. Fact-check everything. Question everything. Sit with the things that produce confusion —

because confusion in genuine inquiry is a sign that something important is being worked through, not a reason to stop.

God made a promise to the truth seeker. He said it in the plainest language available, in the voice of His own Son:

"Ask, and it shall be given you; seek, and ye shall find; knock, and it shall be opened unto you: For every one that asketh receiveth; and he that seeketh findeth; and to him that knocketh it shall be opened." — Matthew 7:7–8 (KJV)

God does not promise to reveal Himself to casual curiosity. He promises to reveal Himself to the person who brings honest intellectual investigation combined with a wholehearted desire to actually find the truth. That combination, in my experience, leads to one place — not because I decided in advance where it would lead, but because I followed it without deciding, and it led me there anyway.

"It is the glory of God to conceal a thing: but the honour of kings is to search out a matter." — Proverbs 25:2 (KJV)

The Hebrew word for search out is chaqar — to penetrate, to examine intimately, to probe beneath the surface. God hid the DNA code. He hid the quantum foundations of matter. He hid the archaeological confirmations of His Word beneath centuries of dust in the ancient Near East. Not to make faith impossible, but to make discovery glorious. He hid these things for us, not from us — like a father hiding treasure for a child to find, knowing the finding will be more precious than simply being handed what was hidden.

And when the doubter named Thomas demanded physical evidence of the resurrection — refusing to believe on the testimony of others, insisting on empirical proof — Jesus did not rebuke him for his skepticism. He walked into the room and offered Thomas exactly what he asked for. He showed him the wounds. He invited the examination. He supplied the evidence first. And only after Thomas's demands were fully satisfied did Jesus offer the gentle, forward-looking observation: blessed are those who have not seen, and yet have believed. God is not afraid of your questions. He is not threatened by your microscope or your telescope or your demand for proof. He built the universe in a way that rewards the honest seeker. The question has never been whether the evidence is there. The question is whether we are willing to follow it without having already decided where it leads.

Science has not disproved God. Science has been, for anyone willing to follow it honestly to its destination, one of the most powerful witnesses He has ever called. The heavens are still declaring. The DNA is still speaking. The ground is still confirming. The Logos is still holding everything together. And the God who spoke the cosmos into existence from nothing, who signed His name in the dimensions of the double helix, who sat at the summit of every mountain the honest scientist has climbed — is the same God who shows up in the hardest moments of a human life, who answers prayers with a precision that leaves no room for coincidence, and who turns the paths we thought were detours into the very destinations He intended all along.

He was never hiding. He was never silent. He has been writing His name into everything He made since before the first moment of time.

The only question left is whether we are willing to read it.

A Prayer for the Reader

Father —

We come to the end of this chapter carrying different things. Some of us carry the relief of seeing what we have always believed confirmed by evidence we did not know existed. Some of us carry the unsettling weight of a question we thought was settled beginning to come undone. Some of us carry years of intellectual pride invested in a position that the evidence in these pages has challenged in ways we are not yet sure what to do with.

For the person who has used science as a shield against You — who has told themselves that choosing reason meant leaving You behind — let the evidence of this chapter do what evidence does when it is honest. Let it dismantle the false choice. Let it show them that the most rigorous, the most honest, the most courageous intellectual path available leads not away from You but toward You.

For the believer who has been shaken — who has sat in a classroom and felt the ground of their faith tremble beneath a scientific argument they could not answer — let this chapter be a foundation. Not because faith requires scientific proof. But because when the honest scientist follows the evidence to its end, they find You there. They have always found You there.

For the genuine truth seeker who is somewhere in the middle — not fully believing, not fully doubting, but honestly looking — honor the looking. You promised to honor it. You promised that the one who seeks with their whole heart will find. We take You at Your word.

Let the saphar of the heavens never lose its power over us. Let the mathematical precision of the cosmos, the information architecture of the cell, the stones of the ancient Near East crying out in confirmation of Your Word — let all of it be a continuous, daily reminder that we do not live in an accidental universe. We live in a created one. And the Creator is not a blind equation. He is a Father. He is present. And He has been sitting at the summit of every mountain the honest seeker has ever tried to climb, waiting for the moment they pull themselves over the final rock and find Him there.

In the name of the Father, the Son, and the Holy Spirit.

Amen.

"For the invisible things of him from the creation of the world are clearly seen, being understood by the things that are made, even

his eternal power and Godhead; so that they are without excuse." —
Romans 1:20 (KJV)

Chapter Eight

Why Are There So Many Religions If There Is Only One God?

"He hath made every thing beautiful in his time: also he hath set the world in their heart, so that no man can find out the work that God maketh from the beginning to the end." — Ecclesiastes 3:11 (KJV)

The Question

It is one of the oldest weapons in the skeptic's arsenal, and it lands with real weight every time it is thrown.

If there is one God, why are there thousands of religions? If the truth is singular and knowable, why has humanity produced such an overwhelming diversity of belief systems, each claiming authority, each demanding devotion, each pointing in a different direction? Does the sheer number of options not prove that the whole enterprise is a human invention — that religion is something people make up to cope with mortality and explain the unexplainable, rather than a response to something genuinely real?

It is a fair question. And it deserves a fair answer — not a defensive deflection, not a theological talking point designed to end the conversation, but an honest engagement with what the evidence actually shows.

Here is what this chapter will argue, carefully and completely: the existence of thousands of religions does not disprove God. It proves Him. Every human civilization in history has produced religion because every human being arrives in this world carrying something God deliberately placed inside them — a longing for eternity, a consciousness of the sacred, an internal compass that points toward a Creator they were designed to find. The diversity of religion is not evidence that the search is meaningless. It is evidence that the search is universal. And a universal search for the same thing, conducted independently by every people group across every century of human history, is powerful evidence that the thing being searched for is real.

The question is not whether God exists. The question is whether, among the thousands of human attempts to find Him, any one of them is actually true.

That is the question this chapter will answer.

The Longing God Planted

Before we examine the religions, we need to examine the longing that produced them.

Ecclesiastes 3:11 contains one of the most quietly devastating observations in all of Scripture. Solomon writes that God has made everything beautiful in its time, and that He has set the world in the human heart — so that no man can find out the work that God maketh from the beginning to the end. The English word translated world in that verse is the Hebrew word olam. It means eternity. Vast, boundless, transcendent existence stretching beyond the edges of what any finite creature can see or comprehend. And God, according to Solomon, has embedded this sense of olam inside the human heart.

This is not a poetic observation. It is a theological diagnosis. God placed within the architecture of the human soul an innate awareness of something infinitely larger than the temporal world we inhabit. We are finite creatures who can perceive infinity. We are mortal beings haunted by the awareness of eternity. We are dust who nonetheless dream of something that does not end. This is not a neurological accident. It is a deliberate act of the Creator — who placed the longing in us so that we would desire, seek, and ultimately find companionship with Him.

The proof that this longing is universal is written across every page of human history. No animal has ever built an altar for worship. Yet everywhere you find human beings, at every point in recorded history, on every continent, in every culture that has ever existed — you find them worshipping. You find them building temples, performing rituals, offering sacrifices, composing prayers, telling stories about gods and creation and death and what lies beyond it. The universality of religious behavior is one of the most consistent findings in all of anthropology. Human beings are, without exception, incurably religious.

The skeptic looks at this fact and concludes that religion is a universal human delusion — a coping mechanism invented independently by every culture to manage the anxiety of mortality. But that conclusion requires a level of arrogance worth examining directly. To be an atheist, you are forced to believe that the vast majority of the human race across the entirety of recorded history has been suffering from one enormous and consistent mistake. You must believe that every civilization that ever produced an altar, a prayer, or a theology was simply wrong — that the universal human intuition of the sacred is a universal human hallucination.

A Christian is not required to believe that. A Christian is free to recognize that the universal human reach toward the divine is exactly what God intended when He placed olam in the human heart. The longing is real. The thing the longing points toward is real. The question is simply whether any of humanity's attempts to satisfy that longing have actually reached the source.

The Logical Fallacy Disguised as Wisdom

Before we go further, the central argument of the skeptic needs to be examined on its logical merits. The argument is this: there are many religions, therefore none of them can be right.

Consider the logic of that claim for a moment. In arithmetic, there is only one right answer to a sum, and all other answers are wrong — but some of the wrong answers are much nearer being right than others. If a classroom of students gives fifty different incorrect answers to a mathematical problem, it does not mean that a correct answer does not exist. It does not invalidate the concept of mathematics. It simply means that most of the students got it wrong. The existence of many wrong answers to a question is not evidence that the question has no answer. It is evidence that the question is difficult and that most people approaching it without adequate guidance will miss the mark.

The argument also commits a deeper logical error. It assumes that widespread disagreement about a subject eradicates the possibility of objective truth. But truth, by definition, is not determined by a vote. If every person on earth believed the world was flat, that belief would not make it flat. If every religion in human history claimed something false, the falseness of those claims would not retroactively make the truth they missed any less true. Reality does not negotiate with consensus.

What the diversity of religion actually demonstrates is that humanity universally senses a reality it cannot fully access without divine guidance. The many wrong maps do not prove that no territory exists. They prove that the territory is real, that humanity desperately wants to reach it, and that finding the true map requires something more than human ingenuity — it requires revelation from the One who designed the territory in the first place.

The War Started Early

I want to be honest about something that took me a long time to understand, because I think it matters for anyone willing to look at the earliest chapters of human religious history with open eyes.

When I began reading other religious texts — ancient texts, the oldest documents humanity has produced — I was not approaching them as a defender of Christianity looking for ammunition. I genuinely wanted to know whether what I had been raised to believe was true, or whether it was simply one more human-made religion among thousands. I read without a predetermined conclusion. I sat with documents that described gods I had never heard of, creation stories that predated the Genesis account in their written form, and religious systems whose imagery sometimes resembled the biblical narrative in ways that initially unsettled me.

What I found, the longer I stayed with the material, was not a disproof of the God I knew. It was a confirmation of something Scripture had been telling me all along.

From the very earliest chapters of Genesis, God is doing something unusual. He is not introducing Himself to a world that has never encountered religion. He is correcting a world that has been worshipping the wrong things. He tells His people directly and repeatedly not to worship the sun, the moon, the stars, the seasons, the forces of nature — not because these things do not exist, but because they are not God.

He is not establishing the first religion in a religious vacuum. He is reclaiming the worship of creatures who have been misdirected.

The Apostle Paul gives us the theological framework for understanding why this happened. In his letter to the Romans, he describes how humanity, having been given the knowledge of God through the created world, chose to worship created things rather than the Creator. They changed the glory of the uncorruptible God into an image made like to corruptible man, and to birds, and fourfooted beasts, and creeping things. The sun gods, the moon gods, the fertility deities, the storm gods of the ancient world — these were not the products of innocent imagination. They were the products of a spiritual misdirection that Paul traces directly to the suppression of truth.

I will tell you what I believe about the earliest false religions, because I think it is both scripturally sound and honest. Satan, from the beginning, knew that a time was coming when God would reveal Himself fully and provide a path of redemption for humanity. And Satan, who is the father of lies and the great counterfeiter, moved ahead of that revelation to confuse and mislead. The ancient world's fixation on stars, suns, moons, and nature deities was not innocent paganism. It was a preemptive misdirection — designed to ensure that when the real God stepped into history, humanity would already have centuries of false worship embedded in its culture, making it easier to dismiss the true revelation as simply one more religion among many.

God knew this would happen. And He responded not by abandoning the nations, but by working through history to correct, reclaim, and ultimately rescue them.

One Foundation, Many Counterfeits

Here is something that every serious student of comparative religion eventually notices, and that I noticed on my own journey through the ancient texts: virtually every major world religion has a relationship with the Old Testament.

This relationship was anticipated by ancient Jewish wisdom. Among the Apocryphal texts preserved in the Greek Septuagint is the Letter of Aristeas — a document from approximately 250 B.C. describing the commissioning of the Septuagint translation. In it, the High Priest Eleazar explains to Ptolemy II of Egypt something remarkable: the same God who gave the Law to Israel is the sovereign God of all the earth, and the wisdom preserved in the Hebrew Scriptures is not Israel's private possession but belongs to all humanity. The Old Testament was not written for a tribe. It was written for the world. Ancient Jewish theology understood this long before Christianity carried it to the nations. The foundation was always intended to be universal.

Judaism is built upon the Old Testament. Christianity fulfills it. Islam claims to complete it. Even traditions further removed from the Abrahamic lineage share conceptual architecture with it — a Creator God, a moral law, a fall from original goodness, a need for redemption, a promised future restoration. The Old Testament is not one religious text among equals. It is the foundation that every subsequent religious tradition has had to either accept, modify, reinterpret, or argue against. That is not what you would expect from a tribal mythology. That is what you would expect from a document that contains the actual record of God's interaction with human history.

The Jewish people received this foundation first. They were the custodians of the covenants, the Law, and the prophets — chosen not for their own greatness but as a vessel through which the light of God's truth would eventually reach the entire world. The prophet Isaiah records God declaring His servant to be a light for the Gentiles, that his salvation may reach unto the end of the earth. The Old Testament was never intended to be Israel's private possession. It was always intended to be humanity's preparation.

And yet, when the fulfillment of everything the Old Testament pointed toward arrived — when Jesus of Nazareth walked into history fulfilling prophecy after prophecy, teaching with an authority no rabbi had ever claimed, forgiving sins on His own authority, healing the sick, raising the dead, and ultimately dying and rising exactly as the prophets had described — the Jewish religious establishment rejected Him. Not because the evidence was insufficient, but because His timeline and method did not match their human expectations of how the Messiah should arrive and what He should accomplish. They expected a military king who would liberate Israel from Rome. They received a suffering servant who liberated the entire human race from sin and death.

This was not a surprise to God. It was predicted. Isaiah 53, written seven centuries before the crucifixion, described it in detail that still stops careful readers cold. The rejection of Jesus by the very people who held the prophecies of His coming was not evidence that He was the wrong Messiah. It was evidence that human beings, even the most religiously devoted among us, have a consistent tendency to impose our own timeline and expectations onto God's plans rather than submitting our expectations to His revelation.

Then, centuries after Jesus, Muhammad appeared. And what happened with Muhammad is what has happened with every major religious founder who came after the completed revelation of Scripture: he took the existing foundation of the Old and New Testaments, the story of Jesus, the history of the patriarchs, and incorporated them into a new narrative that positioned himself as the final and definitive prophet of God. He did not produce a genuinely independent revelation. He produced a revision — one that kept the parts of the biblical story that served his purposes and altered or rejected the parts that did not.

This pattern is not unique to Islam. It is the pattern of every religious system that emerged after the close of the biblical canon: take the existing foundation, claim authority over it, add a new figure or a new doctrine, and declare the previous revelation incomplete without this addition. The pattern itself tells you something important. Counterfeits do not create from nothing. They work from the original. And the fact that so many religious traditions have found it necessary to incorporate, reinterpret, or argue against the biblical narrative is powerful evidence that the biblical narrative is the thing every subsequent tradition is positioning itself in relation to.

There is one more observation worth making. Jesus of Nazareth is acknowledged in every major world religion's sacred texts. Islam acknowledges Him as a great prophet. Judaism acknowledges His historical existence even while rejecting His messianic claims. Even traditions far removed from the Abrahamic lineage have encountered His story and been forced to account for it. No other figure in human history has achieved this universal acknowledgment across competing religious traditions. When every tradition — including the ones that most vigorously oppose Christianity — finds itself compelled to address the person of Jesus, that is not an accident. That is the footprint of Someone whose reality cannot be avoided.

Man Reaching Up, God Reaching Down

To understand why Christianity stands apart from every other world religion, you need to understand the fundamental architecture of human religion — and how Christianity inverts it completely.

Every human-constructed religious system is built on the same foundational premise: that human beings must do something to earn, achieve, or merit a right standing before God or the divine. The Buddhist walks the Eightfold Path toward enlightenment. The Muslim submits to the Five Pillars and observes the code of law. The Hindu pursues liberation through karma and dharma across multiple lifetimes. Every system, at its core, is a ladder. Human beings at the bottom, the divine at the top, and a set of prescribed behaviors, rituals, or spiritual practices that are meant to elevate the practitioner from where they are to where they need to be.

The Tower of Babel in Genesis 11 is the perfect image of this impulse. After the great flood, humanity gathered together and declared: let us build us a city and a tower, whose top may reach unto heaven; and let us make us a name. The Hebrew word for the confusing of their language is balal — to mix, to confuse, to mingle. From it comes the name Babel. God scattered them across the face of the earth, and from that scattering came the diversity of human cultures, languages, and ultimately the diverse religious traditions that each group developed as they spread to the far corners of the world.

But here is what the New Testament reveals about that scattering that changes everything. The Apostle Paul, standing before the Greek philosophers in Athens, declared:

"That they should seek the Lord, if haply they might feel after him, and find him, though he be not far from every one of us." — Acts 17:27 (KJV)

The scattering was not only a judgment on human pride. It was a divine architecture. God localized the nations, determined their boundaries and their epochs, specifically so that every people group would seek Him from within their own cultural context. The diversity of human civilization is not a random accident. It is a purposeful arrangement designed by a God who wanted every people on earth to have a reason to reach toward Him.

The problem is that reaching is all human religion can do. Finite, fallen creatures building ladders toward infinite holiness will always come up short. No amount of moral effort can erase the debt of sin. No ritual observance can bridge the gap between a creature and its Creator. No mystical practice can produce in a human being what only God can supply. The ladder always runs out of rungs before it reaches heaven.

This is why Christianity is not simply the best religion among many. Christianity is categorically different from every other religious system in existence, because it is not a ladder. It is an arrival. Every other religion is humanity reaching up toward God. Christianity is the historical record of God reaching down toward humanity. The Incarnation — God becoming flesh in the person of Jesus Christ, entering the broken world He created, living the life we could not live, dying the death we deserved, and rising to prove that death itself was not the final word — is not a human achievement. It is a divine rescue. God did not wait at the top of the ladder for us to climb to Him. He descended the ladder, found us at the bottom, and carried us.

The Dividing Line

When you lay every major world religion side by side and examine the claims of their founders, one comparison stands above all others in its significance.

Moses never claimed to be God. He claimed to speak for God. Buddha never claimed to be God. He claimed to have found a path to enlightenment and offered to teach it. Muhammad never claimed to be God. He claimed to be the final prophet of God. Confucius never claimed to be God. He offered moral philosophy. Every major religious founder in human history positioned himself as a pointer — a teacher, a prophet, a guide, a messenger. Not one of them claimed to be the destination.

Jesus of Nazareth claimed to be the destination.

He claimed to be the Son of God. He claimed the authority to forgive sins on His own — an authority that the Jewish religious leaders of His day correctly understood to belong to God alone. He told His followers that He and the Father were one. He applied to Himself the divine name I AM that God had spoken to Moses from the burning bush. And when His disciples asked Him to show them the way to the Father, He did not point them down a road. He said:

"I am the way, the truth, and the life: no man cometh unto the Father, but by me." — John 14:6 (KJV)

The Greek word translated way is hodos — a road, a path, the ground on which you walk to reach a destination. Jesus does not claim to know the road. He claims to be it. The Greek word translated truth is aletheia — not merely accurate information, but embodied, living reality. He does not claim to teach the truth. He claims to be it. And the Greek word translated life is zoe — not bios, the temporary biological existence that every creature shares and that will eventually run down and cease. Zoe is the uncreated, timeless, divine life of God Himself. Jesus offers not an improvement to our existing life. He offers to put His own divine life into us, transforming created things into begotten children of God.

C.S. Lewis identified the logical consequence of these claims with an honesty that has never been improved upon. A man who said the kinds of things Jesus said would not be a great moral teacher. He would either know his claims were false, making him a deliberate liar and a hypocrite of monstrous proportions. Or he would sincerely believe his false claims, making him a madman on the level of someone who believes he is a poached egg. The only remaining option, if He is neither liar nor lunatic, is that He is exactly what He claimed to be. Jesus has not left the option of calling Him a great moral teacher open to us. We must either dismiss Him as a fraud or a madman, or fall at His feet and call Him Lord and God.

And Peter, standing before the very Sanhedrin that had orchestrated the crucifixion of Jesus, declared what the resurrection had settled for him beyond any possibility of retreat:

"Neither is there salvation in any other: for there is none other name under heaven given among men, whereby we must be saved." — Acts 4:12 (KJV)

The Greek word soteria — salvation — carries the full weight of deliverance, rescue, wholeness, and restoration. Peter is not making a tribal religious claim. He is making an ontological one. There is one authorized mechanism of rescue between the human soul and its Creator. Not because God is cruel, but because only one Person in human history actually crossed the infinite distance between the divine and the human, paid the full price of human sin, and walked out of a tomb to prove it was finished.

The exclusivity of the Gospel is not arrogance. It is the logical consequence of what actually happened in history. If the Cross accomplished what Scripture declares it accomplished, then there is no second path. Not because God is unwilling to save — but because the price has already been paid, and the door has already been opened, and the only thing left is for human beings to walk through it.

The Ground Beneath the Claim

Every religion makes claims. The decisive question is which claims are anchored in verifiable history.

The philosopher Peter Kreeft observed something that deserves to be heard slowly. The bones of Abraham are in the ground. The bones of Muhammad are in the ground. The bones of Buddha are in the ground. The bones of Confucius, of Lao-Tzu, of Zoroaster — they are all in the ground. The founding figures of every major world religion are dead, and their remains have stayed where they were placed. Jesus Christ's tomb is empty. Not symbolically empty. Physically, historically, verifiably empty — in the city of Jerusalem, weeks after the crucifixion, in the presence of living eyewitnesses, with hostile authorities who had every incentive to produce a body and did not, because there was no body to produce.

The Apostle Paul made a claim in his first letter to the Corinthians that no fabricator would have the audacity to make. He wrote that the risen Christ appeared to Peter, then to the twelve, then to more than five hundred brethren at once, of whom the greater part remain unto this present. That was written within two to five years of the crucifixion. Paul was not issuing a theological statement designed to be verified in a distant future. He was issuing a public challenge to living eyewitnesses: go interview them. If the resurrection did not happen, here are five hundred people who will tell you so.

None of them did. And Paul stated the stakes plainly: And if Christ be not risen, then is our preaching vain, and your faith is also vain. He was not hedging. He was issuing the most honest theological statement a Christian can make — this entire faith rises or falls on whether a dead man walked out of a tomb in Jerusalem two thousand years ago. Paul knew it. And he staked his life on the answer.

Consider also the nature of the people making the resurrection claim. Before the crucifixion, the disciples abandoned Jesus, denied Him, and hid behind locked doors in fear. A crucified messiah was not merely a disappointment to first-century Jewish expectations — it was a sign of divine curse. There was no cultural script for the disciples to follow that would have led them to invent a resurrection story. A fabricated resurrection would have required an immediate, coordinated conspiracy among frightened, grieving men with no precedent for the claim they were making and every reason to stay hidden.

Instead, days after the crucifixion, these same men were standing in the streets of Jerusalem — the very city where Jesus had been publicly executed — declaring that He had risen from the dead. Peter stood before the Sanhedrin. Stephen was stoned. James was beheaded. Paul was beaten, shipwrecked, imprisoned, and eventually executed. Not one of them, under any amount of pressure or threat, recanted.

People will die for what they genuinely believe to be true. History is full of such people. But people do not die for something they know they invented. If the disciples had stolen the body and fabricated the resurrection, every one of them knew it was a lie. And not one of them, facing torture and death, chose to save himself by confessing the conspiracy. That is not the behavior of men protecting a myth. That is the behavior of men who could not deny what they had seen with their own eyes.

There is also the criterion of embarrassment. In first-century Jewish culture, a woman's testimony was considered legally inadmissible. If the disciples were constructing a story designed to convince the Greco-Roman world of the resurrection, the absolute last detail they would have invented is that the first witnesses to the empty tomb and the first people to see the risen Christ were women. The presence of women as the primary witnesses is not a detail a fabricator inserts. It is a detail an honest reporter preserves because it is what actually happened, regardless of how badly it complicates the cultural reception of the story.

And then there is the prophetic architecture. Christianity did not arrive in history as a new religious idea. It arrived as the fulfillment of a centuries-long prophetic foundation. The prophet Micah, writing seven hundred years before the birth of Jesus, named Bethlehem Ephrathah as the birthplace of the one whose goings forth have been from of old, from everlasting. Isaiah 53, also written seven centuries before Calvary, described a suffering servant who would be wounded for our transgressions and bruised for our iniquities, who would be led as a lamb to the slaughter, who would remain silent before His accusers, and who would be buried in a rich man's tomb. Psalm 22, written a thousand years before the Roman invention of crucifixion, described a death in which hands and feet are pierced and garments divided by casting lots. And the prophet Zechariah, five hundred years before the Cross, recorded words that should stop every honest reader cold — God Himself speaking: and they shall look upon me whom they have pierced.

And the community at Qumran — Jewish scribes writing approximately one hundred years before the birth of Jesus — preserved among the Dead Sea Scrolls a text scholars call the Messianic Apocalypse (4Q521). In it, they describe the expected Messiah's ministry in language so precise it should stop every reader cold: the blind will see, the deaf hear, the lame walk, the dead will be raised, and good news will be proclaimed to the poor. This is not a post-Christian interpolation. It was written in the desert a full century before Jesus performed every one of these actions and described His own ministry in identical language to John the Baptist's disciples. The community that produced the Dead Sea Scrolls was expecting the very ministry Jesus performed. He did not invent a messianic role. He fulfilled one that Israel had been anticipating in writing for a hundred years before He arrived.

Professor Peter Stoner calculated the mathematical probability of one person fulfilling just eight of these specific messianic prophecies by coincidence. His answer was one in ten to the power of seventeen. To grasp the scale of that number: imagine a single marked coin dropped somewhere in a field the size of a continent, covered uniformly with coins stretching to the horizon in every direction.

A blindfolded man walks out and reaches down once. The odds of him finding that specific coin on the first attempt is one in ten to the seventeenth power — the same odds that one person fulfills eight messianic prophecies by chance. The odds of forty-eight prophecies being fulfilled in a single person climbs to one in ten to the power of one hundred and fifty-seven. Coincidence is not a serious explanation. The only adequate explanation is that the same Divine Author who spoke the prophecies also engineered the history that fulfilled them, because He was both the Announcer and the Arrival.

The Question of Those Who Never Heard

There is a question that lives underneath this chapter that must be addressed honestly, because it is the question that troubles the most sincere and compassionate hearts. What about the person born in a remote jungle, in a distant century, who never once heard the name of Jesus Christ? Is that person condemned for something they never had the chance to accept or reject?

Scripture does not leave us without an answer. It leaves us without complete certainty — and those are different things.

The Apostle Paul establishes in Romans 2:14–15 that every human being arrives in the world with the work of the law written in their hearts, their conscience also bearing witness, and their thoughts the mean while accusing or else excusing one another. The Greek word translated conscience is syneidesis — the internal moral faculty that evaluates the ethical quality of human thoughts and actions. Paul's argument is that no human being exists in a state of complete moral darkness. Every person, regardless of whether they have ever encountered Scripture, carries an internal witness to the existence of a moral order and the God who established it. They will be judged according to the measure of light they possessed and what they did with it — not according to a revelation they never received.

The story of Cornelius in Acts 10 illuminates this further. Cornelius was a Roman centurion — a Gentile, entirely outside the covenant community of Israel, without access to the Jewish Scriptures or the early Christian community. Yet Scripture describes him as a devout man, one that feared God with all his house, which gave much alms to the people, and prayed to God alway. He was responding with his whole heart to whatever light he had. And God's response was not to leave him in that partial response. God sent an angel to direct him specifically to Peter, who came and preached the full Gospel of Jesus Christ. It was only when Peter shared the truth of Jesus that the Holy Spirit fell upon Cornelius and his household.

The lesson of Cornelius is critical and must be held with precision. God did not look at Cornelius's sincerity and declare it sufficient. He looked at Cornelius's sincere seeking and moved heaven and earth to bring him the complete truth. Sincerity is the posture that invites revelation. Jesus Christ is the only mechanism of salvation. These two facts are not in contradiction. They work together.

The New Testament itself sets the boundary of what we are permitted to claim with confidence: we know that no man can be saved except through Christ. We do not know, because Scripture does not tell us, all the ways in which the completed work of Christ may be applied across circumstances and souls that we, from our limited vantage point, cannot fully map or predict. That is not a door to the idea that all religions lead to God. It is a recognition that the God who is perfectly just and infinitely merciful is capable of what Scripture tells us He is capable of — and His mercy exceeds our ability to chart it.

Deuteronomy 29:29 establishes the boundary of what we are permitted to claim:

"The secret things belong unto the LORD our God: but those things which are revealed belong unto us and to our children for ever." — Deuteronomy 29:29 (KJV)

The eternal disposition of every unevangelized soul belongs to the secret counsels of God, which no human theology has the authority to open or close. Paul echoes this in Romans 11:33 with words that should humble every theologian who has ever tried to map the full reach of divine mercy:

"O the depth of the riches both of the wisdom and knowledge of God! how unsearchable are his judgments, and his ways past finding out!" — Romans 11:33 (KJV)

We are not called to manage the universe's moral accounting. We are called to preach. The Judge of all the earth will do right. That is not a platitude. It is a statement about the character of God that the entirety of Scripture supports.

What Scripture does not support is the idea that sincerity of belief in a false religion is equivalent to faith in Jesus Christ. A person can be deeply devout, morally admirable, and genuinely seeking God within the framework of a false religious system — and still be following a map that does not lead to the destination. The philosopher Peter van Inwagen makes the point with precision: the accuracy of a map has nothing to do with how sincerely the traveler holds it. A map either corresponds to the territory or it does not. The sincerity of the person navigating by it cannot change whether the road it shows leads home. True love does not validate a false map. True love finds the lost traveler and points them, as gently and urgently as possible, toward the only road that actually leads home.

How to Hold the Conversation

Knowing the truth and knowing how to carry it are two different disciplines, and the New Testament is careful to teach both.

The Apostle Peter writes in his first letter: But sanctify the Lord God in your hearts: and be ready always to give an answer to every man that asketh you a reason of the hope that is in you with meekness and fear. The Greek word translated answer is apologia — not an apology in the modern sense of expressing regret, but a reasoned, factual, evidential defense of what one believes. Christians are commanded to know why they believe what they believe and to be able to articulate it clearly. Faith is not the suspension of the mind. It is the engagement of the mind with the evidence God has provided.

But the delivery mechanism for that truth is commanded with equal force. The Greek word translated meekness is prautēs — approaching others, even those who disagree, in a humble and caring spirit, without using force or condescension to get one's way. It is a word used to describe Jesus Himself. The apologia of a scholar must be delivered with the prautēs of a servant. A Christian who wields theological truth as a weapon to batter a family member or a friend into submission is not doing apologetics. They are doing damage — to the person they claim to love and to the faith they claim to represent.

The reason for this posture is found in what Scripture reveals about God's own posture toward a lost world:

"And we have seen and do testify that the Father sent the Son to be the Saviour of the world." — 1 John 4:14 (KJV)

The Greek word translated world is kosmos — and in John's theology, kosmos most often describes not a friendly, receptive world but a world in active rebellion against God, engulfed in spiritual darkness, ruled by the enemy. God did not love a compliant world. He loved a hostile one. And His response to that hostility was not condemnation. It was the Cross.

If the Creator's posture toward a hostile, rebellious world was to absorb its punishment in order to save it, then the Christian's posture toward people of other faiths must mirror that grace. We are not the world's judges. We are the bearers of its only good news. Our engagement with people of other religions should never be marked by superiority, contempt, or the satisfaction of being right. It should be marked by the bleeding-heart urgency of someone carrying a cure to people who do not yet know they are ill.

The Areopagus Model

The most practical biblical model for engaging religious diversity is not found in a theological treatise. It is found in a single afternoon in the city of Athens.

The Apostle Paul arrived in Athens and found a city wholly given to idolatry — a sophisticated, philosophically advanced culture worshipping hundreds of gods with temples, altars, and centuries of religious tradition. His spirit was provoked. But when he stood before the Epicurean and Stoic philosophers on Mars Hill, he did not open with condemnation. He opened with observation.

He acknowledged that as he had passed through the city, he had observed among their devotions an altar bearing the inscription: TO THE UNKNOWN GOD. Paul did not mock it. He recognized it for what it was — a monument to humanity's awareness of a reality it could not name, a blind grasping toward the true Creator they intuitively knew existed. He stepped inside their worldview and showed them that the God they were reaching for in the dark was the same God who had designed their very existence, determined the boundaries of their habitation, and placed within them the longing that had built the altar in the first place.

He even quoted their own poets back to them: For in him we live, and move, and have our being; as certain also of your own poets have said, For we are also his offspring. Paul found the fragments of truth embedded in their pagan tradition — the echoes of a divine preparation scattered across human culture pointing imperfectly toward the full revelation — and honored them by building a bridge from those fragments to the complete truth.

And then, having established that compassionate connection, Paul pivoted without apology to the full and exclusive claim. He introduced the God who is not unknown. He declared that the times of ignorance are past. He announced that God commandeth all men every where to repent because He hath appointed a day, in the which he will judge the world in righteousness by that man whom he hath ordained; whereof he hath given assurance unto all men, in that he hath raised him from the dead.

This is the complete model. Begin with what is true in the other person's seeking. Honor the longing without validating the misdirection. Build the bridge with genuine respect and curiosity. And then, with the warmth of someone who genuinely wants the other person to find what they are looking for, point them to the One who placed the longing there and is the only One who can satisfy it.

Paul proves that true Christian witness does not require insulting another person's religion. It requires loving the person enough to offer them something better than what they have.

The Destination

The story of human religious diversity does not end in confusion. It ends in a vision that should take the breath away from anyone who has ever looked at the fractures and divisions of the religious world and wondered whether reconciliation was possible.

The Apostle John, in the book of Revelation, describes what he saw when the curtain between the present and the eternal was pulled back: After this I beheld, and, lo, a great multitude, which no man could number, of all nations, and kindreds, and people, and tongues, stood before the throne, and before the Lamb, clothed with white robes.

All nations. All kindreds. All people. All tongues. Not a homogenous empire of one culture and one language but a magnificent, multicolored multitude drawn from every people group that ever existed on the face of the earth — each one there not because their particular religious tradition was right, but because they found the One whom every true religious longing was always reaching toward.

The diversity of human culture is not going to be erased in the Kingdom of God. It is going to be redeemed. The scattering at Babel, which produced the diversity of human languages and cultures, will find its resolution in a throne room where that diversity becomes the very instrument of praise. God's grace is so infinitely vast that it requires the combined, redeemed languages and songs of the entire human race to adequately express it throughout eternity.

"Look unto me, and be ye saved, all the ends of the earth: for I am God, and there is none else." — Isaiah 45:22 (KJV)

The scope is universal — all the ends of the earth, every person, every culture, every tradition, no exceptions. The identity is exclusive — I am God, and there is none else. There is not a committee. There is not a spectrum. There is One. And He is throwing the door open to everyone, everywhere, without reservation.

These two realities — the universal invitation and the exclusive identity — are not in tension. They are the same truth seen from two angles. The path is singular because the destination is singular. The door is wide open because the God who opened it desires that none should perish. True love does not offer a hundred different roads to keep everyone comfortable. True love builds one road that actually reaches the destination and invites everyone onto it.

The Invitation

This chapter is for the person living with doubt. Not the person who doubts as a performance — who doubts because it is fashionable or because it keeps the religious people at a safe distance — but the person who genuinely has never had anything about God resonate with them in a way that felt true rather than handed down. The person who has sat in pews or read books or had conversations with very confident religious people and walked away feeling more confused than they came in.

I want you to know that your confusion is not a sign that you are beyond reach. It may be a sign that you have been listening to too many voices and not yet given yourself permission to be alone with the question.

Here is what I would ask you to do. Not to convert. Not to join anything. Not to agree with anything in this chapter before you have tested it. I am asking you to do what I did — to go somewhere alone and quiet, and to say something like this, in whatever words feel honest to you: Whatever or whoever made me — I am not here to defend what I already believe. I am here to find what is actually true. Clear my assumptions. Show me what is real.

And then stay in that posture. Read. Question. Follow the evidence from both directions. Do not let the crowd — the religious crowd or the secular crowd — tell you what to conclude before you have done the work yourself. Keep the investigation private. Let the Holy Spirit guide what your own intellect examines. And be patient, because only you think there is a time limit on this. God has been waiting for you with the same faithfulness with which He has been waiting for every sincere seeker across the entirety of human history.

"Seek ye the LORD while he may be found, call ye upon him while he is near." — Isaiah 55:6 (KJV)

God does not promise to reveal Himself to casual curiosity. He promises to reveal Himself to the person who combines honest intellectual examination with a wholehearted desire to actually find the truth. That combination, in my experience, leads to one place — not because I decided in advance where it would lead, but because I followed it without deciding, and it led me there anyway.

You are not crazy for wondering. You are not beyond God's reach for doubting. You are not disqualified for having grown up in a different tradition, or for having spent years convinced that religion was a human invention, or for carrying wounds from religious people who used the name of God to justify cruelty. None of that closes the door. The door in Isaiah 45 is open to all the ends of the earth. That includes wherever you are standing right now.

Your struggles are not evidence of God's absence. They may be the very thing He is using to get your attention. That addiction you cannot seem to overcome, that grief that will not lift, that persistent sense that something essential is missing — these are not random afflictions. They are the pressure of a soul that was made for something this world cannot provide, pressing against the edges of a life that has not yet found what it was designed for. The brokenness is not the end of the story. It may be the beginning of it.

Stay out of your own way. Keep God private between you and Him. Let Him quietly guide you. Consistency is what He asks for — not perfection, not certainty, not a theological pedigree. Just consistency. Just the daily willingness to keep the search honest and the door open.

Why are there so many religions if there is only one God? Because a spiritually starving human race will reach for anything that might satisfy the hunger God placed in every human heart. But there is only one Bread of Life. Every religion in human history is humanity's attempt to find what only one Person has ever actually provided — not a path, not a philosophy, not a set of rules, but Himself. Fully. Freely. At a cost only He could pay.

He was not waiting at the top of the mountain for us to climb to Him. He came down. He found us. He is still finding people — one honest, searching, broken, willing heart at a time.

Including yours.

My Reflection

There is a version of this chapter that never gets written — the version where I stayed on the outside of the question and argued my way through it. This is not that version.

I did not arrive at my faith in Jesus Christ by being handed it and told not to ask questions. I arrived at it by doing exactly what I am inviting you to do — going alone, without the noise of other people's certainties, and reading everything I could find. Ancient texts. Other religious documents. Archaeological records. Historical accounts. I wanted to know whether what I had been raised to believe was true, or whether it was simply one more human-made system among thousands. I was willing to find out I was wrong. That willingness is what made the journey real.

What I found, the deeper I went, was not a weakening of my faith. It was a foundation I had never seen the full extent of. I found the same God appearing across every point of human history, correcting the misdirected, reclaiming the lost, working through the nations He had scattered toward the moment when He would step into history Himself. I found Jesus acknowledged in texts and traditions that had every reason to make Him disappear, and could not. I found the archaeological ground confirming the biblical record one discovery at a time. I found the prophecies fulfilled with a mathematical precision that accident cannot explain.

But I also found something that no research document can produce. I found that the God I was studying had been present with me in every moment of my life, including the ones I spent trying to verify whether He was real. The private encounters, the moments of inexplicable provision, the times when the only explanation that fit the facts was that Someone had been writing the story long before I could read it — these are not things I can put in a footnote. But they are part of my testimony, and I would not be honest if I left them out.

I also want to tell you something that I think is more important than any of the evidence in this chapter.

I am still broken in some ways. Life is broken, and until we pass from this world into the next, anyone who tells you they have it all figured out is not telling you the truth. I still sin. I still struggle. I still have questions that do not have clean answers. I still have days when the weight of being human is heavier than I know how to carry gracefully. What I have is not the absence of struggle. What I have is the absolute, settled conviction — born out of years of honest seeking, private encounter, and a life that does not add up without God — that Jesus Christ is exactly who He claimed to be. And that conviction holds through everything, not because I have never doubted, but because I paid the price of looking honestly and found that the evidence points in one direction when you follow it without having already decided where it leads.

I fear for those who only know God through other people. I have seen what happens when faith is entirely inherited and never personally owned — when the only reason a person believes is that their family believed, or their community expects it, or the social cost of doubting is too high. That kind of faith does not survive the first serious storm. It was never really faith. It was belonging to a group that used the language of faith.

God does not want your group membership. He wants you. Privately. Personally. He wants to be known by you the way you know your own heartbeat — not because someone described it to you, but because you have felt it for yourself.

A Prayer for the Searching Heart

Father —

We come to the end of this chapter carrying the weight of the question that opened it. Some of us came in as skeptics, using the diversity of religion as a reason to keep You at arm's length. Some of us came in as believers who have never fully worked through why we believe what we believe, who inherited our faith rather than finding it ourselves. Some of us came in quietly desperate — wanting something to be true, not daring to hope that it might be.

For the skeptic — let the evidence in these pages do what honest evidence does when it is followed without a predetermined destination. The longing in every human heart is not an accident. The prophetic architecture of Scripture is not a coincidence. The empty tomb is not a legend. The man who claimed to be the Way, the Truth, and the Life was not a liar or a lunatic. Let the honest mind follow the honest evidence to where it actually leads.

For the inherited believer — let this chapter be a beginning. Not the beginning of doubt, but the beginning of personal ownership. Go alone. Read deeply. Ask the hard questions. You promised to be found by those who seek with their whole heart. We take You at Your word.

For the desperate searcher — the one who has never had anything resonate, who has spent years feeling like everyone else received something they were left out of — hear this: You are not outside the reach of the God who placed the longing in you. The seeking itself is His fingerprint on your soul. He does not plant a hunger He does not intend to satisfy.

And for all of us — remind us that the diversity of human religion is not a reason for despair. It is a testament to the universality of the longing You placed in us. You arranged the nations. You determined the times. You put eternity in our hearts. And You stepped into history Yourself to be the answer to the question that every religion in human history has been trying to answer.

There is only one of You. And that is enough.

In the name of the Father, the Son, and the Holy Spirit.

Amen.

"Look unto me, and be ye saved, all the ends of the earth: for I am God, and there is none else." — Isaiah 45:22 (KJV)

Chapter Nine

Why Is The Church Full of Hypocrites?

"For all have sinned, and come short of the glory of God." — Romans 3:23 (KJV)

The Question

It is one of the most common sentences spoken by people who have walked away from God, and it carries real pain inside it.

I don't go to church. It's full of hypocrites.

Most of the time, the person saying it is not wrong. They have seen something real. A pastor who preached forgiveness on Sunday and practiced cruelty on Monday. A congregation that sang about love and whispered judgment. A church elder who carried a Bible in one hand and a secret life in the other. A Sunday school teacher who grabbed a child by the wrist and cursed in the hallway of God's house. The wound behind the statement is often genuine. The experience that produced it was often real.

And yet the conclusion drawn from that wound — that the hypocrisy of church people disproves God, or justifies walking away from faith entirely — is one of the most dangerous logical errors a searching soul can make. Not because the pain is invalid. The pain is entirely valid. But because the argument confuses two things that Scripture has always kept carefully separate: the perfection of God and the imperfection of His people.

I want to say something honestly before we go further. I do not attend church in the traditional sense. I am not outgoing by nature. Large crowds and loud gatherings pull me away from the kind of focused, private, deeply personal connection with God that I have spent years carefully building. So this chapter does not come from someone standing on the outside throwing stones at people who feel the same way. It comes from someone who understands the wound, who has his own wound, and who has had to learn — slowly, honestly, and sometimes painfully — the difference between the people who fill those buildings and the God who designed the building in the first place.

This chapter will address the wound honestly. It will not minimize what you experienced. It will not tell you that the hypocrites you encountered were not really there, or that what they had done did not matter. It will tell you the truth about what the church actually is, what God actually promised, and why the failure of human beings inside God's house was never — not once — a reason to stop seeking God Himself.

What the Word Actually Means

Before we can answer the question, we need to understand what we are actually saying when we use the word hypocrite. Because most people using it today are using it to mean something very different from what Jesus meant when He said it.

The Greek word is hypokritēs — Strong's G5273. It is a theatrical term. In ancient Greek drama, actors wore physical masks to portray different characters on stage. The hypokritēs was the mask-wearer — a person playing a role, performing a character for an audience, presenting a face to the world that had no connection to the reality underneath. When the performance ended, the mask came off and the true person remained entirely unchanged. The act was not a stumble. It was a design. The deception was not incidental. It was the point.

This is what Jesus condemned with such ferocity in Matthew 23. He was not condemning people who stumbled in their faith. He was not condemning people who struggled with sin, who failed publicly, who could not always live up to what they believed. He was condemning a specific category of person: the one who uses religious performance as a stage. The one who prays loudly in the marketplace so that people will see. The one who widens their religious symbols and seeks the places of honor at gatherings. The one who, as Jesus described, is like unto whited sepulchres, which indeed appear beautiful outward, but are within full of dead men's bones, and of all uncleanness.

The distinction is critical, and it changes everything about this conversation. A biblical hypocrite is not a righteous person who sins. It is an evil person who pretends to be good. A struggling Christian is a broken person begging for mercy. A biblical hypocrite is an imposter wearing a mask, using the church as a stage to project an image they have no intention of actually living.

These are not the same person. And the failure to distinguish between them is the first place the argument against the church goes wrong.

God has never been confused about this distinction, even when we are. He said to the prophet Isaiah: Forasmuch as this people draw near me with their mouth, and with their lips do honour me, but have removed their heart far from me. That was Isaiah 29:13. Lips moving. Heart absent. A performance without a reality. And in 1 Samuel 16:7, when the prophet Samuel was judging by outward appearance, God drew the line that defines this entire chapter:

"For the LORD seeth not as man seeth; for man looketh on the outward appearance, but the LORD looketh on the heart." — 1 Samuel 16:7 (KJV)

The Hebrew word used for man's way of seeing is nabat — a glance at the surface, an assessment of what can be observed. But the Hebrew word used for God's seeing is ra'ah — a penetrating, complete, comprehensive sight that misses nothing. And what God sees all the way down to is the lebab — the heart, the innermost seat of a person's will, motive, and character. The mask fools the congregation. It has never fooled God.

Charles Spurgeon, the great nineteenth-century preacher, put it plainly when he noted that a person can be in the church without being in Christ. The pew can hold a body while the heart remains entirely elsewhere. Spurgeon understood — as Scripture makes clear — that the visible gathering and the genuine spiritual body are not always the same thing. The building can be full. The faith can be absent. And the person who has filled a seat for thirty years can be no closer to God than the person who has never walked through the door.

Jesus Hates Hypocrisy More Than You Do

Here is something that most people who use hypocrisy as a reason to reject Christianity have never fully considered.

The person most offended by hypocrisy in the history of the church is Jesus Christ Himself.

Matthew 23 is the longest, most direct, most devastating confrontation Jesus ever delivered during His earthly ministry. He did not deliver it to tax collectors. He did not deliver it to Roman soldiers. He delivered it to the religious leaders — the most publicly devout, Scripture-educated, temple-attending people of His day. And He called them hypocrites to their faces. Seven times in a single sermon. He told them they were like whitewashed tombs. He told them they were making their converts twice the child of hell that they were. He told them they meticulously tithed their spices while entirely neglecting the weightier matters of the law — judgment, mercy, and faith. He stripped the mask off in public and named the dead men's bones for exactly what they were.

Jesus hates hypocrisy more than the skeptic does. Not almost as much. More. The skeptic is offended by hypocrisy. Jesus was nauseated by it. The skeptic turns away. Jesus turned toward the crowd those hypocrites were harming and walked directly into it — eating with tax collectors, touching lepers, speaking to women that polite religious society had written off entirely.

When a person walks away from God because of hypocrisy in the church, they are expressing an anger that Jesus already expressed more forcefully and more precisely than any skeptic ever has. They share His anger. The difference is only in what they do with it. Jesus' anger at the hypocrites was not a reason to abandon the searching and the wounded. It was a reason to pursue them more urgently. His response to religious corruption was not to walk out the door. It was to walk toward every person the corruption was keeping out.

God Knew This Would Happen

Here is one of the most important arguments in this entire chapter, and it is one that almost never gets made in these conversations.

The presence of hypocrites in the church does not surprise God. He predicted it. He warned about it in explicit detail. And He told us exactly what it would look like.

In Matthew 13:24–30, Jesus told a parable about a man who sowed good seed in his field. While everyone slept, an enemy came and sowed weeds among the wheat and slipped away. As the plants grew, the weeds became visible. The servants asked whether they should pull the weeds out. The master said no — because in pulling the weeds, they might uproot the wheat growing alongside them. Let both grow together until the harvest. At the end, I will separate them.

Jesus later explained the parable directly. The good seed represents the people of the kingdom. The weeds are people of the evil one, planted by the devil, growing in the same field alongside genuine believers. Augustine connected this parable directly to the institutional church, observing that the tares represent those who receive the faith in hypocrisy — possessing the name of a believer while remaining entirely devoid of genuine faith. They sit in the building. They do not sit in Christ.

And the New Testament does not stop there. In Matthew 7:15, Jesus issued a warning that every generation of the church has needed to hear: Beware of false prophets, which come to you in sheep's clothing, but inwardly they are ravening wolves. In Acts 20:29–30, Paul warned the elders of the church at Ephesus: after my departing shall grievous wolves enter in among you, not sparing the flock. Also of your own selves shall men arise, speaking perverse things, to draw away disciples after them. And in 2 Peter 2:1: But there were false prophets also among the people, even as there shall be false teachers among you, who privily shall bring in damnable heresies.

The New Testament did not promise us a perfect institution. It warned us, in careful, specific detail, that the visible church would contain hypocrites, wolves, and false teachers. The presence of these people in the church does not disprove Christianity. It fulfills biblical prophecy. Every hypocrite discovered in a pew is exactly what Scripture told us would be there. The church containing hypocrites is not evidence that the Bible got it wrong. It is evidence that the Bible got it precisely right.

The Hospital and the Physician

There is a question underneath the hypocrisy argument that deserves a direct answer: what exactly did you expect to find when you walked through those doors?

"For all have sinned, and come short of the glory of God." — Romans 3:23 (KJV)

That word all carries no exceptions. Not for pastors. Not for elders. Not for people who have attended church for fifty years. Not for the most theologically educated person in the building. All have sinned. Every single person who walks through a church door on any given Sunday morning is a person who, left to their own devices, falls short of the glory of God. That is not a statement about their effort or their sincerity. It is a statement about the universal human condition.

This is why Augustine described the church not as a museum for perfect saints, but as a hospital. It is a community of sick people, united by their willingness to acknowledge their sin and their hope in the skill of the Physician to whose care they have committed themselves. When you walk into a hospital, you do not expect to find healthy people. You find people who are bleeding, broken, diseased, in pain, and in various stages of recovery. If you walked into a hospital and said, I cannot trust this place, it is full of sick people — you would be missing the entire point of why the institution exists. Their sickness is not a failure of the hospital. It is the reason they are there.

J.I. Packer, one of the most careful theological minds of the twentieth century, made the point that the image of God in the human soul — shattered by sin — is not repaired overnight. The process of being conformed to the character of Christ takes an entire lifetime. A person who walked through the church doors last year is not the same as a person who walked through those same doors thirty years ago. And a person who walked through thirty years ago is still not finished. No one is finished on this side of eternity. That is not an excuse for hypocrisy. It is the reality of what sanctification actually looks like in living, breathing human beings who are still mid-process.

Jesus said it plainly in Matthew 9:12: They that be whole need not a physician, but they that are sick. He did not come to call the righteous. He came to call sinners to repentance. The church is not designed for people who have already arrived at spiritual perfection. It is an emergency room for the spiritually broken. Christians are simply people who have the honesty and the courage to admit that they are sick and that they cannot heal themselves.

"For ye see your calling, brethren, how that not many wise men after the flesh, not many mighty, not many noble, are called: But God hath chosen the foolish things of the world to confound the wise; and God hath chosen the weak things of the world to confound the things which are mighty." — 1 Corinthians 1:26–27 (KJV)

God did not build His church on the most credentialed, the most respected, or the most put-together. He built it on people who had nothing to offer except a willingness to be used. That is the raw material the church has always been made of. It should not surprise us when the raw material looks raw.

When a church member fails publicly — when a leader sins, when a congregation acts in ways that contradict the Gospel they claim to believe — it is painful, and it is wrong, and it must be addressed. But it is not proof that Christianity is false. It is proof that Romans 3:23 is true. And in a way that cuts against everything we would prefer, the disappointment itself is not the end of the story. Disappointment is often the prerequisite for experiencing actual grace. The person who has never needed grace because they have never felt the failure of everything else they trusted rarely knows what grace actually is. The hospital patient who has tried every other remedy and found it wanting is the one who finally stops fighting the Physician and lets Him work.

The Danger of Making Humans Your Foundation

There is a deeper problem underneath the hypocrisy wound that needs to be named, because until it is named, the wound cannot fully heal.

When a person's faith collapses because a pastor fell, or a church leader betrayed them, or a congregation wounded them deeply — the pain is real and the harm was real. But the collapse of faith reveals something important about where the faith was actually built. Because a faith that cannot survive the failure of a human being was never built on the right foundation to begin with.

"Cursed be the man that trusteth in man, and maketh flesh his arm, and whose heart departeth from the LORD." — Jeremiah 17:5 (KJV)

The Hebrew word for trust here is batah — to rely on completely, to feel utterly safe and confident in. And the Hebrew word for flesh is basar — the frail, physical, mortal human structure. God is issuing a warning against leaning your full spiritual weight on another human being. An arm made of flesh will eventually break. And when it breaks, it does not just stop supporting you. It pierces you.

Numbers 23:19 draws the sharpest possible line between God's reliability and human reliability: God is not a man, that he should lie; neither the son of man, that he should repent. And the Psalmist concludes from this truth in Psalm 118:8: It is better to trust in the LORD than to put confidence in man.

When a church leader fails, a man failed. Not God. When a congregation wounds you, broken people did what broken people do. Not

God. When a pastor preaches grace and practices cruelty, a human being revealed the gap between their performance and their reality. Not God. The failure of the human being is painful. It is real. It may have caused damage that will take years to heal. But it does not tell you anything about the character of God, because God never claimed to be that person. He warned you not to put that person in His place.

No human being can bear the weight of being someone else's ultimate savior. It is a weight that will crush anyone it is placed upon, regardless of how gifted or sincere they are. The moment we build our faith on a person rather than on the Person — we have committed a form of idolatry that will always, eventually, result in devastation. Not because God is cruel, but because idols always fail. They are not designed to hold the weight we place on them.

The Apostle Paul asked the question every wounded believer needs to hear:

"Who art thou that judgest another man's servant? to his own master he standeth or falleth." — Romans 14:4 (KJV)

Every person in that church — the struggling one, the failing one, the hypocritical one — answers to God, not to us. And the God they answer to is fully able to make them stand, to correct them, and to judge them with a precision no human being can match. Our responsibility is not to carry that weight. Our responsibility is to ensure that we ourselves are walking honestly before the One we answer to.

What God Actually Built

"Upon this rock I will build my church; and the gates of hell shall not prevail against it." — Matthew 16:18 (KJV)

The Greek word translated church is ekklesia — the called-out assembly. It is never used in the New Testament to describe a building, a denomination, a weekly program, or an institutional structure. It describes a spiritual community of genuine disciples who have been called out of the world and purchased by the blood of Christ. The foundation of this assembly is not the perfection of Peter, who would deny his Lord three times within hours of this very declaration. The foundation is Christ Himself — His identity, His death, His resurrection, His finished work.

"Ye also, as lively stones, are built up a spiritual house, an holy priesthood, to offer up spiritual sacrifices, acceptable to God by Jesus Christ." — 1 Peter 2:5 (KJV)

Not a building. Not an institution. Living stones. Each one placed by the Architect Himself, fitted together into something that no human failure can permanently dismantle.

What Jesus is building transcends every human failure within it. A local pastor may fall into disgrace. A specific congregation may become corrupt and close its doors. A denomination may compromise the truth it was founded on. Every one of these failures is a tragedy that grieves God and wounds His people. But the true ekklesia — the genuine, spiritual body of Christ — survives all of it. Because its Architect, Builder, and Sustainer is not a human being. It is the living God. And the gates of hell cannot prevail against what God Himself is building, no matter how badly the human instruments within it fail.

The earliest followers of Jesus understood this distinction from the very beginning. Among the oldest Christian documents ever discovered — predating many of the New Testament letters being compiled into a single canon — is a text known as the Didache, or Teaching of the Twelve Apostles, written approximately A.D. 50–120. It is the oldest known description of actual Christian community practice in history. What is remarkable about the Didache is what it demands of the people gathering: before approaching the table together, members were to confess their sins honestly — not to perform righteousness before the congregation, but to come to the assembly already having stood before God with their actual condition. The Didache also contains detailed instructions for identifying false prophets within the community: not by their words, which can be crafted for any audience, but by whether their lives match what they preach. The first-century church was not naive about hypocrisy. It built its community practices around the assumption that counterfeits would appear. And it provided tools for discerning the genuine from the performed — tools drawn not from suspicion but from the simple insistence that real faith produces a real life.

Historical theology draws an important distinction between the visible church and the invisible church. The visible church is the institutional gathering — everyone who outwardly professes the name of Christ, attends services, takes communion, and calls themselves a Christian. This body contains wheat and tares, genuine believers and religious performers, the deeply transformed and the deeply deceptive. The invisible church is the true spiritual body — the genuinely regenerate believers whose hearts have been transformed by the Holy Spirit, known perfectly only to God. Augustine described this clearly in The City of God, noting that the institutional church is a mixed body. When a prominent leader falls and the visible institution is shaken, the invisible church is not damaged. The true body of Christ stands entirely secure in Him.

What the visible institution cannot produce in performance, it cannot destroy in failure. Because the thing it was meant to carry — the living, regenerate faith of people genuinely transformed by the Holy Spirit — does not reside in the institution itself. It resides in the people who have actually been changed. Remove the building and the changed people remain changed. The building was never the source.

William Lecky, a nineteenth-century historian who was not himself a believer, was forced to acknowledge something remarkable. Despite the corruption, the scandal, the internal collapse, and the moral failure that marked so many chapters of Christian history, the institution kept surviving and kept producing transformative fruit that no secular institution could explain. Two thousand years of very imperfect human stewardship could not extinguish what was genuinely alive within it. That is not a coincidence. That is an argument — not for the perfection of the people, but for the realness of the God they carried.

"Nevertheless the foundation of God standeth sure, having this seal, The Lord knoweth them that are his. And, Let every one that nameth the name of Christ depart from iniquity." — 2 Timothy 2:19 (KJV)

Two truths in one verse. For the wounded believer wondering if anything inside the church is real: God knows exactly who belongs to Him, and that foundation cannot be moved by human failure. For the person performing religion without genuine faith: God also knows exactly who does not belong to Him, and that accounting will be settled with perfect accuracy. The same foundation that comforts the sincere condemns the pretender.

When a Brother Falls

If the church is a hospital, then we need to talk honestly about how hospitals are supposed to respond when one of their own patients has a crisis. Because the way the church handles the failure of its members — how it treats the fallen, the struggling, the publicly broken — is one of the most important testimonies it has to offer the watching world. And the watching world has noticed, for centuries, when the church gets it catastrophically wrong.

"Brethren, if a man be overtaken in a fault, ye which are spiritual, restore him in the spirit of meekness; considering thyself, lest thou also be tempted." — Galatians 6:1 (KJV)

The Greek word translated restore is katartizō. It is the same word used for mending a torn fishing net — the careful, skilled, patient work of setting broken fibers back into their proper place. It is also the word used in ancient Greek medicine for setting a broken or dislocated bone.

Notice what that word demands. It is not a word for ignoring a broken bone because the sight of it is uncomfortable. It is not a word for attacking the person who broke it. It is the word for sitting down beside them, with skill and with gentleness, and doing the slow, careful work of restoration. Three responses are available when a member of the church falls: pretend it did not happen, condemn and distance, or mend. Scripture gives only one of these the name of faithfulness.

"Judge not, that ye be not judged. For with what judgment ye judge, ye shall be judged: and with what measure ye mete, it shall be measured to you again. And why beholdest thou the mote that is in thy brother's eye, but considerest not the beam that is in thine own eye?" — Matthew 7:1–3 (KJV)

The Greek word for judge here is krinō — the act of pronouncing a verdict, of placing yourself as the final authority over another person's standing before God. Jesus is not prohibiting honest observation or righteous discernment. He is prohibiting the kind of hypocritical condemnation that holds another person to a standard the judge has no intention of applying to themselves. The person with a beam in their own eye has no business performing surgery on someone else's mote.

This is where the hypocrisy argument sometimes turns on itself. Not everyone who uses hypocrisy as a reason to reject the church is entirely without hypocrisy themselves. The person who condemns the church for its judgment while refusing any self-examination has put on a different kind of mask. The log-and-speck passage was not written to give people an excuse to avoid accountability. It was written to establish that accountability must begin with the self.

And yet the community of believers cannot function alone.

"And let us consider one another to provoke unto love and to good works: Not forsaking the assembling of ourselves together, as the manner of some is; but exhorting one another: and so much the more, as ye see the day approaching." — Hebrews 10:24–25 (KJV)

C.S. Lewis used the image of logs burning on a fire to illustrate what isolation does to faith. Several logs burning together sustain a strong, consistent flame. Pull one log away and place it on the hearth alone — and it goes cold. Not because the log was defective. Because fire requires community to sustain itself. This is not a metaphor about physical attendance. It is a truth about what genuine community does for the soul that private study, however deep and sincere, cannot fully replicate. The church at its truest is not a performance. It is a fire kept burning by people who refuse to let each other go cold.

The Warning Jesus Never Softened

There is a passage in Matthew 7 that most people who know about the hypocrisy problem in the church have never been told about, and it is one of the most sobering things Jesus ever said. It is the warning that goes beyond the mask — to the people who wore the mask so long and so convincingly that they convinced even themselves.

"Not every one that saith unto me, Lord, Lord, shall enter into the kingdom of heaven; but he that doeth the will of my Father which is in heaven. Many will say to me in that day, Lord, Lord, have we not prophesied in thy name? and in thy name have cast out devils? and in thy name done many wonderful works? And then will I profess unto them, I never knew you: depart from me, ye that work iniquity." — Matthew 7:21–23 (KJV)

Read that carefully. These are not people who rejected Jesus. These are people who called Him Lord. They prophesied in His name. They cast out devils in His name. They did wonderful works in His name. By any outward measure available to the congregation sitting in the pews around them, they looked like the most committed believers in the room. And yet when they stood before the One they claimed to serve, His answer was: I never knew you.

The theologian A.W. Pink observed that the word knew in that passage carries the weight of intimate, relational knowledge — what the Hebrew would call knowledge of approbation, the deep, personal acknowledgment that comes with genuine relationship. Jesus was not saying He had no information about these people. He was saying He had never entered into a genuine, personal relationship with them. They had religion without relationship. They had activity without intimacy. They had performed in His name without ever actually coming to know Him.

This passage is not written to terrify the sincere believer who worries about their own standing. It is written to terrify the person who has been using the church as a costume. And Jesus delivered it not in anger, but with pastoral precision — because the most merciful thing that can be said to a person performing religion without genuine faith is the truth about what they are doing, while there is still time to stop.

In Revelation 3, Jesus dictated a letter to the church at Laodicea. It is addressed not to pagans or persecutors, but to a gathering of people who called themselves by His name. I know thy works, He says, that thou art neither cold nor hot: I would thou wert cold or hot. So then because thou art lukewarm, and neither cold nor hot, I will spue thee out of my mouth. The violence of that image is intentional. God is not slightly displeased with religious performance. He is nauseated by it. The lukewarm church — the one that goes through the motions of worship without genuine heart — is more offensive to God than honest, cold rejection. Why? Because the cold are not pretending. A person who openly rejects God is not wearing a mask. A lukewarm church has institutionalized the mask. And God finds it intolerable.

But here is what the passage does next that should stop you in your tracks. After that devastating indictment, Jesus does not slam the door. He knocks on it. Behold, I stand at the door, and knock: if any man hear my voice, and open the door, I will come in to him, and will sup with him, and he with me. Even to a performance-driven, spiritually hollow church, the Savior stands outside and offers intimacy. Not condemnation. Not abandonment. An invitation. He is waiting for the one person in that building who is ready to stop performing and start actually opening the door. He is still waiting. In every congregation where the lights are on and the words are right but the hearts are far away. He is standing there, knocking, patient beyond any human patience, offering to any individual who will hear Him the one thing religious performance can never produce: His actual presence.

Asaph's Journey and the Place of Clarity

Three thousand years ago, a man named Asaph sat down and wrote what may be the most honest prayer in the entire book of Psalms. He wrote: My feet were almost gone; my steps had well nigh slipped.

Asaph's crisis was not doubt about the existence of God. It was something more specific and more painful. He was looking at the people around him — the wicked, the hypocritical, the people who lived without any apparent concern for God — and they were prospering. They were comfortable. They were healthy. They were undisturbed. And Asaph, who had tried to live faithfully, was suffering. He wrote: Verily I have cleansed my heart in vain, and washed my hands in innocency. What is the point? Why bother?

He tried to reason his way through it. He turned it over in his mind from every direction. He could not find his way out. The problem, analyzed by human intellect alone, had no solution.

And then something shifted. Until I went into the sanctuary of God, he wrote. Then understood I their end.

When Asaph stopped staring at the hypocrites and entered the presence of God, his perspective was completely realigned. He saw what he could not see from a horizontal view. The prosperity of the wicked was a momentary illusion. The ground beneath their feet was more precarious than it appeared. And more importantly — in the presence of God, the question of what other people were getting away with became very small. Because what Asaph found in the sanctuary was something that made everything else pale by comparison.

He wrote the words that close Psalm 73 with a clarity that only comes from that kind of encounter:

"Whom have I in heaven but thee? and there is none upon earth that I desire beside thee. My flesh and my heart faileth: but God is the strength of my heart, and my portion for ever." — Psalm 73:25–26 (KJV)

We do not overcome disappointment with the church by finding perfect people. Perfect people do not exist. We overcome it by shifting our gaze entirely from the imperfect people to the perfect God. The sanctuary — the place of genuine, private, unperformed encounter with God — is where perspective is restored. It is where the wounds inflicted by hypocrites begin to heal. Not because the wounds are minimized, but because what is found in that place is so much greater than what was lost anywhere else.

The Word to Those Inside

This chapter has spent considerable space addressing the person outside the church looking in through a wound. But there is something that must be said directly to the person inside.

"My brethren, be not many masters, knowing that we shall receive the greater condemnation." — James 3:1 (KJV)

The Greek word krima — condemnation, or judgment — indicates a stricter evaluation, a heavier sentence, a more exacting standard. God does not grade spiritual leaders on the same curve as everyone else. The higher the platform, the greater the accountability for what is done on it.

Why? Because a spiritual leader is not just managing their own soul. They are handling the souls of other people. They are standing between searching, wounded, hungry human beings and the God those people are trying to find. When a leader acts hypocritically — when they preach grace and practice cruelty, when they speak of humility and perform superiority, when they use the authority of the pulpit for personal gain or ego — they do not just damage their own relationship with God. They place a stumbling block in front of the most vulnerable people in the room. The person sitting in the third row who has never been inside a church before, who came because someone they loved invited them, who is watching the person at the front to see whether what is being preached is actually real — that person is watching you. Your life is their first sermon.

"If we say that we have no sin, we deceive ourselves, and the truth is not in us. If we confess our sins, he is faithful and just to forgive us our sins, and to cleanse us from all unrighteousness." — 1 John 1:8–9 (KJV)

The witness of the church to the watching world is not our perfection. It is our transparency. It is the willingness to stand before people and say: I am broken too. I am still being healed. I do not have it all together, and I never claimed to. But I know the One who is putting me back together, and He is real, and He is faithful, and that is why I am still here.

That kind of honesty is not weakness. It is the most powerful testimony the church has ever offered. A perfect performance that eventually cracks destroys people's faith. An honest acknowledgment of ongoing brokenness that is nonetheless sustained by genuine grace builds it.

"And he gave some, apostles; and some, prophets; and some, evangelists; and some, pastors and teachers; For the perfecting of the saints, for the work of the ministry, for the edifying of the body of Christ: Till we all come in the unity of the faith, and of the knowledge of the Son of God, unto a perfect man, unto the measure of the stature of the fulness of Christ." — Ephesians 4:11–13 (KJV)

The word till in that passage carries all the weight. Till we all come. Not when we arrive. Till. The church is a construction site, not a finished building. The people inside it are works in progress, not completed products. If you enter the church expecting finished products and find construction in progress, you have not found evidence that God's work is failing. You have found evidence that it is underway.

Peter's Question and the Honest Answer

John 6 records the moment when Jesus said something so demanding, so difficult, so far from what the crowds had been hoping to hear, that many of His disciples walked away. Not the enemies. Not the religious authorities. The disciples. The people who had been following Him.

Jesus turned to the twelve and asked: Will ye also go away?

Peter answered with the words that have echoed through every generation of believers who have found themselves exhausted, wounded, disillusioned, and still unable to leave:

"Lord, to whom shall we go? thou hast the words of eternal life. And we believe and are sure that thou art that Christ, the Son of the living God." — John 6:68–69 (KJV)

That is the honest answer to the person who wants to walk away from God because of the hypocrites in His house.

Where else are you going to go?

No other philosophy has the words of eternal life. No secular worldview can fill the emptiness that God placed in the human heart and that only He can satisfy. No other religious system provides a God who loved a hostile world enough to enter it, absorb its punishment, and rise from the dead to prove that the rescue was complete. Walking away from the only perfect Savior because of the failures of imperfect people does not protect you from pain. It leaves you with the pain and removes the only One who has ever demonstrated the power to heal it.

Peter was not naive. He knew who was sitting at the table with him. He knew that one of the twelve would betray Jesus before the night was over. He had watched people perform religion his whole life. He would go on to fail spectacularly himself — denying the Lord three times before the rooster crowed. But he had also seen the lame walk and the blind see and the dead come back to life. He had heard teaching that no human mind could have produced on its own. And when the crowds walked away because the demands were too hard, Peter looked around at the alternatives and arrived at the only honest answer a searching soul can reach: there is nowhere else to go. Not because the church is perfect. Not because the people are perfect. Because He is.

The Invitation

This chapter is for everyone who has been put off by the people they found inside God's house and used that experience as a reason to stay away from God entirely.

Your experience was real. The wound was real. The person who hurt you was wrong. And if that person stood in a position of spiritual authority when they did it, they carry a weight of accountability before God that is far heavier than they may realize. He does not ignore pastoral abuse or pulpit hypocrisy. He sees the dead men's bones underneath the whitewashed surface. He knows the difference between the mask and the face. And that accounting will be settled with perfect justice by the only Judge whose sight goes all the way to the heart.

But do not let what that person did become the wall between you and God. That is exactly what the enemy wants. He has used human failure inside the church as a stumbling block for searching souls since the first century, because it is one of the most effective tools available to him. When a person in God's name does something that wounds you, the temptation is to transfer the wound from the person to God — to conclude that if this is what His people are like, He must be like them, or He must not exist at all. That transfer is a lie. God is not that person. He never was. He was the One who was offended by that person long before you were.

Inside or outside the church, remember this: the people you find in those pews are not the finished product. They are the raw material. Some of them are genuinely being transformed by the grace they talk about. Some of them are still early in the process. Some of them — and Jesus said this plainly — are not actually there for transformation at all. They are there for performance, for community, for habit, for appearances. God knows the difference. You cannot always see it. But He can.

What you can do is stop watching the other patients in the waiting room and start looking at the Physician. Because the hospital is not the healer. The Physician is. And He is still seeing patients. He has not turned anyone away who came to Him honestly, without a mask, with their actual condition rather than the one they wanted to project. He receives the broken. He restores the wounded. He does not require you to be well before you enter. He only requires that you come.

The invitation has never been complicated. The Spirit and the bride say, Come. The one who is thirsty is invited. The one who is willing is welcome. Scripture's final invitation does not require a theological pedigree or a spotless record or a church membership card:

"And the Spirit and the bride say, Come. And let him that heareth say, Come. And let him that is athirst come. And whosoever will, let him take the water of life freely." — Revelation 22:17 (KJV)

Whosoever will. The door in those words is as wide as the universe and it leads to one place. Not a building. Not a denomination. Not an institution. To the One who built all of it for the sole purpose of having the people He loves find their way home to Him.

Your life is someone's first sermon. Whatever you carry in you — the broken parts and the healing parts and the honest parts — someone near you is watching to see whether what you believe actually changes how you live. Not because you are required to be perfect. But because the world is full of people looking for evidence that grace is real. Be that evidence. Not with a performance. With a life.

My Reflection

I have spent years building something quietly, in rooms where no one was watching, and I would not trade it for anything the loudest congregation on earth could offer.

I do not attend church in the traditional sense. The crowds, the noise, the social performance of large gatherings — these things pull me away from the kind of focused, private, deeply personal connection with God that I have spent years carefully building. I am not outgoing by nature. I am protective of the space where God speaks to me, and I have found that space most clearly in quietness, in study, in the kind of uninterrupted time alone with Scripture that crowds make difficult.

I hold some honest uncertainty about whether this is entirely right. Hebrews 10:24–25 commands believers not to forsake the assembling of themselves together — and I take that seriously. The image of logs burning together, holding each other's heat, is a real warning about what isolation can do to faith over time. Believers need each other. The friction of real relationship, the accountability of genuine community, the experience of worshipping alongside other broken people who are also reaching toward God — these things have value that private study alone cannot fully replicate.

But what I do know is this. The faith that sustains a person through the hardest moments of life — through losses that have no clean explanation and seasons that strip everything down to what is real — is the faith that was built privately, personally, in the quiet place where it is just you and God and the honest questions you are afraid to ask anyone else. If you have only ever known God through other people — through a church, a community, a family tradition — I am concerned for you. Not because those things are worthless. But because a faith that exists only in company tends to collapse in solitude. And life will put you in solitude.

God does not want your membership in a group. He wants you. Privately. Personally. He wants to be known by you the way you know your own heartbeat — not because someone described it to you, but because you have felt it for yourself. Build that first. Guard it fiercely. And then, from that foundation, the church community becomes what it was always meant to be — not your source of faith, but a place to bring the faith you already carry.

A Prayer for the Wounded and the Watching

Father —

We come to this chapter carrying different kinds of weight. Some of us are carrying wounds given to us in Your name, by people who wore the costume of faith and used it carelessly or cruelly. Some of us are inside the church, and this chapter has held up a mirror we would rather not look into. Some of us are watching from outside, not sure whether any of this is real, not sure whether the gap between what the church preaches and what it practices is too large to ever bridge.

For the wounded — we ask You to do what only You can do. Take the place that person occupied in their faith and fill it with Yourself. Let the collapse of a human foundation become the beginning of a foundation that cannot be moved. Let them hear, in whatever quiet place they will allow You in, that You were never that person. You were the One who was wronged by that person before they were. And You have been waiting — patient beyond any patience they have ever experienced — for them to come to You directly, without intermediaries, without performances, without the crowd.

For those inside the church — remind us that someone is always watching. Not to judge us, but because they are hungry and they are deciding whether what we carry is real. Let us carry it honestly. Not as a performance of spiritual achievement, but as a transparent, living testimony that grace is doing something in us that we could not do ourselves. Let us put down the masks. The dead men's bones underneath them are not hidden from You, and the world is exhausted by whitewashed surfaces.

For the watching, the doubting, the wounded, and the searching — let Asaph's journey be theirs. Let them find the sanctuary. Let them find what he found there. Let them discover that in Your presence, the question of what the hypocrites are getting away with becomes very small, because what is found in that place is so much greater than what was lost anywhere else.

You are not the church. You are the One the church points toward when it is functioning the way You designed it. And when it is not — when it is broken and performing and failing and falling short of everything it was called to be — You are still exactly who You have always been. Unchanging. Unfailing. Standing at the door. Knocking.

In the name of the Father, the Son, and the Holy Spirit.

Amen.

"Nevertheless the foundation of God standeth sure, having this seal, The Lord knoweth them that are his. And, Let every one that nameth the name of Christ depart from iniquity." — 2 Timothy 2:19 (KJV)

Chapter Ten

What Is My Purpose — And Did I Fulfill It?

" The LORD will perfect that which concerneth me: thy mercy, O LORD, endureth for ever: forsake not the works of thine own hands." — Psalm 138:8 (KJV)

There is a particular kind of quiet that settles over a person when the pace of life finally slows down against their will. It might come through illness. It might come through age. It might come through a body that simply refuses to keep moving at the speed the mind still remembers. And in that quiet — sometimes for the first time in decades — a person is left alone with themselves and with a question they have never had the stillness to ask.

What was I here for? And did I do it?

I want you to know that this question does not come from weakness. It does not come from failure. In many cases, it comes from the first honest moment a soul has had in years. The noise of living

— the jobs, the arguments, the bills, the distractions, the years that piled one on top of another — kept this question at arm's length for a long time. But it was always there. Every soul carries it. And when the noise finally stops, the question surfaces like something that was always underneath everything else, waiting patiently for the moment you were ready to face it.

I believe God sometimes creates that quiet on purpose. Not as punishment. Not as abandonment. But as invitation. He slows the body down so He can finally speak to the heart.

This chapter is for the person in that quiet place. It is for the one who lived hard and fast and wonders now whether any of it added up. It is for the one who spent decades chasing things that no longer feel worth what they cost. It is for the one who raised children, buried loved ones, made mistakes they cannot undo, and is now sitting still for the first time — looking back at the full length of their life the way you look at a road in the rearview mirror, trying to make sense of where it went.

Before we go further into this chapter, I want to be honest with you about something regarding the promise of Jeremiah 29:11 — for I know the thoughts that I think toward you, saith the LORD, thoughts of peace and not of evil, to give you an expected end. It is one of the most quoted verses in the modern church. And it is one of the most quoted out of its original context. In the original Hebrew, God spoke these words to the entire nation of Israel while they were in Babylonian captivity. The you throughout this passage is plural — the whole community of exiles. In Jeremiah 29:10, directly before this verse, God tells the nation He will bring them back to their land after seventy years. This was a corporate national promise of restoration — God speaking to His people as a people, not as isolated individuals.

I tell you this not to strip the verse of its meaning. I tell you this because you deserve to know what God's original word actually said — and because the truth is even more beautiful than the institutional shortcut. The God whose character is revealed in that promise — the God who planned shalom and not ra for an entire nation in captivity, the God whose machashavah, whose artisan-designed plans, outlasted seventy years of exile — that God is the same God who knew you before you were formed. He does not lose track of nations in exile and He does not lose track of individual souls. The promise He made to Israel reveals who He is. And who He is applies to every soul He has ever made.

Your life was not an accident. Not one day of it. Not one decision. Not one moment of pain or joy or confusion. God knew you before the first breath entered your lungs. And He has been working in every chapter of your story — even the chapters you are most ashamed of — toward something you may not have had the eyes to see while you were living it.

That is not a comfort I am offering you to make you feel better. That is the testimony of Scripture. And we are going to walk through it together, one truth at a time.

You Were Written Before You Were Born

Before your parents knew your name. Before the first cell of your body was formed. Before any human being on earth was aware you were coming — God knew you.

"The LORD hath called me from the womb; from the bowels of my mother hath he made mention of my name." — Isaiah 49:1 (KJV)

Isaiah spoke these words under the direct inspiration of God, recording what God declared about the one He had summoned before birth. But the theology they contain belongs to every soul. The Hebrew word translated formed elsewhere in the Scriptures is yatsar

— the same word used for a potter working clay. God fashioned your frame the way a master craftsman shapes something with intention and care. But notice that He called by name before He even formed the body. The knowing came first. And in the ancient Hebrew world, the word God uses for that knowing — yada — is not a casual awareness. Yada is an intimate, covenantal word. It means God knew you with a deep, purposeful, relational knowing — a knowledge that included a specific designation and design for your life — before your body even existed.

David understood this. He marveled at it:

"I will praise thee; for I am fearfully and wonderfully made: marvellous are thy works; and that my soul knoweth right well." — Psalm 139:14 (KJV)

He went further, writing that his substance was not hidden from God even when he was made in secret, curiously wrought in the lowest parts of the earth. That God's eyes saw his substance even while it was yet unformed. That in God's book all his members were written, which in continuance were fashioned, when as yet there was none of them. The Puritan theologian John Flavel reflected on this with awe, writing that God did not create haphazardly — that He had his model or pattern before it, according to which it moulded every part. Your body, your mind, your temperament, your particular kind of intelligence, your specific capacity for compassion or courage or creativity — all of it was written out in God's book before a single part of it existed in the world.

The New Testament carries this same truth into the language of the Greek world:

"For we are his workmanship, created in Christ Jesus unto good works, which God hath before ordained that we should walk in them." — Ephesians 2:10 (KJV)

The Greek word translated workmanship is poiema — from which we get the English word poem. A poem is not an accident. A poem is crafted. Every word chosen. Every line considered. Every image placed exactly where the author intended. You are God's poiema. His masterwork. His crafted creation. And the verse does not stop at the fact of your creation — it goes further. It says there were good works that God before ordained that you should walk in them. Prepared in advance. Waiting for you. A specific path, designed before you were born, that God always intended your life to travel.

The theologian A.W. Pink captured this truth precisely: God not only predetermined the salvation of His own but foreordained the good works which they are to walk in. Your salvation was not the end of the plan. It was the beginning of the path.

The philosopher Jean-Paul Sartre — one of the great secular thinkers of the twentieth century — confessed something remarkable near the end of his life. Despite spending his career arguing against God and any transcendent purpose, Sartre admitted that he could not shake the persistent feeling that his existence was not random — that he had been somehow expected, prepared, and intended. Even a man who built his entire philosophy on the rejection of God could not fully escape the intuition that Someone had anticipated him.

You were expected. You were prepared. You were prefigured in the mind of God long before the world knew your name.

The Foundation Every Soul Shares

Before we talk about what makes your purpose unique, we must first establish what every soul shares. Because there is a foundation — a bedrock — beneath every individual calling. And if a person builds their search for purpose without this foundation, they will search their entire life and never fully find what they are looking for.

The wisest man who ever lived searched for it the long way. King Solomon — who had more wealth, more wisdom, more pleasure, and more achievement than any human being of his era — spent the Book of Ecclesiastes documenting what he found at the end of all of it. He chased wisdom. He chased pleasure. He chased work and accomplishment. He chased everything the world offers a person who has the means to pursue it. And at the end of every road, he came back with the same word: hebel. Vapor. Breath. Meaningless.

Not because those things were evil. But because none of them were designed to satisfy the deepest thing in a human heart.

"Let us hear the conclusion of the whole matter: Fear God, and keep his commandments: for this is the whole duty of man." — Ecclesiastes 12:13 (KJV)

The Hebrew phrase here is kol adam — the whole of mankind. Not some men. Not religious men. Not men in a particular culture or era. Every human soul that has ever drawn breath. The universal, non-negotiable foundation of human purpose is this: know God. Fear Him. Walk in His ways. Augustine of Hippo translated this passage with stunning precision: kol adam means that reverencing God and obeying His commandments is not merely a task added to human life. It is the complete summation and definition of what it means to be fully human. A person who has everything but this has nothing that lasts. A person who has nothing but this has everything that matters.

"Thou shalt love the Lord thy God with all thy heart, and with all thy soul, and with all thy mind. This is the first and great commandment. And the second is like unto it, Thou shalt love thy neighbour as thyself." — Matthew 22:37–39 (KJV)

This is the foundation. Love God. Love your neighbor. Everything else — every individual calling, every specific gift, every unique purpose — is built on top of this. Without it, the entire structure has no ground to stand on.

"He hath shewed thee, O man, what is good; and what doth the LORD require of thee, but to do justly, and to love mercy, and to walk humbly with thy God." — Micah 6:8 (KJV)

Do justly. Love mercy. Walk humbly with your God. This is the universal prerequisite. No individual calling can be rightly fulfilled if this covenant baseline is abandoned. Before you can understand the specific, you must be standing on the general. Before the particular path becomes clear, this foundation must be laid.

Purpose Is Revealed in Layers

Here is something I want you to understand, because I believe it will bring a kind of relief that logic alone cannot give you.

God does not hand you the full map on the day you are born. He does not sit a child down and say — here is the complete blueprint of everything your life will mean, every person you will touch, every purpose you will serve. He does not work that way. And the reason He does not work that way is not because He is withholding something from you. It is because the map is too large for a human being to carry all at once. And because the next step is always revealed through the faithful taking of the current step.

"But the path of the just is as the shining light, that shineth more and more unto the perfect day." — Proverbs 4:18 (KJV)

Not a sudden floodlight that exposes everything at once. A shining light that grows brighter as you walk. The next turn on the road becomes visible only after you have walked faithfully through the stretch you are currently on. This is not a design flaw in the way God guides His people. It is an intentional feature. It requires trust. It requires dependence. It keeps you walking close to the One who holds the full map, rather than running ahead on your own.

"I have declared the former things from the beginning; and they went forth out of my mouth, and I shewed them; I did them suddenly, and they came to pass." — Isaiah 48:3 (KJV)

God sees the end from the beginning. The entire arc. The full story. Every domino. Every consequence. Every connection between decisions made in one decade and fruit produced in another. You and I see one frame at a time. He sees the entire film. And His counsel — His design, His purpose for your life — will stand. It cannot be permanently derailed by your wandering. It cannot be cancelled by your failures. Because it was established in His eternal counsel before any of it happened.

The Puritan John Flavel understood this deeply. He wrote that a believer must trust God in the way of your duty rather than demanding to see the future. The theologian J.I. Packer noted that God deliberately makes the path perplexing so that we are driven out of self-confidence and forced to wait on Him. And Proverbs gives us the simplest and most profound instruction for navigating a life whose full purpose has not yet been revealed:

"Trust in the LORD with all thine heart; and lean not unto thine own understanding. In all thy ways acknowledge him, and he shall direct thy paths." — Proverbs 3:5–6 (KJV)

Flavel made the connection between obedience and revelation explicit: Reduce what you know into practice, and you shall know what is your duty to practise. If you want to know God's will for your future, obey His will in your present. Purpose is revealed in layers. And each new layer is unlocked by faithful walking in the layer you already have.

Every Soul Is Unique

The foundation is the same for every soul. But upon that foundation, God builds something that has never existed before and will never exist again — you.

"Now there are diversities of gifts, but the same Spirit. And there are differences of administrations, but the same Lord. And there are diversities of operations, but it is the same God which worketh all in all. But the manifestation of the Spirit is given to every man to profit withal." — 1 Corinthians 12:4–7 (KJV)

The Greek word translated diversities is diairesis — a distribution, an allotment. God does not mass-produce callings. He meticulously distributes unique functions to individual souls. The word for gifts is charisma — a grace gift, a special enablement given freely by God. And notice: these gifts are given to every man to profit withal. Not to make you famous. Not to make you wealthy. To profit the body — to serve the people around you and to build up the kingdom of God.

Paul returns to this theme in his letter to the Romans:

"For as we have many members in one body, and all members have not the same office: So we, being many, are one body in Christ, and every one members one of another. Having then gifts differing according to the grace that is given to us." — Romans 12:4–6 (KJV)

A human body requires every part. The eye cannot do what the hand does. The foot cannot do what the ear does. And the body cannot function if every part insists on being the same part. In the same way, the church — the body of Christ — requires the full diversity of gifts and callings God distributes. The uniqueness of your calling is not accidental. It is architecturally essential. You were designed to fulfill a role that no one else can occupy in exactly the way you can occupy it.

To covet another person's calling is to misunderstand the design. To dismiss your own calling as insignificant is to tell the Architect He made a mistake.

Every soul is different. The beauty of deeply knowing God and living faithfully through Him is that it unveils layer after layer of that difference — layers you would never have seen if you had spent your life running on your own power. No two people in the history of this world have ever had the exact same purpose. The path that was designed for you was designed for the specific combination of your experiences, your wounds, your gifts, your particular way of seeing the world, and your exact place in the story God is writing.

Like a domino effect — who knows what decisions led to what outcomes, what early chapter positioned what later moment. But God knows. He always knew.

The Gift Without the Giver

Now let me address something that every honest person who has lived long enough already knows. A person can operate in their gifts without God. They can build a career on their natural talent, achieve impressive things by their own strength, and go an entire lifetime exercising the very abilities God placed in them — without ever acknowledging Him as the source. The world is full of gifted people who are running entirely on borrowed power and do not know it.

But there is always something missing.

"I am the vine, ye are the branches: He that abideth in me, and I in him, the same bringeth forth much fruit: for without me ye can do nothing." — John 15:5 (KJV)

The Greek word translated without is choris — apart from, separated from. And the word translated nothing is ouden — not a little, not mediocre things, but absolute zero of eternal value. Jesus does not say that apart from Him you cannot achieve things. The world proves that separated people achieve things every day. He says that apart from Him, nothing you produce carries the weight it was designed to carry. A branch can survive a few days after it is cut from the vine. It might still look green. But it cannot bear fruit. It can only wither.

This is why gifts exercised without God always fall short of their true purpose. They may gain earthly applause. They may produce results that impress other people. But they produce no eternal fruit. They glorify the branch and forget the Vine.

"And thou say in thine heart, My power and the might of mine hand hath gotten me this wealth. But thou shalt remember the LORD thy God: for it is he that giveth thee power to get wealth, that he may establish his covenant which he sware unto thy fathers." — Deuteronomy 8:17–18 (KJV)

Do not say in your heart that your own hand did this. The Puritan John Flavel emphasized that the success of your callings and earthly employments is, by the divine blessing, not human diligence alone.

Paul pressed the point further when he asked the Corinthians a question with no comfortable answer:

"For who maketh thee to differ from another? and what hast thou that thou didst not receive? now if thou didst receive it, why dost thou glory, as if thou hadst not received it?" — 1 Corinthians 4:7 (KJV)

Augustine of Hippo responded to that question with a clarity that silences every proud answer: a person only truly understands the Lord when he realizes that his very capacity to understand is a gift from the Lord. To glory in one's own talent as if it were self-generated is supreme foolishness.

"Every good gift and every perfect gift is from above, and cometh down from the Father of lights, with whom is no variableness, neither shadow of turning." — James 1:17 (KJV)

Every good thing you have ever been able to do — every talent, every capacity, every moment of insight or strength or creativity — came down from the Father. To use it without acknowledging Him is not just ingratitude. It turns the blessing into a snare of pride, robbing God of the glory that His initial investment was always designed to produce.

The Parable of the Talents makes the accounting of this unavoidable. The servant who buried his talent was not condemned for evil. He was condemned for doing nothing — for failing to invest what the master had given him in the master's service.

"Well done, thou good and faithful servant: thou hast been faithful over a few things, I will make thee ruler over many things: enter thou into the joy of thy lord." — Matthew 25:21 (KJV)

Agathos — morally excellent. Pistos — faithful, reliable, trustworthy. That is the measure. Not greatness by the world's standard. Faithfulness with what you were given. And faithfulness, at its root, requires knowing whose it was in the first place.

The gift without the Giver is a branch without a Vine. It lives for a season. But it cannot bear the fruit it was created for.

Moses and Paul — Purpose Delayed, Redirected, Redeemed

If you are someone who looks back over your life and sees decades of wandering — years spent in places you should not have been, doing things you wish you had not done, living at a distance from the God who designed you — then I need you to sit with two men before we go any further.

The first is Moses.

Moses began his life with every advantage. Raised in the household of Pharaoh, educated in all the wisdom of the Egyptians, positioned by circumstance to be one of the most powerful men in the ancient world. He also knew, somewhere in his bones, that he was destined to be a deliverer of his people. But he tried to fulfill that destiny through his own strength. He saw an Egyptian beating a Hebrew slave. He looked around. And he killed the man and buried him in the sand.

The plan collapsed immediately. He fled for his life. And for the next forty years, Moses — the man destined to part the Red Sea, to speak face to face with God, to lead two million people out of slavery — tended sheep in the Midianite wilderness. Forty years. An age where most people would have concluded their time for purpose had long passed.

And then God appeared in a burning bush.

"And the LORD said, I have surely seen the affliction of my people which are in Egypt, and have heard their cry by reason of their taskmasters; for I know their sorrows; And I am come down to deliver them out of the hand of the Egyptians... Come now therefore, and I will send thee unto Pharaoh, that thou mayest bring forth my people the children of Israel out of Egypt." — Exodus 3:7–10 (KJV)

Eighty years old. His greatest days still ahead of him.

The wilderness did not disqualify Moses. The wilderness prepared Moses. It stripped away the pride of the palace. It taught him the silence of God's presence before it taught him the power of God's voice. Every year he spent thinking his time had passed was a year God was building in him what Pharaoh's house never could have built.

The ancient world understood this pattern — that God can use the ruins of a wasted life to build something new — better than we often give it credit for. Among the apocryphal texts preserved in the Septuagint tradition is a short prayer attributed to King Manasseh during his captivity in Babylon. It is one of the most raw and personal prayers of repentance in all of ancient literature. Writing from the bottom of his life — a man who had burned his own children in fire, filled Jerusalem with innocent blood, and demolished every altar of righteousness his father had built — Manasseh prayed with a directness that no polished theology can produce: "I have sinned above the number of the sands of the sea... and now I bend the knee of mine heart, beseeching thee of grace." And Scripture records that God heard him. God restored him. A man whose sin had no floor met a mercy that had no ceiling. The Prayer of Manasseh survived in the ancient manuscripts because God intended every generation to know: the door of restoration is open to whoever will bend the knee. No matter what they have done. No matter how many years it cost.

The second man is Paul.

Before he was Paul, he was Saul of Tarsus — a man so violently opposed to the early church that he dragged believers from their homes and delivered them to imprisonment and death. By any measure of human accounting, his past was not a resume. It was a criminal record. He acknowledged this himself:

"For ye have heard of my conversation in time past in the Jews' religion, how that beyond measure I persecuted the church of God, and wasted it." — Galatians 1:13 (KJV)

He did not soften that record. He carried it with him as honest reckoning with what he had been. But on the road to Damascus, something happened that no human plan had prepared for:

"And suddenly there shined round about him a light from heaven: And he fell to the earth, and heard a voice saying unto him, Saul, Saul, why persecutest thou me?... And he trembling and astonished said, Lord, what wilt thou have me to do?" — Acts 9:3–6 (KJV)

The man who had been the church's greatest enemy became its greatest missionary. The man who had stood watching Stephen be stoned to death wrote half of the New Testament. And he never let his past define his future:

"Brethren, I count not myself to have apprehended: but this one thing I do, forgetting those things which are behind, and reaching forth unto those things which are before, I press toward the mark for the prize of the high calling of God in Christ Jesus." — Philippians 3:13–14 (KJV)

Forgetting those things which are behind. Not pretending they did not happen. Not ignoring the wreckage. But refusing to let the wreckage be the final word.

If you look at your past and see things that make you doubt whether God can still use you — Moses tended sheep for forty years. Paul murdered Christians. Manasseh burned his own children in fire. And all of them finished their lives having shaken kingdoms and altered the course of human history. The wilderness does not mean the story is over. Sometimes it means the story is just beginning to take the shape God always intended.

Suffering as Preparation

I want to say something about the pain you have carried. Not to minimize it. Not to explain it away with theological vocabulary that leaves the wound untouched. But to tell you what I believe with everything I am — that your suffering was not wasted. That your pain was not random. That God has been working in it in ways you may not have been able to see while you were inside of it.

"Blessed be God, even the Father of our Lord Jesus Christ, the Father of mercies, and the God of all comfort; Who comforteth us in all our tribulation, that we may be able to comfort them which are in any trouble, by the comfort wherewith we ourselves are comforted of God." — 2 Corinthians 1:3–4 (KJV)

The comfort you receive from God in your darkest moments was never designed to end with you. It was given so you could become a conduit of that exact comfort to someone else in their distress. Your pain — the specific, particular shape of it — qualifies you to reach a person whose pain has that same shape. Someone who has never suffered cannot fully comfort someone who has. The comfort is passed down through the hands of those who received it in the same darkness.

"Wherein ye greatly rejoice, though now for a season, if need be, ye are in heaviness through manifold temptations: That the trial of your faith, being much more precious than of gold that perisheth, though it be tried with fire, might be found unto praise and honour and glory at the appearing of Jesus Christ." — 1 Peter 1:6–7 (KJV)

The fire of trial does not destroy genuine faith. It refines it. It burns away the dross — the performance, the self-reliance, the theoretical belief that sounds convincing in comfortable seasons but has never been tested — and what remains after the fire is something precious and real. This is the actual mechanism by which God uses the hardest seasons of a human life to build something in that person that could not have been built any other way.

Paul called this the pole-star of divine providence when he wrote that all things work together for good to those who love God, who are called according to His purpose. The Puritan John Flavel called this promise the compass by which God's providence flawlessly directs the course of a believer's life. He noted that the all things working for good include not only blessings but things that are evil in themselves, as temptations and afflictions. Even the moral failures and painful setbacks are not outside this sovereign design. God can take what we entertained with sighs and tears and cause us to part with it with joy — because those very afflictions were the instruments of our good.

Augustine of Hippo defended this truth with a force that has never been answered: he asked whether any evil could possibly happen to the faithful that God cannot turn to their absolute profit. The answer Scripture returns is no. Not one trial. Not one failure. Not one season of darkness. God wastes nothing in the life of the person who loves Him.

Your suffering was preparation. For what, you may not fully see yet. But it was not wasted. Not one day of it.

Did I Fulfill It? The Question of Regret

Now we have to face the center of the question directly. Not the easier parts — not the theology of purpose or the beauty of God's design. But the hard, personal, honest part. The part the person asking this question is really asking.

Did I do it? Did I live it? Did I fulfill what I was put here for?

"And I will restore to you the years that the locust hath eaten, the cankerworm, and the caterpiller, and the palmerworm, my great army which I sent among you." — Joel 2:25 (KJV)

The Hebrew word for restore is shalam. In a legal context, shalam means to make restitution — to repay the full value of what was destroyed so that the person who suffered the loss is made completely whole again. God is not offering a partial recovery. He is promising a shalam — a complete restoration of the value of what the locusts devoured. The years of wandering. The years of recklessness. The years spent in the wrong places for the wrong reasons. God says: I can restore what was lost. I can recover its value. I can make you whole.

"Remember ye not the former things, neither consider the things of old. Behold, I will do a new thing; now it shall spring forth; shall ye not know it? I will even make a way in the wilderness, and rivers in the desert." — Isaiah 43:18–19 (KJV)

Do not be paralyzed by the former things. God is not limited by your calendar. He is not constrained by the years that are behind you. He can bring rivers out of the desert. He can do a new thing in a life that the world has already written off. Late-season fruit is still fruit. And a repentant heart is never too old to yield it.

"My grace is sufficient for thee: for my strength is made perfect in weakness. Most gladly therefore will I rather glory in my infirmities, that the power of Christ may rest upon me." — 2 Corinthians 12:9 (KJV)

The Greek word translated sufficient is arkeo — enough, unfailing, satisfactory. The word translated made perfect is teleioo — to complete, to bring to its intended purpose. God's grace does not weakly excuse our failures. His grace completes its intended purpose precisely within our human frailty. When you look at your life and see a massive gap between the perfection you were called to and the brokenness you actually achieved, God declares that His grace is entirely enough to bridge that chasm. Your weakness becomes the necessary platform for the power of Christ to rest upon you.

"It is of the LORD's mercies that we are not consumed, because his compassions fail not. They are new every morning: great is thy faithfulness." — Lamentations 3:22–23 (KJV)

God's mercies are not exhausted by yesterday's sins. His compassions are renewed every single day. Satan will tell you that you are unworthy — but you were always unworthy, and God chose to love you anyway. Therefore past unworthiness cannot be a barrier to fellowship with Him today. You cannot exhaust a grace that is resupplied by the Creator every morning.

It Is Never Too Late

"And about the eleventh hour he went out, and found others standing idle, and saith unto them, Why stand ye here all the day idle? They say unto him, Because no man hath hired us. He saith unto them, Go ye also into the vineyard; and whatsoever is right, that shall ye receive." — Matthew 20:6–7 (KJV)

The eleventh hour. One hour left before the workday ends. And the master still goes out looking for workers. Still finds them. Still hires them. Still pays them the same wage as those who had worked since dawn. No matter when a person comes to God, no matter how late in the day, they receive the same acceptance, the same blessing, the same grace as those who have followed Him from their youth.

It is not too late to come back. It is not too late to be used.

But if there is a single passage in all of Scripture that answers the fear of the person who has lived the most broken, the most distant, the most reckless life — it is this:

"And he said unto Jesus, Lord, remember me when thou comest into thy kingdom. And Jesus said unto him, Verily I say unto thee, To day shalt thou be with me in paradise." — Luke 23:42–43 (KJV)

A criminal. Nailed to a cross. Receiving the due reward of his deeds, as he himself admitted. No time left. No chance to make restitution, join a church, perform good works, or undo what had been done. Nothing to offer. Only a dying request: Lord, remember me.

And Jesus said: To day shalt thou be with me in paradise.

Not tomorrow. Not after a period of reflection. Today. Immediate. Absolute. Complete.

God's willingness to receive a repentant soul has no expiration date prior to death. If you have breath in your body, the offer stands. The grace is available. The door is open. The master is still walking out to the vineyard looking for the eleventh-hour worker.

The Season of Stillness

I said at the beginning of this chapter that God sometimes creates that quiet on purpose. Let me press into that further.

When illness slows a person down, or age begins to limit what the body can do, the world's instinct is to view it as loss. Loss of productivity. Loss of relevance. Loss of purpose. But the Bible frames these seasons with an entirely different language.

"Rest in the LORD, and wait patiently for him." — Psalm 37:7 (KJV)

The Hebrew word behind rest is damam — to be still, to be silent, to cease striving. And the posture of waiting it commands is not passive resignation but the active, expectant stillness of one who has placed their full trust in the character of God. He is commanding two things at once: release your striving — and in that release, come to know God experientially. Not academically. Not intellectually. But the way you know someone you have sat with in the quiet, someone who has spoken directly into your heart.

The busyness of living rarely allows for that kind of knowing. There is too much noise. Too much movement. Too many demands pulling in too many directions. But a season of stillness — even one forced upon you by physical limitation — strips away the noise. And in the quiet, God finally has room to speak.

"Therefore, behold, I will allure her, and bring her into the wilderness, and speak comfortably unto her." — Hosea 2:14 (KJV)

Speak comfortably — literally, in the Hebrew, speak to her heart. God brings people into the wilderness — into the stripped-down, quiet, uncomfortable place — because that is where He can finally speak directly to the heart. Not to the schedule. Not to the ambition. Not to the public face the world sees. To the heart.

If you are in a season of forced stillness right now — I want you to consider the possibility that God did not bring you there to punish you. He may have brought you there to finally have the conversation with you that the noise of your life never allowed.

"They shall still bring forth fruit in old age; they shall be fat and flourishing; To shew that the LORD is upright: he is my rock, and there is no unrighteousness in him." — Psalm 92:14–15 (KJV)

Still. That word is doing a great deal of work in that verse. Not they used to bring forth fruit. Not they brought forth fruit once. Still. Present tense. Ongoing. The spiritually rooted person does not retire from bearing fruit. They bear a different fruit in a different season — the fruit of maturity, of wisdom, of a life that has weathered things and come out still standing.

"That the aged men be sober, grave, temperate, sound in faith, in charity, in patience. The aged women likewise, that they be in behaviour as becometh holiness... teachers of good things." — Titus 2:2–3 (KJV)

Mentorship. Patience. Gravity. Temperance. Sound faith. These are not qualities that come easily to the young. They are hammered out in the crucible of decades. And the church — the family — the next generation — desperately needs the people who carry them.

"And even to your old age I am he; and even to hoar hairs will I carry you: I have made, and I will bear; even I will carry, and will deliver you." — Isaiah 46:4 (KJV)

John Flavel noted that God's providence runs parallel with the line of life. All the way to the end. He does not abandon His workmanship when it grows frail. The One who made you carries you. And the season when you most need to be carried is not the season when your purpose ends — it is often the season when your most important purpose begins.

There is a man in the Bible whose entire life was a long, faithful wait for one specific moment. His name was Simeon.

"And, behold, there was a man in Jerusalem, whose name was Simeon; and the same man was just and devout, waiting for the consolation of Israel: and the Holy Ghost was upon him. And it was revealed unto him by the Holy Ghost, that he should not see death, before he had seen the Lord's Christ... Then took he him up in his arms, and blessed God, and said, Lord, now lettest thou thy servant depart in peace, according to thy word: For mine eyes have seen thy salvation, Which thou hast prepared before the face of all people; A light to lighten the Gentiles, and the glory of thy people Israel." — Luke 2:25–32 (KJV)

To every observer who passed him in the temple courts over those long years, Simeon was simply an old man. Waiting. Living quietly. Not building anything visible. Not producing anything the world could measure. But in the divine architecture, Simeon was holding a pre-ordained appointment with the Messiah. His entire life — all of those years of faithful, quiet presence before God — was the preparation for one moment. And when that moment came, he held the infant Jesus in his arms, and everything he had waited for was fulfilled.

And then he said the most peaceful words ever read from a human mouth.

Lord, now lettest thou thy servant depart in peace.

That is what it looks like when a soul has done what it was put here to do. Not with great fanfare. Not with a monument or a legacy the world would remember. Just peace. The deep, settled, God-given peace of a person who held on, stayed faithful, and finally saw what was promised.

That peace is available to you.

The Changed Life Is Ministry

I want to speak to the person who is sitting with regret about the years that were lived far from God. Who came back — or is considering coming back — but wonders whether it is too late for the return to mean anything.

"And they overcame him by the blood of the Lamb, and by the word of their testimony; and they loved not their lives unto the death." — Revelation 12:11 (KJV)

The Greek word translated testimony is marturia — witness, evidence, record. It is the root from which we get the word martyr. A biblical testimony is not just a story you tell. It is living evidence presented in the courtroom of the spiritual realm. And it is one of the weapons by which the enemy is overcome.

John Flavel wrote that believers reaching the end of their lives must make known to them that survive us, what we have seen and found of God in this world. Your story — including the broken parts, the wandering parts, the parts you are most ashamed of — is evidence. It is marturia. And a life changed late is one of the most powerful forms of that evidence, because it answers the lie that God's grace runs out.

When your children or grandchildren or old friends see that God took what you were and made something different — they cannot argue with it. They were there. They knew you before. And now they see you after. That is not a small thing. That is a ministry. That may be one of the most significant things your life will ever produce.

The enemy will whisper that your past disqualifies you. But the kingdom of heaven runs on redemption. Your failures, your repentance, and your return become your marturia. The very fact that God could take a broken, wasted history and redeem it is the evidence that His grace is inexhaustible.

The Compass of Christ

I said at the beginning of this chapter that the question of purpose cannot be fully answered without knowing the One who designed it. I want to return to that, because I believe it is the hinge everything else swings on.

"For of him, and through him, and to him, are all things: to whom be glory for ever. Amen." — Romans 11:36 (KJV)

Every human being was created of Him, through Him, and for Him. It is therefore a theological and logical impossibility to discover

your true purpose apart from knowing Him. Think of it this way —
a character in a story cannot understand their own purpose without
knowing the author. The character does not know why they were
written. They do not know where the story is going. They do not
know what the author intends for them. Only the author holds that
knowledge. Christ is not merely the Savior of your soul. He is the
revealer of your self. He holds the blueprint of what you were made
for.

"But seek ye first the kingdom of God, and his righteousness; and
all these things shall be added unto you." — Matthew 6:33 (KJV)

The Greek word zeteo — translated seek — does not mean a casual
curiosity. It means to search for as a priority. To crave. To demand.
To orient your entire life around the pursuit. When God becomes the
central pursuit — not the side project, not the Sunday morning obligation, but the actual first priority — He promises to supply everything
else. Including the clarity about purpose that the human heart spends
an entire lifetime searching for.

"Delight thyself also in the LORD: and he shall give thee the desires
of thine heart." — Psalm 37:4 (KJV)

The miracle of this verse is in the mechanism. When you delight
yourself in God — when He becomes the source of your deepest
joy — something happens to the desires of your heart. They change.
The Holy Spirit begins to plant His desires inside you. And those
transformed desires, flowing from intimate fellowship with God, align
perfectly with the specific purpose God designed for your life. You
stop chasing what you want and start wanting what He designed you
for.

Christ is the compass. And a compass only works when you are
willing to follow where it points.

Finishing Well

"I have fought a good fight, I have finished my course, I have kept the faith." — 2 Timothy 4:7 (KJV)

The Greek word for finished is teleioo — to complete, to bring to its intended end, to arrive at the designed conclusion. The word for course is dromos — a specific race, a specific path assigned to a specific person. Paul is saying: I ran the race that was laid out for me. I arrived at the place it was designed to lead. I kept believing through everything that tried to make me stop believing.

That is what finishing well looks like. Not a perfect record. Paul's record included years of murder and persecution. Not a life without failure. Paul's letters document his own struggle with sin. But a life that pressed toward the mark — that kept the faith through the fights — that ran the dromos God assigned without abandoning it.

And the witnesses of Scripture are unanimous on this question: it is absolutely possible to finish well even if the early and middle portions of the race were poorly run. Moses. Paul. The thief on the cross. The eleventh-hour worker. God's redemptive capacity can restore the years the locust has eaten. A life changed late can still cross the finish line in absolute triumph.

But there is an accounting. Paul is clear about this:

"Every man's work shall be made manifest: for the day shall declare it, because it shall be revealed by fire; and the fire shall try every man's work of what sort it is. If any man's work abide which he hath built thereupon, he shall receive a reward. If any man's work shall be burned, he shall suffer loss: but he himself shall be saved; yet so as by fire." — 1 Corinthians 3:13–15 (KJV)

Wood, hay, and stubble — the things done for selfish reasons, for earthly applause, for the wrong purposes — will not survive the fire. Gold, silver, and precious stones — the things done in faithful obedience to God's design — will remain. A person may suffer the loss of rewards. But the text says clearly: he himself shall be saved.

What we do with our lives genuinely matters. The choices carry weight. The faithfulness or unfaithfulness with which we stewarded what God gave us has eternal consequences. But the believer's salvation — their ultimate standing before God — was never based on the flawlessness of their performance. It was always based solely on the foundation of Jesus Christ.

Works matter. Grace saves. Both of these are true. And they are not in conflict.

The Peace That Passes Understanding

If you have read this far and there is still something in you that is afraid — still a voice that counts up the years and the failures and concludes that it does not add up to enough — then I want to give you what Isaiah gave the people of God:

"Thou wilt keep him in perfect peace, whose mind is stayed on thee: because he trusteth in thee." — Isaiah 26:3 (KJV)

The Hebrew word shalom — translated peace — does not merely mean the absence of conflict. It means wholeness. Completeness. A state in which nothing is missing, nothing is broken, nothing is out of place. And God promises to keep that shalom — actively, continuously, as a guard stationed at the gates of the mind — for the person whose mind remains fixed on Him.

The anxiety of wasted years. The fear of not being enough. The haunting question of whether you fulfilled what you were put here for. God's peace, flowing from trust in His character, stands at those gates and says: not here. Not today. This mind is kept by the One who holds all things together.

You do not have to carry the ledger of your life's regrets alone. You can lay it before God — honestly, completely, without pretense — and in exchange, He will give you a peace that bypasses logic. A peace that makes no earthly sense given the circumstances. A peace that the world cannot give and cannot take away.

The Eternity in Your Heart

Solomon put his finger on something in Ecclesiastes that explains why the question of purpose haunts every human being, regardless of what they achieve. He observed that God has made everything beautiful in its time, and that He has set eternity — olam — in the human heart. A deep, unquenchable longing for something far beyond the present moment. For something that lasts. For something that means something beyond the boundaries of a single human life.

This is why wealth does not satisfy it. This is why achievement does not silence it. This is why even the most successful life, measured by earthly standards, can still feel as though something essential is missing. The psalmist named what the olam actually is:

"As the hart panteth after the water brooks, so panteth my soul after thee, O God. My soul thirsteth for God, for the living God." — Psalm 42:1–2 (KJV)

The longing is not for achievement. It is not for legacy. It is for God. C.S. Lewis observed that when a person discovers an inner longing that nothing in this world can satisfy, the most honest explanation is that the person was built for a different world entirely. The olam in your heart cannot be filled by anything this world offers. It was placed there by God. And it can only be satisfied by God.

An earthly life cannot be called a failure simply because it lacked wealth or recognition. Those things were never designed to satisfy the olam. They were never designed to answer the deepest question. The person who reverenced God, who loved their neighbor, who showed kindness and acted selflessly — even imperfectly, even with years of wandering along the way — has done the thing that was always the point.

The Real Measure

The final reframing I want to offer you is this.

We have spent our entire lives measuring purpose by achievement. By career. By what we built or what we produced or what other people said about us. But God declared His primary purpose for every believer with a clarity that changes everything:

"But we all, with open face beholding as in a glass the glory of the Lord, are changed into the same image from glory to glory, even as by the Spirit of the Lord." — 2 Corinthians 3:18 (KJV)

Changed into the same image. From glory to glory. This is the active, ongoing, Spirit-driven process by which God transforms every believer into the likeness of Christ — not all at once, not without struggle, not without setback, but continuously, relentlessly, and by His power rather than ours. God's primary purpose for every believer is not a career milestone. It is not a ministry achievement. It is not the size of a legacy. It is that they be conformed to the image of His Son.

This shifts the question entirely.

Not: Did I achieve the right things? But: Did I allow God to shape me through everything I experienced?

The trials. The suffering. The failures. The years of wandering that you look back on with regret. All of it — every chapter, including the painful ones — is part of God's masterful design to humble us, strip away our self-reliance, and sculpt us into the image of Christ. J.I. Packer wrote: God is at work in Christian believers to repair his ruined image by communicating these qualities to them afresh. The shaping never stops. And every experience — including the ones we would not have chosen — is part of the shaping.

If you have allowed God to shape you — if through the hard years and the quiet years and the honest moments of surrender, you have been slowly, imperfectly, genuinely conformed more and more to the character of Christ — then you have fulfilled the deepest purpose God had for your life.

The rest was always His to complete.

The Invitation

If you are reading this and you have never surrendered your life to Jesus Christ — I want to speak directly to you.

It is not too late. The master is still walking out to the vineyard at the eleventh hour. The thief on the cross proves that grace is available in the final breath. That moment of surrender does not have to happen in any particular place. It can happen right now, wherever you are, in whatever condition you are in.

I believe the soul knows its own condition. I believe that the person who has been running their own way for years or for decades knows, somewhere underneath all the noise, that something is missing. That the olam in their heart has never been satisfied. That the question of purpose has been there all along, waiting to be answered honestly.

The answer is not a checklist of good works. It is a person. His name is Jesus Christ. He is the One who designed you. He is the One who holds the blueprint of everything you were made for. And He is the One who, through His death and resurrection, made it possible for you to know God not as a distant authority but as a Father who welcomes you home.

The prayer is not complicated. It does not require religious vocabulary or perfect words. It requires honesty. Tell Him the truth about what you have been and what you have done. Tell Him you believe He is who He says He is. Ask Him to receive you. Ask Him to forgive you.

And ask Him to show you — one step, one layer at a time — what He put you here for.

He will answer. He has always been the one who answers.

I want to close with the words of God through the prophet Isaiah — the invitation that sums up everything this chapter has been building toward:

"Hearken diligently unto me, and eat ye that which is good, and let your soul delight itself in fatness. Incline your ear, and come unto me: hear, and your soul shall live; and I will make an everlasting covenant with you." — Isaiah 55:2–3 (KJV)

Your soul shall live. Not merely survive. Not limp along. Live — fully, abundantly, in the purpose God designed for you — connected to the Vine, shaped by the Potter, kept by the peace that passes understanding, and walking one faithful step at a time toward the end of a course that was always in His hands.

Did you fulfill your purpose?

If you have accepted Jesus Christ as your Lord and Savior. If you have asked for forgiveness and received it. If you have loved the people around you — imperfectly, in the way broken human beings love — but genuinely and selflessly, with moments that cost you something. If you have shown kindness that had nothing in it for you and everything in it for someone else.

Then you have done the thing that was always the thing.

The rest belongs to God. And God finishes what He starts.

My Reflection

I want to tell you what I know, not what I was taught.

I have not seen the full map of my own life. There are chapters I do not understand and seasons I am still processing. There are decisions I cannot fully explain and outcomes I did not see coming — both the ones I would have chosen and the ones I would not have. But I have seen enough to know the map exists.

I have had moments — quiet moments, unexpected moments — where something shifted and I knew, without being able to explain it, that God was pointing to something. A direction. A confirmation. A fingerprint left in a circumstance that had too much precision to be coincidence. Those moments were not coincidences. They were layers being revealed.

I believe with everything I have that the domino of a person's life is being arranged with far more intention than we can see while we are living it. The thing that seemed like a detour was the route. The chapter that felt like failure was the preparation. The season that felt like abandonment was the one where the most important work was being done — quietly, below the surface, in the person rather than the circumstances.

And I want to say this to the person reading this chapter who is afraid they came too late. Who is looking at the years and doing an accounting that does not feel like it balances.

God does not keep the same ledger you do. He does not measure a life the way the world measures it — by productivity or legacy or the number of people who remember your name after you are gone. He measures it by the thing He always said He was looking for: a heart that was genuinely His. Not perfect. Not unbroken. Not without failure. His. The person who, through all of it — the wandering and the returning and the wandering again and the final coming home — never fully let go of the God who never fully let go of them. That person fulfilled the deepest purpose God had for their life. The rest belongs to Him. And He finishes what He starts.

A Prayer for the Soul Asking This Question

Lord God, I come before You on behalf of every soul reading these words who has picked up this question and carried it for a long time. The person who has lived hard and fast and is finally sitting still. The person who looks back on years spent in the wrong places for the wrong reasons. The person who loved imperfectly and wonders if the people who needed them knew they were loved. The person who gave their best years to things that could not hold what they poured into them.

I ask You to speak to them now with the same voice You used in the wilderness. With the same peace You have always stationed over the minds and hearts of those who laid their broken story at Your feet.

Remind them that they were written in Your book before the foundations of the world. Remind them that their suffering was not wasted. Remind them that the locust years can be restored. Remind them that it is never too late — that the master is still walking out to find the eleventh-hour worker, and that the door has not closed.

And if there is a soul reading this who has not yet surrendered to You — who is at the end of themselves, in the quiet, with nothing left but the truth — let this be the moment. Let this be the page where everything changes.

You are the God who keeps His word. You are the God who finishes what He starts. And You are the God who said: I will make an everlasting covenant with you. Incline your ear, and your soul shall live.

Receive them. Hold them. And bring them home.

In the name of Jesus Christ, the Author and Finisher of our faith. Amen.

"Let us run with patience the race that is set before us, Looking unto Jesus the author and finisher of our faith; who for the joy that was set before him endured the cross, despising the shame, and is set down at the right hand of the throne of God." — Hebrews 12:1–2 (KJV)

Chapter Eleven

What Actually Happens When We Die?

"Jesus said unto her, I am the resurrection, and the life: he that believeth in me, though he were dead, yet shall he live: And whosoever liveth and believeth in me shall never die." — John 11:25–26 (KJV)

I want to tell you about two moments that changed the way I understand death.

They did not happen in a church. They did not happen during a sermon, a Bible study, or any moment I had planned or prepared for. They happened in quiet rooms, beside beds that had become altars, holding the hands of two women whose faith had shaped everything I believe about God and about what waits for us on the other side of this life.

Both of my grandmothers were women who knew God the way some people know the air they breathe — without effort, without performance, without any need to announce it. Their faith was not decoration. It was the structure of everything. And I was given the profound and sacred gift of being present in their final hours. I held their hands. I prayed over them. I spoke into whatever awareness remained — telling them they were loved, that they would be missed, that God was calling them home, and asking them to look over me from wherever they were going.

I do not know exactly what they could hear. Their bodies had already begun the long letting go. But I believe, with everything in me, that my voice reached them. I believe God used those words as a lantern held at the threshold of a door I could not yet pass through. Because even in states where the body is no longer coherent, the spirit is still present. And I believe the spirit hears what the body can no longer register.

What I felt in those rooms was not grief alone. It was something I can only describe as the nearness of God. A presence. A stillness that did not feel empty but full. The kind of quiet that does not belong to this world. Death is one of those things that either pulls us toward God or pushes us away. For me, it pulled me close. And it is because of those moments — because of what I felt, and what I have studied, and what Scripture so clearly and consistently declares — that I write this chapter not from a comfortable distance, but from the certainty of someone who has stood at that edge and knows what is waiting on the other side of it.

Because here is the truth that needs to be said before anything else: you are not wrong to ask this question. You are not faithless for needing an answer. Whether you are standing at a deathbed right now, lying awake at three in the morning terrified of your own mortality, or grieving someone whose absence feels like a wound that will never close — this question deserves more than comfort. It deserves the truth.

And the truth is this: God has not left us without an answer. From the earliest pages of Genesis to the final vision of Revelation, Scripture speaks to death with a clarity and compassion that no philosophy and no science has ever matched. The Bible does not flinch from death. It walks directly into it. And it walks back out.

Why Death Feels So Wrong

Before we can understand what happens when we die, we need to understand something that most people sense but cannot name — the reason death feels so profoundly, so violently wrong.

It is not weakness to feel that way. It is not a lack of faith. It is the most spiritually honest response a human being can have. The reason death feels unnatural is because it is unnatural. It was never part of God's original design.

When God formed the first man from the dust of the ground and breathed into his nostrils the breath of life, He created a being fashioned for eternity. The Garden of Eden was not a temporary arrangement. It was the intended permanent state of humanity — life in the unbroken presence of God, without suffering, without decay, and without death. God's warning in Genesis was not a prediction of something inevitable. It was a warning against a door that was never meant to be opened.

"But of the tree of the knowledge of good and evil, thou shalt not eat of it: for in the day that thou eatest thereof thou shalt surely die." — Genesis 2:17 (KJV)

The door was opened anyway. And death entered the world not as a natural process but as a consequence — an alien intruder into a creation that was made for life. Augustine of Hippo, writing in his monumental work The City of God, argued this point with force.

He insisted that we are subject to the death of the body not by the law of nature, by which God ordained no death for man, but by His righteous response to the entrance of sin. Had humanity not fallen, Augustine wrote, they would not have been dismissed from their bodies by any death, but would have been endowed with immortality.

The Apostle Paul confirmed this in his letter to the Romans:

"Wherefore, as by one man sin entered into the world, and death by sin; and so death passed upon all men, for that all have sinned:" — Romans 5:12 (KJV)

Death is not God's creation. It is sin's consequence. And the revulsion you feel when you stand over a casket, when you watch a body that once held laughter and memory and love reduced to stillness — that revulsion is spiritually correct. You are not overreacting. You are recognizing the intrusion of something that was never supposed to be here.

But there is another reason death feels wrong that goes even deeper. God placed something inside every human being that refuses to accept death as final. The writer of Ecclesiastes named it plainly:

"He hath made every thing beautiful in his time: also he hath set the world in their heart, so that no man can find out the work that God maketh from the beginning to the end." — Ecclesiastes 3:11 (KJV)

The word translated as "world" in that verse is the Hebrew word olam — which means eternity. Not the world as in the planet. Eternity itself. God has planted an unquenchable longing for something beyond the boundary of this life into every soul He has ever created. This is why no human civilization in the history of the world has ever simply accepted death as a full stop. Every culture, in every age, has reached toward something beyond the grave. Not because they invented the idea — but because God planted it there.

C.S. Lewis observed that if we find in ourselves a desire that no experience in this world can fully satisfy, the most reasonable explanation is that we were made for another world. The longing is the evidence. The ache is the argument. We ask what happens when we die because something deep inside us already knows that death is not the end of who we are.

What the Old Testament Tells Us

Long before Jesus stood at the tomb of Lazarus and declared Himself the resurrection and the life, the Old Testament was already speaking about what lies beyond the grave. It did not speak with the fullness of the New Testament revelation, but it was not silent.

The Hebrew word that the Old Testament uses most consistently for the realm of the dead is Sheol. According to Strong's Concordance, Sheol derives from a root meaning to inquire or to ask, and is translated variously in the King James Bible as the grave, hell, and the pit. It refers to the netherworld — the shadowy dwelling place of the departed. But Sheol is not simply a hole in the ground. It is a realm. And three passages make this unmistakably clear.

First, the Psalmist writes in Psalm 16:10:

"For thou wilt not leave my soul in hell; neither wilt thou suffer thine Holy One to see corruption." — Psalm 16:10 (KJV)

Here, Sheol is depicted as a realm that attempts to hold the soul captive — but God's power transcends it. The New Testament apostles would later cite this very verse as the proof-text for the resurrection of Christ. And just one verse further, the Psalmist adds this word of confidence:

"Therefore my heart is glad, and my glory rejoiceth: my flesh also shall rest in hope." — Psalm 16:9 (KJV)

Even the body resting in the grave rests in hope. Not in despair. Not in nothing. In hope. Because the God who holds the soul also holds the body in His intention.

Second, the Psalmist declares in Psalm 139:8:

"If I ascend up into heaven, thou art there: if I make my bed in hell, behold, thou art there." — Psalm 139:8 (KJV)

Even the deepest abyss of the afterlife is fully exposed to the Creator. There is nowhere the soul can go that lies outside the reach of God. This is not a threat. It is a comfort. Even in death, you are not beyond Him.

Third, and most vividly, the prophet Isaiah writes about the realm of Sheol in terms that leave no room for the idea that the dead are simply unconscious:

"Hell from beneath is moved for thee to meet thee at thy coming: it stirreth up the dead for thee, even all the chief ones of the earth; it hath raised up from their thrones all the kings of the nations. All they shall speak and say unto thee, Art thou also become weak as we? art thou become like unto us? Thy pomp is brought down to the grave, and the noise of thy viols: the worm is spread under thee, and the worms cover thee." — Isaiah 14:9–11 (KJV)

The departed kings — described in the ancient Hebrew as the Rephaim, the shades of the underworld — recognize the arriving King of Babylon. They remember their own histories. They speak. They taunt. They retain identity and awareness. Their existence in Sheol is diminished compared to earthly life, but it is not nothing. They are conscious. The Old Testament picture of the afterlife is not annihilation. It is a reduced, shadowy existence that awaits the full revelation of what God would accomplish through His Son.

The Old Testament also records a moment that most people overlook when thinking about the nature of the afterlife — the account of

King Saul and the medium at Endor. Saul, desperate for guidance and abandoned by God because of his disobedience, sought a woman who practiced forbidden contact with the dead. He asked her to bring up the spirit of the prophet Samuel, who had died some time before.

"Then said the woman, Whom shall I bring up unto thee? And he said, Bring me up Samuel... And the woman said unto Saul, I saw gods ascending out of the earth. And Samuel said to Saul, Why hast thou disquieted me, to bring me up?" — 1 Samuel 28:11, 13, 15 (KJV)

Samuel appeared. He was recognizable. He was aware of what had happened since his death. He delivered a divine message of judgment against Saul. Thomas Aquinas, writing in the Summa Theologica, addressed this passage directly and argued that such an event could occur either by the special dispensation of God — meaning God Himself permitted Samuel's spirit to appear in order to deliver a sentence of judgment — or through the activity of deceiving spirits. Most orthodox theologians hold to the former view. But regardless of which interpretation a scholar takes, the passage establishes something undeniable: the ancient Israelites understood that the soul retains conscious awareness, recognizable identity, and the capacity for communication after physical death. Samuel was not erased. He was present. He was himself. And he could be disturbed.

Beyond Sheol, the Old Testament gives us two extraordinary exceptions that establish something even more profound. Enoch walked with God, and was not, for God took him — Genesis 5:24. And Elijah was carried into heaven by a whirlwind of fire — 2 Kings 2:11. These two men bypassed death entirely and entered the presence of God in bodily form. They established the theological precedent, written into the oldest pages of Scripture, that conscious life with God beyond this world is not only possible but real.

The Old Testament closes its witness to the afterlife with its most explicit declaration. The prophet Daniel wrote:

"And many of them that sleep in the dust of the earth shall awake, some to everlasting life, and some to shame and everlasting contempt." — Daniel 12:2 (KJV)

The Hebrew word translated "sleep" here is yashen — which describes the physical body resting in the grave. It is not a description of the soul's state. It is a figure of speech pointing to the temporary nature of the body's rest before the great awakening. Augustine, commenting on this verse in The City of God, noted that Daniel's declaration stands as a direct forerunner of the resurrection doctrine declared in the New Testament. The hope of rising from the dead did not originate with Christianity. It was planted in the heart of Israel centuries before the empty tomb.

What Jesus Taught About the Moment of Death

If you want to know what happens the moment a believer dies, the most direct answer in all of Scripture comes from the lips of Jesus Himself — spoken not from a pulpit, not to His disciples, but to a dying criminal who had no religious credentials, no baptism, no church membership, and no time left to earn anything.

As Jesus hung on the cross in the final hours of His own life, the man dying beside Him turned to Him and said: Lord, remember me when thou comest into thy kingdom. And Jesus answered:

"And Jesus said unto him, Verily I say unto thee, To day shalt thou be with me in paradise." — Luke 23:43 (KJV)

Every word of this verse carries weight. The Greek word translated "paradise" is paradeisos — which derives from an ancient Persian word, pairidaeza, meaning a walled royal garden. When the Old Testament was translated into Greek, paradeisos was the specific word chosen to describe the Garden of Eden. Jesus is not pointing the thief toward a vague spiritual holding place. He is pointing him toward the restored garden — the recovered Edenic presence of God, the immediate and conscious fellowship of the righteous with their Creator.

And the word "To day" cannot be moved. The thief had asked to be remembered when Jesus came into His kingdom — assuming a long delay. Jesus corrected his timeline on the spot. Not eventually. Not after a period of unconscious waiting. Today. The moment the thief breathed his last, his spirit was consciously, immediately present with the Messiah.

Some have attempted to shift the punctuation of this verse to read, "Verily I say unto you today, you shall be with me in paradise" — implying the word "today" modifies the saying rather than the timing of paradise. Orthodox theology rejects this grammatical distortion entirely. The Greek construction does not support it, and the entire weight of scriptural witness runs against it. Today means today.

That same Jesus — the One who made that promise from the cross — modeled it Himself in His own dying. When He had cried with a loud voice, He said:

"Father, into thy hands I commend my spirit: and having said thus, he gave up the ghost." — Luke 23:46 (KJV)

And the first martyr of the church, Stephen, dying under a hail of stones, followed His Lord's example:

"And they stoned Stephen, calling upon God, and saying, Lord Jesus, receive my spirit." — Acts 7:59 (KJV)

Jesus committing His spirit to the Father. Stephen committing his spirit to Jesus. Both in the very moment of death. Both as conscious, deliberate acts of trust. The pattern is unmistakable: at death, the spirit of the believer departs — not into darkness, not into unconscious sleep — but directly into the hands of the God who gave it.

What Paul Teaches About Death and the Soul

No writer in all of Scripture speaks about death with more confidence, more joy, and more theological precision than the Apostle Paul. He had been beaten, shipwrecked, imprisoned, and left for dead. He had seen the risen Christ face to face on the road to Damascus. And because of that encounter, death held no terror for him whatsoever.

In his second letter to the Corinthians, Paul gives us what may be the single most precise statement in all of Scripture about what happens when a believer dies:

"Therefore we are always confident, knowing that, whilst we are at home in the body, we are absent from the Lord: (For we walk by faith, not by sight:) We are confident, I say, and willing rather to be absent from the body, and to be present with the Lord." — 2 Corinthians 5:6–8 (KJV)

Paul uses two Greek verbs built on the same root. Endemeo means to be at home, to reside among your own people. Ekdemeo means to be away from home, to migrate out of a place. As long as the believer's spirit is at home in the physical body, it exists at a distance from the immediate, visible presence of Christ. The moment death comes, the spirit departs — away from home in the body — and simultaneously arrives — at home with the Lord. There is no gap. There is no waiting room. The departure from the body and the arrival into the presence of Christ are the same moment.

Just a few verses earlier in that same letter, Paul gives the believer one of the most sustaining descriptions of what it means to face the dying of the body with faith:

"For which cause we faint not; but though our outward man perish, yet the inward man is renewed day by day. For our light affliction, which is but for a moment, worketh for us a far more exceeding and eternal weight of glory; While we look not at the things which are seen, but at the things which are not seen: for the things which are seen are temporal; but the things which are not seen are eternal." — 2 Corinthians 4:16–18 (KJV)

This is the perspective that changes everything. The outward man — the body — is perishing. That is not something Paul denies. He faces it honestly. But he says simultaneously that the inward man is being renewed. The soul is not diminishing while the body declines. It is being prepared. It is being made ready. The dying of the body is not the destruction of the person. It is the releasing of them.

His letter to the Philippians carries that same triumphant certainty:

"For to me to live is Christ, and to die is gain. But if I live in the flesh, this is the fruit of my labour: yet what I shall choose I wot not. For I am in a strait betwixt two, having a desire to depart, and to be with Christ; which is far better:" — Philippians 1:21–23 (KJV)

The Greek word Paul uses for "depart" is analuo — a word used in the ancient world for unloosing a ship from its moorings so it could set sail, or for striking a tent to break camp and move on. Death, for Paul, is not an ending. It is a casting off from the dock. It is the ship finally freed to sail toward its true home.

If departing meant entering an unconscious void, Paul could never have described it as gain, or as far better than his active, conscious fellowship with Christ on earth. The only way death is gain is if something is waiting on the other side that surpasses everything available here. Paul knew what was waiting. He called it by name: to be with Christ.

And near the end of his life, writing from a Roman prison as execution approached, Paul wrote these words to Timothy that stand as one of the great deathbed declarations in all of Scripture:

"For I am now ready to be offered, and the time of my departure is at hand. I have fought a good fight, I have finished my course, I have kept the faith: Henceforth there is laid up for me a crown of righteousness, which the Lord, the righteous judge, shall give me at that day: and not to me only, but unto all them also that love his appearing." — 2 Timothy 4:6–8 (KJV)

There is no fear in those words. There is no regret. There is the calm, steady confidence of a man who has lived for something that death cannot take from him. He is ready. The departure is at hand. And what waits on the other side is not darkness but a crown. That is what faith looks like when it finally arrives at the door of death. Not gripping. Not fighting. Ready.

Finally, Paul writes to the Thessalonian believers who were grieving their dead — afraid that those who had already died would somehow miss the resurrection:

"But I would not have you to be ignorant, brethren, concerning them which are asleep, that ye sorrow not, even as others which have no hope. For if we believe that Jesus died and rose again, even so them also which sleep in Jesus will God bring with him... Then we which are alive and remain shall be caught up together with them in the clouds, to meet the Lord in the air: and so shall we ever be with the Lord. Wherefore comfort one another with these words." — 1 Thessalonians 4:13–14, 17–18 (KJV)

Notice that Paul says God will bring with Jesus the souls of those who have fallen asleep. They are already with Him. They are not waiting in a holding place. They are already in His presence, and at the resurrection they will be brought back with Him to be reunited with their glorified bodies. The sleep Paul speaks of is the sleep of the physical body in the grave — not the suspension of the soul. The soul of every believer who has ever died is awake, aware, and with Christ right now.

The Intermediate State — What Happens Between Death and the Resurrection

Christian theology has a name for the condition of the soul between physical death and the final resurrection. It is called the intermediate state — the in-between time when the spirit of the believer is consciously present with God, but has not yet been reunited with a glorified physical body.

This state is not purgatory. It is not soul sleep. It is not an unconscious void. It is paradise — exactly the word Jesus used when He spoke to the dying thief. And Scripture gives us a vivid picture of what it looks like.

In the sixth chapter of Revelation, when the apostle John is given a vision of heaven, he sees something astonishing:

"And when he had opened the fifth seal, I saw under the altar the souls of them that were slain for the Word of God, and for the testimony which they held: And they cried with a loud voice, saying, How long, O Lord, holy and true, dost thou not judge and avenge our blood on them that dwell on the earth?" — Revelation 6:9–10 (KJV)

These are souls in the intermediate state — not yet reunited with their resurrection bodies, not yet in the final state of glory. And they are fully conscious. They remember what happened to them on earth. They cry out with a loud voice. They are aware of time passing. They receive white robes. This is not the picture of souls suspended in dreamless sleep. This is the picture of conscious, aware, worshiping individuals who are alive in God's presence and waiting for the final chapter.

The Transfiguration provides perhaps the most breathtaking proof of conscious identity in the intermediate state. Jesus took Peter, James, and John up a high mountain, and there they witnessed something impossible by every natural law:

"And, behold, there appeared unto them Moses and Elias talking with him." — Matthew 17:3 (KJV)

Moses had died and been buried centuries before that mountain. Yet there he stood — recognizable, articulate, conscious, actively conversing with Jesus about His coming death in Jerusalem, as Luke 9:31 records. His identity had not dissolved. His memory had not been erased. His personality had not been absorbed into some cosmic energy. He was Moses. He was present. He was real. And the disciples knew exactly who he was without being told.

This is what the intermediate state looks like. The believer who dies does not cease to be themselves. They are more themselves than they have ever been — freed from the weight of the body's decay, freed from the fog of pain and confusion, freed from every burden of this fallen world, and standing in the presence of the One who called them by name before the foundations of the earth were laid.

The Nature of the Soul and Spirit

To understand what survives death, we must understand what the Bible means when it speaks of the soul and the spirit — because these two words are often used interchangeably in everyday conversation, but the original languages of Scripture distinguish them carefully.

The Hebrew word for soul is nephesh. According to Brown-Driver-Briggs, nephesh — used over seven hundred times in the Old Testament — literally means breath, but encompasses the entire living being: the seat of the will, the emotions, the personality, the desires. It is the "I" at the center of every human person — the one who wills, who feels, who chooses, who grieves, who loves. The Greek equivalent in the New Testament is psyche — the living self, the inner life, the seat of all that makes a person distinctively themselves.

This matters because one of the most significant distortions in Western Christianity's understanding of the soul did not come from the Hebrew Bible. It came from Plato. Plato taught that the soul is an immortal spiritual substance naturally imprisoned in a physical body

— that the real you is a deathless spiritual entity that merely inhabits flesh, and that the body is inferior to the soul's true spiritual existence. This is not what the Hebrew nephesh means. Genesis 2:7 does not say man received a soul into a body. It says man became a living nephesh — the whole animated person, body and breath and life together as one unified whole. The Hebrew vision of a human being is not divided. You are not a soul trapped in a body. You are a whole person whom God breathed into existence.

This distinction matters deeply for what follows in this chapter, because God's answer to death is not the escape of a soul from a body — it is the resurrection of the whole person. That is why Jesus rose bodily. That is why the hope of Scripture is not a soul floating free but a whole self raised and restored.

The Hebrew word for spirit is ruach — which literally means wind or breath in movement. It is the faculty within a human being through which God most immediately encounters them. The Greek equivalent is pneuma. While the soul is the seat of human personality, the spirit is the seat of divine communion — the part of us designed for direct relationship with God. Jesus told the woman at the well that God is a Spirit, and they that worship him must worship him in spirit and in truth — John 4:24. The spirit is the gateway between the human person and the divine presence.

The writer of Hebrews draws this distinction with great precision:

"For the Word of God is quick, and powerful, and sharper than any twoedged sword, piercing even to the dividing asunder of soul and spirit, and of the joints and marrow, and is a discerner of the thoughts and intents of the heart." — Hebrews 4:12 (KJV)

Soul and spirit are distinct but inseparable. And when physical death occurs, what happens to both is answered with absolute clarity by the writer of Ecclesiastes:

"Then shall the dust return to the earth as it was: and the spirit shall return unto God who gave it." — Ecclesiastes 12:7 (KJV)

The body returns to dust. The spirit — carrying with it the soul, the personality, the memory, the identity of the person — returns to God who gave it. Death does not erase you. It returns you. And what returns is not a shadow or a fragment. It is the complete immaterial person, fully intact, fully conscious, fully themselves.

Answering the Hard Objections

There are several objections to everything we have covered that deserve an honest answer. The first comes from within the church. The second comes from the secular world. The third is one that even sincere believers wrestle with quietly.

Within certain Christian traditions, a doctrine called soul sleep has been taught — the idea that after death, the soul enters a state of complete unconscious rest until the final resurrection. The theologian Louis Berkhof, in his Systematic Theology, traces this view through history and notes it was held by small fringe groups in the early church, by certain Reformation-era sects, and by some traditions today. The great reformer John Calvin considered this doctrine so dangerous that he wrote an entire treatise specifically against it, titled Psychopanny-chia.

Berkhof dismantles the soul sleep position with a precise and decisive linguistic observation: the Bible never says that the soul falls asleep. The word sleep is used in Scripture to describe the dying person — specifically the physical body resting in the grave. It is a figure of speech pointing to the temporary nature of death in light of the coming resurrection. It is not a description of the soul's condition. Luke 23:43, 2 Corinthians 5:8, and Philippians 1:23 all establish beyond reasonable theological dispute that the soul of the believer is conscious and present with Christ immediately upon death. If soul sleep were true, Paul could not have called death gain. He could not have preferred departure to continued earthly life. He could not have called the intermediate state far better. Unconsciousness is not better. Presence with Christ is better. And presence requires consciousness.

The second objection comes from a secular and scientific worldview. Modern materialism argues that human consciousness is simply a product of brain activity. The brain produces thought the way the liver produces bile — and when the brain dies, consciousness must cease. Under this framework, no afterlife is possible because there is no "you" apart from your neurons.

Berkhof responds with clarity. The materialist argument confuses the instrument with the worker. The fact that consciousness currently transmits itself through the brain does not mean consciousness cannot exist apart from the brain. A musician plays through an instrument — but the musician is not the instrument. When the instrument is destroyed, the musician does not cease to exist. The brain is the temporary physical instrument of the soul. What happens when the instrument is laid down is precisely what Scripture declares: the spirit returns to God who gave it.

It is worth noting that near-death experience research — accounts of people who have been clinically dead and then revived, reporting conscious awareness, encounters with light, and encounters with deceased loved ones — has grown substantially in recent decades. While apologists have found this evidence useful in challenging strict materialism, careful theologians urge that we place no final theological weight on subjective human experience, however compelling. These accounts are interesting. They are sometimes remarkable. But our confidence in conscious life after death rests not on the reports of those who have brushed against it and returned. It rests on the infallible Word of the God who designed it. Scripture is not strengthened by human experience. Human experience, when it points toward Scripture, is simply catching a glimpse of something Scripture already declared with full authority.

The third objection is subtler. Some have argued that because the New Testament so strongly emphasizes the bodily resurrection, the soul cannot possibly survive death independently — that if resurrection is necessary, it implies the person completely ceased to exist at death and God must recreate them. Herman Bavinck addresses this with precision. These two doctrines are not in tension — they are complementary. The intermediate state is real but provisional. The soul without the body is not the final design for the human person. God created human beings as body and soul together, and the final act of redemption is not the escape of the spirit from matter but the glorification of the complete person. Resurrection is not recreation. It is re-formation — the surviving, conscious soul reunited with a glorified, incorruptible body. As Paul declares in 1 Corinthians 15:53:

"For this corruptible must put on incorruption, and this mortal must put on immortality." — 1 Corinthians 15:53 (KJV)

The Resurrection Body

The intermediate state — as wonderful and real as it is — is not the final chapter. Paradise is not the destination. It is the waiting room before the destination. And the destination is the resurrection.

Paul describes this with the most careful and precise language in his entire ministry:

"So also is the resurrection of the dead. It is sown in corruption; it is raised in incorruption: It is sown in dishonour; it is raised in glory: it is sown in weakness; it is raised in power: It is sown a natural body; it is raised a spiritual body. There is a natural body, and there is a spiritual body." — 1 Corinthians 15:42–44 (KJV)

Paul contrasts two Greek terms: soma psychikon — the natural body, animated by the soul and subject to weakness, decay, and death — and soma pneumatikon — the spiritual body, animated fully by the Spirit of God, incorruptible and immortal. This distinction is critical, because the word "spiritual" here does not mean ghostly or invisible or made of spirit-matter. NT scholar William Lane Craig notes that scholars agree pneumatikos speaks to orientation, not substance. The resurrection body is not a ghost. It is matter redeemed — flesh and bone glorified, freed from every limitation of the fallen world, exactly as the body of the risen Christ was glorified.

When the disciples encountered the risen Lord and doubted, He said to them:

"Behold my hands and my feet, that it is I myself: handle me, and see; for a spirit hath not flesh and bones, as ye see me have." — Luke 24:39 (KJV)

Jesus after the resurrection could eat fish, could be touched and handled, and yet could also appear in a locked room and ascend into heaven. His resurrection body was the prototype of what awaits every believer. Augustine, writing in The City of God, makes a point that is both theological and deeply pastoral: the soul's happiness in the intermediate state is not complete until it is reunited with its body. The resurrection is the completion of salvation — the moment when the full human person, body and soul together, enters the eternal state permanently and perfectly. Even the wounds of the martyrs, Augustine wrote, will remain in their glorified bodies — not as defects, but as shining marks of honor, transformed from signs of suffering into signs of glory.

This is the final answer to the ancient human fear of death. Not the mere survival of a ghost. Not the vague continuation of a disembodied spirit floating in an indefinite somewhere. But the resurrection of the complete person — renewed, glorified, incorruptible — living on a redeemed new earth in the unbroken, face-to-face presence of God forever.

Will We Know Our Loved Ones?

This is the question beneath the question. When people ask what happens when we die, what they are often really asking is: will I see them again? Will I know them? Will the love I have for them survive the grave?

The answer Scripture gives is unambiguous. Moses and Elijah were immediately recognizable on the Mount of Transfiguration. The disciples knew who they were without being told. Moses had been dead for centuries. Yet his identity was fully intact — his personality, his presence, his distinctiveness as a person had not been dissolved or absorbed. He was himself. And he was known.

The martyrs in Revelation 6 remember what was done to them on earth. Memory is intact. Identity is intact. The capacity for relationship is intact. Richard Baxter, the great Puritan pastor, wrote with joy about the reunion that awaits — being gathered to the glorified spirits of the saints, recognizing the faces of those whose faith shaped our own. Those who went before us in faith are not strangers in the presence of God. They are more fully themselves than they ever were here.

And Paul, writing to believers devastated by the deaths of their loved ones, did not tell them to stop grieving. He told them to grieve differently — as those who have hope rather than those who have none. And the ground of that hope was reunion. There is no genuine comfort in the promise of 1 Thessalonians 4:17 if the reunion it describes is a reunion with strangers. Paul's entire argument for comfort rests on the word together — you and the person you lost, together, caught up, united. The parting at the deathbed is not a permanent severance. It is a temporary interruption in a love that God Himself designed.

And Paul closes his great treatise on resurrection hope with a promise about knowledge itself:

"For now we see through a glass, darkly; but then face to face: now I know in part; but then shall I know even as also I am known." — 1 Corinthians 13:12 (KJV)

Eternity does not bring a diminishing of knowledge. It brings a completion of it. Everything unclear becomes clear. Everything seen through a glass darkly is finally seen face to face. You will know. And you will be known. Fully. Completely. Without confusion, without distance, without the fog that this fallen world throws across every relationship we have ever treasured.

What the Great Voices of the Faith Have Said

I am not the first person to have stood at a deathbed and wondered what lay beyond it. The greatest minds in the history of the Christian faith have stood in that same place — and what they found there is worth hearing.

Augustine of Hippo argued in his City of God that the soul's conscious joy remains perfectly intact even while the body waits in the grave. He pointed to Psalm 16:9 — my flesh also shall rest in hope — as the believer's confidence that even the sleeping body is held in the care of God. He insisted that the resurrection is not God creating someone new, but God completing and glorifying the person who already exists and has been with Him all along. And he did not shy away from the physical reality of the resurrection body — teaching that it will be real, tangible, glorified flesh, animated entirely by the Holy Spirit, incorruptible and immortal.

John Flavel, the Puritan pastor whose writings on God's providence have anchored believers for three centuries, offered practical wisdom about both dying and praying over the dying. He observed that the hour of death is often a time of intense spiritual pressure, where the departing soul may be assaulted by doubt and fear. He counseled those standing at deathbeds to speak words of faith over the dying — reminding them of the unchangeable love of Christ, anchoring them to the promises of God when their own mind may be clouded. And he modeled the prayer of release after Christ and Stephen: committing the departing spirit into the hands of God as the final act of faith. Flavel also described something that I believe, and I believe because I have experienced it: the believer who has walked with God through a lifetime of trials arrives at the deathbed with a kind of accumulated evidence — a treasury of specific moments where God came through, where God showed up, where God proved faithful. Recounting those moments, Flavel wrote, is one of the most powerful things a dying person can do. It sweetens the crossing.

Charles Spurgeon, the prince of preachers, taught that for the believer, death holds no ultimate terror because of what has already been settled. Because there is therefore now no condemnation to them which are in Christ Jesus, who walk not after the flesh, but after the Spirit — Romans 8:1 — the Christian stands not on the shifting sand of their own obedience but on the eternal rock of a work Christ has already completed. Spurgeon described the intermediate state as wading deeper into a river to swim in — the joy the Holy Spirit begins in us on earth is the exact same joy we enter into at death. The river does not end at the grave. It deepens. And Spurgeon assured his dying congregants that God's love would not withdraw from them in their final moments. He was emphatic: the Father who loved you in your strength will not abandon you in your weakness. He cannot. He will not. His love is not conditional on your ability to feel it.

C.S. Lewis, writing after the devastating loss of his wife, documented with painful honesty the grief that death brings and the silence that can seem to follow when a person reaches out to God in the rawest moments of loss. But Lewis ultimately arrived at the same place every honest seeker arrives when they push through the silence: not an empty house, but a God who was there all along — who used the very agony of grief to strip away every false comfort and leave the soul with nothing left to hold onto but Him. Lewis argued in The Problem of Pain that a Christian account of suffering is incomplete without the afterlife — that the joys of heaven must be placed on the scale against the sufferings of earth, or no honest answer to human pain is possible. He also insisted that heaven is not a pale, vague reward. It is the most solid and most real thing that exists — more real than anything this world has ever offered.

Grief as a Doorway to God

Death is not only something that happens to the person who dies. It happens to the people who are left behind. And the grief that follows loss is one of the most powerful forces in human experience. It strips away everything that is not essential. It silences every distraction. And it leaves a person face to face with questions that ordinary life allows us to avoid.

Philip Yancey observes that tragedy and death force the human soul to ask, "Where is God?" Those who expect God's primary role to be the shielding of His people from all physical harm find their faith shattered when death comes — because it always comes. But those who push through that shattering often find on the other side of it something they could not have found any other way: the reality of a God who does not stand at a safe distance from human suffering but descends into it. The God of Scripture is not a God who explains grief from a position of comfort. He is the God who entered our grief, took on our mortality, and walked through death Himself.

C.S. Lewis described grief as a kind of house where every door you try seems to be locked from the inside. The silence is deafening. The absence is overwhelming. But Lewis discovered, and documented it honestly, that the silence was not abandonment. It was preparation. God was not hiding. He was waiting for Lewis to stop trying to manage his own grief and simply fall into His hands.

Spurgeon taught that bereavement burns like a furnace. And furnaces, he observed, burn away everything that cannot withstand the heat. What survives a furnace is what is real. The person who walks through genuine grief and finds God waiting on the other side of it has found something that comfortable, undisturbed faith can never produce — a faith that has been tested and did not collapse. A faith that knows, not theoretically but actually, that God is present even when everything around you says He is not.

"The LORD is nigh unto them that are of a broken heart; and saveth such as be of a contrite spirit." — Psalm 34:18 (KJV)

God does not stand distant from human grief. His presence is most acutely manifested exactly where the heart is most shattered. And the ancient shepherd's prayer that has comforted more dying people than any other passage in Scripture puts it this way:

"Yea, though I walk through the valley of the shadow of death, I will fear no evil: for thou art with me; thy rod and thy staff they comfort me." — Psalm 23:4 (KJV)

Death casts a shadow. It is real. It is dark. The Psalmist does not pretend otherwise. But a shadow only exists because there is a light shining behind it. The valley of the shadow of death is shadowed because the light of God is on the other side of it. And the sheep walking through that valley is not walking alone. The shepherd is there. His rod and His staff — the instruments of guidance and protection — are present. The comfort is not that the valley is not dark. The comfort is that the One who walks with you through it is greater than the darkness.

And where does the shepherd lead? The Psalmist answers at the very end of that same psalm:

"Surely goodness and mercy shall follow me all the days of my life: and I will dwell in the house of the LORD for ever." — Psalm 23:6 (KJV)

All the days of my life. And then the house of the Lord, forever. The shepherd does not abandon the sheep at the edge of the valley. He leads them through it, and out the other side, and home.

How to Prepare for Death with Faith and Peace

I want to speak to something that most people never talk about directly, even in the church. How do you prepare for death — not morbidly, not obsessively, but with the kind of faith and peace that Paul modeled when he wrote that the time of his departure was at hand and he was ready?

The first thing to understand is that preparing for death is not a morbid exercise. It is the most honest thing a person of faith can do. Every human being who has ever lived has died. Every human being alive today will die. The question is not whether death is coming. The question is whether you will meet it as someone who has made peace with it, or as someone it ambushes.

John Flavel offered practical counsel for this that has lost none of its power in three centuries. He advised believers to spend time intentionally recounting the specific ways God has cared for them throughout their lives. Not in a general way — not just "God has been good to me" — but specifically. The time He came through when there was no human explanation for it. The moment the fear broke and peace came. The provision that arrived exactly when it was needed. Flavel wrote that it must sweeten a deathbed to recount the specific passages of God's care from the beginning of a person's life to that very day. Because what that recounting does is build a case — an evidential case, in the court of the believer's own soul — that the God who was faithful through all of that will not suddenly become unfaithful at the final crossing.

Charles Spurgeon anchored this preparation in the completed work of Christ. The believer does not prepare for death by accumulating enough good works to feel worthy. The believer prepares for death by understanding what has already been done on their behalf. Because there is therefore now no condemnation to them which are in Christ Jesus, who walk not after the flesh, but after the Spirit — Romans 8:1 — the ground beneath a believer's feet is not their own righteousness but the eternal rock of what Christ accomplished. Death cannot touch that. The grave cannot undo that. The believer stands on finished work, and finished work does not unfinish.

And the prayer of the church over its sick and dying is itself an act of preparation. James writes:

"Is any sick among you? let him call for the elders of the church; and let them pray over him, anointing him with oil in the name of the Lord: And the prayer of faith shall save the sick, and the Lord shall raise him up." — James 5:14–15 (KJV)

We often read this passage with our eyes fixed entirely on physical healing. But the deepest raising up God promises His people is not the restoration of the mortal body. It is the resurrection of the whole person into eternal life. The prayer of faith over the dying is not a failure if the body does not recover. It is the church doing exactly what it was designed to do — standing at the threshold between this world and the next, speaking the name of Jesus over a departing soul, and trusting the One who said, To day shalt thou be with me in paradise.

An Invitation

If you have read this chapter and you are not yet certain of your own destination, I want to speak to you directly.

The answer to what happens when we die is not the same for everyone. Scripture is honest about this. Daniel declared a resurrection to everlasting life and a resurrection to shame and contempt. Jesus confirmed it. Paul unpacked it. And the difference between the two is not the quality of a person's life, not the length of their religious history, not whether they have done more good than bad. The difference is a relationship.

The thief on the cross had done nothing to earn paradise. He had no time left to earn anything. All he did was turn to Jesus in his final moments and ask to be remembered. And Jesus said: today. That is how fast grace moves. That is how wide the door stands open.

It has never been complicated. It has never required credentials. It has always required only one thing: the honesty to admit that you need what only Christ can give, and the willingness to ask for it.

Even Jesus wept at the tomb of His friend Lazarus — John 11:35. He did not rebuke the weeping. He joined it. It is not faithless to grieve. It is not weakness to be undone by death. It is human. And Jesus met humanity in that grief, in that exact place of undoing, and then declared Himself to be the resurrection and the life. He said so Himself. He proved it by walking out of His own tomb. And everything Scripture has declared, everything history has confirmed, and everything written on the human heart by the God who made it, agrees.

If you have never given your life to Christ, today is the day. Not because death might be near, though it might be. But because what waits on the other side of that decision is more real, more solid, and more alive than anything this world has ever offered you. And the God who planted eternity in your heart has been waiting, with extraordinary patience and extraordinary love, for you to come home.

My Reflection

There are moments in a life that do not fade with the passing of years — not because the memory is extraordinary, but because what occurred in them was. I have carried two such moments since the seasons in which they happened, and I carry them still.

Both unfolded in quiet rooms beside beds that had become, in the truest sense, altars. Beside each of my grandmothers in the final hours of their earthly lives, I was granted something I did not deserve and could not have anticipated — the sacred privilege of presence at the threshold between this world and whatever lies immediately beyond it. I held their hands. I prayed over them with whatever words I could find, aware even as I spoke that I was addressing not merely the women whose bodies lay before me, but the spirits that inhabited those bodies and that would survive them.

I do not know with certainty what they could perceive in those hours. The physical mechanisms of hearing and comprehension had largely withdrawn. But I know what Scripture declares — that the spirit remains present and active even as the body begins its long relinquishment — and I know what I felt in those rooms: a quality of atmosphere that belongs to no ordinary space, a nearness and a fullness and a stillness that did not originate from anything in the natural world. The presence of God was not an impression or a consolation I manufactured for myself. It was a weight in the room. A warmth at the edges of things. The unmistakable sense of standing very close to something vast.

I have spent considerable time since those hours in the company of theologians, exegetes, and patristic scholars — tracing the Hebrew and Greek of every passage this chapter has covered, examining the arguments of Augustine and Berkhof and Calvin and Spurgeon on the nature of the soul, the reality of the intermediate state, and the certainty of the resurrection. All of that study has served one primary purpose. It has given language and structure and evidential weight to what I already knew in those rooms.

The spirit endures. The person continues. What appeared, in the language of the world, to be an ending was, in the language of Scripture, a departure — and departures have destinations.

I want to speak directly to anyone reading this who has stood in a room like those rooms, or who is standing in one now, or who lies awake in the small hours of the morning with the weight of someone's absence pressing down on a silence that will not lift. The grief is legitimate. The ache is not weakness. It is the cost of love operating at full intensity in a world where love is required to endure separation. And it will not last forever.

The person you loved did not cease to exist. They departed — as Paul understood departure, as a ship loosed from its moorings to sail toward the harbor it was always built for. Their identity is intact. Their consciousness is undiminished. Their capacity for love and recognition and joy has not been reduced — it has been liberated from every constraint this fallen world imposed upon it. And the reunion that is coming is as certain as the empty tomb that made it possible.

I held my grandmothers' hands at the edge of something I could not yet cross. I spoke into a stillness that held more than silence. And what I encountered in those rooms — confirmed now by everything this chapter contains — is not a comfort I have constructed to soften an unbearable reality.

It is the reality itself.

Death is not the end of those who belong to Christ. It is the moment their story finally becomes everything it was always meant to be.

A Prayer for the One Who Is Asking This Question

Lord,

I come to You with this question because I do not know how to carry it alone anymore. Death is too large for me. The grief is too heavy. The fear is too quiet and too persistent. And I do not know what to do with any of it.

If I am standing at a deathbed right now — if I am watching someone I love cross a threshold I cannot follow — give me the grace to trust what I cannot see. Let me hold their hand and speak Your name over them. Let my voice be a lantern at the edge of the darkness. And let me trust that You are standing on the other side of that door, ready to carry them the rest of the way.

If I am grieving someone already gone — if the silence of their absence is louder than anything else in my life right now — remind me that they are not lost. Remind me that they are with You. Remind me that the parting is temporary and the reunion is coming, and that You who hold them also hold me.

If I am afraid of my own death — if mortality has found its way through every distraction I have built against it and is sitting with me in the quiet — let Your Word be louder than my fear. Let the promise of the thief's today reach me. Let Paul's confidence become mine. Let me know in my deepest place that to depart is not to be lost, but to arrive.

And if I do not yet know You — if I have read these words as someone standing outside the door, uncertain, perhaps wanting, but not yet sure — then let this be the moment. I do not need to understand everything. The thief did not understand everything. I only need to turn to You and ask. And so I am asking.

Receive my spirit, Lord. Not at my death. Now. Today. Into Your hands I commend everything I am.

In the name of Jesus, who is the resurrection and the life.

Amen.

"And God shall wipe away all tears from their eyes; and there shall be no more death, neither sorrow, nor crying, neither shall there be any more pain: for the former things are passed away." — Revelation 21:4 (KJV)

Chapter Twelve

Why Did God Create Me Knowing I Would Struggle?

"**B**y thee have I been holden up from the womb: thou art he that took me out of my mother's bowels: my praise shall be continually of thee." — Psalm 71:6 (KJV)

There is a particular kind of tired that has nothing to do with sleep.

It is the tired that settles into a person after the third job loss, or the second broken marriage, or the fourth time they tried to get clean and failed. It is the tired that follows a diagnosis that changed everything, or a phone call that divided life into before and after. It is the tired of a mother who has done everything right and watched it fall apart anyway. The tired of a man who built something with his hands and saw it taken. The tired of a young person who entered this world already carrying a weight they did not choose and cannot explain.

And somewhere inside that tired — usually in the quiet, usually at night — a question forms that most people are afraid to say out loud.

Why did You make me like this? Why did You put me here, in this life, knowing it would hurt this much? If You are God, and if You knew — if You truly knew before I was born every breaking point, every loss, every season of darkness I would have to walk through — then why did You create me at all?

I want you to know something before we go one word further into this chapter.

That question does not frighten me. It does not embarrass me. And it does not embarrass God.

I have heard it asked by people who were angry. I have heard it whispered by people who had nothing left. I have seen it written on the face of someone sitting in a hospital waiting room, staring at the floor, too exhausted even to pray. And every single time I have encountered it, I have seen the same thing underneath it — not rebellion, not atheism, not a desire to tear down faith. What I have seen is a soul in genuine pain reaching out toward the only One who might have an answer.

That is not a faithless act. That is one of the most honest things a human being can do.

So if that is where you are right now — if you picked up this book from the bottom of a hard season, carrying that question like a stone — then I want you to stay with me through every page of this chapter. Because the answer is not a dismissal of your pain. It is not a theological lecture delivered from a comfortable distance. And it is not a list of reasons designed to make your suffering feel smaller than it is.

The answer is something far more staggering than that. The answer is that God knew. He always knew. And He created you anyway — not in spite of the struggle, but because of what He intended to build in you through it.

I want to tell you how I see the person asking this question.

When I hear these words — why did God create me knowing I would struggle — I do not picture a hardened skeptic. I picture someone who still believes, or wants to believe, but has been worn thin by the weight of their own story. I picture someone who was taught that faith was supposed to feel like shelter, and instead has spent years feeling exposed. Someone who looked at their life and saw not a masterpiece in progress, but a series of fractures they cannot explain and cannot fix.

What I want that person to hear first — before anything else — is this.

Your struggles are not evidence that God made a mistake. They are evidence that He is making something. Every great story ever told, every book that has ever moved a human heart, every life that has ever mattered has had the same architecture — a beginning, a conflict, a cost, and a purpose that only becomes visible when enough of the story has been written. That is not an accident of storytelling. That is a reflection of the structure God built into existence itself.

The struggle does not define your soul. Only surrendering to the lie that it does gives it that power.

Your flaws, your failures, your hardest seasons — they are the tools God uses to break the cycle of self-sufficiency that keeps human beings from finding Him. They are not your identity. They are your invitation.

And every single one of them was seen — fully, completely, without surprise — before you drew your first breath.

What It Means That God Knew

Most people, when they hear the word foreknowledge, think of it the way they think of a weather forecast. God looked ahead, saw what was coming, and noted it down. Clinical. Distant. The way a scientist records data without emotional investment in the outcome.

That is not what the Bible means when it says God knew you.

In Jeremiah 1:5, God speaks directly to the prophet with words that carry a weight most English translations can only partially convey. He says: "Before I formed thee in the belly I knew thee; and before thou camest forth out of the womb I sanctified thee; and I ordained thee a prophet unto the nations."

Four words in that single verse carry the architecture of God's entire relationship to every human life He has ever created. Formed. Knew. Sanctified. Ordained.

But it is the second word — knew — that I want to stay with for a moment, because it changes everything about how we understand this chapter's question.

The Hebrew word translated as knew is yada. Yada is not a cold, intellectual word. It is not the word you would use to describe a scientist cataloguing data. The scholars who have spent their lives studying this word in its original context describe it as a sovereign-grace word — a word that carries within it the idea of personal affection, relational choosing, covenant faithfulness, and providential care. When God says He knew Jeremiah before he was formed, He is not saying He had information about Jeremiah. He is saying He had set His love upon Jeremiah. He had chosen him. He had already determined to walk with him, sustain him, and bring him through every hard thing his life would contain.

A.W. Pink, in his study of divine foreknowledge, made this precise point — that biblical foreknowledge is not cold intellectual awareness.

It carries the weight of God having set His love upon specific persons, a sovereign act of relational choosing before time began. This is not foreseeing an action or event. It is God foreknowing persons with approbation and relational purpose.

Think about what that means for you.

Before you were born, God did not merely observe the outline of your life and make notes about the hard parts. He set His love upon you. He chose you. He knew every breaking point, every loss, every season of darkness — and He looked at all of it and said, this one is mine.

That is not the action of a God who made a mistake. That is the action of a God who made a decision.

Written Before You Existed

David understood something about this that he could barely contain in language. In Psalm 139, he writes words that become more staggering the more slowly you read them.

"For thou hast possessed my reins: thou hast covered me in my mother's womb. I will praise thee; for I am fearfully and wonderfully made: marvellous are thy works; and that my soul knoweth right well. My substance was not hid from thee, when I was made in secret, and curiously wrought in the lowest parts of the earth. Thine eyes did see my substance, yet being unperfect; and in thy book all my members were written, which in continuance were fashioned, when as yet there was none of them." — Psalm 139:13–16 (KJV)

That word translated as substance — yet being unperfect — is the Hebrew word golem. It refers to an unformed, wrapped, embryonic mass. The image is of a human being before it has fully taken shape — still in the process of becoming what it will be. And David says that even then, even in that unfinished state, God's eyes were already there. Already watching. Already writing.

In thy book all my members were written, which in continuance were fashioned, when as yet there was none of them.

John Flavel, the Puritan pastor and writer, meditates on this verse with a reverence that is hard to match. He writes that before the golem even took physical shape, the exact architecture of that life was already meticulously recorded by God — that God sculptured our bodies according to an exact model He had already drawn in His own gracious purpose before we had a being.

What Flavel is pointing at — and what David is singing about — is not merely that God saw your body before it was formed. He saw your days. He saw your story. He saw the moments that would make you, and the moments that would break you, and the moments that would bring you — if you let them — all the way home to Him.

Charles Spurgeon, preaching from this very psalm, says it plainly: God predetermined the days of each life before a single one of them came to be. Not one dark season is an accident. Not one breaking point is a surprise. Every hard thing you have ever carried was already known — and already accounted for — before you drew your first breath.

That is not cruelty. That is craftsmanship.

The Potter Does Not Make Mistakes

There are two Hebrew words in Isaiah 43:1 that I want you to hear side by side, because together they say something about how God made you that no single word can carry alone.

"But now thus saith the LORD that created thee, O Jacob, and he that formed thee, O Israel, Fear not: for I have redeemed thee, I have called thee by thy name; thou art mine." — Isaiah 43:1 (KJV)

The first word — created — is the Hebrew bara. This is a word used exclusively with God as the subject throughout the Old Testament.

No human being bara anything. It is reserved entirely for the divine act of bringing something into existence from nothing.

The second word — formed — is the Hebrew yatsar. This word carries the image of a potter working at a wheel, hands pressed into clay, shaping and pressing and deliberately forming the vessel into exactly the shape he intends it to be. Yatsar is not a word of mass production. It is a word of patient, deliberate, skilled craftsmanship.

God uses both words in the same breath when speaking of Jacob. Of Israel. Of you.

He did not merely bring you into existence. He shaped you. He pressed you. He formed you with the intentionality of a master crafts-man who knows exactly what the finished vessel is supposed to be — and who understands that the shaping process is inseparable from the finished product.

"But now, O LORD, thou art our father; we are the clay, and thou our potter; and we all are the work of thy hand." — Isaiah 64:8 (KJV)

The clay does not get to tell the potter that the pressing is a mistake. The clay does not have the vantage point to see what the potter sees. The clay is in the middle of the process. The potter is holding the end in mind.

And then — this is the part I do not want you to miss — God fol-lows the declaration of His craftsmanship in Isaiah 43 with a promise that is one of the most important in all of Scripture for anyone carrying the question of this chapter.

"When thou passest through the waters, I will be with thee; and through the rivers, they shall not overflow thee: when thou walkest through the fire, thou shalt not be burned; neither shall the flame kindle upon thee." — Isaiah 43:2 (KJV)

When. Not if.

God does not say if you pass through waters. He says when. The struggle is not a possibility He is warning you about. It is a certainty He is preparing you for. He designed the life knowing the waters were coming. He shaped the vessel knowing the fire was part of the process. And He made the promise — I will be with you inside it — before you ever took your first step toward the flame.

Philip Yancey, reflecting on this promise, writes that because of this we know God truly understands our pain — that when we endure trials, He stands beside us, just as the fourth man stood in the fiery furnace with Shadrach, Meshach, and Abednego in Daniel 3. Thomas Watson, the Puritan writer, puts it this way: God does not bring His people into troubles and leave them there. He holds their heads and their hearts when they are fainting.

The struggle was foreknown. So was the grace appointed to sustain you through it.

What the Struggle Is Actually Doing

I want to tell you something that took me years to understand. And I want to say it plainly, because this is the heart of everything this chapter is trying to answer.

The struggle is not the enemy of your soul. It is the instrument of its formation.

Peter writes to believers under genuine trial with words that carry the weight of someone who has personally known both failure and restoration:

"But the God of all grace, who hath called us unto his eternal glory by Christ Jesus, after that ye have suffered a while, make you perfect, stablish, strengthen, settle you." — 1 Peter 5:10 (KJV)

After that ye have suffered a while. Not in spite of it. After it. The perfecting, establishing, strengthening, settling is what comes on the other side of the suffering. Not around it. Through it.

The Apostle Paul provides the precise mechanics of what that process looks like. The Greek word he uses for tribulation in Romans 5 is thlipsis. And if you look at the root of that word, you find an image that is not gentle. Thlipsis comes from the verb thlibo — which means to press, to squeeze, to crush. It was the word used to describe a sledge pressing down on stalks of grain to thresh them. The crushing of olives to extract oil. The stomping of grapes to press out wine.

In every single one of those images, the pressure is not destroying what it is applied to. It is extracting what is most valuable from it.

That is what God is doing when He permits thlipsis — crushing, pressing tribulation — in a life He designed. He is not destroying you. He is extracting from you the faith, the endurance, the character, and the hope that cannot be produced any other way.

Paul traces the chain reaction precisely. Thlipsis — the crushing pressure — produces hupomone — patient endurance. The word hupomone is built from two roots: hupo, meaning under, and mone, meaning dwelling place. It literally means to live under something — to remain steady beneath the weight rather than collapsing or running. And that patient endurance produces dokime — a word drawn from the ancient practice of testing metal coins to prove they are genuine and not counterfeit. The believer who endures the crushing pressure emerges as dokime — authenticated, proven, spiritually fit. And proven character produces elpis — hope. Not wishful thinking. Solid assurance. Confident expectation.

This is the chain God is building in a life that includes struggle. This is what the pressure is for.

The writer to the Hebrews captures the same truth from the angle of divine discipline:

"For they verily for a few days chastened us after their own pleasure; but he for our profit, that we might be partakers of his holiness. Now no chastening for the present seemeth to be joyous, but grievous: nevertheless afterward it yieldeth the peaceable fruit of righteousness unto them which are exercised thereby." — Hebrews 12:10–11 (KJV)

No chastening for the present seemeth joyous, but grievous. That is the honest acknowledgment. God does not ask you to pretend the pressing is pleasant. He acknowledges that it is hard. Nevertheless afterward — this is the turning point of the verse. The peaceable fruit of righteousness is not produced by comfort. It is produced by being exercised thereby. The Greek word for perfect in this context — teleios — does not mean sinless or flawless. It means mature. Complete. Having reached the full end of what it was designed to be. The goal God is working toward through every trial in your life is not your comfort. It is your completion.

God Said So Himself

There is a moment in the Gospel of John that I want to take you to, because it is one of the most direct answers Jesus ever gave to the question of why suffering exists in a life God designed.

His disciples see a man who has been blind since birth. And they ask Him the question that feels most natural — who sinned? Was it this man? Was it his parents? Somebody must be responsible for this. Somebody must have done something wrong to deserve a life like this.

And Jesus stops them entirely. He tells them that the man's suffering is not a punishment. It is not a consequence. It is not evidence of failure or fault or divine displeasure. The Greek word He uses — phaneroo — means to reveal, to disclose, to bring into the open what was not previously visible. Jesus is saying that the man's darkness was the specific, sovereignly designed canvas upon which the light and the healing power of God would be displayed in a way it could not have been displayed any other way. The darkness was not an accident. It was an appointment.

Peter understood this and wrote to suffering believers with the same reframing:

"Beloved, think it not strange concerning the fiery trial which is to try you, as though some strange thing happened unto you: But rejoice, inasmuch as ye are partakers of Christ's sufferings; that, when his glory shall be revealed, ye may be glad also with exceeding joy." — 1 Peter 4:12–13 (KJV)

Think it not strange. This is not an accident. This is not punishment. This is participation — a sharing in the sufferings of the only Person in history who was fully innocent and fully in pain simultaneously. And the participation leads somewhere. When his glory shall be revealed. The suffering is not the destination. It is the road.

There are struggles in your life that are not punishments. They are not mistakes. They are not evidence that you are cursed or forgotten or beyond reach. They are the specific, purposefully designed circumstances through which God intends to make Himself visible — through which the works of God are about to be made manifest — in a way that no amount of comfort or ease could ever produce.

Your darkness, whatever form it takes, may be the very thing God uses to show the world who He is.

The Chain That Cannot Be Broken

Paul writes eight of the most extraordinary words in the New Testament in Romans 8:28 — and then in the two verses that follow, he pulls back the curtain on why they are true.

"And we know that all things work together for good to them that love God, to them who are the called according to his purpose." — Romans 8:28 (KJV)

All things. Not some things. Not the comfortable things. Not the things that make sense. All things — including the hardest, darkest, most confusing things in your life — are being actively worked together by God for the good of those who love Him and are called according to His purpose.

But how? How can that be true? How can genuine suffering, real loss, authentic pain — how can all of it be working toward good?

Paul answers that question in Romans 8:29–30 with what theologians have called the golden chain.

"For whom he did foreknow, he also did predestinate to be conformed to the image of his Son, that he might be the firstborn among many brethren. Moreover whom he did predestinate, them he also called: and whom he called, them he also justified: and whom he justified, them he also glorified." — Romans 8:29–30 (KJV)

The Greek word translated as foreknew is proginosko. And like the Hebrew yada we looked at earlier, this word carries far more than intellectual awareness. Theologian Herman Bavinck explains that proginosko is not passive precognition — it is God's active self-determination to relate in love to the objects of His choosing. B.B. Warfield, in his study of this passage, describes the chain of Romans 8:30 as five golden links — foreknew, predestinated, called, justified, glorified — welded together so that all who are set upon in God's gracious distinguishing view are carried on by His grace, step by step, to the great consummation.

The struggle is not outside the chain. It is inside it. The conforming to the image of Christ — which is the stated goal of the foreknowing and predestinating and calling — does not happen in spite of the hard things. It happens through them. The golden chain runs directly through the fire.

J.I. Packer observes something about verse 30 that I have never forgotten. The word glorified is written in the past tense — as though it has already happened. Because in God's mind, the completion of the believer's journey is already as certain as if it were done. The struggle you are in right now is not a detour. It is not a delay. It is a link in a chain that God finished forging before the foundation of the world.

The Hardest Objection

Before we go further I want to stop and face something directly. Because if I do not, I am not being honest with you. And this book was never written to give you easy answers. It was written to give you true ones.

The hardest version of the objection behind this chapter's question goes something like this. If God is truly good, He would want His creatures to be free from suffering. If God is truly all-powerful, He would be able to make that happen. But His creatures are not free from suffering. They suffer enormously, repeatedly, and sometimes without any visible resolution. Therefore, either God is not as good as He claims, or He is not as powerful as He claims, or He simply does not exist at all.

This is not a new argument. It traces back to the ancient philosopher Epicurus and has been sharpened by skeptics ever since. And I am not going to wave it away. It deserves a real answer.

There is a second form of the objection that cuts even deeper. If God foreknew every struggle before He created you — if He saw every dark season, every breaking point, every unanswered prayer before you were formed — then was not your suffering inevitable from the moment He decided to create you? And if it was inevitable, does that not make God directly responsible for it? Does it not make human beings something closer to puppets than people — walking a script that was written before they were born?

These are honest questions. And they deserve honest answers.

The first answer is this. The objection assumes that the highest form of love is the removal of all discomfort. But that is not love — that is indulgence. C.S. Lewis dismantles this with clarity in The

Problem of Pain. He argues that what we really want when we make this objection is a grandfather in heaven — a deity whose only concern is that we remain comfortable, undisturbed, and perpetually satisfied. But a God who wanted only our comfort would not be giving us the greatest gift. He would be leaving us exactly as we are — self-sufficient, self-centered, and incapable of the love and depth and character that suffering alone can produce. Lewis argued further that pain operates in human experience as God working to break through the wall of self-sufficiency — forcing open the soul that has closed itself to anything beyond its own comfort, insisting on being heard when every other voice has been drowned out.

God did not create a world without suffering because a world without suffering would be a world without growth, without love, without the soul-making that turns incomplete creatures into something worthy of eternity.

The second answer addresses the foreknowledge objection directly. There is a critical distinction between knowing something will happen and causing it to happen. Philosopher Alvin Plantinga and theologian Louis Berkhof both anchor this point carefully. Foreknowledge is not causation. If I know that a friend will make a particular choice tomorrow, my knowledge of that choice does not cause it. The choice is still freely made. God's foreknowledge of your struggles does not mean He scripted them like a puppeteer pulling strings. It means He saw them — all of them — and in His wisdom determined that a world in which real human freedom existed, with all the pain that freedom can produce, was a world worth creating. Because it was also a world in which real love could exist. Real faith. Real courage. Real redemption. Berkhof makes the distinction plainly: God's eternal knowledge of an event no more makes Him its author than a witness's knowledge of a crime makes that witness the criminal.

And He did not watch from a distance. He entered the suffering He foreknew. That is the cross. That is the answer God gave with His own body to every person who has ever asked why He would create a world like this.

"Nay but, O man, who art thou that repliest against God? Shall the thing formed say to him that formed it, Why hast thou made me thus? Hath not the potter power over the clay, of the same lump to make one vessel unto honour, and another unto dishonour?" — Romans 9:20–21 (KJV)

Paul is not dismissing the question. He is redirecting it. He is pointing out that the creature does not have the vantage point of the Creator. The clay is in the middle of the shaping. The potter sees the finished vessel. And the question — why hast thou made me thus — is answered not by an explanation but by an invitation. Trust the potter. Not because He owes you an explanation. But because His hands have never once produced a vessel that was not exactly what He intended it to be.

What the Greatest Minds Said

I want to bring you now to some of the men who have wrestled most honestly and most deeply with this question — not from the safety of comfortable theology, but from lives that knew genuine suffering and emerged with convictions forged in the fire.

John Calvin, in his Institutes of the Christian Religion, will not allow us to imagine a God who sits at a distance watching events unfold. He writes that divine providence is not an unconcerned sitting of God in heaven from which He merely observes the things done in the world, but an all-active governance by which He directs everything He has made. Nothing takes place by chance. And to the person who accuses God of cruelty for creating a life He foreknew would include pain, Calvin's answer is anchored not in argument but in the wisdom and purpose of God — that He always has the best reason for His plan, whether to instruct His people in patience, to correct their wrong affections, or to subdue them to self-denial.

Calvin is also careful — and this matters — to draw a line between God ordaining the use of suffering and God being the author of evil. The distinction is precise. The motives of God and the motives of the evil that sometimes produces suffering are entirely different. God uses what evil intends for destruction and turns it to redemption. The sin comes from the creature. The purpose comes from the Creator.

Augustine, writing centuries earlier out of a life he himself described as years of rebellion, intellectual pride, and moral failure, came to a similar conclusion through a more personal road. He understood from his own biography that the restlessness and fracturing of a soul in rebellion was not God's absence — it was God's pressure. His famous declaration in the opening pages of Confessions captures it perfectly: "Thou madest us for Thyself, and our heart is restless, until it repose in Thee." The suffering of a life not yet surrendered is not evidence that God made a mistake. It is evidence that the soul has not yet found the only thing that can satisfy it.

Augustine came to understand suffering as what he called severe mercy — a divine therapy that heals by stripping away the wrong attachments that keep us from the only One who can give us rest.

C.S. Lewis, in The Problem of Pain, takes on the accusation most directly. He writes that our problem with a God who allows suffering is almost always rooted in a trivial understanding of the word love. We want, Lewis says, a grandfather in heaven — a benevolent deity whose only goal is our comfort and whose highest achievement is our undisturbed happiness. But that is not love. That is indulgence. And indulgence, Lewis argues, is not what a God who truly loves us would offer. God does not exist for the sake of man's comfort. Because He loves us, He insists on making us truly lovable — which requires our purification. Lewis argued that pain operates in human experience as God working to break through the wall of self-sufficiency that keeps human beings from surrendering to the only One who can actually give them what they are looking for.

Thomas Watson, the Puritan writer, uses the image of the goldsmith to say the same thing from a different angle. No vessel can be made of gold without fire, Watson writes. It is impossible to be made a vessel of honor unless you are melted and refined in the furnace of affliction. And then he adds something that has stayed with me — what hurt does the fire do to the gold? It only purifies it.

John Flavel, in The Mystery of Providence, counsels the believer who cannot yet see the hand of God inside their suffering with an image I have returned to many times. He compares providence to a ship at sea following the compass of Romans 8:28. Looking back, Flavel says, we will see that the very events we could neither reconcile with the promise nor with each other were the right way to a city of habitation — that what felt like a wilderness was, in fact, the designed path home.

Charles Spurgeon echoes this with the pastoral honesty that marks everything he wrote. He teaches that even when the darkest midnight falls upon a believer, the penury, the sickness, the bereavement, the contempt — all of it is as much ordained and settled in the path of providence as the wealth, the comfort, and the joy. God scars the soil of a life, Spurgeon says, that He may cleanse it and turn up the subsoil. He ploughs deep that He may bring forth something that the surface alone could never produce.

And Dietrich Bonhoeffer, writing from a Nazi prison cell while facing execution, understood something about this that few people have ever had the opportunity — or the cost — to understand from quite so close. He wrote that when believers are brought to the place where they participate in the sufferings of God — when they enter the darkness not running from it but walking through it in faith — they are drawn into a communion with Christ that no amount of ease or comfort could ever produce. The suffering is not an obstacle to knowing God. For Bonhoeffer, it was the doorway.

The God Who Is Not Distant

I need to address something directly before we go further, because it is the accusation that sits underneath this chapter's question for a great many people.

If God knew all of this was coming — every tear, every diagnosis, every betrayal, every breaking point across every human life — and created the world anyway, does that not suggest that He simply does not care? That He watches from a safe distance, immune to the suffering He foreknew?

Scripture will not allow that conclusion. Not even close.

"In all their affliction he was afflicted, and the angel of his presence saved them: in his love and in his pity he redeemed them; and he bare them, and carried them all the days of old." — Isaiah 63:9 (KJV)

The Hebrew word translated as affliction is tsarah — rooted in the word tsar, which means narrow, tight, cramped, restricted. The image is of being pressed into a space so tight there is no room to breathe. That is the word God uses for what His people experience.

And then — this is the part that stops me every time — He uses the same category of word for Himself. In all their affliction, He was afflicted.

There is a remarkable textual detail in the ancient Hebrew manuscripts here. Two different readings of this verse exist side by side in the tradition. One renders it as He was not an adversary in their affliction. The other renders it exactly as the KJV — that their affliction was affliction to Him. Remarkably, both readings point to the same theological truth. God is not the enemy standing over the suffering. God is present inside it. He feels what His people feel. He carries what they carry.

Terryl Givens, drawing on this verse alongside Genesis 6:6 — where human rebellion grieved God to His very heart — dismantles completely the idea of an emotionally distant, philosophically impassible deity. The God of Scripture is a God whose bowels are moved with mercy, whose heart beats in sympathy with human pain, who weeps because He feels perfect compassion for the creatures He made and loves.

But it does not stop there. Because Isaiah 63:9 only shows us the shadow of what the New Testament reveals in full.

God did not only feel the suffering of His people from a distance. He entered it. He put on human flesh and walked into the worst of it — rejection, betrayal, grief, physical torment, and the cosmic abandonment of the cross — so that there would never be a moment of human suffering that He had not personally entered and personally redeemed.

"For we have not an high priest which cannot be touched with the feeling of our infirmities; but was in all points tempted like as we are, yet without sin." — Hebrews 4:15 (KJV)

We are not bringing our struggle to a God who watches from above the clouds, unmoved and untouched. We are bringing it to a High Priest who has felt what we feel. Who was tempted in every point as we are. Who knows the weight of unanswered prayer, of betrayal, of physical suffering, of the silence before dawn.

He did not design a painful path for humanity while keeping Himself immune to the pain. He walked it first. He walked it further than any of us will ever have to walk. And He is walking it still — beside every soul in every narrow, crushing, breathless moment of their lives.

That is not the behavior of a God who does not care. That is the behavior of a God whose love has no outer boundary.

You Are Allowed to Cry Out

I want to say something to the person who has been carrying this question in silence, afraid that asking it out loud is somehow a failure of faith.

It is not.

The Bible does not ask you to pretend. It does not ask you to perform a peace you do not feel or manufacture a joy you have not found. The great men and women of Scripture who are held up as models of faith were not people who smiled through their pain and kept it to themselves. They were people who brought their pain — raw, unfiltered, and sometimes furious — directly to God.

David, the man Scripture calls a man after God's own heart, wrote from the floor of a darkness he could not explain:

"I cried unto the LORD with my voice; with my voice unto the LORD did I make my supplication. I poured out my complaint before him; I shewed before him my trouble." — Psalm 142:1–2 (KJV)

This is not a man who has it figured out. This is a man pouring out his complaint in the dark. And God did not strike him down for it. He did not disqualify him from the catalog of faith. He preserved those words in Scripture for three thousand years so that every person who has ever felt forsaken could find their own voice in them.

Psalm 88 is perhaps the most honest passage in the entire book of Psalms. It is a lament that offers almost no resolution. It ends in darkness. The ancient community that preserved these psalms kept it in the canon precisely because God honors the cry that is addressed to Him even when the cry has no resolution. Even when the soul cannot find its way to the answer. Bringing the pain to God rather than carrying it away from Him is itself an act of trust. It is saying — I do not understand this. I cannot reconcile it. But I am bringing it to You rather than carrying it away from You.

"My soul longeth, yea, even fainteth for the courts of the LORD: my heart and my flesh crieth out for the living God." — Psalm 84:2 (KJV)

"Why art thou cast down, O my soul? and why art thou disquieted in me? hope thou in God: for I shall yet praise him for the help of his countenance." — Psalm 42:5 (KJV)

David does not answer his own question with a theological argument. He answers it with a declaration of forward trust — I shall yet praise Him. Not yet, not now in the middle of this darkness. But yet. It is coming. And the lament itself is the bridge that carries him there.

The defining difference between questioning faith and abandoning faith is not the intensity of the pain or the honesty of the cry. It is the direction. Job, in the depths of his suffering, declared something that became one of the most powerful statements of faith in all of Scripture.

"Though he slay me, yet will I trust in him." — Job 13:15 (KJV)

That is not the statement of a man who has no questions. That is the statement of a man who has decided that God is trustworthy even when He cannot be understood. The questions are still there. The pain is still there. The darkness has not lifted. But the direction of the soul has been chosen. Toward God rather than away from Him.

You are allowed to cry out. You are allowed to bring the full, unedited weight of your pain to God. What you are not allowed to do — what will only deepen your isolation — is carry it away from Him entirely. Bring it to Him. Leave it at His door. And wait. He will answer. He always does.

The Proof Written Into Scripture

There is a life recorded in the book of Genesis whose conclusion speaks directly to this chapter's question in a single sentence that I want to place before you.

Joseph's story — examined in full in Chapter Three — is the most detailed case study Scripture gives us of a designed life that ran through betrayal, injustice, slavery, and imprisonment before arriving at purpose. Twenty-two years from the pit to the palace. And when the full picture was finally revealed, the Psalmist captures what God had been doing across all of it:

"He sent a man before them, even Joseph, who was sold for a servant: Whose feet they hurt with fetters: he was laid in iron: Until the time that his word came: the word of the LORD tried him." — Psalm 105:17–19 (KJV)

He sent a man before them. Not — He permitted a man to be sent. Not — He watched as a man was sold into slavery. He sent. The sovereign agency is unmistakable. Joseph's brothers meant it for evil, chashab-ing destruction against him — they calculated, they plotted, they wove together a plan of harm. And God simultaneously chashab-ed good through those exact same events. The Hebrew word means to weave, to calculate, to fabricate a design with precision. The same years. The same darkness. The same wounds. Two different calculations. And God's calculation was larger.

The word of the LORD tried him. The iron was not the enemy's work alone. It was also the instrument of God's preparation. The fetters were the shaping.

The suffering was not a detour from the purpose. The suffering was the path to it.

I want to say that again, because I believe it is the sentence this entire chapter is built around.

The suffering was not a detour from the purpose. The suffering was the path to it.

When God Does Not Remove the Thorn

There is one more piece of this answer that I cannot leave out, because for many of the people asking this chapter's question, the hardest part is not the suffering itself. The hardest part is that they have prayed — earnestly, repeatedly, with real faith — and the suffering has not been removed. And now they wonder if that means something has gone wrong. If God has forgotten them. If their faith is insufficient.

Paul speaks directly to this.

In 2 Corinthians 12, Paul describes what he calls a thorn in the flesh — the Greek word is skolops, which means a sharp, pointed stake or thorn that embeds itself deeply and cannot be easily extracted. He does not tell us exactly what it was. But he tells us everything we need to know about what it meant.

He asked God three times to remove it. Three times. This is the Apostle Paul — the man who wrote half the New Testament, who was caught up to the third heaven, who had seen and experienced more of God's power than almost anyone who had ever lived. And his prayer was not answered the way he asked.

And God's response was this:

"And he said unto me, My grace is sufficient for thee: for my strength is made perfect in weakness. Most gladly therefore will I rather glory in my infirmities, that the power of Christ may rest upon me." — 2 Corinthians 12:9 (KJV)

J.I. Packer observes that the thorn was sent specifically to keep Paul humble — to prevent the spiritual pride that might have come from the extraordinary revelations he had received. The affliction itself was the provision. What looked like a hindrance to Paul's ministry was actually the instrument God used to keep the vessel clean enough to be useful. As Hebrews confirms, the discipline is for our profit, that we might be partakers of His holiness.

The Greek word translated sufficient is arkeo — enough, unfailing, satisfactory. The word translated made perfect is teleioo — to complete, to bring to its intended purpose. God's grace does not weakly excuse our weakness. It completes its intended purpose precisely within our human frailty.

My grace is sufficient. My strength is made perfect in weakness.

The removal of the pain is not the only way God shows His love. Sometimes the continuous supply of His grace inside the pain is the greater miracle. Sometimes the unresolved struggle is the specific place where God's power is most completely and most visibly at work. Because when you have been stripped of every resource of your own — when you have nothing left — God's strength operates in you without competition. There is nothing in the way. And what comes through a vessel that empty is something the world cannot produce and cannot explain.

Paul moved from pleading for deliverance to declaring that he would rather glory in his infirmities, that the power of Christ may rest upon him. The weaker the vessel, the more completely Christ fills it.

The Question That Changes Everything

There comes a moment in the life of every person who has wrestled honestly with the question of this chapter — a moment when something shifts. When the question stops being why did God create me knowing I would struggle and becomes what is God building in me through this struggle.

That shift is not automatic. It does not happen because the pain lifts. It does not happen because the circumstances change. It happens when the human will makes a decision — a specific, costly, sometimes agonizing decision — to stop demanding an explanation and start trusting the design.

Oswald Chambers, in My Utmost for His Highest, describes what that decision actually requires. He writes that the imperative spiritual need is to sign the death warrant of my claim to my right to myself. That is the language of complete surrender. Not partial. Not conditional. Not I will trust God if He explains Himself. But the full, unconditional laying down of the demand that my life make sense to me on my timeline.

Chambers is not romantic about this. He knows what it costs. He knows the spiritual restlessness that arises when we are in pain and God is silent and the explanation we desperately need does not come. And his counsel is not to try harder or believe more intensely. His counsel is to stop dictating to God and yield completely to the process that is producing something in you that you cannot yet see.

Because here is what Chambers promises on the other side of that surrender. When a person truly yields — fully, without reservation — the supernatural rush of the life of God invades them instantly. Not eventually. Not after enough time has passed. Instantly. Because surrender is not the end of something. It is the opening of a door.

And what comes through that door is not just comfort. It is purpose. Chambers draws a hard but necessary line between what he calls plaintive, self-centred prayer — the kind that petitions God for relief while quietly demanding He operate on our schedule and according to our plan — and the raw, honest ravings that God actually honors. God is not repelled by the unfiltered cry. He is repelled by the performance of piety that refuses to let go of self. The anguish that surrenders is the anguish He meets.

Chambers writes that through a broken heart — through a life that has been pressed and crushed and poured out — God can bring His purposes to pass in the world. That a person who has been through the fire becomes broken bread and poured out wine to feed and nourish others. And then he says something that I have returned to in my own hardest moments, because it is the most counterintuitive and most liberating thing I have ever read about suffering: thank God for breaking your heart.

Not because the breaking is pleasant. Not because the pain was deserved. But because a broken heart that has been surrendered to God becomes the very instrument through which He does His deepest and most lasting work. The breaking is not the end. It is the opening.

The crushing of the olive does not destroy the oil. It releases it.

Philip Yancey adds something essential to this. He draws a distinction that I believe is one of the most practically useful things ever written about suffering: stop asking the backward-looking question — Why is this happening to me — and start asking the forward-looking one — To what end is God using this? The first question looks at the wound. The second looks at the work. And he observes that the people who make that turn — who move through suffering toward God rather than away from Him — do not arrive at a place where the pain makes perfect logical sense. They arrive at a place where the pain has been dignified. Where it has been given a deeper level of meaning — a sharing in Christ's own redemptive victory. They move from being victims of their story to being participants in something God is doing through it.

That movement is the whole point.

The Apostle Paul says it with a compression of language that takes your breath away when you feel the full weight of who is writing it.

"For our light affliction, which is but for a moment, worketh for us a far more exceeding and eternal weight of glory." — 2 Corinthians 4:17 (KJV)

This is not a man who has been spared suffering. This is a man who has been beaten, shipwrecked, imprisoned, stoned, and left for dead. When Paul calls affliction light and momentary, he is not minimizing pain. He is establishing proportion. He has seen enough of eternity to know that the weight of glory waiting on the other side of this life is so staggering that it reframes everything on this side of it.

The Work He Will Finish

James Montgomery Boice, writing on the great promises of the New Testament, brings us to one of the most quietly powerful verses in all of Paul's letters. Philippians 1:6 contains a promise that directly answers the fear that the struggle means something has gone permanently wrong.

"Being confident of this very thing, that he which hath begun a good work in you will perform it until the day of Jesus Christ." — Philippians 1:6 (KJV)

The Greek word translated as perform — epiteleo — means to complete, to bring fully to its intended end. It is not a word of hopeful intention. It is a word of guaranteed completion. God is not merely trying to finish what He started in you. He is committed to it. He has staked His own name and nature on it.

Boice reflected that this verse speaks directly to the believer who is suffering. He observed that while the Christian life is a fierce battle, the outcome is not bleak or uncertain — it is glorious — because of God. God permits difficulties to come to test and train. He works as a Master Engineer, allowing the weight of trial not because the construction of your soul has been halted, but because epiteleo is at work, bringing you to the ultimate completion He planned before you were formed.

The work is not abandoned. It is not failing. It is being finished.

And when it is finished — when the glass that now shows us only a dark reflection is finally removed — what was suffered in this life will be seen in the full light of what it was always producing. Every tear redeemed. Every breaking point revealed as a turning point. Every dark season exposed as the very road that led you home.

My Reflection

I have carried a lot of hard things in my life. Some of them I have written about in this book. Others are still too close to name. But I will tell you this — there has not been a single season of genuine suffering in my life that, looking back, I cannot see the hand of God working in ways I could not see from inside it.

The years that felt like failure were the years He was building the foundation. The moments that looked like closed doors were redirections toward something I would not have had the wisdom to choose on my own. The breaking points were not the end of the story. They were the turning points.

And I will tell you something else. This book — the very pages you are holding — exists in large part because of the hard things. Not in spite of them. Because of them. God used the pressure to produce something I would never have sat down to write from a place of comfort and ease. The crushing produced something. And I hope — I believe — it will feed someone who is hungry.

But here is the thing I want you to hear most clearly from my own life.

My story is still being written. I do not say that with anxiety. I say it with a settled, hard-won peace. More challenges are coming. More seasons I will not understand while I am inside them. More moments that will require me to choose — to trust what I cannot see, or to collapse under what I cannot explain.

And my honest prayer is that the words of this book will be there waiting for me when those moments come. That I will pick it up and be reminded — not by theology from a distance, but by the Word of

God and the testimony of people who walked through fire before me — that tough times are learning moments. They are not a curse. They are not evidence that God made a mistake. They are the tools He uses to build something in us that comfort alone could never build.

The struggle does not define your soul. What you do with it does.

An Invitation

If you have read this far and you are not yet sure that you know the God this chapter has been talking about — the God who saw you before you were formed, who wove your story with the same word He used to weave the stars, who stepped into human suffering rather than watching from a distance — then I want to speak directly to you now.

You did not pick up this book by accident.

The very fact that this question lives in you — why did God create me knowing I would struggle — is itself evidence of something. It means you are not indifferent to God. You are wrestling with Him. And in my experience, and in the testimony of every great life of faith I have ever studied, wrestling with God is not the opposite of faith. It is one of the earliest forms of it.

The God this chapter describes is not a distant administrator who set the universe running and walked away. He is a Father who knelt in the dirt of a Palestinian road to wash feet. Who wept at a tomb. Who did not remove the cup of suffering when it came, but drank it all the way to the bottom — so that you would never have to wonder whether there is a God who understands what it means to hurt.

You do not have to have it figured out to come to Him. You do not have to have resolved the question of suffering before you are allowed to approach. You can come with the question still in your hand, still bleeding, still making no sense — and He will meet you there.

He was already there before you arrived.

If you want to know this God, you can speak to Him right now. You do not need a building or a ceremony or a clean record. You need only the willingness to say — I cannot carry this alone. I believe You are real. I believe You see me. Help me trust You with the parts of my story I do not yet understand.

That is the beginning. And from that beginning, everything else in this book becomes not just theology — but a letter from a Father who knew you before you were formed and has been weaving your story with purpose from the very first breath.

A Prayer for the One Who Is Tired

Lord God,

I am praying right now for the person holding these pages who is tired in the way that has nothing to do with sleep. The person whose breaking points have stacked up so high they can no longer see over them. The person who looked at their own life and asked — why? Why would You make me this way? Why would You place me here, in this story, knowing it would cost this much?

I am praying that right now, in this moment, You would make Yourself known to them — not as a distant architect, but as a present Father. Remind them that You are not watching their suffering from the outside. You entered it. You know what the narrow, crushing places feel like from the inside, because You walked them. You know what betrayal feels like, and grief, and unanswered prayer, and the silence that comes before the dawn.

Let them hear the truth of Psalm 71:6 — that before they were formed, You held them from the womb. That You have been present since before the beginning of their story. That Your holding has never stopped and will not stop.

Let them see the gold that the fire is producing in them, even now, even in the middle of what they cannot yet understand. Let them feel the sustaining grace that is sufficient — the grace that is most fully present when everything else has been stripped away.

And Lord — when they are tempted to believe that You made a mistake by creating them — let them hear Your answer in the voice of Paul writing from a prison cell, in chains, at peace: the suffering was not a detour from the purpose. The suffering was the path to it.

Give them the grace to stop asking only why You made them, and to begin asking what You are making them into.

For the one who has been crying out in the dark like David, unable to see the dawn — remind them that the lament is not the end of the song. That You preserved those cries in Scripture because You honor them. That turning toward You with the pain is the very act of faith that carries a soul from the cry at midnight to the declaration of praise.

May the one who began this chapter asking why finish it knowing — You created me for this. And You are with me in it.

In the name of Jesus Christ, who entered the suffering so we would never face it alone.

Amen.

"He will swallow up death in victory; and the Lord GOD will wipe away tears from off all faces; and the rebuke of his people shall he take away from off all the earth: for the LORD hath spoken it." — Isaiah 25:8 (KJV)

Chapter Thirteen

Why Does God Allow Children to Suffer?

"Suffer little children, and forbid them not, to come unto me: for of such is the kingdom of heaven." — Matthew 19:14 (KJV)

There are places in this world where the question of this chapter is not theoretical. It is not a seminary debate or a philosophy lecture. It is the air itself — breathed in and breathed out with every shift, every chart, every small hand that grows cold before it should.

I think about the people who walk those hallways. The ones who have given their lives to fighting for children — and who have had to watch, sometimes, when the fight could not be won. People of extraordinary intelligence and extraordinary compassion who began their work with faith, and who have found over time that the sheer weight of what they witness has created a distance between themselves and the God they once knew.

Philip Yancey, in Where Is God When It Hurts?, describes what happens to those who work in the middle of suffering every day. He writes that they can enter a place where the volume of pain they encounter forces a breakdown of meaning that ordinary theology cannot easily reach. The neat explanations that comfort people who observe suffering from a distance become hollow to the people who are inside it every day. They do not need a formula. They need something that can reach them where they actually are.

I understand that distance. I am not going to pretend I do not.

What I am going to do is take you somewhere most people have never been taken. Into the Scripture. Into the original languages. Into the writings of the men and women who wrestled with this question across two thousand years of church history. Because when I arrived there — when I really arrived there — I found something I did not expect.

I found that God has spoken to this question with more tenderness, more specificity, and more hope than most people ever knew was there.

This chapter is for the person who has seen too much to settle for easy answers. Good. Easy answers are not what we are offering here.

Before we go anywhere else, I want to say something that I believe is critically important for the person carrying this question.

Your grief, your confusion, your anger, your distance — none of that disqualifies you from God. None of it offends Him. And none of it is evidence that your faith was not real.

The Bible has a word for what you are feeling. The word is lament. And lament is not a failure of faith. It is one of the most ancient and honored forms of prayer in all of Scripture.

Job lost everything in a single day — his wealth, his health, and all ten of his children. And Job did not offer a quiet, composed theological response. He tore his robe. He fell to the ground. He demanded an audience with God Himself.

"Then Job arose, and rent his mantle, and shaved his head, and fell down upon the ground, and worshipped, And said, Naked came I out of my mother's womb, and naked shall I return thither: the LORD gave, and the LORD hath taken away; blessed be the name of the LORD. In all this Job sinned not, nor charged God foolishly." — Job 1:20–22 (KJV)

God's verdict on Job's honest ravings was far more generous than His verdict on the tidy, careful speeches of Job's friends. God told those friends — you have not spoken of me the thing that is right, as my servant Job hath. Job's broken honesty was more pleasing to God than polished religious language that protected itself from the full weight of the pain.

The entire book of Lamentations exists in the Bible because God wanted us to know that there is a language for seasons when words fail. Jeremiah sat in the rubble of Jerusalem and wrote — Is it nothing to you, all ye that pass by? behold, and see if there be any sorrow like unto my sorrow. That cry is in the Bible. God put it there.

Even Jesus, on the cross, spoke the opening words of Psalm 22 — My God, my God, why hast thou forsaken me? In the ancient Jewish tradition, quoting the first line of a Psalm was the accepted way of invoking the entire text. Jesus was not expressing confusion or abandonment. He was declaring from the cross that Psalm 22 — written a thousand years before, describing the crucifixion in precise detail, and ending in worldwide victory — was being fulfilled in that exact moment. He was pointing every Jewish witness to the ending they already knew. And God preserved those words in Scripture forever.

There is a critical difference between lament and the loss of faith. Lament turns toward God with a broken heart, beats its fists against

His chest, and says — I do not understand what You are doing, this hurts beyond what I can carry, but You are the only hope I have, so I am not leaving. Loss of faith turns its back on God, declares Him absent or cruel, and walks away into the dark.

Lament stays. It stays in the pain. It stays in the questions. But it stays with God.

If you are in that place right now — if you are angry, confused, exhausted, and barely holding on — you are not outside the reach of God. You are exactly where the Psalms were written. You are exactly where Job sat. You are in the place where some of the most profound encounters with God in all of history have begun.

What This World Actually Is

To understand why children suffer, we have to understand what this world actually is in its present condition. Not what we wish it were. Not what God originally designed it to be. What it is right now.

The Apostle Paul tells us plainly:

"For the creature was made subject to vanity, not willingly, but by reason of him who hath subjected the same in hope, Because the creature itself also shall be delivered from the bondage of corruption into the glorious liberty of the children of God. For we know that the whole creation groaneth and travaileth in pain together until now." — Romans 8:20–22 (KJV)

This world is groaning. That is not poetry. That is diagnosis. Paul is telling us that the entire physical universe — every cell, every chromosome, every gene that can mutate into disease — is operating under a weight it was never designed to carry.

The Greek word Paul uses for groaneth is stenāzō — meaning to groan inwardly, to express deep internal anguish. And the word systenāzō — groaneth together — captures something even more profound. It is the groan of something in labor. James Montgomery

Boice, in his Romans commentary, observed that Paul deliberately compares the groaning of creation to the pains of childbirth. And that comparison changes everything. The pains of childbirth are not the groan of something dying. They are the groan of something being born. They are excruciating, but they are not endless, and they are not hopeless. They are the pressure of a new creation struggling into existence.

The suffering in this world — including the suffering of children — is not the meaningless decay of a dying planet. It is the labor pain of a New Creation being born. The groaning will not last forever. Something is coming.

Herman Bavinck, the great Dutch Reformed theologian, wrote that Scripture never presents death or suffering as natural or necessary. It is a hostile intruder. An unnatural power. A consequence of humanity choosing to walk away from God — and taking the entire created order along when we fell.

When a child suffers, God is not the author of that suffering. He is not reaching down and selecting children for pain. He is watching His creation groan under the weight of what sin introduced. And He weeps over every moment of it.

Paul tells us that God is actively working even through the pain — weaving things that appear broken into something that, in eternity, will be recognized as whole. For the child who never had the chance to consciously experience God's redemptive plan on earth, God's ultimate good is not earthly comfort. It is eternal glorification. The child is delivered from the bondage of decay and brought instantly into the presence of Christ.

God Was With That Child

Here is the first thing I want you to know, and I want you to hold it before we go anywhere else.

God was with that child. In every moment. In every breath. The Holy Spirit does not abandon the suffering child to face it alone.

I believe this with my whole heart. I believe that when a child is in pain, God does not watch from a distance. The presence of God surrounds that child in a way that the people standing in the room cannot fully see or measure. God, who knit that child together before a single day of their life had yet been lived, does not leave them in their darkest hour.

"Thou tellest my wanderings: put thou my tears into thy bottle: are they not in thy book?" — Psalm 56:8 (KJV)

God keeps a record of every tear. He counts every wandering. He collects every tear shed over a suffering child in His bottle and writes it in His book. No moment of grief escapes His notice. No tear falls unwitnessed. No child suffers in a room where God is not present. He is nigh — the Hebrew word qarowb, meaning near, close, present — not watching from somewhere beyond the stars, but nearer than breath.

And I believe with everything in me that this nearness extends to the child who cannot speak their suffering. God is there. He has never not been there. In all their affliction, He is afflicted. He bears it alongside them. He carries them.

Gathered, Not Lost — Isaiah 57:1–2

Now I want to take you to a passage that changed the way I understand this question entirely. Most people have never encountered it in this context. I want you to sit with every single word.

"The righteous perisheth, and no man layeth it to heart: and merciful men are taken away, none considering that the righteous is taken away from the evil to come. He shall enter into peace: they shall rest in their beds, each one walking in his uprightness." — Isaiah 57:1–2 (KJV)

Look at these words carefully. Especially one of them.

The Hebrew word translated taken away is asaph. And asaph does not mean what we typically picture when we hear those words. It does not mean destroyed. It does not mean abandoned. It does not mean lost to the dark.

Asaph means to gather. To harvest. To pull into the fold.

When God takes a child home early, Isaiah is telling us He is gathering them. He is harvesting them. He is pulling them into His arms before the coming storm can reach them. The text says it specifically — the righteous is taken away from the evil to come. God sees what lies ahead on this broken planet. He sees the disease, the heartbreak, the temptations, the suffering that the years of this fallen life would bring. And sometimes — not always, but sometimes — He reaches down before any of that can reach His child, and He pulls them home.

And where do they go? The verse tells us plainly.

He shall enter into peace.

The Hebrew word is shalom. And shalom is not merely the absence of war or conflict. Shalom means absolute completeness. Total wholeness. Perfect safety. The full and unbroken flourishing of the soul in the unmediated presence of God.

Among the ancient texts preserved in the Septuagint tradition — the Greek Old Testament that Jesus and His first followers regularly read and quoted — there is a passage that articulates this same truth with stunning clarity. The Wisdom of Solomon, written before the New Testament era, speaks directly into the grief of those who watch the righteous die young:

"But the souls of the righteous are in the hand of God, and no torment shall touch them. In the eyes of the foolish they seemed to have died, and their departure was thought to be a disaster, and their going from us to be their ruin: but they are in peace... Having been disciplined a little, they will receive great good, because God tested them and found them worthy of himself." — Wisdom of Solomon 3:1–6 (Septuagint)

In the eyes of the foolish they seemed to have died. The world looks at the bed, at the stillness, at the absence, and calls it loss. But the ancient wisdom tradition — centuries before Paul wrote Romans, centuries before John wrote Revelation — already knew what God had revealed to those with eyes to see: but they are in peace. The child is not in the place the grief says it is. The child is in the hand of God, and no torment shall touch them there.

The child is not lost. The child has been gathered. There is a profound difference between those two things — and that difference is the gift this chapter most wants to place in your hands.

David Washed His Face

The man who understood this most clearly in all of Scripture may have been a grieving father.

King David's infant son was dying. David was desperate. He fasted. He lay on the ground through the night. He pleaded with God for seven days. He refused to eat, refused to be comforted. He was a man in complete anguish.

And then the child died.

"Then David arose from the earth, and washed, and anointed himself, and changed his apparel, and came into the house of the LORD, and worshipped: then he came to his own house; and when he required, they set bread before him, and he did eat... And he said, While the child was yet alive, I fasted and wept: for I said, Who can tell whether GOD will be gracious to me, that the child may live? But now he is dead, wherefore should I fast? can I bring him back again? I shall go to him, but he shall not return to me." — 2 Samuel 12:20–23 (KJV)

When the servants saw David's sudden calm, they were confused. The same man who had torn his clothes and refused to eat for seven days was now washing his face and eating bread?

David's answer is one of the most quietly profound statements in all of Scripture.

I shall go to him, but he shall not return to me.

The Hebrew word for child throughout this passage is yeled — the most tender Hebrew word for a child, used eighty-nine times in the Old Testament to denote offspring, from a newborn infant to a young boy. Yeled comes from the root yalad, meaning to give birth. It emphasizes the fragile, dependent, deeply beloved nature of the child.

And here is something that should stop every reader in their tracks. That same word — yeled — appears in one of the most glorious prophetic promises in the entire Bible:

"For unto us a child is born, unto us a son is given: and the government shall be upon his shoulder: and his name shall be called Wonderful, Counsellor, The mighty God, The everlasting Father, The Prince of Peace." — Isaiah 9:6 (KJV)

The word for child in that verse is yeled. The exact same word David used for his dying infant. Every child who dies is called by the same word as the promised Messiah Himself. That is not an accident in the language of Scripture. God chose that word deliberately, and it carries the weight of His love for every yeled — every tender, beloved child — who has ever been gathered home to Him.

The Hebrew word for go in David's declaration is halak — meaning a literal walking toward a specific destination. David is not saying I will also die one day and become a corpse in the ground. He is saying I know where my son is, and one day I will walk toward him and reach him. This is the language of reunion. This is the language of a man who knows his child is alive somewhere that he cannot yet go.

And this is the moment the grieving king washed his face, went to the house of God, and worshipped.

Not because the pain was gone. But because he knew something his servants did not. His son was not lost. His son was with God. And the separation, though real and painful, was not permanent.

Randy Alcorn, in his work on heaven, observes that David's behavior in this moment constitutes one of the most powerful biblical arguments for infant salvation ever recorded in Scripture. A man does not wash his face and go worship because his child has ceased to exist. He washes his face and goes to worship because he knows his child is safe.

What Jesus Said About Children

There is a moment in the Gospels that deserves to be read very slowly.

"Then were there brought unto him little children, that he should put his hands on them, and pray: and the disciples rebuked them. But Jesus said, Suffer little children, and forbid them not, to come unto me: for of such is the kingdom of heaven. And he laid his hands on them, and departed thence." — Matthew 19:13–15 (KJV)

The disciples tried to turn the children away. They thought Jesus was too important and too busy for small children. Mark's Gospel tells us He was much displeased — the Greek word aganakteō meaning deeply, genuinely offended — and He rebuked the disciples sharply.

The Greek word translated suffer in suffer little children is aphiemi — meaning allow, permit, let come freely. Jesus is not merely tolerating children. He is welcoming them with urgency and rebuking any force that would keep them from Him.

The Greek word behind of such is toioutos — meaning of this kind, of this class, belonging to this category. Jesus is not using children as a cute illustration. He is declaring that children are the very portrait of who the Kingdom belongs to. The helpless. The dependent. The ones who cannot earn their way in and do not try.

The word nepios, used throughout the New Testament for infant or babe, carries this same weight. In Matthew 11:25, Jesus prays — I thank thee, O Father, Lord of heaven and earth, because thou hast hid these things from the wise and prudent, and hast revealed them unto babes. The Greek word there is nepios. Jesus directly connects the infant state to spiritual purity and to God's willingness to reveal Himself. And in Matthew 21:16, Jesus defends the praises of the young by quoting Psalm 8:2 — Out of the mouth of babes and sucklings thou hast perfected praise. God receives and deeply honors the worship of the nepios — the infant, the young, the one who comes to Him with nothing but need.

Earlier in this same conversation, Jesus had said something even more direct:

"Even so it is not the will of your Father which is in heaven, that one of these little ones should perish." — Matthew 18:14 (KJV)

It is not the will of God. Jesus does not say it is unlikely, or that God hopes it will not happen. He says it is not the will of the Father. The children belong to Him. He said so. He has never taken it back.

Charles Spurgeon, the great nineteenth-century preacher, declared that every parent who watches a child die should hold these words like a lamp in the dark. Jesus did not say the Kingdom belonged to the educated, the converted, or the baptized. He said it belonged to such as these. And Spurgeon was certain — completely, joyfully certain — that the child who dies is not lost but is immediately gathered into the loving arms of the Savior who said, forbid them not.

Job and the God Who Shows Up

There is a man in Scripture who asked the hardest version of this question anyone has ever asked. And what God said in response —

or more precisely, what God chose not to say — may be the most important thing in this entire chapter.

Job lost his wealth, his health, and all ten of his children in a single catastrophic series of events. His friends, well-meaning but profoundly wrong, insisted that his suffering must be punishment for hidden sin. Job knew he was innocent. He cried out for a direct audience with God to explain why this tragedy had occurred.

When God finally answered Job out of the whirlwind, the theological significance lies in what God did not say. God never gave Job a direct explanation for his suffering. He never mentioned the cosmic events that had allowed it. Instead, He asked Job a series of magnificent questions about the creation of the world — the morning stars, the foundations of the earth, the wild animals, the storehouses of snow.

God did not explain Himself. He revealed Himself.

Philip Yancey observes that God deflected attention from the issue of cause to the issue of who He is. Instead of an explanation, Job received a revelation. And remarkably — it was enough. Job was not given the answer to his why. He was given a deeper encounter with the Who. And that encounter transformed everything.

This is one of the most honest pastoral truths in all of Scripture. On this side of eternity, we may never receive the specific answer to why a particular child suffered or died. The infinite architecture of divine providence is too vast for the finite human mind to fully receive. What God offers in its place is not a formula but a presence — the same presence He offered Job out of the whirlwind. A God who shows up. A God who is not intimidated by the question. A God who does not flinch when we cry out.

And God's verdict on Job's honest, anguished cry was this — you have spoken of me the thing that is right. Honesty before God is not faithlessness. It is the highest form of trust.

The Lament Psalm

There is a psalm of raw, honest anguish that the ancient community of faith preserved precisely because God honors the cry that turns toward Him rather than away. The Psalmist writes:

"Hear my prayer, O LORD, and let my cry come unto thee. Hide not thy face from me in the day when I am in trouble; incline thine ear unto me: in the day when I call answer me speedily." — Psalm 102:1–2 (KJV)

This is the cry from inside the darkness. Hide not thy face. Answer me speedily. The urgency of a soul that cannot wait. God preserved this cry in Scripture for three thousand years so that every person who has ever felt that urgency — every nurse, every parent, every anyone who has ever stood at a small bedside — could find their own voice in it.

The defining difference between questioning faith and abandoning faith is not the intensity of the pain or the honesty of the cry. It is the direction. Even in Psalm 22, the cry that begins My God, my God, why hast thou forsaken me — the cry Jesus spoke from the cross — the psalmist does not leave. He does not abandon the address. He is still speaking to God, still reaching toward God, still anchoring himself in the history of God's faithfulness. Even the feeling of abandonment does not become the conclusion. The psalm that begins in total darkness ends in total victory, with all the ends of the world turning to worship the God who was present through every moment of it.

And because Jesus took the true abandonment — the real azab, the turning away of the Father from the weight of human sin — upon Himself at the cross, the person crying out in the darkness today is never truly alone in it. The worst version of the cry has already been absorbed. What remains for every grieving soul is a God who hears, who is near, and who has already paid the price to make the reunion certain.

The Theology of Infant Salvation

I want to answer this question as directly and as honestly as I know how.

I believe — with peace, with scriptural grounding, and with the full backing of the greatest theological minds in church history — that children who die young go immediately and completely into the presence of God.

Not because they are without a fallen nature. Every human being born since Adam carries the weight of humanity's rebellion. Paul is clear:

"Wherefore, as by one man sin entered into the world, and death by sin; and so death passed upon all men, for that all have sinned." — Romans 5:12 (KJV)

Original sin is real. Children are born into a broken world, subject to its consequences. That is why they can suffer. That is why they can die. The disease is real.

But here is where the grace of Jesus Christ says something that most grieving people have never heard said with this kind of force:

"But not as the offence, so also is the free gift. For if through the offence of one many be dead, much more the grace of God, and the gift by grace, which is by one man, Jesus Christ, hath abounded unto many... Therefore as by the offence of one judgment came upon all men to condemnation; even so by the righteousness of one the free gift came upon all men unto justification of life. For as by one man's disobedience many were made sinners, so by the obedience of one shall many be made righteous." — Romans 5:15–19 (KJV)

Twice in this passage the Apostle Paul uses the Greek phrase pollō mallon. It is translated much more. According to Thayer's Greek Lexicon, mallon means more, to a greater degree — and combined with pollō it becomes an overwhelming, superabundant, immeasurable excess. A surplus that swallows the deficit entirely.

Paul is building a direct comparison. Adam's one sin was powerful enough to bring physical death to every human being born after him — including innocent children. But Paul says the grace of Jesus Christ is not equal to the curse. It is not merely as strong. It is pollō mallon — infinitely, superabundantly greater.

How much more is the blood of Christ able to cover what Adam did? That is Paul's question. And his answer is that it is not even a contest.

James Montgomery Boice, reflecting on the theology of infant death, captured the entire argument with simple precision — noting that the curse of Adam brings physical death to children, while the grace of Jesus Christ brings them to life. The curse was real. The remedy is infinitely greater.

B.B. Warfield, one of the most rigorous theological minds of the nineteenth century, built his case for infant salvation directly on this foundation. He argued that the Reformed doctrine of sovereign grace is the only theology that provides an absolute, ironclad guarantee of infant salvation. If salvation depended on human choice or conscious faith, no infant could be saved — because an infant cannot make those choices. But because salvation is entirely the sovereign work of God, an infant's inability to choose presents no obstacle to the Holy Spirit whatsoever.

Warfield concluded with words that every grieving family deserves to hear: when we look at the death of an infant, we can know with confidence that they die in infancy not because they are reprobate, but because they are elect. That they die in infancy is not the cause but the effect of God's mercy toward them. God simply takes them home before the world can break them.

John Calvin understood that God's electing love is not bound by ceremony or by the circumstances of birth. God's grace reaches the child before any human action can either grant or withhold it. The Westminster Confession of Faith, the great seventeenth-century summary of Reformed theology, states it plainly — elect infants dying in infancy are regenerated and saved by Christ, through the Spirit who worketh when, and where, and how he pleaseth.

John Owen extended this further. He wrote that God's grace rescues children regardless of who their earthly parents were — that he made no doubt that God takes many children unto Himself in Christ whose parents never knew the Gospel, or had been despisers of it.

The salvation of a child is not limited by what their parents believed. It is not contingent on a ceremony. It does not depend on anything the child could do, say, or understand. It rests entirely in the sovereign mercy of Jesus Christ.

"For by grace are ye saved through faith; and that not of yourselves: it is the gift of God." — Ephesians 2:8 (KJV)

The salvation of a child is the purest picture of this verse in all of human experience. The infant cannot walk an aisle. Cannot pray a prayer. Cannot read a Bible. Cannot do anything. And yet the grace of God reaches them entirely — not because of anything they did, but because salvation has never depended on what we do. It has always been entirely the gift of God.

Charles Spurgeon said it in the most direct way possible: children do not go to heaven because they are inherently sinless. They enter heaven by the very same way that we do. They are received in the name of Christ.

The Age of Accountability

I want to be completely honest about one thing before we continue. The phrase age of accountability does not appear anywhere in the Bible. I want to be clear about that. But the concept it points toward is woven throughout Scripture in ways that deserve to be seen.

"For before the child shall know to refuse the evil, and choose the good, the land that thou abhorrest shall be forsaken of both her kings." — Isaiah 7:16 (KJV)

"Moreover your little ones, which ye said should be a prey, and your children, which in that day had no knowledge between good and evil, they shall go in thither, and unto them will I give it, and they shall possess it." — Deuteronomy 1:39 (KJV)

Both passages describe a period in early life when a child has not yet reached the moral and cognitive capacity to make a willful, knowing, hardened rejection of God. A child who has no knowledge between good and evil cannot be judged for a rebellion they never consciously committed.

Jonathan Edwards, Richard Baxter, and the Puritan theologians consistently pointed grieving believers away from dark speculation about the fate of children and directed their eyes to the infinite mercy of Christ's cross. They agreed completely on this: the salvation of a child never relies on the child's works, nor is it ultimately limited by the parents' failures. It rests solely in the hands of a God whose grace is deeper and wider than any human failure can reach.

God does not punish a soul for rejecting a Gospel it did not have the cognitive capacity to understand. He does not hold accountable those who lack the knowledge or the ability to be accountable. This is consistent with everything Scripture reveals about the character of God. He is just. And justice does not condemn the innocent for what they could not yet comprehend.

When the Suffering Does Not End Quickly

I want to pause here and address something that the theology of where children go does not fully answer on its own. Because some children do not die quickly. Some suffer. And the suffering itself — the time between the beginning and the gathering — is the part of this question that cuts the deepest for the people who have to stand in the room and watch it.

The Greek word used throughout the New Testament for suffering and tribulation is thlipsis — appearing forty-five times. It comes from the verb thlibō, which literally means to press, to squeeze, to crush. It is the word for being put under pressure so severe that it feels like you are being compressed from every side.

It is a massive theological error to assume that thlipsis always implies God's punishment. Jesus did not say tribulation was punishment. He said it was the reality of living in a fallen world. And He gave His followers this promise:

"For whatsoever is born of God overcometh the world: and this is the victory that overcometh the world, even our faith." — 1 John 5:4 (KJV)

The victory is already decided. The world's suffering does not determine the outcome of anyone who belongs to God. John Owen wrote extensively on this, teaching that when tragedy strikes — even the agonizing suffering of an innocent child — it is not God pouring out His wrath, because all wrath was already poured out on Christ at Calvary. What remains is the pressing of a broken world on souls that God is shaping. And Richard Baxter counseled that in those seasons, the believer must stop looking at the present darkness and instead fix their eyes on the eternal weight of glory that Paul promises is being produced even through the pressing. The eternal perspective — the things which are not seen are eternal — is the only scale large enough to contain the full weight of what God is doing through pain.

And there is something else I have come to believe, and I hold it with both humility and conviction. When a child suffers, I believe God minimizes that suffering in ways we cannot measure or see. I believe the Holy Spirit is present in that child's experience in a manner that goes beyond what the clinical picture in the room reflects. I do not believe God leaves a child to absorb the full weight of their suffering alone. He is there. He bears it with them. He counts every tear.

The Hardest Objection — Ivan's Ticket

I want to stop and face the hardest version of this question directly. Because this chapter is not for people who have thought about child suffering from a safe distance. It is for people who have lived inside it. And those people deserve an honest engagement with the strongest objection — not a dismissal of it.

Fyodor Dostoevsky, through the character Ivan Karamazov in The Brothers Karamazov, made the most emotionally devastating argument against God ever put into literature. Ivan recounts the suffering of children in heartbreaking detail and declares that even if God's eternal plan eventually produces something beautiful and just, it is simply not worth the tears of one tortured child. He hands back his ticket to the harmony.

I am not going to dismiss that argument. I am going to face it.

C.S. Lewis, who came to faith as a hardened atheist and then had his neat theological categories demolished by the death of his own beloved wife, understood this objection from the inside. In The Problem of Pain, Lewis argued that what skeptics actually want is something like a grandfather in heaven — a benevolent deity whose only goal is to ensure that a good time was had by all. But Lewis argued that God is a Father, not a grandfather. True love is not about keeping someone comfortably numb. A surgeon who loves his patient does not refuse to operate because the operating will cause pain. The loving thing is not always the comfortable thing. God's love for human souls is not shallow and does not end at the grave. It is infinite and reaches into eternity.

The fatal flaw in Ivan Karamazov's argument is the assumption that if a human mind cannot see a reason for a tragedy, no reason can possibly exist. That is an enormous act of faith — faith in the completeness of human understanding. I cannot hold that faith. I have experienced too much that I could not understand in the moment, and later came to see clearly, to believe that my inability to comprehend something proves it has no meaning.

But more than that — the answer to this question is not an argument at all. It is a Person.

God did not watch children suffer from a safe distance and decline to explain Himself. He stepped directly into it. He put on human flesh. He was born as a helpless infant Himself — dependent, vulnerable, hunted by Herod before He could walk. He grew up in a broken world. He suffered. He was tortured. He died.

When Herod massacred the infant boys of Bethlehem in his attempt to destroy Jesus, Matthew connected that horror directly to the cry of Jeremiah:

"Then Herod, when he saw that he was mocked of the wise men, was exceeding wroth, and sent forth, and slew all the children that were in Bethlehem, and in all the coasts thereof, from two years old and under... Then was fulfilled that which was spoken by Jeremy the prophet, saying, In Rama was there a voice heard, lamentation, and weeping, and great mourning, Rachel weeping for her children, and would not be comforted, because they are not." — Matthew 2:16–18 (KJV)

Children were murdered by a tyrant in an attempt to destroy the Son of God. God allowed it. The Scripture records it without softening. And then God spoke directly into the lamentation — not with an explanation, but with a promise. The same God who watched those children be taken promised that death would not keep them.

The God who asks us to trust Him through the suffering of children is the same God who descended all the way to the bottom of human pain Himself. He is not insulated from our grief. He is the Man of Sorrows. And He went to the bottom of human suffering so that the bottom would not be permanent for anyone who belongs to Him.

Peter Kreeft, the Christian philosopher, argues that the only answer to human suffering that actually reaches a person in the dark is not a philosophical argument but a personal presence. That is not a philosophical argument. That is a presence. And sometimes presence is the only answer that actually reaches a person in the dark.

Rachel's Promise

"Thus saith the LORD; A voice was heard in Ramah, lamentation, and bitter weeping; Rachel weeping for her children refused to be comforted for her children, because they were not. Thus saith the LORD; Refrain thy voice from weeping, and thine eyes from tears: for thy work shall be rewarded, saith the LORD; and they shall come again from the land of the enemy. And there is hope in thine end, saith the LORD, that thy children shall come again to their own border."
— Jeremiah 31:15–17 (KJV)

Rachel is weeping. She refuses to be comforted. Her children are gone. God does not tell her that her grief is wrong. He does not ask her to stop feeling what she feels. He validates the weight of it entirely by speaking directly into it.

But then He says something that changes everything.

Refrain thy voice from weeping — not because the loss was not real, but because it is not permanent. They shall come again from the land of the enemy.

Who is the enemy? Paul answers that directly — the last enemy that shall be destroyed is death. God promises that death will not get to keep these children. They are not lost to the void. Because of the finished work of Jesus Christ, they will come back from the land of the enemy. The separation is real. The grief is real. But the promise of God stands over both of them — there is hope in thine end.

The Glass Will Not Stay Dark

One of the most honest things Scripture ever says about the human condition is that right now, we see only in part. Paul tells us that we are looking at the tapestry of God's providence from the back side, seeing only a tangled mess of threads and dark colors. The pattern is there. The design is real. But from where we stand right now, we cannot see it.

Richard Baxter, the great Puritan pastor who spent his life writing to people in grief, counseled believers not to marvel at the darkness of their current understanding — because this limitation is not permanent. When we finally stand face to face with Jesus Christ, the glass will be shattered. We will not only be reunited with those we lost, but God will give us the full, beautiful, and complete understanding of His design. And in that moment, the eternal joy of the answer will infinitely outweigh the temporal pain of the question.

A.W. Tozer observed that genuine faith is never contingent on complete understanding — that we trust the character of God even when His actions lie beyond our comprehension. We trust His heart even when we cannot trace His hand.

And the eternal perspective Paul gives us reframes everything:

"While we look not at the things which are seen, but at the things which are not seen: for the things which are seen are temporal; but the things which are not seen are eternal." — 2 Corinthians 4:18 (KJV)

The things which are seen are temporal. The bed. The stillness. The grief on the faces of the people in the room. Temporal. The things which are not seen — the gathered child in shalom, the reunion that is coming, the eternal weight of glory being produced even in this moment — are eternal. The scale that makes sense of it is simply too large for this side of eternity to contain.

The Resurrection Is the Answer

The Apostle Paul makes the most decisive statement in the New Testament about what the death of anyone — including a child — ultimately means in light of what God has already done:

"But now is Christ risen from the dead, and become the firstfruits of them that slept. For since by man came death, by man came also the resurrection of the dead. For as in Adam all die, even so in Christ shall all be made alive... The last enemy that shall be destroyed is death." — 1 Corinthians 15:20–26 (KJV)

Death is the last enemy. Paul does not say it has been eliminated from this world yet. He says it is the last enemy that shall be destroyed. The battle is still happening. But the outcome is already decided.

Because Jesus Christ physically walked out of His tomb on the third day, the physical death of a child is not the final word on that child's existence. The word firstfruits — Paul's specific Greek word in verse 20 — was a term every first-century reader understood. It was the first portion of a harvest that guaranteed the rest of the harvest was coming. N.T. Wright argues that Christ's resurrection is not a spiritual metaphor — it is the first physical, historical down payment on a new creation that God has guaranteed will come.

And then Paul reaches back to the ancient promise God made over death and the grave centuries before the empty tomb:

"I will ransom them from the power of the grave; I will redeem them from death: O death, I will be thy plagues; O grave, I will be thy destruction." — Hosea 13:14 (KJV)

This is the ancient divine oath that Paul quotes when he writes O death, where is thy sting. Centuries before the cross, God declared it over the grave: I will ransom them. I will redeem them. The grave does not get to keep what it takes. Death does not win. The enemy does not get the final word. And on the day when the trumpet sounds and the dead are raised incorruptible — the children will rise. Every small hand. Every child gathered too soon from this groaning earth. They will rise.

The Promise to Those Who Grieve

I want to close the body of this chapter with the promise I believe is the most personal and most powerful in all of Scripture for the person who has lost a child — or who has watched children be taken.

"But I would not have you to be ignorant, brethren, concerning them which are asleep, that ye sorrow not, even as others which have no hope. For if we believe that Jesus died and rose again, even so them also which sleep in Jesus will God bring with him... Then we which are alive and remain shall be caught up together with them in the clouds, to meet the Lord in the air: and so shall we ever be with the Lord. Wherefore comfort one another with these words." — 1 Thessalonians 4:13–14, 17–18 (KJV)

Paul is writing to people who are grieving. People who have lost loved ones and are terrified the story is over. And he tells them — do not sorrow as those who have no hope.

He is not telling them not to grieve. He is telling them not to grieve as though the story has ended. Because it has not ended.

The Greek word used in verse 17 for meet is apantesis. In the ancient Greco-Roman world, this was a technical term for a specific and deeply joyful civic event. When a king or triumphant dignitary was approaching a city, the citizens would leave the city walls and go out to meet him on the road — not to stay on the road, but to escort him back into the city in a great, triumphant procession. The meeting was not a farewell. It was the beginning of the return home together.

This is what Paul is describing. We will not float endlessly in the clouds. We will meet the Lord — and those who have gone before us — and together we will escort the King of Kings back to a renewed, physical earth where we will live together in the shalom that God always intended.

And Jesus Himself said it with complete authority. He is the one who holds the keys:

"I am he that liveth, and was dead; and, behold, I am alive for evermore, Amen; and have the keys of hell and of death." — Revelation 1:18 (KJV)

He holds the keys. Not death. Not the grave. Not the disease. Not the suffering. Not the enemy. He holds the keys. And what He opens, no one closes. And what He closes, no one opens. Your child is not beyond His reach. The child is in the very hands that hold the keys to every door.

Spurgeon said to the grieving parents of his congregation — ye shall hear those sweet voices once more. Ye shall yet know that those whom ye loved have been loved by God.

I believe that with my whole heart.

My Reflection

I will tell you something that is not easy for me to say.

This question breaks me. I do not hold it at a safe distance. When I think about a child suffering, something in me rises up and refuses to be calm about it. I feel the weight of other people's pain even when they are working very hard to hide it. I can be across a room from someone carrying grief and sense it without a single word being spoken. I believe that capacity — that sensitivity — is something the Lord gave me. I think it resembles something in Jesus Himself, who felt the weight of human suffering so deeply that He wept at a tomb even when He was about to open it.

I choose to believe — as an act of my will, in the moments when my feelings cannot carry me there alone — that God and the Holy Spirit are present with every child in every moment of suffering. That the child is never alone. That the presence of God surrounds them in a way the people standing in the room cannot see or measure.

And I hold something else. I hold it with peace, even when it is hard to say aloud.

A soul that passes at or near the beginning of life may be so untouched by willful, knowing, hardened rebellion — so completely dependent, so entirely without the accumulation of conscious refusal — that it needs only a brief entry into this world before God is ready to receive it fully. The children who are gathered home early are not the ones who lost. They are the ones who went ahead. They are already in a place I will not reach until my own journey is finished. They are already serving God in ways that are fully alive, fully divine, and fully at peace.

The pain that remains is ours. It is human. It is real. And God does not dismiss it. But I do not believe the child is suffering it with us. I believe the child is already home.

I sit with that, and I find a peace that I cannot fully explain. Not the absence of grief. But the peace of a man who washed his face, went to the house of God, and worshipped. Because he knew where his son was.

An Invitation

If you are reading this chapter and you have drifted from God because of what you have seen — because the weight of witnessing innocent suffering has made it feel impossible to reconcile a loving God with what your eyes have shown you — I want to speak to you directly and honestly.

I am not going to tell you that your distance from God is wrong. I am going to tell you that it makes sense. That the things you have seen are genuinely hard. That the question you are carrying is one of the most difficult any human being can carry. That God is not offended by your struggle. He is not fragile. He welcomed Job's honest, anguished cry with more warmth than He welcomed the tidy theological speeches of Job's friends.

But I want to ask you something.

Is it possible — not certain, just possible — that the God who watched children suffer is the same God who came down and suffered alongside them? Is it possible that the cross was not God watching from a distance, but God descending all the way to the bottom of human pain so that the bottom would not be the final destination for anyone? Is it possible that the child you watched suffer was not abandoned — but gathered?

If there is even the smallest possibility that those things are true, then there is a door worth walking toward.

You do not have to have all your questions answered before you can walk through it. Faith is not the absence of questions. Faith is the decision to trust the character of God even when His actions are beyond our comprehension. It is trusting His heart even when we cannot trace His hand.

He has not forgotten you. He has not forgotten the children. And He is not finished with the story yet.

"Who is among you that feareth the LORD, that obeyeth the voice of his servant, that walketh in darkness, and hath no light? let him trust in the name of the LORD, and stay upon his God." — Isaiah 50:10 (KJV)

Even in total darkness. Even with no light. Lean hard on the name of Jesus. He is strong enough to hold the weight of every question you carry.

A Prayer for the Ones Who Have Seen Too Much

Lord, I am bringing before You someone who has seen too much.

Someone who has stood in places where children suffer and die — who has given their strength, their skill, and their heart to fight for those children — and who has had to watch, sometimes, when the fight could not be won. Someone whose image of You has been worn down by the weight of what they carry every single day.

I am asking You to meet them in this moment with something that goes deeper than any word I have written.

I am asking You to let them feel, for just one moment, what David felt when he washed his face and went to worship. That quiet, impossible, unexplainable peace that only comes from knowing that the child is not lost — the child is gathered. The child is safe. The child is already ahead of all of us, already in shalom, already in Your arms.

I am asking You to remind them that You were present in every room they have ever stood in. That You were at every bedside. That You never once left a child alone in their suffering. That You were there — closer than breath, closer than heartbeat — in every single moment. In every moment they could not reach.

Help them to hear what You said to Rachel — refrain thy voice from weeping, for there is hope in thine end. Help them to believe it. Not because the grief is not real, but because the promise is more real than the grief.

I am asking You to use the pain that this person is carrying. Do not let it destroy them. Let it open them. Let the grief that has driven them away from You become the very thing that drives them back — the way a broken heart, when brought to You, becomes the beginning of the deepest faith.

There is hope. The tomb is empty. The grave does not win. And the children — every one of them — will rise.

Hold this person, Lord. Sit with them the way You sat with Job. The way You wept with Mary at the tomb of Lazarus. The way You have always been close to the brokenhearted.

Bring them home to You.

Amen.

"And the ransomed of the LORD shall return, and come to Zion with songs and everlasting joy upon their heads: they shall obtain joy and gladness, and sorrow and sighing shall flee away." — Isaiah 35:10 (KJV)

Chapter Fourteen

How Could a Loving God Send Anyone to Hell?

"As I live, saith the Lord GOD, I have no pleasure in the death of the wicked; but that the wicked turn from his way and live: turn ye, turn ye from your evil ways; for why will ye die, O house of Israel?" — Ezekiel 33:11 (KJV)

There is a question that stops people more completely than almost any other in all of theology. It does not come from philosophy classrooms or seminary debates. It comes from ordinary people. People who have buried someone they loved and are not sure where that person went. People who have been handed this doctrine like a weapon and flinched from it ever since. People who genuinely want to believe in a God of love but cannot reconcile that image with the picture of that same God consigning souls to an eternal fire.

The question is this.

How could a loving God send anyone to Hell?

I want to say something directly to you before we go one word further into this chapter.

This question does not embarrass me. It does not embarrass God. And if it has been the wall between you and a faith you have always wanted but could not fully embrace — I am glad you are still here. Because this chapter is going to give you an honest answer. Not a comfortable one. Not a sanitized one designed to make the doctrine disappear by redefining it into something easier to swallow. An honest one. And when you hold that honest answer in your hands, I believe you will find not a contradiction to God's love — but one of the most breathtaking proofs of it that Scripture contains.

A Distinction Most People Have Never Been Taught

One of the deepest sources of confusion in this conversation is that most people — including most people who grew up in the church — have never been taught a distinction that the Bible makes with absolute precision. Without this distinction, the doctrine of Hell becomes muddled, easy to misrepresent, and almost impossible to defend honestly. With it, the biblical picture becomes not only coherent but staggeringly beautiful.

Hell. Hades. The Lake of Fire. Most people use these terms interchangeably, as though they all describe the same thing. They do not. They are three distinct realities on a biblical timeline, and understanding each one changes everything about how you see this question.

The Old Testament word is Sheol. The Hebrew text uses this word — Strong's H7585 — to describe the realm of the dead in a way that carries both breadth and weight. Brown-Driver-Briggs defines Sheol as the subterranean holding place of departed souls, the world of the dead in all its dimensions. In the earliest Old Testament usage, Sheol is the common destination of both the righteous and the unrighteous at the moment of physical death. But as the Old Testament develops, a distinction begins to emerge. The wicked are described as being appointed for Sheol. The righteous cry out with confidence that God will redeem their soul from its power.

"The wicked shall be turned into hell, and all the nations that forget God." — Psalm 9:17 (KJV)

Psalm 16:10 contains David's prophetic cry that God will not leave his soul in Hell — a verse Peter quotes directly at Pentecost as a prophecy of the resurrection of Christ. The trajectory of Sheol in the Old Testament runs from a general term for the realm of the dead toward an increasingly specific association with divine judgment and divine wrath against persistent, unrepentant rebellion.

In the New Testament this realm is called Hades — Strong's G86 — the Greek equivalent of the Hebrew Sheol. Jesus Himself pulls back the curtain on Hades in the parable of the Rich Man and Lazarus, and what He reveals is not a vague shadow-land but a place of conscious, wakeful existence divided by a great gulf fixed between those who rest in God's peace and those who are already experiencing the beginning of judgment.

"And in hell he lift up his eyes, being in torments, and seeth Abraham afar off, and Lazarus in his bosom." — Luke 16:23 (KJV)

The rich man in Hades is not asleep, not annihilated, not unconscious. He lifts up his eyes. He sees. He speaks. He feels. He remembers his family still living. He begs for a drop of water to cool his tongue. And he is told that between where he is and where Lazarus rests, there is a gulf that no one can cross.

Hades, then, is the intermediate state — the temporary holding place between physical death and the final judgment. It is not the final destination. Christ holds the keys of Death and Hades, meaning nothing enters and nothing leaves without His governance. The souls held there are not beyond His reach. They are in His territory, awaiting the final judgment that Revelation 20 places at the end of the age.

Then there is the Lake of Fire. This is the final destination — what Revelation calls the second death. At the Great White Throne Judgment, Hades itself is emptied. Every soul that has been held there stands before God. The books are opened. The Book of Life is opened. And those whose names are not found written there are cast into the Lake of Fire.

"And death and hell were cast into the lake of fire. This is the second death. And whosoever was not found written in the book of life was cast into the lake of fire." — Revelation 20:14–15 (KJV)

And here is what I want you to understand about the timeline you are living inside right now. The Lake of Fire has not yet received its inhabitants. The final judgment has not yet occurred. No human soul has yet been cast there. We are still in the age of patience — the age in which God is longsuffering toward us, not willing that any should perish. The alarm is still sounding. The door is still open.

Now — what did the cross change? Everything.

Before the death and resurrection of Jesus Christ, even the souls of the faithful dead could not enter the full presence of God. The blood of bulls and goats covered sin temporarily but could not remove it permanently. But when Jesus cried out from the cross, It is finished, the debt was paid. Not covered — paid. The veil of the temple was torn from top to bottom by hands that were not human. And the believing dead who had been waiting were freed.

Because of what Jesus did, the believing soul today does not descend into Hades to wait. It departs and is with Christ. Paul, facing the prospect of his own execution, wrote with a peace that no philosophy could manufacture: For to me to live is Christ, and to die is gain. He was not afraid. He knew exactly where he was going. And so does every soul who is covered by the blood of the Lamb.

The Foundation in the Old Testament

The doctrine of Hell does not appear suddenly in the New Testament as though God changed His character between the Testaments. It is built on a foundation laid across the entire Old Testament — a foundation of divine holiness, divine justice, and divine wrath that the New Testament does not contradict but reveals in its full and final form.

The Hebrew word for God's justice is mishpat — Strong's H4941. Brown-Driver-Briggs defines it as justice, ordinance, the act of deciding a case, the fundamental moral order of the universe established by God as its sovereign King.

"He is the Rock, his work is perfect: for all his ways are judgment: a God of truth and without iniquity, just and right is he." — Deuteronomy 32:4 (KJV)

A.W. Tozer understood justice as the moral architecture of the universe itself — the application of equity to every moral situation, grounded in the character of God rather than in any external standard above Him. God's justice is not a reactive emotion. It is the stable, consistent moral architecture of creation. J.I. Packer argued that a judge who ignores the murder, the abuse, the cruelty that ravages his court is not merciful. He is corrupt. God's perfect justice is what makes the universe trustworthy. It is what guarantees that evil will not ultimately triumph. It is what makes love safe.

The Old Testament also gives us the Hebrew word chema — Strong's H2534 — translated as burning wrath, fierce anger, or indignation. It frequently appears alongside aph — Strong's H639 — which literally means nostril, or the rapid, heated breathing of intense reaction. Together they describe divine wrath in terms that are neither cold nor clinical. God's wrath is alive and personal. But the scholars who have studied these words most carefully are consistent in their conclusion: unlike human anger, which is often volatile and morally compromised, divine wrath is a settled, judicial, and holy reaction to objective moral evil.

"Who can stand before his indignation? and who can abide in the fierceness of his anger? his fury is poured out like fire, and the rocks are thrown down by him." — Nahum 1:6 (KJV)

The destruction of Sodom and Gomorrah is not a story the Old Testament records with embarrassment. It is presented as a deliberate, irreversible act of divine judgment against hardened, unrepentant wickedness. Augustine identified this event as something more than a historical record: it was a divine preview, built into the fabric of redemptive history, of the final and eternal judgment. God has always been willing to amputate what is destroying His creation to protect what He loves.

And Isaiah 66 — the final chapter of the greatest prophetic book in the Old Testament — closes with an image that Jesus would later quote verbatim when describing Hell:

"And they shall go forth, and look upon the carcases of the men that have transgressed against me: for their worm shall not die, neither shall their fire be quenched; and they shall be an abhorring unto all flesh." — Isaiah 66:24 (KJV)

The undying worm. The unquenchable fire. These are not New Testament inventions. They are Old Testament declarations, spoken by Isaiah centuries before the incarnation. When Jesus walked into the synagogues of Galilee and Judea and spoke about Gehenna, He was not introducing a foreign concept. He was bringing the fullness of divine revelation to bear on an image His audience already knew.

What Jesus Said

Here is one of the most important and most frequently overlooked facts in this entire conversation. The most loving, compassionate, and merciful figure who has ever walked the earth — Jesus Christ, the Son of God who wept at a tomb, who healed the sick, who told the story of the prodigal son welcomed home by a running father — spoke about Hell more than any other person in the entire Bible.

Not the prophets. Not Paul. Not John in the Apocalypse. Jesus.

The word He used most often was Gehenna — Strong's G1067 — which appears twelve times in the New Testament and eleven of those times in the direct speech of Jesus Christ. Gehenna is the Greek rendering of the Hebrew Gei Hinnom — the Valley of Hinnom, a literal geographical location just southwest of Jerusalem. During the reigns of the wicked kings Ahaz and Manasseh, the Valley of Hinnom had been used as a site for child sacrifice. The righteous King Josiah later desecrated it, turning it into the city's refuse dump. The fires there burned continuously. Maggots and worms infested the rotting flesh. The smoke never stopped rising. When Jesus said Gehenna to His hearers, He was not pointing at an abstraction. He was pointing at a place they knew, with a history they knew.

"And if thy hand offend thee, cut it off: it is better for thee to enter into life maimed, than having two hands to go into hell, into the fire that never shall be quenched: Where their worm dieth not, and the fire is not quenched." — Mark 9:43–44 (KJV)

This matters profoundly to the question this chapter is asking. The secular world has built an image of a gentle Jesus who taught love and forgiveness — in contrast to the harsh Old Testament God who judged and condemned. That image is false. The most detailed, the most vivid, the most repeated descriptions of eternal punishment in all of Scripture come from the lips of the Man of Sorrows. And He did not speak of Hell the way a theologian discusses an uncomfortable doctrine at a safe intellectual distance. He spoke of it with urgency, with tears, with the desperate earnestness of a Savior who knew what was at stake and refused to hide the truth from the people He loved enough to die for.

A loving Savior does not hide the reality of a burning bridge from the people walking toward it. He warns them. That is what the warnings of Jesus are. Not threats from a cruel God. Desperate warnings from a God whose love is fierce enough to tell the truth even when the truth is hard.

The Greek Language and the Permanence of Judgment

The most common theological escape hatch from the doctrine of eternal punishment is the argument that the Greek word aionios — translated as everlasting or eternal — does not really mean eternal. Aionios derives from the noun aion, which means an age, an era, a period with a discernible character and duration. Greek had a separate word available for genuinely infinite duration without end — aidios — which appears in Romans 1:20 and in Jude 6. The New Testament writers chose aionios rather than aidios when describing the final state. What aionios clearly communicates is ultimate, final, age-defining weight.

But the Greek text makes the weakening argument impossible to maintain. And the reason it is impossible is contained in a single verse.

"And these shall go away into everlasting punishment: but the righteous into life eternal." — Matthew 25:46 (KJV)

In Matthew 25:46, Jesus uses the word aionios twice in the same sentence — once to describe the punishment of the condemned, and once to describe the life of the righteous. The same Greek adjective. The same grammatical weight. The same force. If aionios means temporary when applied to punishment, it means temporary when applied to eternal life. If the punishment of the condemned will eventually end, then the life of the righteous will eventually end. You cannot have it both ways. The same word cannot mean permanent in one clause and temporary in the next clause of the same sentence. Every believer who wants to hold onto the promise of eternal life must accept the corresponding permanence of eternal punishment. They are anchored to the same word.

The Greek phrase in Revelation 20:10 is the strongest description of endless duration available in the entire New Testament: they shall be tormented day and night eis tous aionas ton aionon — unto the ages of the ages. This is the identical phrase used in Revelation 4:9 to describe the eternal existence of God Himself. The duration is not different. The fire is the same fire.

The word basanizo — tormented — is equally unambiguous. It means to torture, to afflict with acute suffering. It is not the word for sleep, not the word for cessation, not the word for unconscious rest. It is the word for conscious, ongoing, acute distress. The rich man in Luke 16 used the related noun basanos when he cried out that he was tormented in the flame. This is not poetry for nonexistence. It is the language of conscious, wakeful, unending anguish.

The Nature of God — Why Holiness and Love Are Not in Conflict

The perceived contradiction at the heart of this question rests on a misunderstanding of God's character. People assume they are holding two incompatible attributes — God is love, and God judges eternally — and they cannot see how both can be true at once. But the contradiction only exists if you begin with a deficient understanding of what love is and what holiness demands.

A.W. Tozer understood that the foundational attribute of God — the one that defines and shapes every other attribute — is not love. It is holiness. The Bible never uses a triple repetition to describe God's love.

It does not say God is love, love, love. It says He is holy, holy, holy. The seraphim before the throne of God do not cry mercy, mercy, mercy.

"Who shall not fear thee, O Lord, and glorify thy name? for thou only art holy: for all nations shall come and worship before thee; for thy judgments are made manifest." — Revelation 15:4 (KJV)

Thou only art holy. God's love is holy love. His mercy is holy mercy. His patience is holy patience. And His justice — the justice that the doctrine of eternal punishment reflects — is not an embarrassing attribute that has to be apologized for or balanced against His love. It is the expression of His holy love fiercely protecting the moral health of His creation against the deadly poison of sin.

Tozer captured God's wrath with a striking image: not cold cruelty but the fierce, protective opposition of a loving parent to the disease destroying what she loves. That is what divine wrath is. The settled, consistent, holy opposition of a perfect God to everything that degrades and destroys the human beings He created in His own image.

J.I. Packer argued that divine wrath is not volatile or morally compromised. It is the right and measured response of a perfectly good God to objective moral evil — the wrath of the Judge, administering justice with perfect consistency and perfect knowledge.

"Behold therefore the goodness and severity of God: on them which fell, severity; but toward thee, goodness, if thou continue in his goodness: otherwise thou also shalt be cut off." — Romans 11:22 (KJV)

Goodness. And severity. Both. From the same God. In the same verse. Paul did not experience these as a contradiction. He experienced them as a description of the same perfectly unified character.

Thomas Aquinas addressed the deeper philosophical question through what theologians call Divine Simplicity — the truth that God's nature is perfectly unified and undivided. God is never at cross-purposes with Himself. His justice and His mercy are not two competing forces in an internal divine struggle. They are the same perfect nature expressing itself consistently from two directions of the same reality. Aquinas wrote that the work of divine justice always presupposes the work of mercy, and is founded upon it. Mercy does not override justice. Justice does not cancel mercy. At the cross of Jesus Christ they meet, they kiss, they become one act of perfect love.

"Mercy and truth are met together; righteousness and peace have kissed each other." — Psalm 85:10 (KJV)

And Jonathan Edwards gave the most complete answer to the proportionality objection — the question of how a finite lifetime of sin can justify an eternal punishment. Edwards argued that we are measuring the crime by the wrong standard. Human beings measure severity by duration. Biblical justice measures severity by the dignity and holiness of the One against whom the offense is committed. He wrote that if there be any being that we are under infinite obligations to love and honor and obey, the contrary towards him must be infinitely faulty. God is not merely a head of state. He is the infinite, eternal, perfectly holy Creator of all existence. To spend a lifetime in deliberate, persistent, fully-informed rejection of the God whose image you bear is not a minor offense.

"Against thee, thee only, have I sinned, and done this evil in thy sight: that thou mightest be justified when thou speakest, and be clear when thou judgest." — Psalm 51:4 (KJV)

God Does Not Send Anyone — He Honors the Choice

The image most people carry when they think about Hell is of an angry God reaching down and throwing unwilling, terrified, apologetic souls into an eternal fire. That image is not in the Bible. It is a caricature that has been used to manipulate people for centuries, and it has done enormous damage to the honest understanding of this doctrine.

What the Bible actually describes is something altogether different. C.S. Lewis argued that the doors of Hell are locked from the inside — not because God bars souls from escaping, but because the soul has chosen the lock. In The Great Divorce, Lewis examined what it means for a soul to be offered Heaven and refuse it — not because God turns it away, but because remaining in Heaven would require releasing pride, grievance, self-will, and the insistence on remaining the center of one's own universe. Lewis observed that the final separation between the saved and the lost is not a divine act of exclusion but the honoring of what each soul chose across the whole of its existence. Every soul arrives at the destination toward which it has been pointing itself. Those who surrendered to God receive what they chose. Those who refused Him to the end receive what they chose as well. The difference is never God's willingness to receive. It is the soul's willingness to be received.

God did not design Hell for human beings. Jesus Himself declared in Matthew 25:41 that the everlasting fire was prepared for the devil and his angels — not for people. Hell entered human history as a consequence of human choice, not as a divine intention.

"O Jerusalem, Jerusalem, thou that killest the prophets, and stonest them which are sent unto thee, how often would I have gathered thy children together, even as a hen gathereth her chickens under her wings, and ye would not!" — Matthew 23:37 (KJV)

Would not. Not could not. Would not. This is not a God dragging people to their doom. This is a God standing with arms open, offering everything, and watching with a grief that no human language can adequately describe as some souls choose to walk away from every single thing He offered them.

The Apostle Paul described the divine response to persistent rebellion with some of the most sobering language in the New Testament.

God gave them up. He said it three times in Romans 1. Three times. Not as an angry act of punishment, but as the solemn, settled, grieving honoring of what human beings had chosen with the freedom God gave them.

"Wherefore God also gave them up to uncleanness through the lusts of their own hearts..." — Romans 1:24 (KJV)

If God forced every rebellious soul into Heaven against its will, He would not be showing greater love. He would be invalidating human dignity. He would be treating human beings as less than persons — as objects to be moved around rather than souls to be loved. The very seriousness with which God takes human freedom is the proof of how seriously He takes human dignity. We are not puppets. Our choices are real.

God sets the choice before every human being. He sends prophets. He provides Scripture. He writes His signature into creation and His moral law into conscience. He sent His own Son. And then He honors the choice.

"Choose you this day whom ye will serve... but as for me and my house, we will serve the LORD." — Joshua 24:15 (KJV)

Answering Universalism

There is a theological position that has gained significant traction in recent years, particularly in circles where the discomfort with eternal punishment is greatest. It is called Universalism — the belief that God's love is so vast, His atonement so complete, and His patience so infinite that every soul will ultimately be reconciled to Him. That in the end, Love wins, and nobody stays in Hell.

The desire behind this position is deeply human and deeply understandable. I understand it. The thought of any soul being permanently separated from God is genuinely terrible. And there are Bible verses that universalists point to that, read in isolation, seem to support their hope.

"Who will have all men to be saved, and to come unto the knowledge of the truth." — 1 Timothy 2:4 (KJV)

These truths are real. God does not desire the death of the wicked. God is longsuffering toward us, not willing that any should perish, but that all should come to repentance — 2 Peter 3:9 declares this plainly. And this raises the question that many believers quietly carry but rarely ask out loud: if God already knows who will end up in heaven and who will end up in the lake of fire, why did He create the ones He knew would reject Him? The answer is not comfortable but it is true. He created them because love that cannot be rejected is not love. A God who only created souls He knew would choose Him would be creating a universe of programmed responses, not genuine relationship.

But the universalist makes a fatal error by confusing God's desire with God's decree. God desires all to be saved. He has provided the rescue for all. But the rescue must be received. And God, who honors human freedom as a sacred gift of dignity, will not force it on a soul that persistently refuses it. His longsuffering is genuine. His invitation is universal. But overriding the final, settled choice of a soul would mean destroying the very freedom that made the love real in the first place.

J.I. Packer made what I believe is the most decisive single observation against universalism. He noted that if universalism is true, Judas Iscariot will ultimately be saved. But Jesus said of Judas that it would have been better for that man if he had never been born. A life that would have been better never lived is not a life on its way to eternal joy.

"The Son of man goeth as it is written of him: but woe unto that man by whom the Son of man is betrayed! it had been good for that man if he had not been born." — Mark 14:21 (KJV)

Augustine made the philosophical argument with characteristic clarity. If universalism is true, then human history is ultimately meaningless. Every horrific act of evil — every cruelty, every abuse, every destruction of innocent life — is eventually whitewashed and absorbed into a universal reconciliation that renders the choices made in this life irrelevant. A God who guarantees that outcome does not honor human freedom. He renders it hollow. And He tells every victim of human evil that what was done to them ultimately does not matter, because the one who did it will be in Heaven anyway. That is not greater love. That is the abolition of moral reality.

The rescue has been provided. The invitation has been issued. The choice belongs to the soul. And a God who overrides the final, persistent, fully-informed no of a human being to drag that soul into Heaven is not showing it greater love. He is showing it the ultimate disrespect.

Answering Annihilationism

A second alternative to the traditional doctrine of eternal conscious punishment is called Annihilationism — the belief that the condemned do not suffer eternally but are simply extinguished. They cease to exist. The fires of judgment consume them completely, and what remains is simply nothing.

On the surface this seems more merciful. But the Bible does not support it. And the Greek language makes it impossible to maintain consistently.

Annihilationists lean heavily on the Greek word apollumi — Strong's G622 — translated as destroy or perish. They point to

Matthew 10:28, where Jesus says God is able to destroy both soul and body in Hell.

"And fear not them which kill the body, but are not able to kill the soul: but rather fear him which is able to destroy both soul and body in hell." — Matthew 10:28 (KJV)

But a complete study of apollumi across the New Testament makes this reading untenable. The word apollumi is used three times in Luke 15 in the parables of the lost sheep, the lost coin, and the lost son. The shepherd has a sheep that is apollumi — lost. The woman has a coin that is apollumi — lost. The father has a son who is apollumi — lost. In every single case, the lost thing still exists. The sheep did not cease to be a sheep. The coin did not cease to be a coin. The son did not cease to be a son. To be apollumi is not to be annihilated. It is to be separated from your rightful owner, ruined for your intended purpose, lost to the fellowship you were designed for.

"For the Son of man is come to seek and to save that which was lost." — Luke 19:10 (KJV)

Jesus came to seek and save the apollumi — the lost. Not the nonexistent. The ones who still exist but are separated from God. To be destroyed in Hell is to be a total spiritual wreck, permanently ruined and eternally separated from the joy and presence of God. Not vaporized. Ruined.

Furthermore, annihilation would not actually be a punishment. It would be an escape. A soul that has spent its entire life refusing God, refusing accountability, refusing the moral order of the universe — that soul would gladly choose to simply cease existing rather than stand in the light of God's perfect holiness and face the full weight of what it chose. Annihilationism gives the rebellious soul exactly what it wants. That is not justice. That is the final capitulation of moral reality to the soul that refused it.

What the Original Words Leave Open

This chapter has been honest about the reality and seriousness of final judgment. Now it must be equally honest about what the original words of Scripture actually say and what they leave genuinely open.

Four different original words — Sheol in the Hebrew, and Hades, Gehenna, and Tartarus in the Greek — have all been translated as the single English word hell throughout most English Bibles. They do not all mean the same thing. Sheol in its original Hebrew usage is the place of all the dead, under God's presence. Psalm 139:8 says directly: if I make my bed in Sheol, behold thou art there. God is present even there. Hades is the temporary holding place that will itself be destroyed at the final judgment — Revelation 20:14 says Death and Hades were cast into the lake of fire. Hades ends. It is not the final state.

This is the timeline Scripture actually gives. Physical death leads to Hades. Hades holds the dead under Christ's keys and authority. The final judgment comes. Then and only then the second death. There is a significant space in that timeline, and in that space Christ holds the keys and God is present.

"For Christ also hath once suffered for sins, the just for the unjust, that he might bring us to God, being put to death in the flesh, but quickened by the Spirit: By which also he went and preached unto the spirits in prison." — 1 Peter 3:18–20 (KJV)

Between His death and resurrection Christ went and preached to the spirits in prison. This is in the canon. It is in the KJV. A God who descended into the place of the dead and preached is not a God who finishes pursuing a soul the moment physical death occurs.

The full character of God assembled across both Testaments points in a consistent direction. He takes no pleasure in the death of the wicked — Ezekiel 18:23 and 33:11, stated twice, plainly. He desires all people to be saved — 1 Timothy 2:4. The risen Christ declares in

Revelation 3:20 that He is still standing at the door and knocking. Paul declares in 1 Corinthians 15:28 that the final end of all things is that God will be all in all. Not God and eternal torment running alongside each other forever. God. All. In all.

"And when all things shall be subdued unto him, then shall the Son also himself be subject unto him that put all things under him, that God may be all in all." — 1 Corinthians 15:28 (KJV)

None of this removes the urgency of the Gospel. It sharpens it. Come to Christ now — in this life, in this moment — because now is the fullness. Now is the feast. Now is the door open and the shepherd present and the invitation extended with everything Christ purchased on the cross. That is not a small thing. That is everything.

Christ is the only means of reconciliation. Colossians 1:20 says it is through the blood of the cross that God reconciles all things to Himself. Philippians 2:10–11 says every tongue will confess that Jesus Christ is Lord. The necessity of Christ is not softened by anything in this section. It is the foundation of everything.

These truths are held with open hands. Not as a replacement for the doctrine of final judgment. The judgment is real. The second death is real. The exclusion from the Kingdom is real and serious and not to be minimized. What is being held with honest humility is the tradition's claim that it has fully mapped what the original words left genuinely open. The God who holds the keys of Death and Hades, who takes no pleasure in the death of the wicked, who descended into the place of the dead and preached, who will be all in all — that God's final word on every soul He made belongs to Him and to the judgment He has prepared. It is enough to trust Him with it.

What the Earliest Christians Believed

There is an objection sometimes raised against the doctrine of eternal punishment that claims it was a later invention — an addition to the original gentle message of Jesus imposed by medieval theologians or church councils. That claim is historically false. And the evidence against it dates from the generation immediately following the apostles.

Among the earliest Christian documents outside the New Testament canon is a text known as the Apocalypse of Peter, written approximately A.D. 100 to 150 — within living memory of the apostolic generation. It was read in churches alongside the New Testament writings. The Muratorian Fragment, one of the oldest lists of accepted Christian texts dated to approximately A.D. 170, includes it. Clement of Alexandria quoted it with full authority. This was not a fringe document. It represented what the earliest Christian communities believed and taught.

What the Apocalypse of Peter describes is a vision of both the blessed and the condemned — with the condemned depicted in conscious, ongoing torment corresponding to the nature of their choices in life. The text does not present this as a dark theological novelty. It presents it as the natural consequence of having rejected the God who came to rescue them. The earliest Christian communities — the ones who had sat under the teaching of the apostles themselves, who had received the Gospel from the mouths of those who walked with Jesus — held without apology that final judgment was real, that Hell was real, and that the rescue Christ accomplished made its reality all the more urgent to declare.

This matters because it answers the historical objection directly. The doctrine of eternal punishment was not imposed on Christianity from outside. It was there from the beginning. It was held by the people who were closest in time and relationship to the One who warned about it most frequently and most urgently.

What About Those Who Never Heard?

This is the objection I take most seriously, because it comes from the most honest place. Not cynicism or a desire to argue. But genuine moral concern. What about the person who grew up in a remote part of the world with no access to the Bible, no knowledge of the name of Jesus, no exposure to the explicit Gospel? Can a just God condemn someone for failing to believe a message they never had the chance to hear?

The answer the Bible gives is clear, and it is both honest and just.

God does not condemn anyone for failing to respond to a message they never received. What He judges is the light they were given. And according to Romans 1 and Romans 2, every human being who has ever lived has been given light. Two kinds. Without exception.

The first is the witness of creation. Paul writes that the invisible things of God — His eternal power and divine nature — are clearly seen in the things He has made, so that every human being is without excuse.

"For the invisible things of him from the creation of the world are clearly seen, being understood by the things that are made, even his eternal power and Godhead; so that they are without excuse." — Romans 1:20 (KJV)

The second is the witness of conscience. Paul writes in Romans 2 that the Gentiles — those without the written law of Moses — nevertheless show the work of the law written on their hearts. Their conscience bears witness. Their thoughts accuse and excuse one another. Every human culture that has ever existed has carried a moral intuition about justice and betrayal, about the difference between right and wrong. That intuition is not an accident of evolution. It is the voice of God written inside every soul He has made.

The sobering reality is this: no one is truly innocent. Every human being, when honestly measured against the light they were given through creation and conscience, falls short. The person who has never heard the Gospel is not condemned for failing to believe a message they never heard. They are judged on the basis of what they knew, what they were given, and what they chose to do with it. And by that standard, every human being stands in need of the rescue that only the cross of Christ provides.

As for the specific, final judgment of every individual soul that lived without the explicit Gospel — that belongs to the God whose judgments are perfect. What we know is what Abraham declared from the oldest pages of Scripture:

"Shall not the Judge of all the earth do right?" — Genesis 18:25 (KJV)

He will. He has never made a single error in judgment. He will not begin at the Great White Throne.

The Cross Proves Hell — and Hell Explains the Cross

I want to bring you now to what I believe is the most important argument in this entire chapter. Everything we have said about holiness and justice and human freedom and divine wrath — all of it is true and essential. But none of it reaches the final depth of what the Bible reveals about the relationship between God's love and the reality of Hell.

The cross does.

If you want to understand what Hell actually is — not as a cartoon image of fire and pitchforks, but as the true, terrible spiritual reality of permanent separation from the source of all life and light and love — you do not need to look at medieval paintings. You need to look at Jesus Christ in the Garden of Gethsemane.

That night, the eternal Son of God — who had existed in perfect, unbroken, joyful communion with the Father from before the foundation of the world — fell on His face in the dirt and sweated drops of blood. He prayed, Let this cup pass from me. He was not afraid of the whip. He was not afraid of the nails. He was facing something infinitely worse than physical suffering. He was facing the full, concentrated, unmitigated weight of the divine judgment that every human sin deserved. And He trembled.

And then He went to the cross anyway.

When the darkness came over the land at midday and the Son of God hung dying, Christ bore the full weight of human sin. He stood in the place where every separated soul had ever stood. He experienced from the inside what it costs to carry what we could not carry.

"Christ hath redeemed us from the curse of the law, being made a curse for us: for it is written, Cursed is every one that hangeth on a tree." — Galatians 3:13 (KJV)

He was made a curse. Not merely sympathetic with our curse. Made it. The full weight, the full condemnation, the full separation — absorbed by Him, in Him, on Him. So that every soul covered by His blood would never have to bear it.

Charles Spurgeon preached this truth with a force that few have matched before or since. He taught that Jesus stood as our substitute, and that Hell's waves rolled over Him, the eternal wrath of God spending itself upon His blessed head. And then Spurgeon asked his congregation with a holy astonishment: What! Did Christ at one tremendous draught of love, drink my damnation dry? Yes. That is exactly what happened. And that single question contains more theology about Hell and grace than most people encounter in a lifetime of Sunday mornings.

The New Testament uses a specific Greek word for what happened at the cross. The word is hilasērion — Strong's G2435 — translated as propitiation. Paul uses it in Romans 3:25. It is the same word used in the Greek Old Testament for the Mercy Seat — the golden cover on the

Ark of the Covenant in the Holy of Holies. On the Day of Atonement, the high priest would enter that sacred space and sprinkle blood on the Mercy Seat to shield the people from the consuming wrath of a holy God. Jesus Christ is our hilasērion. His blood did not merely cover our sin as a temporary measure. It absorbed the full, undiminished, eternal wrath of God against it. Completely. Permanently. Finally.

"Whom God hath set forth to be a propitiation through faith in his blood, to declare his righteousness for the remission of sins that are past, through the forbearance of God; To declare, I say, at this time his righteousness: that he might be just, and the justifier of him which believeth in Jesus." — Romans 3:25–26 (KJV)

Just. And the justifier. Both in the same verse. Both accomplished by the same act. The cross is not God compromising His justice to show mercy. It is God satisfying His justice so completely and permanently that mercy becomes possible without a single compromise.

J.I. Packer described the cross as the moment where the demands of divine justice and the impulse of divine love were satisfied simultaneously in a single act — that at Calvary, God showed Himself to be just, and the justifier of him that hath faith in Jesus.

Now here is the argument that I want you to sit with.

If Hell is not real — if the punishment for sin is not severe, not permanent, not truly terrible — then the cross of Jesus Christ was a massive divine overreaction. The death of the eternal Son of God was catastrophically disproportionate to the problem. Why would a God of love put His own Son through that for a penalty that was temporary? Or mild? Or that He was going to waive for everyone eventually anyway?

But if Hell is exactly what the Bible says it is — if permanent separation from God is the ultimate catastrophe of a free soul that chose to reject the only source of all good that exists — then the cross makes complete sense. Not as an overreaction. As the only possible response of a God whose love was great enough and whose justice was perfect enough to do the only thing that could actually solve the problem. He stepped in front of it. He absorbed it. And He offers the result freely to every soul that will receive it.

"And as it is appointed unto men once to die, but after this the judgment: So Christ was once offered to bear the sins of many; and unto them that look for him shall he appear the second time without sin unto salvation." — Hebrews 9:27–28 (KJV)

The incarnation was not God deciding to come down and teach us better morals. It was God the Son taking on a body capable of bearing the weight of eternal judgment so that every soul who trusted in Him would walk free. The reality of Hell is not a dark, embarrassing corner of Christian theology. It is the very reason the Gospel exists. It is the engine that makes the incarnation, the cross, the resurrection, and the promise of eternal life make any sense at all.

The writer of Hebrews captures the full scope of what the incarnation accomplished:

"That through death he might destroy him that had the power of death, that is, the devil; And deliver them who through fear of death were all their lifetime subject to bondage." — Hebrews 2:14–15 (KJV)

Through death, He destroyed death. He dismantled the enemy's greatest weapon by walking directly into it. And He set free every soul that had been held in bondage to the fear of it. That is what the cross accomplished. And it only makes complete sense against the backdrop of what it was saving us from.

What the Church Gets Wrong — And What It Must Get Right

I need to say something plainly, because it is a conviction I carry about this doctrine that I cannot leave out.

I deeply dislike what has been done with Hell in too many churches and too many pulpits. Not what the Bible teaches about it. What has been done with it.

I have seen Hell used as a weapon. A scare tactic. A tool of manipulation designed to frighten people through the door of faith rather than inviting them through it with the love and beauty of the God who is waiting on the other side. The doom and gloom. The theatrical horror show of eternal torment delivered without tears, without brokenness, without any apparent love for the souls in the room. That approach has done profound damage. It has driven people away from the very God who died to reach them. And it is not the Gospel.

The Apostle Paul, who had stared into the full reality of divine judgment and eternal accountability, described his own evangelistic approach with two carefully chosen words:

"Knowing therefore the terror of the Lord, we persuade men..." — 2 Corinthians 5:11 (KJV)

We persuade men. Not we terrify men. Not we threaten men. Paul knew the terror. He held it honestly and fully. And his response was to persuade — to reason, to argue, to beg, to plead with tears in every city he entered — because he understood what was at stake and loved the people he was speaking to.

Charles Spurgeon modeled this balance better than almost anyone in the history of preaching. He thundered about eternal judgment — honestly, vividly, without softening a syllable. And in the very same sermon he would dissolve into tears and beg his hearers to look to Christ. He cried out: My hearer, give me thine hand. Never did father plead with son with more impassioned earnestness than I would with thee. Why wouldst thou sit still, when hell is burning in thy face?

And then Spurgeon staked his own eternal destiny on the Gospel invitation. He declared from the pulpit: Sinner, trust in Jesus: and if thou dost perish trusting in Jesus, I will perish with thee. I will make my bed in hell, side by side with thee — if thou canst perish trusting in Christ. But that can never be.

That is what honest preaching about Hell looks like. Not a lecture. A plea. Not a threat. A declaration of love so fierce it will not look away from the truth.

But I want to speak to the other failure as well — because it may be doing even more damage in the modern church than the first.

There are churches and preachers today who have effectively removed Hell from the conversation. Not because they have studied the Greek and found it insufficient. Because it is uncomfortable. Because it is offensive to a culture that wants a God who costs them nothing. And so they mumble on about God's kindness while saying virtually nothing about His judgment.

J.I. Packer was blunt about what this produces. He argued that without a clear understanding of the judgment from which Christ saves us, neither the Gospel, nor the cross, nor the wonder of God's love can be properly understood. Remove Hell and you remove the need for propitiation. Remove the need for propitiation and the cross becomes a moral example rather than a cosmic rescue. Remove the cosmic rescue and grace becomes cheap. And cheap grace holds nothing together when the hard seasons come.

Tozer noted that the absence of the fear of God produces a culture where transgression becomes effortless — where moral boundaries erode because the consequence has been made to seem abstract, distant, or temporary.

And God Himself stated the pastoral heart of this doctrine with more clarity and more tenderness than any preacher ever has:

"Say unto them, As I live, saith the Lord GOD, I have no pleasure in the death of the wicked; but that the wicked turn from his way and live: turn ye, turn ye from your evil ways; for why will ye die, O house of Israel?" — Ezekiel 33:11 (KJV)

Turn ye. Turn ye. Not a threat. A pleading. God does not want anyone to perish. He is not waiting impatiently for the chance to condemn. He is calling, warning, pleading, longsuffering, patient — doing everything consistent with His holy nature and the dignity of human freedom to make sure that every soul has every possible opportunity to choose life. The alarm about Hell is not cruelty. It is the most urgent act of love available to anyone with a voice.

My Reflection

I have carried that fear myself.

There is someone in my own life whose relationship with God I could not see clearly from the outside. Someone I loved. Someone who sat in a church pew one time in my memory, and whether that was for family, for obligation, for something stirring quietly inside them that I was not close enough to see — I cannot tell you. I do not know what conversation that soul had with God in the private places of a lifetime. I do not know what happened in the dark of the night I was not there for.

And I want to be honest with you: I do not know where that soul is. I carry that uncertainty. What I will not do is offer you false comfort. I will not tell you that love wins no matter what, that God grades on a curve, that everyone ends up in the same place. That would be kind in the moment and cruel in the long run. You deserve honesty.

But here is what I do know.

We cannot see what a person's soul and mind talked with God about during the span of their life. We see the outside. The church attendance or the lack of it. The declarations made or not made. God sees everything. Every private moment of reaching. Every whispered question in the dark. Every time, however weakly and imperfectly, a soul turned — even slightly — toward the God it was not sure was there.

Philip Yancey, writing about this kind of grief, counseled that when we love someone who has died and we do not know where they stand with God, the most honest and most faithful place to stand is not in judgment and not in false assurance, but in the character of God Himself. We trust not what we know about the person. We trust what we know about the God who was present in their life every moment we were not.

Abraham stood before God and staked everything on a truth that has never been revoked:

"That be far from thee to do after this manner, to slay the righteous with the wicked: and that the righteous should be as the wicked, that be far from thee: Shall not the Judge of all the earth do right?" — Genesis 18:25 (KJV)

He will. God does not make mistakes. He does not overlook the tiny sliver of faith that reached toward Him in a life that looked faithless from the outside. He does not ignore the soul that turned toward Him in the last moment of a life we thought we understood. His judgments are perfect. His knowledge is complete. And the weight of what we do not know — the private conversations, the dark-hour prayers, the hidden wrestlings of a soul with its Maker — belongs entirely in His hands.

For the heart that is broken and carrying this fear right now:

"He healeth the broken in heart, and bindeth up their wounds." — Psalm 147:3 (KJV)

God is close to you in this. Not watching from above. Close. The grief you are carrying is known to Him. And the soul you are grieving for was loved by Him even more than you loved them — and was pursued by Him in ways you never saw and may never know on this side of eternity.

You do not have to resolve this question to be at peace. You have to trust the Judge. And He has given us every reason to trust Him.

Three Truths That Hold This Together

Let me bring this chapter toward its close with three truths that, held together, form the most complete and honest answer to the question this chapter is asking.

Hell is necessary — because love without truth is not love. The God who shrugs at the evil that destroys His creation, who declares that the cruelty and rebellion of human history amounts to nothing in the end, who guarantees that every soul ends up in the same place regardless of what it chose — that God would not be more loving than the God of Scripture. He would be indifferent. Tozer was right: a God without wrath against sin is a God who does not care. And Aquinas was right: goodness without justice is not goodness. God's wrath against sin is the proof of His love for the human beings sin destroys.

Hell is serious — because eternity is real. Edwards was right: sinning against an infinite and holy God carries a moral weight that finite human categories cannot measure. And the biblical language is not ambiguous: everlasting, forever and ever, the worm that dieth not, the fire that is not quenched. These are not metaphors for a temporary unpleasantness. They are descriptions of a permanent reality.

Hell is merciful — because the warning is being given right now. Jesus Christ — the most loving figure in the history of the world — spoke about Hell more than any other person in all of Scripture. Not because He was cruel. Because He loved the people walking toward it and refused to keep silent. The cross only shines with its full, staggering brilliance against the backdrop of what it was saving us from. Hell is the darkness that makes the light of Calvary visible.

No one has to go there. That is the point of everything this chapter has said. God desires all to be saved. He provided the rescue at infinite personal cost. He is longsuffering toward every soul. The door is still open. The invitation is still extended. And the same God who permits Hell to exist is the One who went to every possible length to make sure you never have to.

An Invitation

If you have carried this question as the wall between yourself and God — if Hell has been the reason you kept your distance from a faith you have always wanted but could not fully embrace — I want to speak to you now.

The God this chapter has been describing is not the God of the scare tactics. He is not a prosecuting attorney building a case against you. He is not a celestial accountant waiting impatiently to find grounds for your condemnation. He is the God who went to every possible length — including the cross — to make sure you never have to face what the cross absorbed.

He wept over Jerusalem. He left the flock to search for the one who was missing. He ran down a dusty road because He saw His child coming home from a long way off. He stood at the tomb of His friend and wept. He chose the cross over the escape that was available to Him because He loved you and would not leave you without a rescue.

You do not need a clean record to come to Him. You do not need to have resolved every theological question in this chapter before you approach. You can come exactly as you are — with the grief, the doubt, the questions still in your hands — and He will meet you there. He was already there before you arrived.

If you want to receive what He did for you at the cross, you can do it right now. No ceremony required. No special building. No perfect prayer. Only the willingness to say: I believe You are real. I believe You came for me. I receive what You did on the cross. I am Yours.

That is the beginning of everything. And from that beginning, the question that opened this chapter stops being a barrier — and becomes one of the most breathtaking proofs of love you have ever held in your hands.

And for the soul carrying the weight of everything they have been — everything they have done, everything they were certain put them beyond the reach of a God they were not sure still cared:

"He will turn again, he will have compassion upon us; he will subdue our iniquities; and thou wilt cast all their sins into the depths of the sea." — Micah 7:19 (KJV)

All their sins. Into the depths of the sea. Submerged. Unreachable. Gone. That is not a soft Gospel. That is the most radical declaration of divine mercy in all of Scripture. And it is available to you right now.

A Prayer for the One Who Is Wrestling

Lord God,

I am praying for the person holding these pages who came to this chapter not from curiosity but from pain. The one afraid for someone they lost. The one hurt by a cold and weaponized version of this doctrine who flinches every time the word Hell is spoken because of what it has been used to do to them. The one genuinely trying to hold together the God who is love and the God who judges — and finding the tension almost too much to carry.

Let Your Word do what only Your Word can do. Let it cut through every distortion and every wound and reach the place in each of these souls where You have always been working and have never stopped. Remind them that You are not a distant verdict waiting to be rendered. You are the One who breathed life into their first moment and has been writing toward their last with purpose they cannot yet see from inside the story.

For the one carrying grief for a soul they could not see clearly — let Genesis 18:25 be their resting place tonight. Shall not the Judge of all the earth do right? He will. Release into those perfect hands what no human heart was ever meant to carry alone. Let the God who sees every private reaching, every silent prayer, every moment a soul turned toward the light it wasn't sure was there — let Him be trusted with the weight of what we do not and cannot know.

For the one still standing at a distance because this question has kept them there — let this be the hour the distance closes. Not because we have answered everything. Because You are enough. Because the cross was enough. Because the One who was made a curse for us so that we would never have to bear it — that One is still calling. Still waiting. Still holding the door open with nail-scarred hands.

We do not ask You to explain everything. We ask to be trusted. And we believe You are worthy of that trust — because of everything You have already done to prove it.

In the name of Jesus Christ, who drank the cup that we deserved, so that we could receive the cup that He earned.

Amen.

"But God, who is rich in mercy, for his great love wherewith he loved us, Even when we were dead in sins, hath quickened us together with Christ, (by grace ye are saved.)" — Ephesians 2:4–5 (KJV)

Chapter Fifteen

Why Does Psychosis Target God?

G ot it. Cleaning chapter 15 now.

"The spirit of man is the candle of the LORD, searching all the inward parts of the belly." — Proverbs 20:27 (KJV)

There is a question behind the question that was asked here — and anyone who has watched someone they love break down inside a psychotic episode already knows it. They have seen it. They have stood in a room while someone who never chose religion in their calm life suddenly screamed about God. They have watched a person weep over divine visions one moment and then curse holy things the next moment with language that shocked everyone in the room — language the person themselves would never have chosen, would never have used, would be horrified to learn they said. And those watching ask the question that has no easy answer: what is happening inside that person? Is that God? Is that Satan? Is that just the illness? And if a good God really exists — why would He allow any of this at all?

These are not academic questions. They are the questions of families. They are the questions of people who have watched suffering up close and cannot find an adequate answer anywhere. Religious institutions have too often offered either shallow comfort or terrifying condemnation — and neither serves the people living inside this reality.

So this chapter does something different. It goes to two sources that most people have never seen brought together honestly: the medical and neuroscientific research on what actually happens inside a schizophrenic brain, and the original Hebrew and Koine Greek text of Scripture — not filtered through centuries of institutional theology, but read as the ancient authors wrote it. When these two sources are allowed to speak together, the picture that emerges is one of the most profound and sobering things in this entire book.

It begins with understanding what we are.

The Architecture of the Human Person — What God Said He Built

Before we can understand what breaks, we have to understand what God originally designed. And to do that we have to go to the Hebrew text of Genesis 2:7 — not the English translation alone, which flattens what the original says — but the actual words Moses wrote, the words God chose to describe what He did when He made the first human being.

The King James Version reads: And the LORD God formed man of the dust of the ground, and breathed into his nostrils the breath of life; and man became a living soul. That is accurate. But in the Hebrew it reads: wayyîṣer YHWH Elohim et-hā'ādām 'apār min-hā'ă-damâ wayyippaḥ bə'appāyw nišmat ḥayyîm wayəhî hā'ādām lənepəš ḥayyāh. Three words in that sentence carry the entire weight of what this chapter is about.

"The Spirit of God hath made me; and the breath of the Almighty hath given me life." — Job 33:4 (KJV)

(□□□□□□□neshamah) — The breath of God — the divine spark, intellect, and lamp placed inside every human. This is translated "breath of life" in Genesis 2:7 and "breath of the Almighty" in Job 33:4. The root nāšam is the physical act of puffing or breathing. But neshamah is not ordinary air — it is the direct exhalation of God Himself into the human person. Job 32:8 says: there is a spirit in man: and the inspiration (neshamah) of the Almighty giveth them understanding. And most powerfully, Proverbs 20:27 declares: The spirit of man is the candle (nêr) of the LORD, searching all the inward parts of the belly. Literally: the neshamah of the human person is God's own lamp, placed inside us, pointing inward. It searches. It reaches. It is, by its nature and design, oriented toward its source — which is God. This divine breath does not disappear when the brain malfunctions. It does not go out during a psychotic break. It is the deepest structural layer of what every human being is, and when the outer mind collapses, the neshamah is what remains — unfiltered, unmediated, and reaching toward the only thing it was designed to reach for.

(□□□□□□nephesh) — The whole living being — body and breath unified as one, not separated. Translated "living soul" in Genesis 2:7, nephesh appears 755 times in the Hebrew Old Testament, and the KJV alone uses 28 different English words to translate it. This variety exists because nephesh does not mean what Greek philosophy meant by "soul" — a separate, immaterial thing imprisoned inside a body like a ghost in a machine. That Greek dualism entered Christian theology through centuries of Platonic influence, not from the Hebrew text. In the original, nephesh is the whole, unified, living person: dust plus the breath of God, inseparable, forming one creature. You do not have a nephesh the way you have a wallet. You are one. This is why mental illness affects everything simultaneously — the physical brain, the emotional life, the spiritual reach — because in God's original design, these are not separate compartments. They are one unified person. When the brain breaks, the whole person is in the storm. And the neshamah inside the storm does not stop burning.

"And God said, Let us make man in our image, after our likeness: and let them have dominion over the fish of the sea, and over the fowl of the air, and over the cattle, and over all the earth, and over every creeping thing that creepeth upon the earth." — Genesis 1:26 (KJV)

(□□□□□tselem) — The image — the representative stamp of the King placed in every human person. In the ancient Near Eastern world where Moses wrote, a king's tselem was a physical statue placed throughout his territory to represent his authority in every place he could not personally stand. When God declared He would make humanity in His tselem, He was making a royal proclamation: every human being is a walking, breathing representative of the living God. The stamp of the King. This image does not leave a person because of illness. It is not diminished by disability. It does not fade because the brain is broken. To be human is to bear the image of God — and no medical condition, no psychotic break, no number of lost years changes that.

These three words together — neshamah, nephesh, tselem — give us the original Hebrew picture of what every human being is: a creature formed from dust, animated by the direct breath of God, bearing the royal image of the Creator, living as a whole unified person in whom body and spirit cannot be separated. This is the person who breaks. This is the person whose brain malfunctions. This is the person who screams in the night — and this is the person God does not abandon.

What Medicine Has Discovered About the Schizophrenic Brain

Schizophrenia is a genuine medical condition. It is not demonic possession in every case. It is not caused by personal sin or spiritual failure. It is a disorder of how the brain develops, processes information, and regulates behavior — and it affects approximately one percent of the global population, across every culture, every religion, and every era of recorded human history.

The Prefrontal Cortex — The Gatekeeper That Goes Offline

The prefrontal cortex is the region of the brain directly behind the forehead. Neuroscientists describe it as the brain's executive center. It controls rational decision-making, planning, the ability to regulate impulses, and most critically — it controls the filter between what a person thinks and what a person says or does. In healthy individuals, this region acts as a gatekeeper at every moment: monitoring thoughts as they arise, evaluating them, and determining which ones are appropriate to express and which ones to suppress.

Multiple neuroimaging studies, including a landmark review in Translational Psychiatry, have confirmed that the dorsolateral prefrontal cortex is one of the most consistently impaired regions in schizophrenia — showing reduced gray matter volume, decreased metabolic activity, and abnormal functional connectivity. Researchers at Yale University documented that patients with schizophrenia show significantly reduced prefrontal activation during tasks requiring cognitive inhibition, working memory, and impulse control. The prefrontal cortex does not simply slow down in schizophrenia. Its network connections — the pathways that link it to the rest of the brain — become disordered. The gatekeeper does not just become less effective. It loses its ability to coordinate with other regions.

What this means in plain language is this: the person experiencing a psychotic episode has lost, to varying degrees, the brain system that normally controls what comes out of their mouth. The intrusive thoughts, the inappropriate words, the blasphemies, the rages — these are not chosen. The filter that would catch them in a healthy mind and prevent their expression is not functioning. The person living inside this experience has described it as watching themselves from the outside, unable to control what is happening. The scientific literature confirms what they describe is neurologically real.

The Temporal Lobe — The Meaning-Engine That Fires Toward God

If the prefrontal cortex is the gatekeeper, the temporal lobe is the meaning-generator. Located on the sides of the brain above the ears, the temporal lobes process language, memory, emotion, and most significantly for our purposes — the sense of meaning, significance, and transcendence. Research in neurotheology, the scientific study of the brain and spiritual experience, has consistently shown that the temporal lobes are the primary region associated with experiences of awe, presence, and transcendent significance.

Neurologist Norman Geschwind first documented in the 1970s what is now called Geschwind Syndrome — a cluster of behavioral traits associated with temporal lobe disorders, including hyperreligiosity. Subsequent brain imaging studies published in Biological Psychiatry confirmed that religious delusions in psychosis strongly correlate with temporolimbic overactivity — excessive, irregular firing in the limbic system and temporal lobe regions. A 2021 study published in Biological Psychiatry mapped a specific neural circuit for spirituality centered on the periaqueductal gray — a brainstem region involved in meaning-processing — and found that brain lesions causing hyper-religiosity intersected this same circuit. Dr. Andrew Newberg at Thomas Jefferson University has spent decades imaging the brains of people engaged in spiritual practice across multiple traditions and found consistent temporal lobe activation during experiences of transcendent significance.

The reason this matters is straightforward and profound: the temporal lobe fires toward the most significant, meaning-saturated things it knows. For most human beings, in most cultures, across all of recorded history, the most significant and meaning-saturated thing in human experience is God — the sacred, the divine, the question of ultimate reality. When the temporal lobe is disordered by schizophrenia and firing abnormally, it fires toward what it has always fired toward when overwhelmed with significance: the sacred.

This is the medical explanation for why psychosis targets God. The brain's meaning-generator is misfiring — and meaning, at its highest frequency, points toward the divine.

But this is only the first half of the answer. It explains the reaching. It does not yet explain the rage, the blasphemy, the uncontrollable cursing of the very God the other part of the mind is simultaneously reaching for.

The Collision — When Both Systems Fail Together

In schizophrenia, both systems fail simultaneously and in opposite directions.

The temporal lobe fires with overwhelming, uncontrolled intensity — generating experiences of meaning, spiritual presence, divine significance, and terror all at once. The person is flooded with what feels like the most important experience of their life, coming at them faster than they can process it.

At the same time, the prefrontal cortex — the gatekeeper, the filter, the regulator — has been compromised by the same disorder. It cannot shape the overwhelming input coming from the temporal lobe.

It cannot distinguish what should be expressed from what should be suppressed. It cannot moderate the terror from the awe, the worship from the rage.

A study published in the Journal of Neuropsychiatry and Clinical Neurosciences documented that patients with schizophrenia show a fundamental impairment in self-monitoring — the brain's ability to recognize that a thought originated internally rather than externally. In healthy individuals, the frontal cortex generates what researchers call a corollary discharge — an internal signal that says this thought came from you. In schizophrenia, this signal is absent or severely diminished. The person genuinely does not experience their own inner voice as their own. They experience it as something else speaking through them or to them.

This is the neurological reality of what someone in a psychotic episode is living inside: not a choice, not a spiritual state, but a system failure so severe that the boundaries between self and other — between my thought and an external voice — collapse entirely.

The result is what families observe: a person who is simultaneously drawn toward God and raging against Him. Who weeps with what appears to be genuine spiritual longing one moment and screams obscenities at sacred things the next. Who, if you could ask them on a quiet day, would be horrified by what came out of their mouth.

Believe them when they say it was not them. Because the neuroscience confirms that is exactly right. It was not the person choosing those words. It was a regulatory system in catastrophic failure, unable to shape what the disordered meaning-engine was generating.

The Man Among the Tombs — Mark 5

Before we continue to the question of what God does with suffering, there is a man in the Gospel of Mark who deserves to stand here. Because of all the figures in the entire New Testament, he is the one who most closely resembles what a family with a severely mentally ill loved one actually observes.

Mark 5:1–20 introduces him without a name — and that namelessness is itself significant, because this chapter is not about a single historical individual. It is about a condition. The text says he lived among the tombs. He could not be bound, not even with chains — the chains had been broken and the fetters torn asunder. Night and day he was in the mountains and in the tombs, crying and cutting himself with stones. He was violent. He was isolated. He was destroying his own body. He had been this way long enough that the community had stopped trying to help him and had learned to go around him.

When Jesus came out of the boat, this man ran to Him and worshipped Him.

That detail is not incidental. It is the neshamah. The deepest part of this man — the breath of God that no condition can extinguish — recognized what his disordered mind could not coherently process, and it ran. It fell at the feet of the only One who could actually reach it.

What happened next is the most carefully described healing in all four Gospels. Jesus did not shout at the man. He did not rebuke him from a distance. He engaged him in conversation. He asked his name. And the Greek word translated restored — in verse 15, where the healed man is described as sitting, and clothed, and in his right mind — is sōphroneō (σωφρονέω). It means to be of sound mind. To be in possession of one's mental faculties. To think with discipline and clarity.

It is the only time in the entire New Testament that a healing is described specifically as the restoration of right mind. Not physical healing. Not forgiveness of sin. The recovery of the mind itself.

And what did Jesus say to this man after? He sent him back — to his house, to his own people. Go home to thy friends, and tell them how great things the Lord hath done for thee, and hath had compassion on thee — Mark 5:19 (KJV). The restored man became the first evangelist to the Decapolis. His story — the most extreme case of disorder and loss that anyone in that region had witnessed — became the testimony that opened an entire community to the Gospel.

God did not waste the worst years of that man's life. He used them as the most credible possible evidence that His power had no limit.

What the Ancient Text Says About the Battle Inside

Medicine explains the mechanism. But it does not explain the battle. And Scripture does not leave us without language for what the medical framework cannot reach.

The Apostle Paul, writing in Koine Greek — the original language of the entire New Testament — described something in Romans 7 that the neuroscientist would recognize immediately. He was writing about his own inner experience, the war between his deepest values and his involuntary actions. He was not describing schizophrenia. But what he described maps onto it with a precision that is difficult to dismiss.

"For that which I do I allow not: for what I would, that do I not; but what I hate, that do I. For I know that in me (that is, in my flesh) dwelleth no good thing: for to will is present with me; but how to perform that which is good I find not. For the good that I would I do not: but the evil which I would not, that I do." — Romans 7:15–16, 18–19 (KJV)

Paul was describing a war happening inside a person between what they want and what they do — between their will and their actions. For someone living inside a psychotic episode, this description is not metaphorical. It is the literal description of what they experience every waking moment. They do not allow what they do. They do not want what comes out of their mouth. And the evil they would not — the blasphemy, the rage, the terror — that is exactly what pours out.

The Greek word Paul uses for I allow not is ou ginōskō — literally, I do not acknowledge it, I do not recognize it as mine. The person with a severely broken regulatory system says exactly the same thing about the words their disordered brain produces. Those words are not mine. I do not recognize them. I do not acknowledge them.

Before any neurologist ever imaged a human brain, God's Word described what it feels like to be trapped in a mind that does not obey you.

The Adversary — What the Hebrew Text Actually Reveals

Now we must address the question that every family eventually asks: is this Satan? Is what is happening to my loved one a spiritual attack?

To answer honestly, we have to return to the Hebrew text — because what most people think they know about Satan is not what the original Scripture says.

(□□□□□ha-satan) — The Accuser — the Adversary — a title describing a role, not a personal name. The Hebrew word śāṭān ( )□□□□□ is a generic noun meaning adversary, accuser, or opposer — derived from a verb meaning to obstruct or stand against. It appears 27 times in the Hebrew Old Testament, and in most of those appearances it refers to human adversaries, not a supernatural being. When it refers to a supernatural adversary, it appears with the definite article ha- meaning the — ha-satan, the Accuser. It is a job description, not a personal name. He is not God's equal. He is not a second god of evil. He is a created, fallen being operating within the limits God sets. In Job 1:12, God explicitly constrains him: Behold, all that he hath is in thy power; only upon himself put not forth thine hand. The Accuser cannot touch a person beyond what God permits. His power is real but bounded.

The most direct picture of ha-satan at work in the entire Old Testament is found in a vision given to the prophet Zechariah — and what God does in that vision changes everything about how we understand spiritual warfare and the broken mind.

"And he shewed me Joshua the high priest standing before the angel of the LORD, and Satan standing at his right hand to resist him. And the LORD said unto Satan, The LORD rebuke thee, O Satan; even the LORD that hath chosen Jerusalem rebuke thee: is not this a brand plucked out of the fire? Now Joshua was clothed with filthy garments, and stood before the angel." — Zechariah 3:1–3 (KJV)

The Hebrew word translated filthy here is ṣôʾîm — a word so strong that it refers specifically to human excrement. The most extreme language of defilement available in the Hebrew vocabulary. Joshua is standing before God's court wearing the worst thing imaginable. The Accuser has a case. By every external appearance, this man has nothing to bring before the throne.

And then God does something the Accuser cannot answer. He does not defend Joshua. He does not explain the filthy garments. He does not debate the evidence. He commands: take away the filthy garments from him. And unto Joshua He says — Behold, I have caused thine iniquity to pass from thee, and I will clothe thee with change of raiment — Zechariah 3:4 (KJV).

The Hebrew word for change of raiment is maḥălāṣôt — ceremonial garments of honor, the opposite of what was removed. God's response to the Accuser's most devastating case was not a legal argument. It was a garment change. Not earned. Not negotiated. Simply given, by the sovereign will of the One who had the authority to give it.

The Oldest War — What the Dead Sea Scrolls Knew

The Qumran community — the Jewish community that preserved the Dead Sea Scrolls — understood the Accuser's strategy in ways that speak directly into what this chapter describes. Among the scrolls discovered at Qumran are texts designated 4Q510–511, known as the Songs of the Sage, written approximately two centuries before the birth of Christ. These are not merely liturgical hymns. They are anti-demonic protection psalms — the earliest Jewish prayer texts specifically designed to establish spiritual boundaries against evil spirits and to declare the sovereignty of God over the afflicting powers.

The maskil — the teacher of wisdom — would sing these songs to terrify and confuse the spirits that harassed and oppressed the vulnerable members of the community. What is remarkable about the Songs of the Sage is what they assume: that evil spirits target human beings not from a position of power over God but from a position of strategy. They look for openings. They exploit weakness. They work through what is already broken.

This is exactly what ha-satan does in Zechariah's vision. He does not create the filthy garments. He presents them as the final word. His strategy with a broken mind is the same as it has always been: to present the evidence of the brokenness as the definition of who that person is. Look at what they said. Look at what came out of their mouth. Look at the disorder. Look at the shame.

And the Songs of the Sage declare, in the tradition of Zechariah's vision, that the Accuser's testimony is not the court's verdict. God speaks last. And when God speaks, the charge is absorbed, the garments are changed, and the Accuser who had the most devastating case in his files finds that case dismissed by a decree he could not anticipate and cannot appeal.

The neshamah inside the broken mind is still burning. And the Accuser who exploits the open door of a disordered prefrontal cortex has never, in all of human history, successfully extinguished it.

"For I know that my redeemer liveth, and that he shall stand at the latter day upon the earth: And though after my skin worms destroy this body, yet in my flesh shall I see God." — Job 19:25–26 (KJV)

The Hebrew word for redeemer here is gō'el (—)□□□□□□the kinsman-redeemer, the one with both the right and the responsibility to pay the price and set the captive free. Job had no medical terminology for what was happening to him. He had no theological system that explained it. He had no friends left who believed him. But the neshamah inside him reached through all of it and found the one true thing: God is real, God is my Redeemer, and I will see Him.

The person with schizophrenia who reaches for God in the middle of a psychotic break — even in broken, even in distorted, even in terror-soaked words — is doing what Job did. Not coherently. Not in words that make sense to everyone watching. But the deepest part of what they are is reaching for the only thing it was ever made to reach for.

The Exhausted Prophet — When the Body Breaks First

There is one more figure Scripture gives us who belongs in this chapter — not because he experienced psychosis, but because he experienced what clinicians today would diagnose as a severe depressive episode, and because God's response to it is one of the most carefully observed pieces of pastoral care in the entire Bible.

His name was Moses. He had led two million people out of slavery, stood before Pharaoh, seen the Red Sea part, and received the law of God face to face. But in Numbers 11, the weight had accumulated beyond what one human being could carry. The people were weeping again, demanding meat, complaining about manna. And Moses, the man who had spoken directly with God, reached his breaking point.

"I am not able to bear all this people alone, because it is too heavy for me. And if thou deal thus with me, kill me, I pray thee, out of hand, if I have found favour in thy sight; and let me not see my wretchedness."
— Numbers 11:14–15 (KJV)

The collapse was total. Moses was not weak in faith — he was the man who had stood before the burning bush. He was not a sinner being punished — God's response in the verses that follow contains no word of rebuke whatsoever. He was a human being at the absolute limit of what the nephesh — the whole unified person — can endure. And the weight had become too great.

What did God do? Not what most religious people would have done. He did not tell Moses to pray harder. He did not deliver a sermon on the faithfulness of God. He did not rebuke him for asking to die. He provided something immediate and practical: seventy elders to share the burden. He redistributed the weight. He gave Moses what his situation required — not a spiritual lecture, but structural relief.

This is the God of the neshamah. He understands what the neuroscientist also knows: you cannot minister to the spirit while the body is in crisis and expect the spirit to receive it. The person must be stabilized before they can be reached. Rest before revelation. Relief before renewal. The still small voice comes after the weight has been addressed, not instead of addressing it.

The Hebrew word used elsewhere for God's most intimate communication is qôl dəmāmāh daqqāh — literally, a sound of fine silence. Not wind. Not earthquake. Not fire. The smallest, most delicate, most interior sound imaginable. The opposite of the dramatic. And it is in that sound that God speaks. To the one who has been given food. Who has been given rest. Who has been given care for the body first.

Why Does a Good God Allow This? — The Biblical Answer

This is the question that outlasts all the others. Medicine can explain the mechanism. Scripture can explain the battle. But nothing silences the hardest question: if God is loving and powerful and good, why does He allow a person to be imprisoned inside a mind that does not work?

The answer begins with what happened at the fall.

"And unto Adam he said, Because thou hast hearkened unto the voice of thy wife, and hast eaten of the tree, of which I commanded thee, saying, Thou shalt not eat of it: cursed is the ground for thy sake; in sorrow shalt thou eat of it all the days of thy life; Thorns also and thistles shall it bring forth to thee." — Genesis 3:17–18 (KJV)

Thorns and thistles. The creation itself, subjected to brokenness because of the fall. The Greek word the Apostle Paul uses elsewhere for this condition is mataiotēs (ματαιότης) — futility, decay, subjection to brokenness. The entire created order — every cell that can malfunction, every brain that can break, every system in the human body that can decay — was subjected to this futility when sin entered the world. The broken brain is a wound of a broken world. It is not punishment. It is not abandonment.

God did not design mental illness. He designed the human brain perfect — capable of thought, creativity, reasoning, and above all, genuine relationship with its Creator. The fall broke it. Not as targeted punishment for individual people. As a consequence of a broken world. And every person living inside a disordered mind is carrying a wound that the world gave them — not a judgment that God placed on them.

Jesus demonstrated this definitively. When His disciples saw a man who had been blind from birth, they asked the question most religious people still ask when they see severe suffering: who sinned? Jesus answered them directly, and His answer was a refusal. He told them the man's blindness was not punishment but a stage — the Greek word phaneroo, to make visible, to bring into the open what was hidden. His illness was an appointment. God does not answer the question of suffering from a distance. He enters it. He is already there, in the room, working toward something that will one day be made visible.

"But the Lord said unto him, Go thy way: for he is a chosen vessel unto me, to bear my name before the Gentiles, and kings, and the children of Israel: For I will shew him how great things he must suffer for my name's sake." — Acts 9:15–16 (KJV)

God choosing the vessel through the suffering, not in spite of it. The illness is not the obstacle. It is the road. And the promise given through Paul to those chosen to bear suffering in their weakness is one of the most specific in all of Scripture:

"But we have this treasure in earthen vessels, that the excellency of the power may be of God, and not of us." — 2 Corinthians 4:7 (KJV)

The Greek word for earthen vessels is ostrakinos (ὀστράκινος) — clay pots, the cheapest and most breakable containers in the ancient world. Vessels that cracked in the heat. Vessels that shattered when dropped. Paul is describing human beings whose outer life is under siege. And he says: the treasure is still in the pot. The cracking does not remove the treasure. The shattering does not extinguish the light inside.

This is the answer to the question every family asks when they watch someone they love break: is God still in there? Is the faith still real? Is anything of who they were still present?

The vessel is cracked. The clay is breaking. And the treasure — the neshamah, the breath of God, the lamp of the LORD searching the inward parts — is still inside. Still burning. The breaking of the outer container does not diminish the excellency of the power. It exposes it.

For the Family Standing Outside the Storm

If you are reading this because someone you love is living with schizophrenia or severe mental illness, this section is for you specifically. Not for the person who is suffering — for you. Because you are suffering too, in a different way, and the questions you carry are as heavy as anyone else's.

You have watched someone you love become someone you cannot always recognize. You have heard words come out of their mouth that you know they would never choose. You have watched them reach for God and rage against God in the same week. You have wondered whether you did something wrong, whether they did something wrong, whether God is listening at all. You have been exhausted in ways that most people do not understand, because caring for someone whose mind is at war with itself is one of the heaviest things a human being can carry.

Here is what the original text of Scripture speaks directly into your situation.

First: the blasphemy and the rage that come out of your loved one during an episode are not the confession of who they are. They are the output of a broken regulatory system — a prefrontal cortex that cannot perform the filtering it was designed to perform. Every neurologist who has studied this disorder agrees on this point. The person is not choosing those words. The filter is gone. God does not hold the broken mind accountable for what the broken filter produces, and neither should you.

Second: get them the best medical care available to you. Antipsychotic medications, when they work, can restore enough prefrontal function to allow the gatekeeper to come partially back online. Therapy, structured environment, community support, and consistent medical care can all reduce the frequency and severity of episodes.

Seeking this help is not a failure of faith. The God who made the human brain also gave human beings the intelligence to study it, understand it, and develop treatments for when it breaks. Using those treatments is an act of faithfulness.

One more image belongs in this section — one that most people walking through this situation have never been shown.

In Luke 13:10–16, Jesus was teaching in a synagogue on the Sabbath when He saw a woman who had been bent double for eighteen years. The Greek word Luke uses for her condition is pneuma asthenias — literally, a spirit of infirmity, a spirit of weakness. She could not straighten herself. The text says she was bowed together and could in no wise lift up herself. Eighteen years of being unable to stand upright. Unable to see the sky. Unable to look anyone in the face at eye level.

Jesus called her to Him. He did not wait for her to navigate to the front. He called her. And He said: Woman, thou art loosed from thine infirmity — Luke 13:12 (KJV). The Greek word is apoluō — released, set free from bondage, discharged.

But what matters most for the family reading this chapter is not the healing. It is what Jesus called her in the verse that follows, when the religious leaders objected to the healing on the Sabbath. He called her a daughter of Abraham. Not a sick woman. Not a disabled woman. Not a disruption to the synagogue service. A daughter of Abraham — fully belonging to the covenant, fully included in the promises, fully a member of the family of faith.

Before He restored her posture, He restored her identity.

The person in your life whose mind is bent under the weight of illness — whatever they look like from the outside, whatever their behavior, whatever has come out of their mouth during the worst episodes — they are not defined by the bending. They are a daughter of Abraham. A son of Abraham. Fully made in the tselem of God.

Fully carrying the neshamah of their Creator. Fully the person Jesus would call across a crowded room by name.

Third: the neshamah inside your loved one — the breath of God, the lamp of the LORD — is still burning. Schizophrenia cannot reach it. No psychotic episode can extinguish it. No number of lost years can remove the image of God from a person He formed with His own hands and breathed His own life into. They are still His. The storm surrounding them is not the whole story of who they are.

"Whither shall I go from thy spirit? or whither shall I flee from thy presence? If I ascend up into heaven, thou art there: if I make my bed in hell, behold, thou art there. If I take the wings of the morning, and dwell in the uttermost parts of the sea; Even there shall thy hand lead me, and thy right hand shall hold me. If I say, Surely the darkness shall cover me; even the night shall be light about me." — Psalm 139:7–11 (KJV)

The Hebrew word translated hell in that passage is Sheol — the lowest depth, the place of the dead, the most extreme edge of human experience. And David says: thou art there. Not thou wilt come there eventually. Not thou canst be reached from there. Thou art there. Already present. Already inhabiting the lowest place a human soul can occupy.

That means God is in the hospital room at three in the morning. God is present inside the psychotic break, in the darkness your loved one cannot navigate and you cannot enter. God is in the locked psychiatric unit, in the place that feels most forsaken and most removed from anything sacred. The neshamah inside your loved one is not isolated from its Creator by the disorder surrounding it. God does not lose track of souls in Sheol. He is already there before they arrive.

The Hebrew word for hold in verse 10 — thy right hand shall hold me — is 'āḥaz (.)□□□□□□It means to grasp firmly, to seize, to grip with strength. Not a gentle cradling. An active, firm grip. The God of Psalm 139 does not loosely accompany His people into the darkness. He grips them. In the darkest place available. With His right hand.

Fourth: the Scriptures that speak most directly to the condition of someone whose mind is in collapse are not the ones about distant healing. They are the ones written from inside the collapse itself.

"I called upon thy name, O LORD, out of the low dungeon. Thou hast heard my voice: hide not thine ear at my breathing, at my cry. Thou drewest near in the day that I called upon thee: thou saidst, Fear not." — Lamentations 3:55–57 (KJV)

The Hebrew word for dungeon here is bôr — a pit, a cistern, the lowest place available. It is the word used for the pit Joseph was thrown into. It is the word used for the dungeon where prisoners were held without light. Jeremiah was not speaking metaphorically. He was describing what it feels like when the outer world has collapsed and the inner world offers no shelter. And from that place — not from healing, not from resolution, not from understanding — he called on the name of the LORD. And the LORD heard. Thou drewest near. The Hebrew word is qārab — to come close, to approach, to be in immediate proximity. God did not answer from a distance. He drew near. To the dungeon. To the broken-down city. To the collapsed inner world. He came close.

Fifth: it is right to ask God why. It is right to be angry. It is right to weep and to demand answers. Job did it for thirty-seven chapters. God did not punish him for it. God answered him. Not with an explanation of why suffering exists, but with a revelation of who God is — and that was enough for Job. Keep bringing the question to God. He is listening.

The prophet Isaiah described the posture of the Messiah toward fragile and damaged things in a single sentence that has no equal in all of prophetic literature.

"A bruised reed shall he not break, and the smoking flax shall he not quench: he shall bring forth judgment unto truth." — Isaiah 42:3 (KJV)

The Hebrew word for bruised is rāṣaṣ — to crack, to splinter, to be broken without being fully severed. A bruised reed is not a healthy reed. It cannot make music the way it was designed to. It bends wrong. It sounds wrong. The practical thing, the efficient thing, is to snap it off and use a new one. But the Messiah does not break the bruised reed. He carries it with him as it is.

The smoking flax is even more evocative. Flax — the material used to make lamp wicks — when it is dying, produces not light but smoke. The flame is gone. What remains is a smoldering thread barely holding warmth. The practical thing is to pinch it out and replace it. The Messiah does not quench the smoking flax. He protects the ember that is barely there.

For every family watching a loved one whose mind is broken — whose faith seems extinguished, whose words seem wrong, whose life seems to produce smoke instead of light — Isaiah 42:3 is the answer to the question you are really asking. Has God given up on them? Is there too much damage? Is the flame too low?

The Messiah does not break bruised reeds. He does not quench smoking flax. The ember that barely flickers in a disordered mind is not too small for Him to protect. The faith that cannot form coherent sentences is not too damaged for Him to carry. He brings forth judgment unto truth — the original Hebrew word for truth here is 'ĕmet, the word for firm, faithful, unshakeable reality — and He does

it through the ones the world has already dismissed as too broken to
matter.

The Answer, Brought Together

Why do psychotic breaks lead to hyper-religious episodes? Because
the neshamah — the breath of God, the lamp of the LORD, the divine
spark placed inside every human person at creation — is the deepest
layer of what we are. It was designed to reach for God. It searches the
inward parts. It points toward its source the way a compass points
north. When the outer mind collapses under the weight of illness, the
neshamah is what remains, unfiltered and reaching. At the same time,
the temporal lobe — the brain's meaning-generator, confirmed by
decades of neuroscience research — fires toward the most significant
things it knows. And for most human beings, in most cultures, across
all of human history, the most significant thing is God. Both explanations are true. They are the same truth seen from two directions.

Why does the same illness also produce uncontrollable blasphemy
and rage against the sacred? Because the prefrontal cortex — the gatekeeper, the filter — fails simultaneously. The person loses the ability
to moderate what the overdriven temporal lobe is generating. The
result is raw, unmediated, uncontrolled — both the reaching and the
raging come through at full force, unshielded. And the Adversary —
ha-satan, the Accuser, the Opposer — exploits the open door of a
mind with no gatekeeper, presenting the evidence of the brokenness
as the final word. But the neshamah is still burning inside the storm,
still pointing toward its Creator, even when the words coming out of
the broken filter say otherwise.

Why does God allow it? Because we live in a world subjected to
mataiotēs — the futility and decay that entered creation when the
fall broke what God made perfect. The broken brain is a wound of
a broken world. It is not punishment. It is not abandonment. And

God does not manage suffering from a distance — He enters it. He is qārôb, already near, already present inside every shattered mind, working toward a phaneroo — a making-visible of His glory in a way that nothing else could accomplish.

My Reflection

The closing promise of this chapter does not belong to the end of time. It belongs to the nature of God. And the most specific promise God has ever made about what He will do with a broken mind is found in the book of Ezekiel — spoken to a people in exile, in a foreign land, whose national identity had been stripped from them and whose inner life had been shattered by loss.

"A new heart also will I give you, and a new spirit will I put within you: and I will take away the stony heart out of your flesh, and I will give you an heart of flesh." — Ezekiel 36:26 (KJV)

The Hebrew word for new in that promise is ḥādāš — not repaired, not restored, not patched. New. The promise is not that God will fix what is broken. The promise is that He will replace it entirely. The stony heart — the hardened, impenetrable, unresponsive stone — will be removed. And in its place, a heart of flesh. The Hebrew word bāśār — living, responsive, capable of feeling, capable of relationship, alive in the way only living tissue is alive.

God is not offering to improve the broken mind. He is offering to give a new one. Not in an afterlife someday. In the promise of His covenant nature — the same God who spoke these words is the same God who breathed the neshamah into the first human being and has never stopped breathing life into what He made.

The day is coming — and has in some measure already broken in through the resurrection of Jesus Christ — when every shattered mind will receive what Ezekiel describes. Not a patch. Not a partial recovery. A new heart. A new spirit. Put within you by the hands of the God who formed you from dust and breathed Himself into you and has never, not once, let go of what He made.

The Greek word exaleíphō — to wipe completely clean, with no trace left. Every tear. Every shattered year. Every broken mind. Every family worn to the bone by watching. Wiped away, completely, by the hand of God Himself. Not because suffering does not matter. But because the God who enters suffering also has the power to end it, and He has promised that He will.

He keeps His promises. Every single one of them. This one included.

A Prayer for the Broken Mind and the Watching Family

Father — You breathed Your own life into us.

Every human being alive carries the neshamah You placed in them — and that breath has not gone out in any of them, not even the ones whose minds are broken and whose words are strange and whose families are afraid. You are qārôb — already near, already present, already in the room before anyone calls out to You.

We bring before You every person living inside a storm they cannot control. Every person who cannot stop the words that come out of their mouth. Every person trapped inside a mind at war with itself, terrified by their own thoughts, unable to trust what they hear or see or feel. Be near to them with the nearness only You can give. Bring healing. Bring the right medical care, the right doctors, the right medication, the right people who will not give up on them.

We pray for every family member who is exhausted — worn to the bone, heavy-laden, carrying something that is too heavy for any human being to carry alone. We ask for Your rest. Not the rest that means the problem disappears. The rest that means You are carrying it with us.

Thank You that the former things shall pass away. Thank You that every tear will be wiped. Thank You that the day is coming when there will be no more pain. And until that day — be with us.

In the name of Yeshua — Jesus the Messiah — who entered the brokenness of this world so He could heal it from the inside out.

Amen.

"A bruised reed shall he not break, and the smoking flax shall he not quench: he shall bring forth judgment unto truth." — Isaiah 42:3 (KJV)

Closing Prayer

F ather God,

We have come to the end of these pages together. But I want to say plainly — the questions do not end here. They were never supposed to.

What I hope is different now, for every person who has walked through these chapters, is not that the questions are gone. It is that the questions have somewhere to go. That they are no longer carried alone in the dark but brought directly, honestly, without performance or pretense, to the God who was never frightened by them in the first place.

So I come before You now on behalf of the reader who has just closed this book.

For the one who arrived as a skeptic and left with something they did not expect — a crack in the wall, a thought that will not leave, a question that has now become a search — I ask You to honor that. You promised to be found by those who seek with their whole heart. Let this be the beginning of that search. Follow them into whatever quiet room they return to. Be louder than their doubt. Be realer than their hesitation. And let the crack become a door.

For the one who arrived as a believer and found in these pages a faith that is now deeper, more honest, more anchored than the one they brought in — protect what You have built. The enemy will come for it. The noise of ordinary life will try to bury it. Let the truths that landed in these chapters become roots rather than memories — things that hold them when the storms come rather than things they once read in a book.

For the one who is still in the middle of the hardest season of their life — who read these chapters from inside a suffering that has not yet resolved, who found comfort in some pages and frustration in others, who closed the book still carrying more than they feel they can hold — stay near to them. Do not let the silence feel like absence. Remind them that the God who met Job in the whirlwind, who wept at Lazarus's tomb, who sweat drops of blood in Gethsemane and chose to feel every moment of it — that God is present in their exact room, in their exact pain, in their exact moment of barely holding on.

For the one who read Chapter Thirteen and recognized themselves in it — the one who walks hallways where children suffer, who has given everything to a fight they sometimes cannot win — I ask You to speak to them specifically. Let them feel what David felt when he rose from the ground, washed his face, and went to worship. Not because the grief was gone. Because he knew where his child was. Let them know. Let that knowledge reach a place that theology alone cannot reach.

For everyone who found a question in this book that was never answered to their complete satisfaction — I ask You to be the answer that these pages could only point toward. No book can hold You fully. No chapter can contain what You are. Every word written here was an attempt to point in Your direction. You are the destination these pages were always aimed at.

And for me — the broken man You chose to write through — I ask only this. Let nothing in these pages have been about me. Let any credit belong entirely to You. Let the person who was helped by something in this book trace it not to the author but to the God who authored the truth the author only tried to reflect. I am nothing more than a signpost. You are the road. You are the destination. You are the One who was waiting at every chapter's end.

This book is Yours. It always was. I was only ever holding it for You.

Go now with the one who just put it down. Be in the car when they drive home. Be in the room when they lie down tonight. Be in the first thought they have when they wake up tomorrow. And let what began on these pages become something they carry for the rest of their lives — not as a memory of a book they once read, but as the beginning of a faith they can never put down.

In the name of the Father, the Son, and the Holy Spirit.

Amen.

"He shall call upon me, and I will answer him: I will be with him in trouble; I will deliver him, and honour him." — Psalm 91:15 (KJV)

A Note to The Reader

From the bottom of my heart — thank you.

Thank you for picking up this book, for giving your time to these pages, and for trusting me with questions that matter deeply. This was my first book — my first attempt at putting something this personal and this important into the world — and bringing it from an idea all the way to your hands has been one of the most humbling experiences of my life.

My greatest hope is that something within these pages met you where you needed it most. That a question you carried found some peace. That a doubt found some light. That wherever you are in your journey with God, this book moved you even one step closer to Him.

If there is one thing I want you to leave with, it is this — Jesus Christ is real, He is near, and He is worth knowing fully. Not as a religious idea, but as a living Savior who already knows your name and already loves you without condition.

I am grateful beyond words that you were here.

God bless you richly.

— R.P. Priddy

Scripture Reference Index

All Scripture quotations are from the King James Version (KJV)

OLD TESTAMENT

Genesis

Genesis 1:1 Genesis 1:26 Genesis 2:7 Genesis 2:17 Genesis 3:17–18 Genesis 5:24 Genesis 6:1–2 Genesis 6:6 Genesis 14:18–19 Genesis 15 Genesis 16:13 Genesis 18:25 Genesis 22:12 Genesis 39:21 Genesis 50:20

Exodus

Exodus 3:7–10 Exodus 3:14 Exodus 9:14 Exodus 12 Exodus 17 Exodus 29:38–39 Exodus 32 Exodus 34:6–7

Numbers

Numbers 11:14–15 Numbers 23:19

Deuteronomy

Deuteronomy 1:39 Deuteronomy 8:17–18 Deuteronomy 29:29 Deuteronomy 30:19 Deuteronomy 31:17–18 Deuteronomy 32:4

Joshua — 2 Chronicles

Joshua 24:15 1 Samuel 15 1 Samuel 16:7 1 Samuel 28:11, 13, 15 2 Samuel 12:13 2 Samuel 12:20–23 1 Kings 19:4, 7, 11–12 1 Kings

19:4–5 1 Kings 19:12 2 Kings 2:11 2 Chronicles 33:9 2 Chronicles 33:12–13

Job

Job 1:1 Job 1:8 Job 1:12 Job 1:20–22 Job 3:3 Job 3:20–21 Job 13:15 Job 19:25–26 Job 26:7 Job 32:8 Job 33:4 Job 38:4 Job 42:2 Job 42:5 Job 42:6 Job 42:7

Psalms

Psalm 5:3 Psalm 8:2 Psalm 9:17 Psalm 13 Psalm 16:9–10 Psalm 19:1 Psalm 22:1 Psalm 23:4, 6 Psalm 28:1 Psalm 30:5 Psalm 33:6 Psalm 34:18–19 Psalm 37:4 Psalm 37:7 Psalm 42:1, 5 Psalm 44:23–24 Psalm 46:10 Psalm 51:4 Psalm 56:8 Psalm 69:3 Psalm 71:6 Psalm 73:17 Psalm 73:25–26 Psalm 84:2 Psalm 85:10 Psalm 88 Psalm 90:2 Psalm 91:15 Psalm 92:14 Psalm 102:1–2 Psalm 105:17–19 Psalm 118:8 Psalm 119:105 Psalm 138:8 Psalm 139:7–11 Psalm 139:8 Psalm 139:13–16 Psalm 142:1–2 Psalm 145:3 Psalm 147:3 Psalm 147:5

Proverbs

Proverbs 3:5–6 Proverbs 4:18 Proverbs 8:22–23 Proverbs 20:27 Proverbs 25:2

Ecclesiastes

Ecclesiastes 3:11 Ecclesiastes 12:7 Ecclesiastes 12:13

Isaiah

Isaiah 1:18 Isaiah 6:1 Isaiah 6:3 Isaiah 6:5 Isaiah 7:16 Isaiah 9:6 Isaiah 14:9–11 Isaiah 25:8 Isaiah 26:3 Isaiah 29:13 Isaiah 35:10 Isaiah 40:25–26 Isaiah 40:31 Isaiah 41:10 Isaiah 42:3 Isaiah 43:2 Isaiah 43:10 Isaiah 43:18–19 Isaiah 44:6 Isaiah 45:15 Isaiah 45:22 Isaiah 46:4 Isaiah 46:9–10 Isaiah 48:3 Isaiah 49:1 Isaiah 50:10 Isaiah 52:13 Isaiah 53:3 Isaiah 53:4 Isaiah 53:10–11 Isaiah 55:2–3 Isaiah 55:6 Isaiah 57:1–2 Isaiah 61:1 Isaiah 63:9 Isaiah 64:8 Isaiah 66:24

Jeremiah — Malachi

Jeremiah 1:5 Jeremiah 7:25 Jeremiah 17:5 Jeremiah 19:5 Jeremiah 29:10–11 Jeremiah 29:13 Jeremiah 31:3 Jeremiah 31:15–17 Jeremiah 33:3 Lamentations 3:22–23 Lamentations 3:26 Lamentations 3:55–57 Ezekiel 18:23 Ezekiel 33:11 Ezekiel 36:26 Daniel 4:34 Daniel 12:2 Hosea 2:14 Hosea 13:14 Joel 2:25 Jonah 3:10 Micah 6:8 Micah 7:19 Nahum 1:6 Habakkuk 1:2 Habakkuk 2:1 Habakkuk 3:17–18 Zephaniah 3:17 Zechariah 3:1–3 Zechariah 3:4 Malachi 3:6

NEW TESTAMENT

Matthew

Matthew 2:16–18 Matthew 5:17 Matthew 6:33 Matthew 7:1–3 Matthew 7:7–8 Matthew 7:15 Matthew 7:21–23 Matthew 9:12 Matthew 10:28 Matthew 11:25 Matthew 11:28 Matthew 12:31 Matthew 13:24–30 Matthew 16:18 Matthew 17:3 Matthew 18:6 Matthew 18:14 Matthew 19:13–15 Matthew 20:6–7 Matthew 21:16 Matthew 22:37–39 Matthew 23:37 Matthew 25:21 Matthew 25:41 Matthew 25:46 Matthew 27:46

Mark — Luke

Mark 5:1–20 Mark 9:43–44 Mark 11:25 Mark 14:21 Mark 15:25 Luke 2:25–32 Luke 4:18 Luke 8:17 Luke 9:31 Luke 13:10–16 Luke 15:20 Luke 16:23 Luke 19:10 Luke 22:44 Luke 23:34 Luke 23:39–43 Luke 23:43 Luke 23:46 Luke 24:39

John

John 1:1–3 John 1:14 John 1:18 John 3:16–17 John 4:24 John 5:46 John 6:44 John 6:68–69 John 8:56 John 8:58 John 8:59 John 9:3 John 10:10 John 11:3–4 John 11:25–26 John 11:35, 37 John 14:6 John 14:16, 18 John 15:5 John 16:33 John 19:30

Acts — Romans

Acts 4:12 Acts 7:59 Acts 9:3–6 Acts 9:15–16 Acts 10 Acts 17:23 Acts 17:27 Acts 20:29–30 Romans 1:19–20 Romans 1:20 Romans 1:24 Romans 2:14–15 Romans 3:23 Romans 3:25–26 Romans 5:3–5

Romans 5:8 Romans 5:12 Romans 5:15–19 Romans 6:23 Romans 7:15–16 Romans 7:19 Romans 8:1 Romans 8:18 Romans 8:20–22 Romans 8:26–27 Romans 8:28 Romans 8:29 Romans 8:30 Romans 9:20–21 Romans 10:13 Romans 11:22 Romans 11:33 Romans 11:36 Romans 12:2 Romans 12:4–6 Romans 12:19 Romans 14:4

1 Corinthians — Galatians

1 Corinthians 1:26–27 1 Corinthians 3:13–15 1 Corinthians 3:16 1 Corinthians 4:7 1 Corinthians 9:19–20, 22 1 Corinthians 10:13 1 Corinthians 12:4–7 1 Corinthians 13:12 1 Corinthians 15:20–26 1 Corinthians 15:28 1 Corinthians 15:42–44 1 Corinthians 15:53, 55–57 2 Corinthians 1:3–4 2 Corinthians 1:20 2 Corinthians 3:18 2 Corinthians 4:7 2 Corinthians 4:16–18 2 Corinthians 4:17 2 Corinthians 5:6–8 2 Corinthians 5:11 2 Corinthians 12:9 Galatians 1:13 Galatians 3:13 Galatians 3:24–25 Galatians 6:1 Galatians 6:7

Ephesians — Philippians

Ephesians 1:4 Ephesians 1:7 Ephesians 2:4–5 Ephesians 2:8–9 Ephesians 2:10 Ephesians 4:11–13 Ephesians 4:32 Ephesians 6:12 Philippians 1:3 Philippians 1:6 Philippians 1:21–23 Philippians 2:10–11 Philippians 3:13–14 Philippians 4:6–7

Colossians — Revelation

Colossians 1:16–17 Colossians 1:20 1 Thessalonians 4:13–14 1 Thessalonians 4:17 1 Timothy 1:15 1 Timothy 2:4 1 Timothy 6:16 2 Timothy 2:19 2 Timothy 4:6–8 Titus 2:2–3 Hebrews 1:1–2 Hebrews 1:3 Hebrews 2:14–15 Hebrews 4:12 Hebrews 4:15 Hebrews 5:6 Hebrews 9:16–17 Hebrews 9:27–28 Hebrews 10:1 Hebrews 10:4 Hebrews 10:12 Hebrews 10:24–25 Hebrews 11:3 Hebrews 12:1–2 Hebrews 12:6 Hebrews 12:10–11 Hebrews 13:5 James 1:2–4 James 1:17 James 3:1 James 5:14–15 1 Peter 1:6–7 1 Peter 2:5 1 Peter 3:18–20 1 Peter 4:12–13 1 Peter 5:8 1 Peter 5:10 2 Peter 2:1 2 Peter 3:9 1 John 1:8–9 1 John 4:10 1 John 4:14 1 John 5:4 Jude 1:22–23 Revelation 1:8 Revelation 1:18 Revelation 3 Revelation 3:20 Revelation 4:9 Revelation 4:11 Revelation 6:9–10 Revelation 12:11 Revelation 13:8 Revelation 15:4 Revelation 20:10, 14–15 Revelation 21:4 Revelation 22:13 Revelation 22:17

Dedication

To My Wife —

You have been my greatest supporter and my most honest mirror. You stood beside me through failure, through health battles, and through seasons where my leadership fell short. But something shifted. My health turned. My commitment to God deepened. And we became a true team. We learned to find peace in the hard moments instead of letting conflict consume us. Thank you for enduring my intensity, my overthinking, and the seasons when I was present in body but somewhere far away in mind. You are not just my family. You are the reason I want to be better. I love you with a depth I am still learning to fully express — and I am grateful every day that God chose you for me.

To My Oldest Son —

You were the one who made me a father. Long before I knew what I was doing, before I had figured out how to lead or how to love with patience and steadiness — you were there. A little boy who needed someone to show up, and somewhere along the way, showing up for you taught me everything. You did not just receive my love. You shaped it. You made me better simply by needing me to be.

You are not my son by blood. You are my son by choice — mine and God's. And I want you to know that there is no version of my life, no chapter of my story, no moment of growth I am proud of that does not have your fingerprints on it somewhere.

I see the man you are becoming. I see the quiet work you do every day to choose better, to hold yourself accountable, to resist what everyone around you has simply accepted as normal. That kind of integrity does not announce itself. It just shows up.

You were my first. You will always be my first. I love you son — with everything in me — and I am so proud to be your father. I love you, Bud.

To My Beautiful Daughter —

You have stopped me in my tracks more times than you know. Without the walls of a church building, without a youth group, without the social pressure that pushes most young people toward faith — you found God on your own and you held onto Him. You open Scripture not because someone told you to but because something in you hungers for it. And when the world around you challenged what you believe, you did not shrink. You stood. You spoke. You loved them anyway and tried to bring them with you. I do not have words for what it feels like to be a father and to watch your child do that. I only know that God sees it too, and He is proud of you. And so am I. I love you more than you know baby girl, to the moon and back.

To My Youngest Son —

There are not enough pages in this book for what I want to say about you. You came into this world small. You faced things at an age when most children are just learning to tie their shoes. You endured a surgery that would have broken most grown men, and you came out the other side with a smile on your face and fire in your eyes. And then — as if God wanted to make absolutely certain I understood what a miracle looks like — He gave you sports. Not just an interest in them. A gift. A natural, impossible, joyful gift that appeared almost overnight as though it had been waiting inside you all along, held in reserve for the season when your body was finally ready to carry it. Watching you play, watching you compete, watching you light up — I have had to stop and ask myself if this is real.

It is. You are real. You are mine. I love you more than these words can carry — and that cross around your neck tells me everything I need to know about the man you are already becoming.

I love each of you with everything I have. You are not just my children. You are evidence of God's goodness in my life — walking, breathing, living proof that He is faithful. I love you, T.

To My Father, Bud —

I have never once called you Dad. Not because the love was not there — but because we have always been something more than that. We call each other Bud. For buddy. And that one word says everything about the kind of relationship God built between us. Father and son, yes. But also brothers. Two people cut from the same cloth, wired the same way, carrying the same gifts.

Your passion for music — your singing, your playing, your creating — planted something in me that God has been growing ever since. Watching you pour yourself into music inspired me to find my own. The natural abilities I carry, you carry too. That is not a coincidence. That is a father passing something real to his son without even trying to.

You were a stern father growing up — and now that I am a father myself, I understand completely. The weight of responsibility, the depth of love behind the firmness, the way a father's patience gets tested by the very children he would lay down his life for. I would not change a thing about how you raised me. It shaped the man I am. And the man you are today — gentle, warm, proud, supportive — is one of my greatest joys to witness.

Over the last decade you have become my biggest supporter. Every talent. Every project. Every step toward discovering what God placed inside me — you have been there, watching with pride. That means more to me than I know how to say. I love you, Bud.

To My Mother, Momma —

You love the way Jesus instructed us to love — steadfast, gentle, honest, and faithful. You have never judged me. Your first instinct has always been to care, to pray, and to point me back to God. The way you quietly carry the burdens of others and appear at exactly the right moment is not ordinary — it is Christ-like.

You made birthdays feel like something out of a dream. Not store-bought, not basic — handcrafted, carefully planned, and made entirely out of love. A Nike birthday cake that matched my shirt. A monster truck cake with hills, tracks, and actual toy trucks built into the design. Hours of your time poured into something just to make me feel special. You could have had a career doing that and you would have been extraordinary at it. Instead you gave that gift to your children — freely, every year, without being asked.

And the everyday things — the ones I did not fully appreciate until I became a parent myself. Every morning getting my sister and me ready for school. Teaching a full classroom of students all day. Coming home and cooking a full dinner, packing lunches for the next morning, handling laundry and the house and helping us with homework for however many hours it took. I look back now and honestly do not know how you managed all of it. That was not just good parenting. That was a kind of love that does not run out.

When moments became difficult during the writing of this book, I reminded myself of the comment you made about how you know Pap-paw is proud of the man I am becoming. I hope the words written in this book make him smile, and I know I served God's Word well because you showed me what faithful love looks like lived out loud, every single day. I love you, Momma.

To My Sister —

Most people will never fully understand what you do or what it costs you. They see the surface — the showing up, the caring, the giving — but they do not see what happens behind closed doors when the weight of it all settles on your shoulders. I do. I have always seen it.

What you carry for others, God carries for you. That is not a poetic idea — it is a covenant promise from a Father who has never once looked away from your life. He placed inside of you a heart so attuned to the needs of others, so willing to pour itself out, that it could only have come from Him. And He has never asked you to do it alone.

You were chosen for the lives you touch. Not randomly. Not reluctantly. With full knowledge of everything it would require of you — and with the absolute intention of walking every step of it beside you.

You are seen. You are known. You are deeply and unconditionally loved.

And your big brother — who has been watching your entire life with nothing but pride and admiration — is always, without question, in your corner.

With all my love — Your Big Brother, R.P. Priddy

"Blessed be God, even the Father of our Lord Jesus Christ, the Father of mercies, and the God of all comfort; Who comforteth us in all our tribulation, that we may be able to comfort them which are in any trouble, by the comfort wherewith we ourselves are comforted of God." — 2 Corinthians 1:3–4 (KJV)

To A.J. —

My sister could not have been given a better husband, and I mean that from the bottom of my heart. The way you take care of her, love her, and stand beside her is everything a brother could ask for the person he loves most. Thank you for the years of friendship you have given me as well — for showing up, for being solid, and for putting up with all my antics through the years. You deserve an award for that alone. I love you, A.J.

To Nanny P. —

You were the hardest working woman I have ever known. While the rest of the world was still sleeping, you were already in that kitchen at three or four in the morning — pots on the stove, the smell of a full breakfast filling the house, clothes already washed and hung up from the day before. Nobody asked you to do those things. Nobody expected them. We tried for years to slow you down, to let you rest, to tell you it was enough. You would not hear it. That was not stubbornness. That was love — the kind that does not announce itself, it just shows up before sunrise and keeps going until everyone else has gone to bed.

You grew up with very little. Hard times. Poverty that would have broken most people and closed most doors. You never let it define you. The world tried to limit what you could become, and you simply refused. You were fluent in three languages, brilliant in ways that had nothing to do with a classroom, and sharp in every room you ever walked into. You and Grandpaw opened your hands to families in need without keeping score, without waiting to be asked, without expecting anything back.

Your faith was not something you wore on Sunday. It was the architecture of your entire life. I believe God looked at the way you lived — the quiet sacrifice, the unending generosity, the faithfulness that never wavered — and was deeply, genuinely pleased. I carry you with me still. I love you, Nanny P. And I will see you again.

To Grandpaw P. —

I miss you more than I know how to say. I still think about you — that powerful handshake, that warm embrace that made you feel like everything was going to be alright simply because you were there. You were a true Texas man. A rancher. A cowboy in every honest sense of the word.

I remember the mornings counting cattle — hundreds of them across that land — and then the evenings doing it all over again to make sure not one was missing or hurt. I remember the metal Coke can airplanes you built for my cousins and me with your own hands. The hummingbird houses you crafted so carefully, and how we would sit on that porch together watching them feed. The tall tales you would tell with a straight face while we laughed and played along because the story was so good we did not want it to end.

And the fishing trips. Those enormous fields of grasshoppers you would have us gather before we ever touched the water. The way you set up every pole, cleaned every catch, and gave us an entire day without a single moment of it feeling rushed. That was who you were — a man who gave his time like it was the most natural thing in the world, because for him it was.

Wherever you went, you had a friend within minutes. That kind of warmth does not come from effort. It comes from genuinely loving people. You and Nanny P. built something together that I am still grateful to have grown up inside of. I know we will see each other again. I love you, Grandpaw P.

To Aunt T.K. —

As far back as my memory reaches, you have been a woman who brought faith into every room you entered and every moment life presented. Not as a performance — as a reflex. As the most natural response you know. I have watched you apply God to the ordinary and the extraordinary with the same steady conviction, and it has always left a mark on me whether I acknowledged it in the moment or not.

I love you, Aunt T.K. — thank you for never letting faith be just a Sunday thing.

To S.K. —

You are a great man and I mean that without reservation. You have shown up when it mattered — hospital rooms, hard moments, the kind of situations where most people find reasons not to come — you came. You walk your faith and you know it personally. Thank you for the man you are to your family and the example you have been to me. I love you and I am grateful for you.

To Mee-Maw J. —

Your smile could change the entire feeling of a room. The warmth and love that radiated from you was the kind that made everyone around you feel safe, seen, and completely at home. That is not a small gift. That is a grace. I carry the memory of it with me still. I love you, Mee-Maw — and I am grateful for every moment I had in your presence.

To Uncle A.Z. —

For years I have always admired how hard a worker you are. The way you keep going even when most would rest or say enough — you carry an ability that life just cannot compete with. You are a living example of the old saying that you cannot keep a good man down. I love you, Uncle A.

To Pap-paw Z. —

You stood behind a pulpit as a Baptist preacher and delivered the Gospel with a conviction I could feel even as a small child sitting in those pews. I remember looking up at you leading that church full of people and thinking how remarkable it was that my grandfather was the one up there. I told people back then that I wanted to be a preacher too — partly the innocence of a child who thought his grandfather was the greatest man in the room, but partly something real that God had already placed inside me before I had the maturity to understand it. That seed you planted without even knowing it has never stopped growing.

I remember standing at the edge of your pond as a boy, fishing pole in hand, watching you toss dry cat food across the water with a grin on your face. And then it happened — the surface would explode. Catfish jumping, lines going tight, hooks disappearing before you could blink. In five minutes we had enough for a full dinner. I have never had fishing like that before or since, and I have never laughed that hard doing it. That pond, that cat food, that enormous smile of yours — I carry all of it.

And then there was the drive you made to take me to my first college football game when I was just a little boy. Walking that campus, buying jerseys and hats, feeling like the whole world was open and generous and full of wonder. That is one of those days a child stores somewhere deep and never lets go of. I never let go of it.

I can still see those bright green country fields. Still feel what it was like to sit in your lap on that riding lawn mower, small enough that the whole machine seemed enormous, and just ride. No destination. Just you and me.

I love you, Pap-paw.

To R.B. —

When I was a young man with no direction and a work ethic that still needed serious work, you opened a door anyway. You put tools in my hands, taught me crafts and lessons I carry to this day, and remained committed to a twenty year old who was late more than he was on time. A godparent is someone trusted with the spiritual covering of a child — you took that seriously and never let it become just a title. I love you. Thank you for the many years of patience and life lessons.

To S.B. —

Your love has always been consistent, warm, and faithful. A god-parent is someone trusted with the spiritual covering of a child — you took that seriously and never let it become just a title. I love you. Thank you for always being there for us.

To The W. Family —

There is a kind of family that is not built by blood but by choosing — over and over, through every season, to love someone as their own. That is what you are to me. From the moment you opened your door you never once made me feel different or out of place. Not then. Not now. Not ever.

To Momma J. —

The foundation of this family is evident in every one of your children. Thank you for opening your home and your heart. You were tough, honest, and you did not let anything slide. But that toughness was love — the kind of love that refuses to let the people it cares about become less than what God made them to be. I love you, Momma J.

To B.W. — Big Brother —

You became a big brother to me in every sense of the word. You taught Cody and I how to carry ourselves with confidence and how to keep our focus on what is good. You made us tough, you taught us how to be a man, but most importantly you showed us what loving your family truly means. I love you, big bro.

To C.W. —

My brother in every way that actually counts. We have been through the kind of seasons together that either break a friendship or forge it into something permanent. Ours got forged. And almost thirty years ago two kids made a decision that became a lifelong commitment — the Oregon Ducks would be our team. Last year we finally made the trip. We stood in Eugene, Oregon together and watched our team play. Some things are worth waiting almost thirty years for. That was one of them. Go Ducks. I love you, brother.

To B.W. — Bonus Sister —

You are your mother's daughter through and through. I have watched you grow into a woman and a mother that I am proud of. I love you — and I am grateful to have you as my bonus sister.

To B.W. — My Brother's Better Half —

The woman who said yes to my best friend and has been keeping him together ever since. Many years of marriage, two beautiful children, and a life built together. I could not be more proud that you are the one standing beside him. Thank you for taking care of my brother. I love you for that.

To C.S. —

You are woven into the fabric of our daily life and our family would not be the same without you. You have been there through the hard seasons, the celebrations, and everything in between. My children love you dearly and watching that bond brings me joy. You are family — real family — and I love you for everything you are to us.

To T.S. —

Thank you for trusting me with your daughter. That is not a small thing and I have never taken it lightly. There were seasons in our marriage that were hard and uncertain, and I will never forget the moments you spoke truth into your daughter about the nature of commitment — that marriage is tough, that struggle does not mean failure, and that you do not walk away from a person simply because the road gets difficult. That kind of wisdom from a father to his child at the right moment carries more weight than you may know. It carried our marriage. I am grateful for you. I love you for the wisdom you gave us when we needed it most.

To J.V. —

Brother, where do I begin. You have shown up during every one of my difficult seasons of life — when my son was fighting for his health and my own body was failing me at the same time — you sat with me. Not with empty words or rehearsed comfort. But with Scripture. With presence. With the kind of honest, Spirit-led conversation that only comes from someone who has pursued God with genuine depth and devotion. You met me in the middle of the storm and pointed me back to the only One who could actually calm it.

You told me to read the Book of Job. I had heard of Job. I may have even read it before. But I had never read it the way I read it after your guidance — with fresh eyes, an open heart, and a season of personal suffering that made every word land differently than it ever had before. No book of the Bible — outside of the story of Jesus Himself — has ever connected with me so deeply or stayed with me so powerfully. Job became a mirror. And what I saw in that mirror changed the way I understood my own story.

What you did not know — what perhaps God had already planned — is that our conversation that day became one of the seeds that eventually grew into this book. Thank you, J.V. I am proud of the man of God you have become. I love you, brother — and I am grateful God placed you in my life.

To A.C. —

You have known me longer than almost anyone. You knew where I came from, who I was raised to be, and what was in my heart even when my actions were trying to say something different. You held me accountable when I was headed the wrong direction. You reminded me who I truly was when life and circumstances and the noise of growing up were trying to convince me otherwise.

That is a rare gift. Most people tell you what you want to hear. You always told me the truth. I am a better man because you never let me forget where I came from. I love you, brother.

To K.J. —

I have watched you walk through valleys that most men do not survive. There was a season where the road you were on had only one destination — and it was not life. But God had other plans for you. You fought your way through the darkest version of yourself and came out the other side not just restored but transformed. And now you have dedicated your life to helping others find Christ. That is not recovery. That is resurrection. I am truly proud of you and I love you, brother.

To S.T. —

I am amazed by the father and the man you have become. Long before the hard seasons came, you and I spent countless hours together creating music. Those hours mattered. And when the hard seasons did come, you showed up for those too. You checked on us. You made sure we did not face it alone. I love you, brother.

To C.G. —

You are one of the busiest people I know. And yet you have always been one of the first to show up for me. Birthdays. Holidays. The hard seasons when most people go quiet. You write. You check in. You remember. That kind of faithfulness from someone who has every legitimate reason to be consumed by their own full and beautiful life is not something I take lightly. I love you, brother.